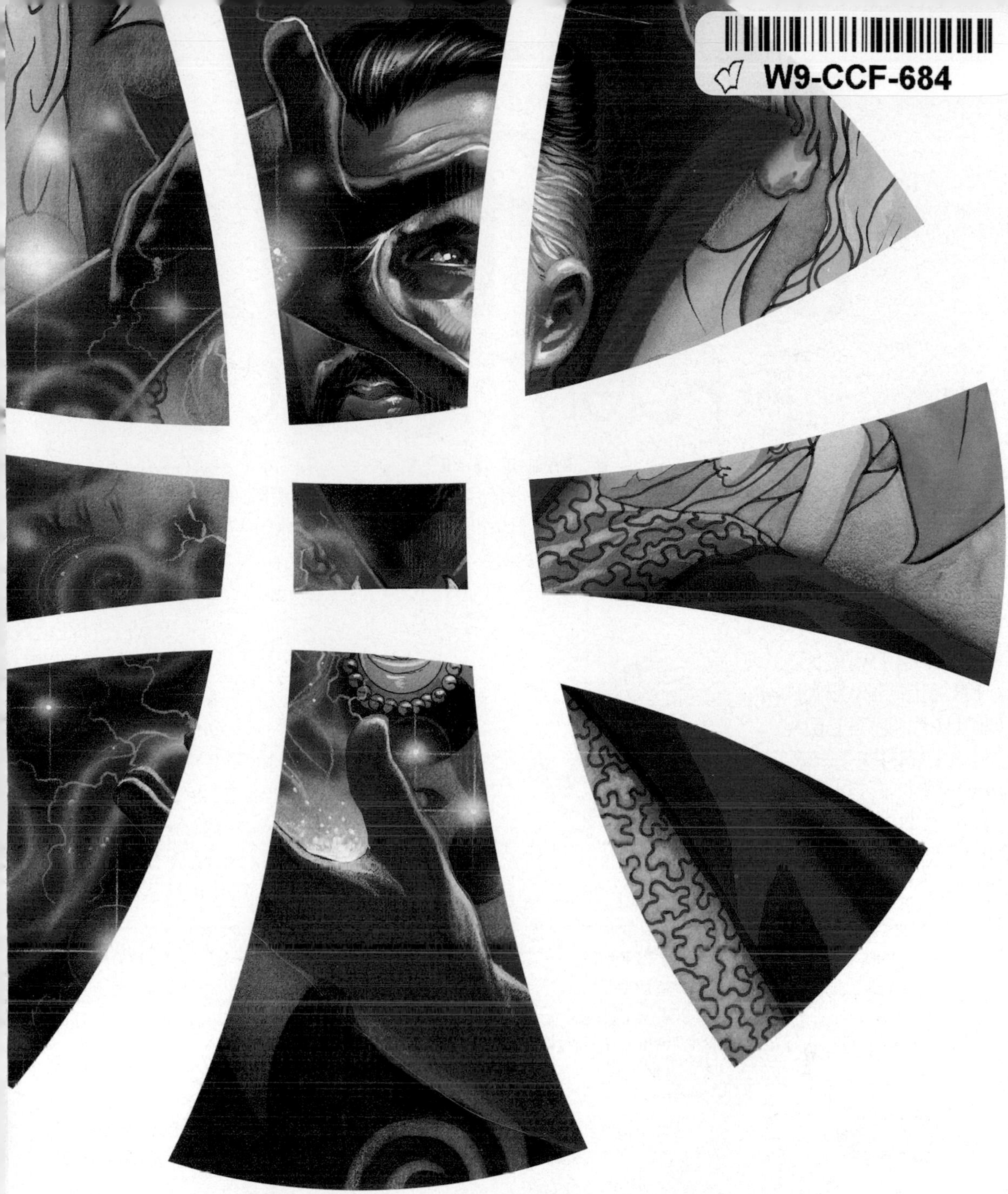

DOCTOR STRANGE

The Flight of Bones

DOCTOR STRANGE

THE FLIGHT OF BONES

WRITERS

DAN JOLLEY & KIERON GILLEN WITH TONY HARRIS, RAY SNYDER, MICHAEL GOLDEN, JIM STARLIN, MICHAEL T. GILBERT, PETER MILLIGAN, TED McKEEVER & MIKE CAREY

PENCILERS

TONY HARRIS, PAUL CHADWICK & FRAZER IRVING WITH MICHAEL GOLDEN, JIM STARLIN, MICHAEL T. GILBERT, FRANK BRUNNER, TED McKEEVER & MARCOS MARTIN

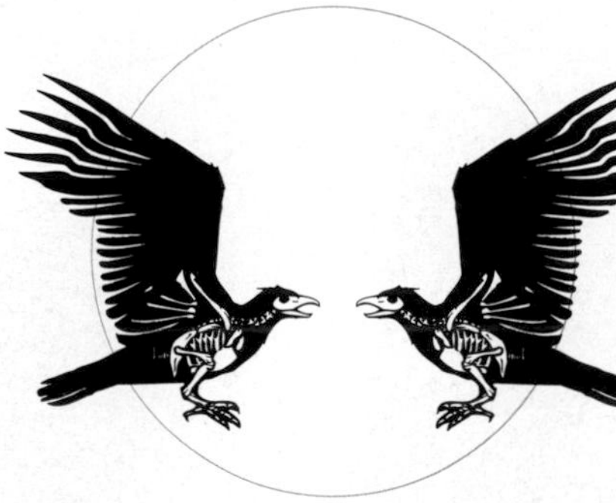

INKERS

RAY SNYDER, JIMMY PALMIOTTI & FRAZER IRVING WITH JOHN BEATTY, AL MILGROM, JIM STARLIN, MICHAEL T. GILBERT, FRANK BRUNNER, TED McKEEVER & MARCOS MARTIN

COLORISTS

MATT HOLLINGSWORTH & CHRIS SOTOMAYOR WITH MICHAEL T. GILBERT

LETTERERS

JOHN ROSHELL, VC'S JOE CARAMAGNA AND RICHARD STARKINGS & COMICRAFT INC. DAVE LANPHEAR & WES ABBOTT, WITH JACK MORELLI & KEN BRUZENAK

MANAGING & ASSISTANT EDITORS

NANCI DAKESIAN WITH PETE FRANCO & ANDY SCHMIDT

EDITORS

JOE QUESADA, JIMMY PALMIOTTI, JODY LEHEUP & JOHN BARBER WITH MARK POWERS, JOE ANDREANI & MARC SUMERAK

FRONT COVER ARTIST: J.G. JONES

BACK COVER ARTIST: TONY HARRIS

DOCTOR STRANGE CREATED BY STAN LEE & STEVE DITKO

COLLECTION EDITOR: MARK D. BEAZLEY | **ASSOCIATE MANAGING EDITOR:** KATERI WOODY
ASSOCIATE EDITOR: SARAH BRUNSTAD | **ASSOCIATE MANAGER, DIGITAL ASSETS:** JOE HOCHSTEIN
SENIOR EDITOR, SPECIAL PROJECTS: JENNIFER GRÜNWALD | **VP PRODUCTION & SPECIAL PROJECTS:** JEFF YOUNGQUIST
RESEARCH: MIKE HANSEN | **LAYOUT:** JEPH YORK | **PRODUCTION:** RYAN DEVALL
BOOK DESIGNER: RODOLFO MURAGUCHI | **SVP PRINT, SALES & MARKETING:** DAVID GABRIEL

EDITOR IN CHIEF: AXEL ALONSO | **CHIEF CREATIVE OFFICER:** JOE QUESADA
PUBLISHER: DAN BUCKLEY | **EXECUTIVE PRODUCER:** ALAN FINE

SPECIAL THANKS TO DOUG SHARK OF MYCOMICSHOP.COM & DENNIS BARGER OF WONDERWORLD COMICS

DOCTOR STRANGE: THE FLIGHT OF BONES. Contains material originally published in magazine form as DOCTOR STRANGE #1-4, MYSTIC HANDS OF DOCTOR STRANGE #1, MARVEL SHADOWS AND LIGHT #1, SHADOWS & LIGHT #2 and MARVEL DOUBLE-SHOT #4. First printing 2016. ISBN# 978-1-302-90167-7. Published by MARVEL WORLDWIDE, INC., a subsidiary of MARVEL ENTERTAINMENT, LLC. OFFICE OF PUBLICATION: 135 West 50th Street, New York, NY 10020. **Printed in the U.S.A.** ALAN FINE, President, Marvel Entertainment; DAN BUCKLEY, President, TV, Publishing & Brand Management; JOE QUESADA, Chief Creative Officer; TOM BREVOORT, SVP of Publishing; DAVID BOGART, SVP of Business Affairs & Operations, Publishing & Partnership; C.B. CEBULSKI, VP of Brand Management & Development, Asia; DAVID GABRIEL, SVP of Sales & Marketing, Publishing; JEFF YOUNGQUIST, VP of Production & Special Projects; DAN CARR, Executive Director of Publishing Technology; ALEX MORALES, Director of Publishing Operations; SUSAN CRESPI, Production Manager; STAN LEE, Chairman Emeritus. For information regarding advertising in Marvel Comics or on Marvel.com, please contact Vit DeBellis, Integrated Sales Manager, at vdebellis@marvel.com. For Marvel subscription inquiries, please call 888-511-5480. **Manufactured between 8/26/2016 and 10/3/2016 by R.R. DONNELLEY, INC., SALEM, VA, USA.**

10 9 8 7 6 5 4 3 2 1

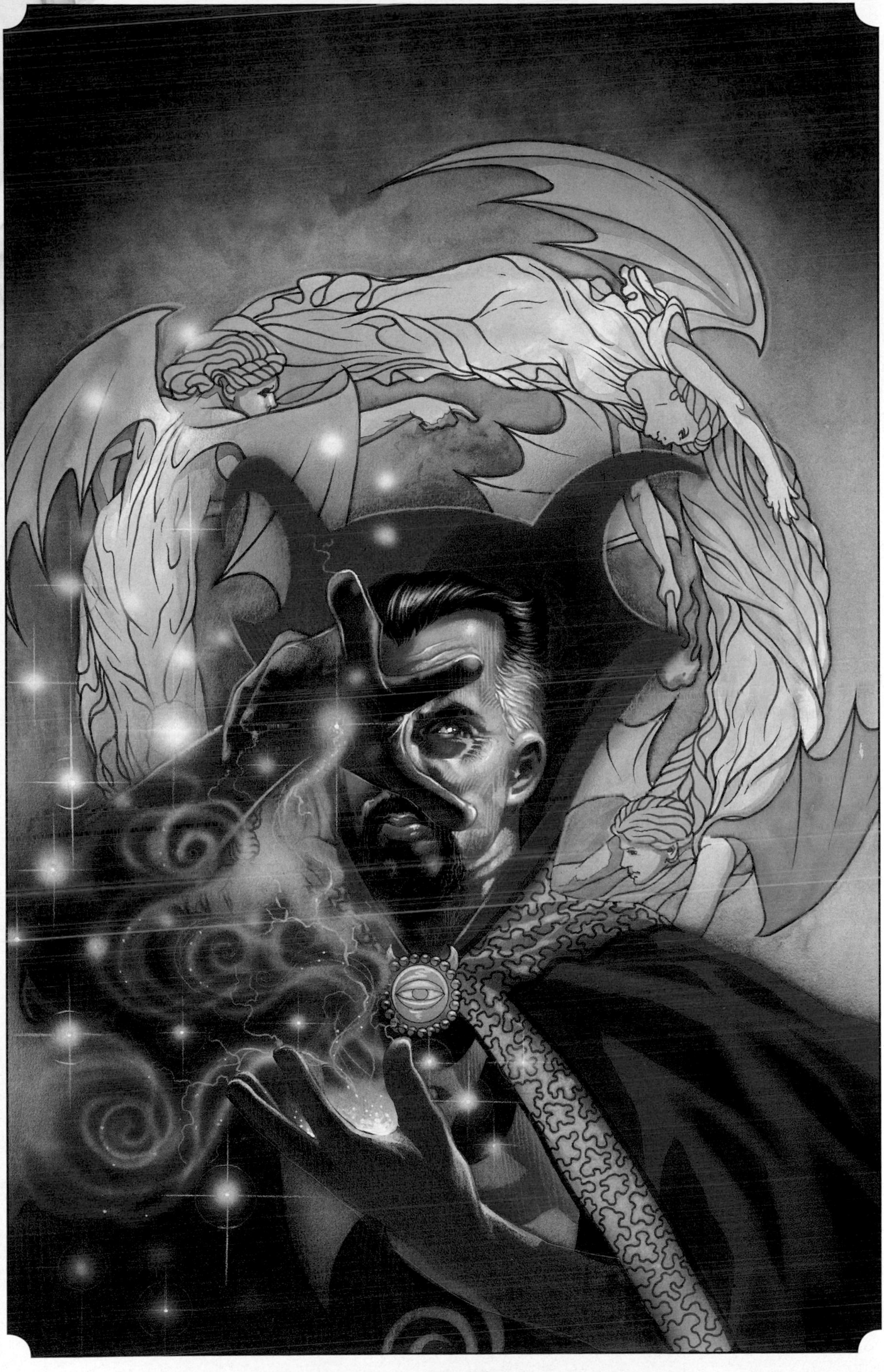

DOCTOR STRANGE #1

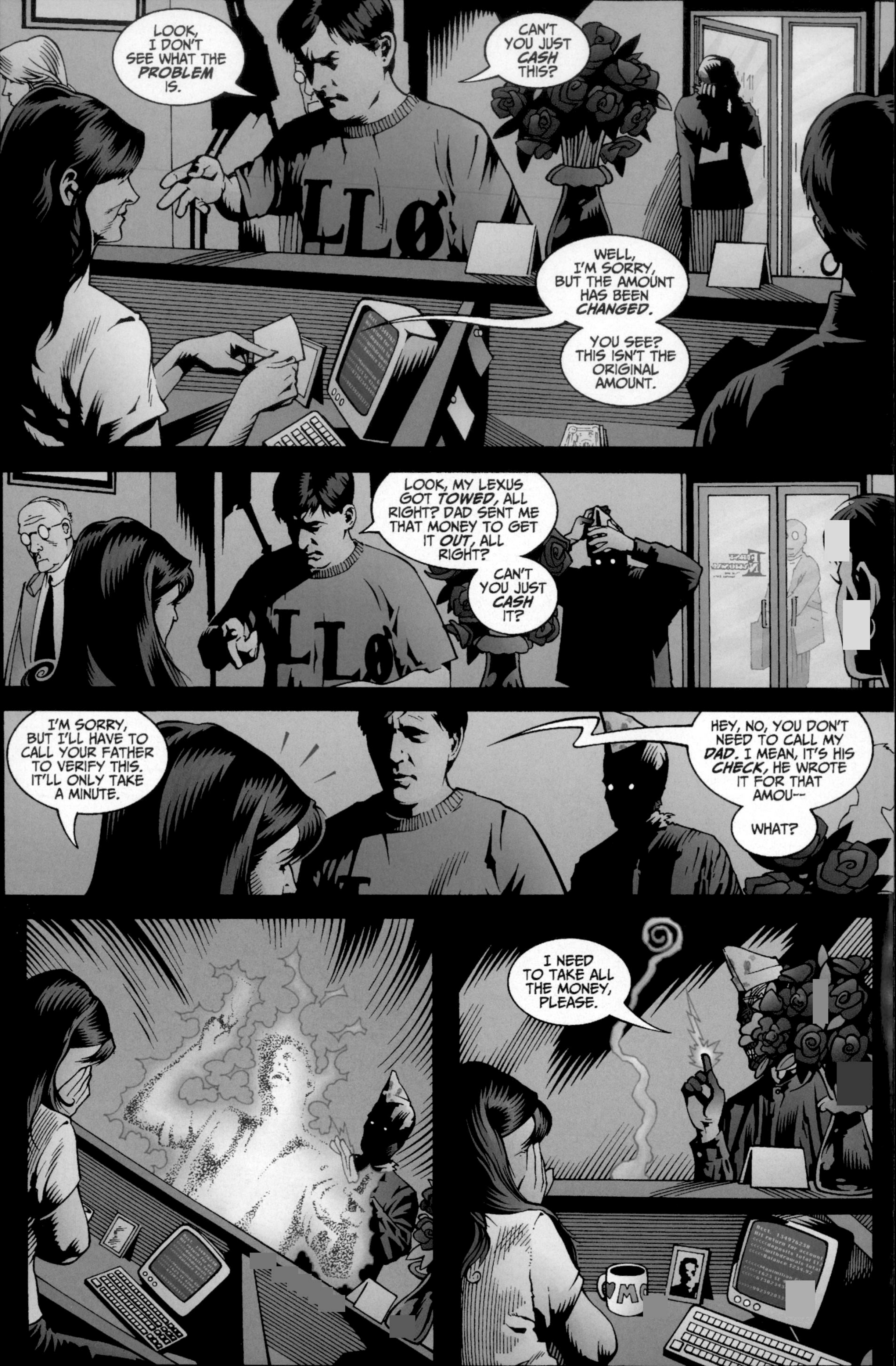
LOOK, I DON'T SEE WHAT THE PROBLEM IS.
CAN'T YOU JUST CASH THIS?
WELL, I'M SORRY, BUT THE AMOUNT HAS BEEN CHANGED.
YOU SEE? THIS ISN'T THE ORIGINAL AMOUNT.
LOOK, MY LEXUS GOT TOWED, ALL RIGHT? DAD SENT ME THAT MONEY TO GET IT OUT, ALL RIGHT?
CAN'T YOU JUST CASH IT?
I'M SORRY, BUT I'LL HAVE TO CALL YOUR FATHER TO VERIFY THIS. IT'LL ONLY TAKE A MINUTE.
HEY, NO, YOU DON'T NEED TO CALL MY DAD. I MEAN, IT'S HIS CHECK, HE WROTE IT FOR THAT AMOU--
WHAT?
I NEED TO TAKE ALL THE MONEY, PLEASE.

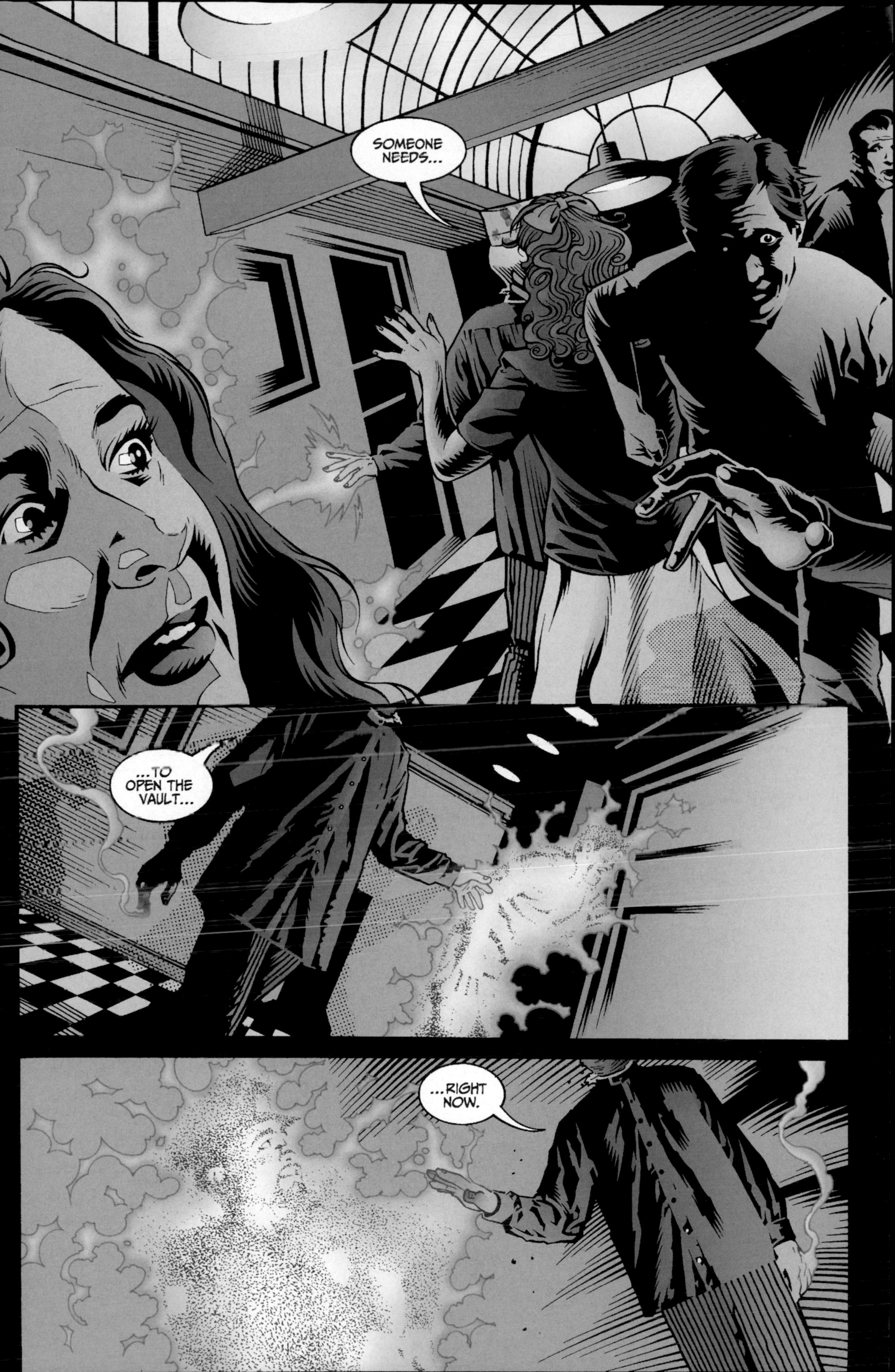
SOMEONE NEEDS...
...TO OPEN THE VAULT...
...RIGHT NOW.

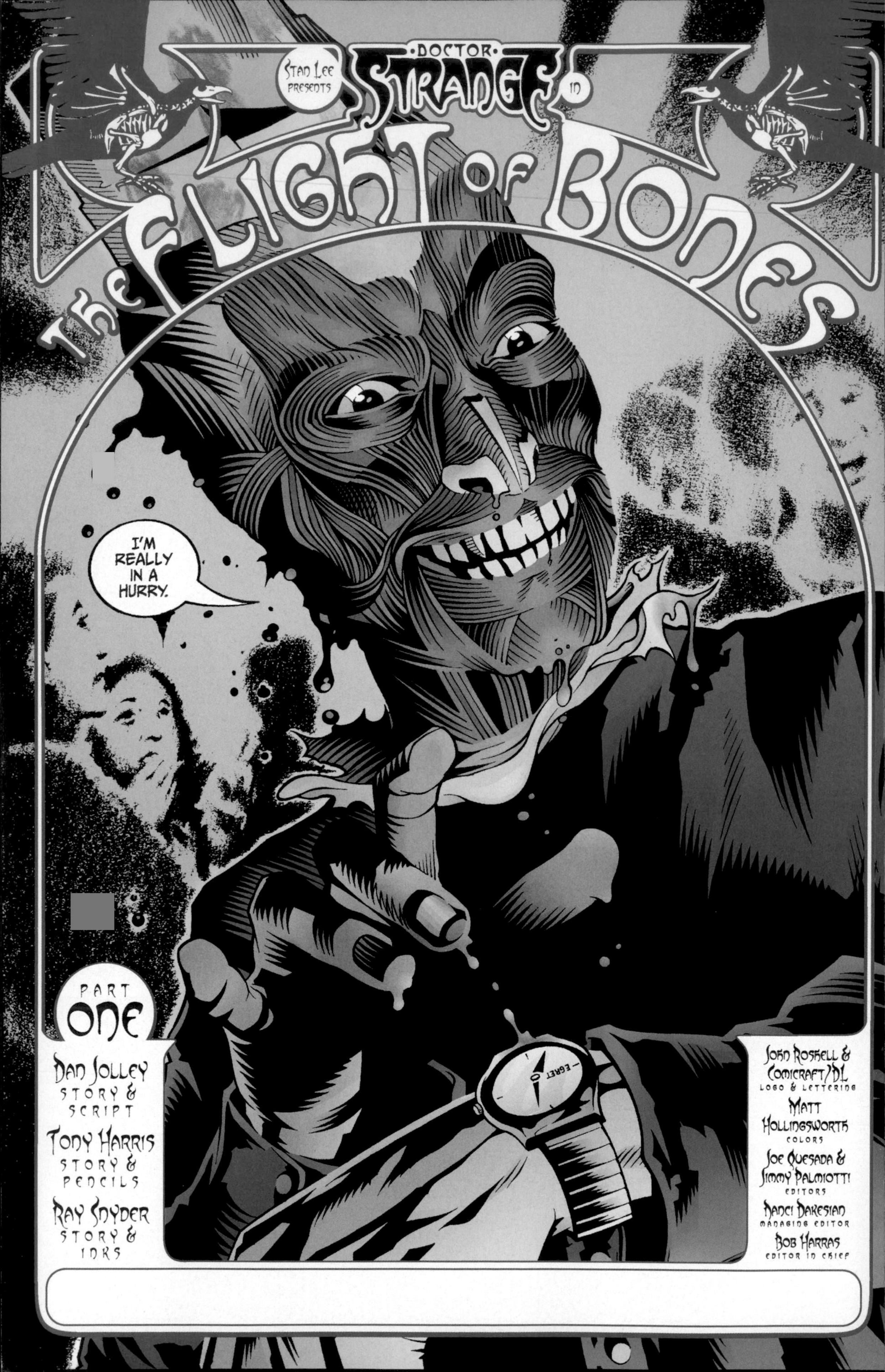
Stan Lee presents
Doctor Strange in
The Flight of Bones
I'M REALLY IN A HURRY.
Part One
Dan Jolley Story & Script
Tony Harris Story & Pencils
Ray Snyder Story & Inks
John Roshell & Comicraft/DL Logo & Lettering
Matt Hollingsworth Colors
Joe Quesada & Jimmy Palmiotti Editors
Nanci Dakesian Managing Editor
Bob Harras Editor in Chief

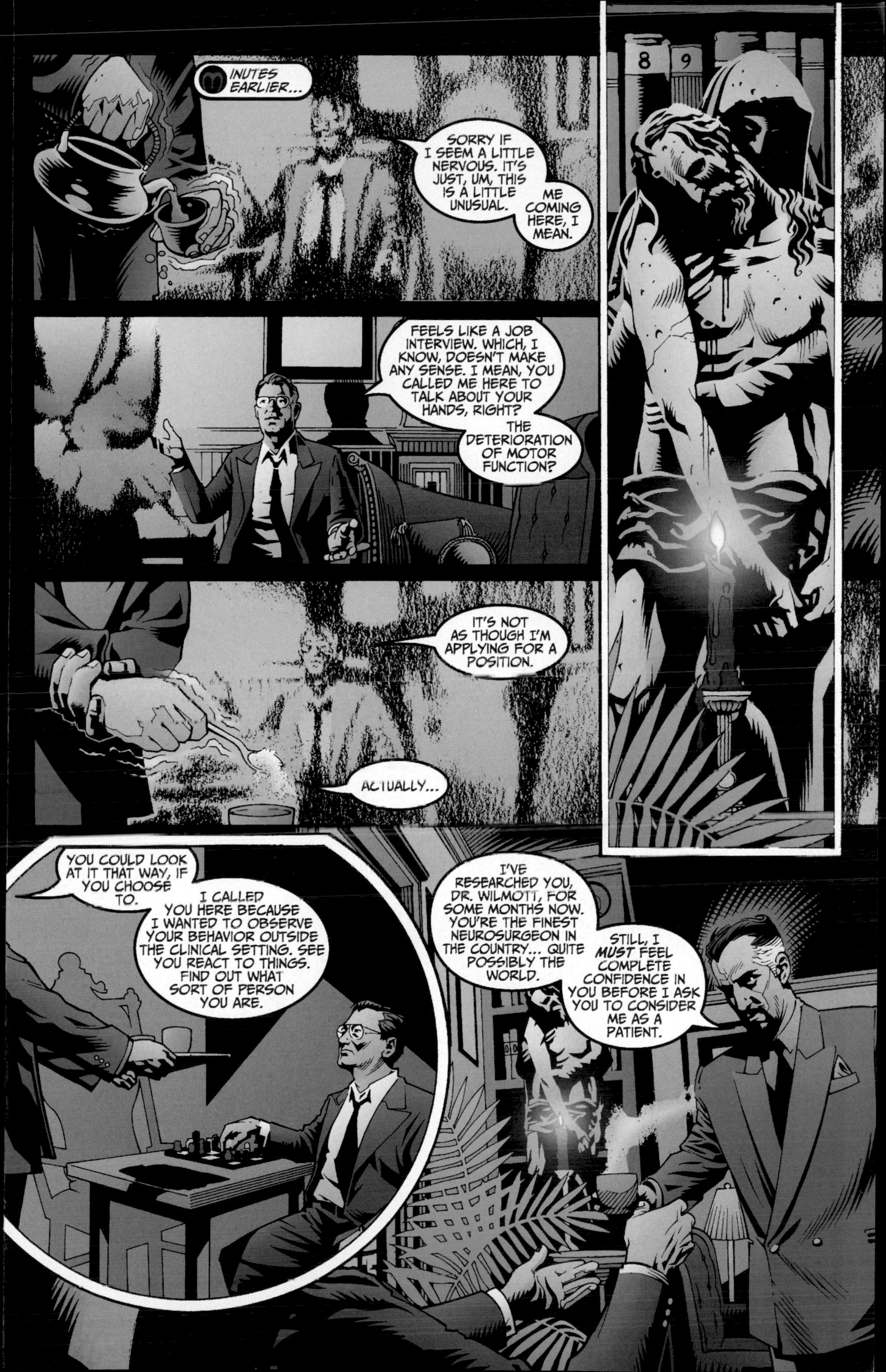
MINUTES EARLIER...
SORRY IF I SEEM A LITTLE NERVOUS. IT'S JUST, UM, THIS IS A LITTLE UNUSUAL.
ME COMING HERE, I MEAN.
8
9
FEELS LIKE A JOB INTERVIEW. WHICH, I KNOW, DOESN'T MAKE ANY SENSE. I MEAN, YOU CALLED ME HERE TO TALK ABOUT YOUR HANDS, RIGHT?
THE DETERIORATION OF MOTOR FUNCTION?
IT'S NOT AS THOUGH I'M APPLYING FOR A POSITION.
ACTUALLY...
YOU COULD LOOK AT IT THAT WAY, IF YOU CHOOSE TO.
I CALLED YOU HERE BECAUSE I WANTED TO OBSERVE YOUR BEHAVIOR OUTSIDE THE CLINICAL SETTING. SEE YOU REACT TO THINGS. FIND OUT WHAT SORT OF PERSON YOU ARE.
I'VE RESEARCHED YOU, DR. WILMOTT, FOR SOME MONTHS NOW. YOU'RE THE FINEST NEUROSURGEON IN THE COUNTRY... QUITE POSSIBLY THE WORLD.
STILL, I MUST FEEL COMPLETE CONFIDENCE IN YOU BEFORE I ASK YOU TO CONSIDER ME AS A PATIENT.

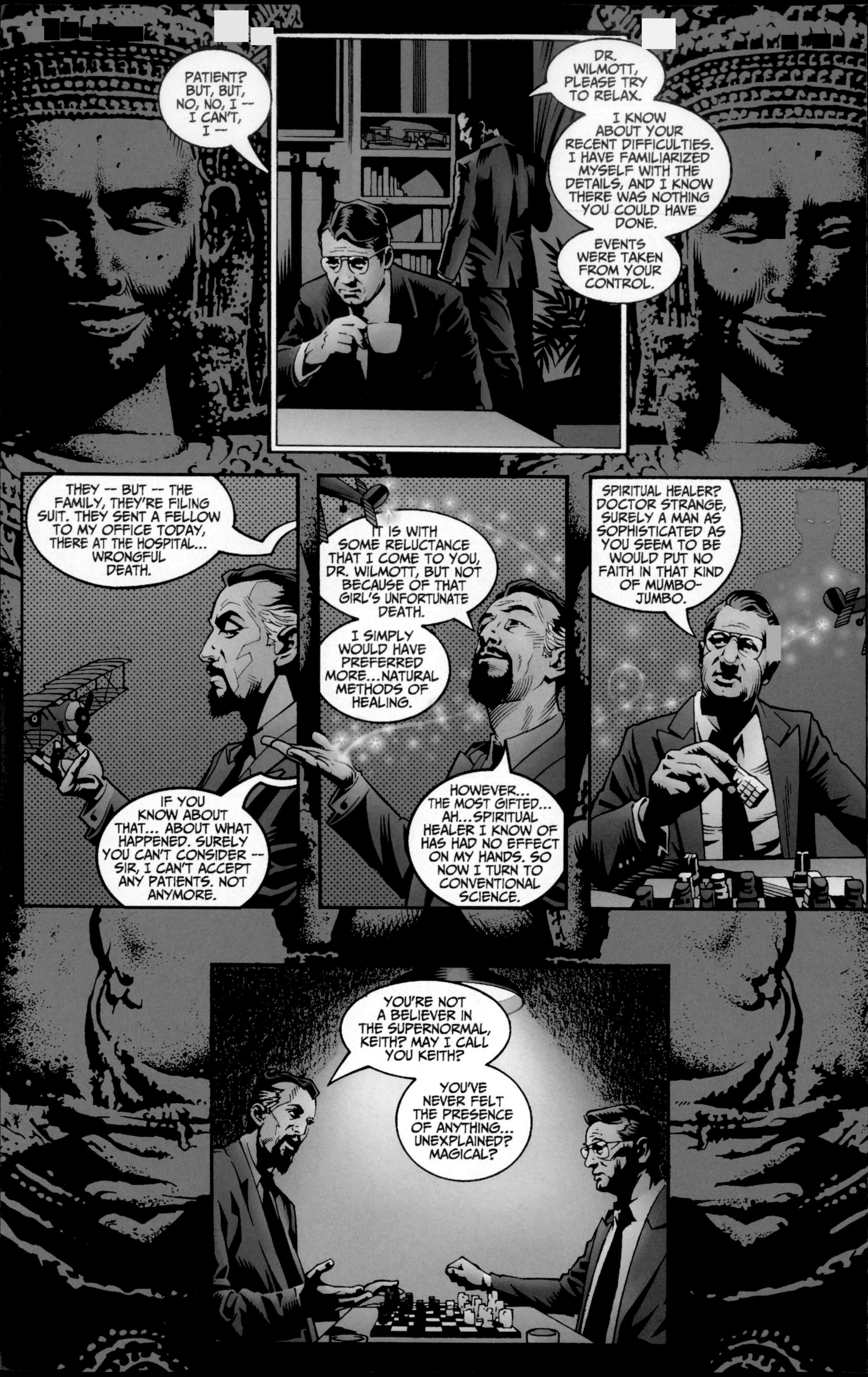
PATIENT? BUT, BUT, NO, NO, I -- I CAN'T, I --
DR. WILMOTT, PLEASE TRY TO RELAX.
I KNOW ABOUT YOUR RECENT DIFFICULTIES. I HAVE FAMILIARIZED MYSELF WITH THE DETAILS, AND I KNOW THERE WAS NOTHING YOU COULD HAVE DONE.
EVENTS WERE TAKEN FROM YOUR CONTROL.
THEY -- BUT -- THE FAMILY, THEY'RE FILING SUIT. THEY SENT A FELLOW TO MY OFFICE TODAY, THERE AT THE HOSPITAL... WRONGFUL DEATH.
IF YOU KNOW ABOUT THAT... ABOUT WHAT HAPPENED. SURELY YOU CAN'T CONSIDER -- SIR, I CAN'T ACCEPT ANY PATIENTS. NOT ANYMORE.
IT IS WITH SOME RELUCTANCE THAT I COME TO YOU, DR. WILMOTT, BUT NOT BECAUSE OF THAT GIRL'S UNFORTUNATE DEATH.
I SIMPLY WOULD HAVE PREFERRED MORE...NATURAL METHODS OF HEALING.
HOWEVER... THE MOST GIFTED... AH...SPIRITUAL HEALER I KNOW OF HAS HAD NO EFFECT ON MY HANDS. SO NOW I TURN TO CONVENTIONAL SCIENCE.
SPIRITUAL HEALER? DOCTOR STRANGE, SURELY A MAN AS SOPHISTICATED AS YOU SEEM TO BE WOULD PUT NO FAITH IN THAT KIND OF MUMBO-JUMBO.
YOU'RE NOT A BELIEVER IN THE SUPERNORMAL, KEITH? MAY I CALL YOU KEITH?
YOU'VE NEVER FELT THE PRESENCE OF ANYTHING... UNEXPLAINED? MAGICAL?

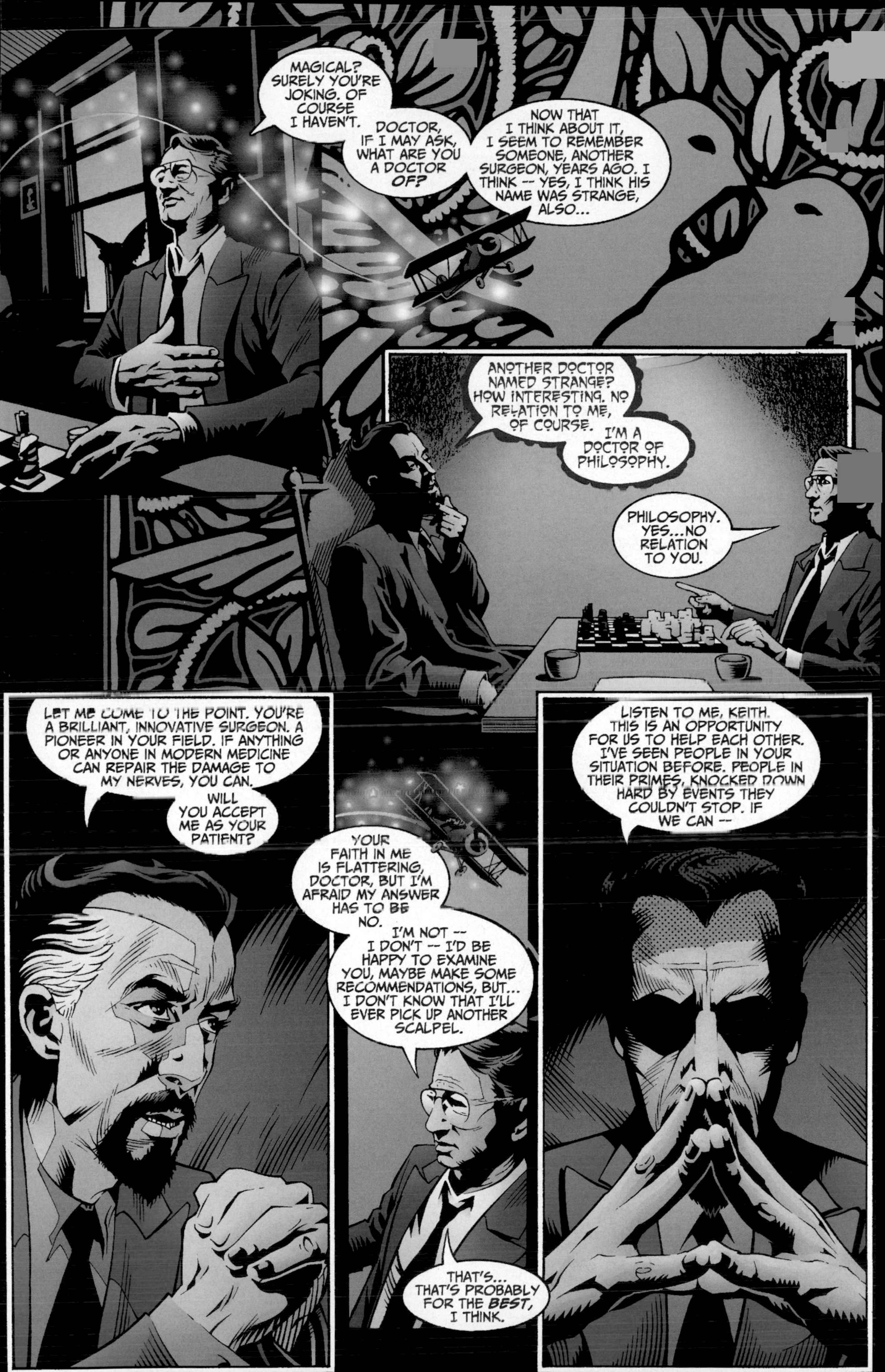
MAGICAL? SURELY YOU'RE JOKING. OF COURSE I HAVEN'T.
DOCTOR, IF I MAY ASK, WHAT ARE YOU A DOCTOR OF?
NOW THAT I THINK ABOUT IT, I SEEM TO REMEMBER SOMEONE, ANOTHER SURGEON, YEARS AGO. I THINK -- YES, I THINK HIS NAME WAS STRANGE, ALSO...
ANOTHER DOCTOR NAMED STRANGE? HOW INTERESTING. NO RELATION TO ME, OF COURSE.
I'M A DOCTOR OF PHILOSOPHY.
PHILOSOPHY. YES...NO RELATION TO YOU.
LET ME COME TO THE POINT. YOU'RE A BRILLIANT, INNOVATIVE SURGEON. A PIONEER IN YOUR FIELD. IF ANYTHING OR ANYONE IN MODERN MEDICINE CAN REPAIR THE DAMAGE TO MY NERVES, YOU CAN.
WILL YOU ACCEPT ME AS YOUR PATIENT?
YOUR FAITH IN ME IS FLATTERING, DOCTOR, BUT I'M AFRAID MY ANSWER HAS TO BE NO.
I'M NOT -- I DON'T -- I'D BE HAPPY TO EXAMINE YOU, MAYBE MAKE SOME RECOMMENDATIONS, BUT... I DON'T KNOW THAT I'LL EVER PICK UP ANOTHER SCALPEL.
LISTEN TO ME, KEITH. THIS IS AN OPPORTUNITY FOR US TO HELP EACH OTHER. I'VE SEEN PEOPLE IN YOUR SITUATION BEFORE. PEOPLE IN THEIR PRIMES, KNOCKED DOWN HARD BY EVENTS THEY COULDN'T STOP. IF WE CAN --
THAT'S... THAT'S PROBABLY FOR THE BEST, I THINK.

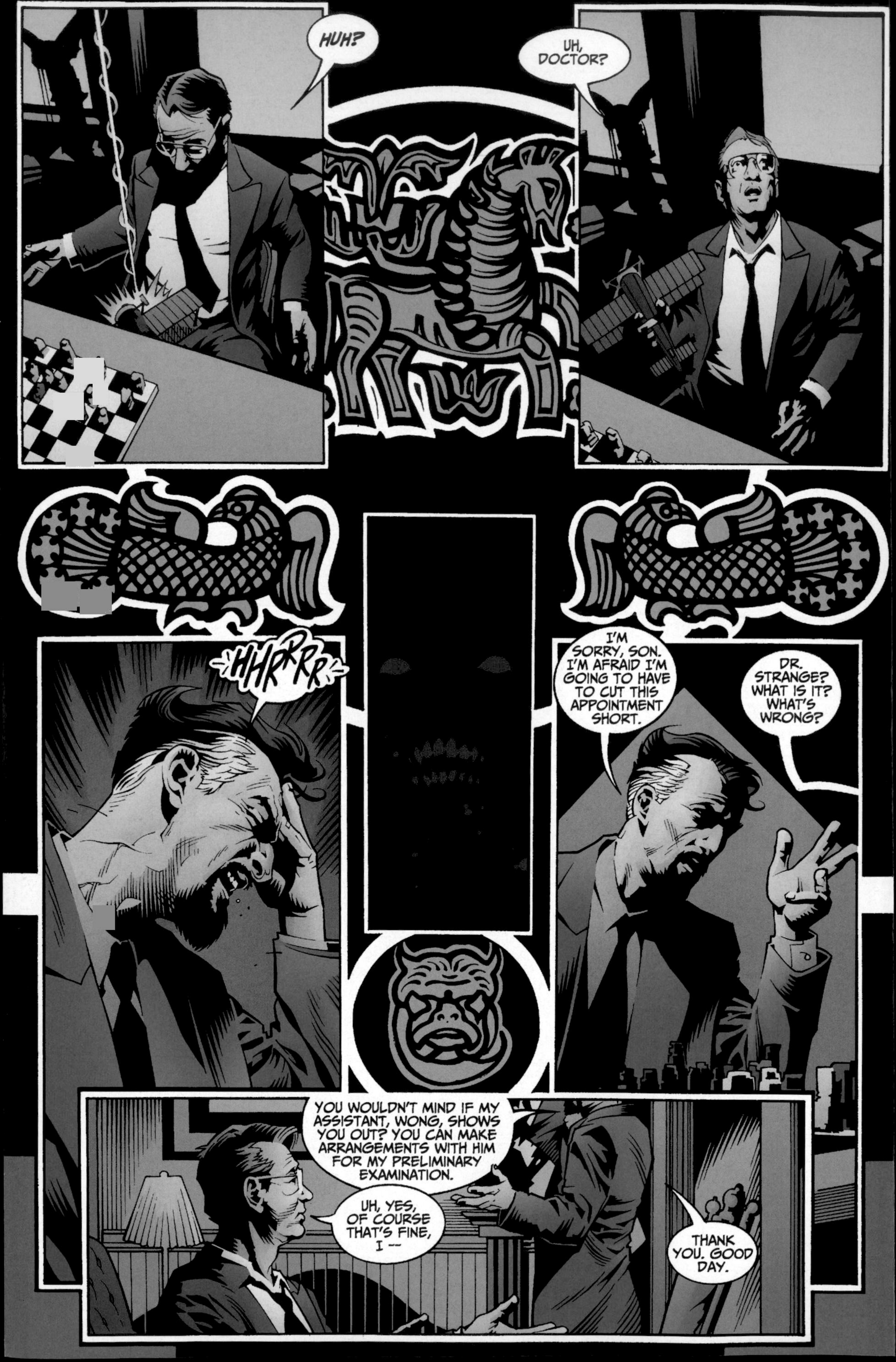
HUH?
UH, DOCTOR?
HHRRRR
I'M SORRY, SON. I'M AFRAID I'M GOING TO HAVE TO CUT THIS APPOINTMENT SHORT.
DR. STRANGE? WHAT IS IT? WHAT'S WRONG?
YOU WOULDN'T MIND IF MY ASSISTANT, WONG, SHOWS YOU OUT? YOU CAN MAKE ARRANGEMENTS WITH HIM FOR MY PRELIMINARY EXAMINATION.
UH, YES, OF COURSE THAT'S FINE, I --
THANK YOU. GOOD DAY.

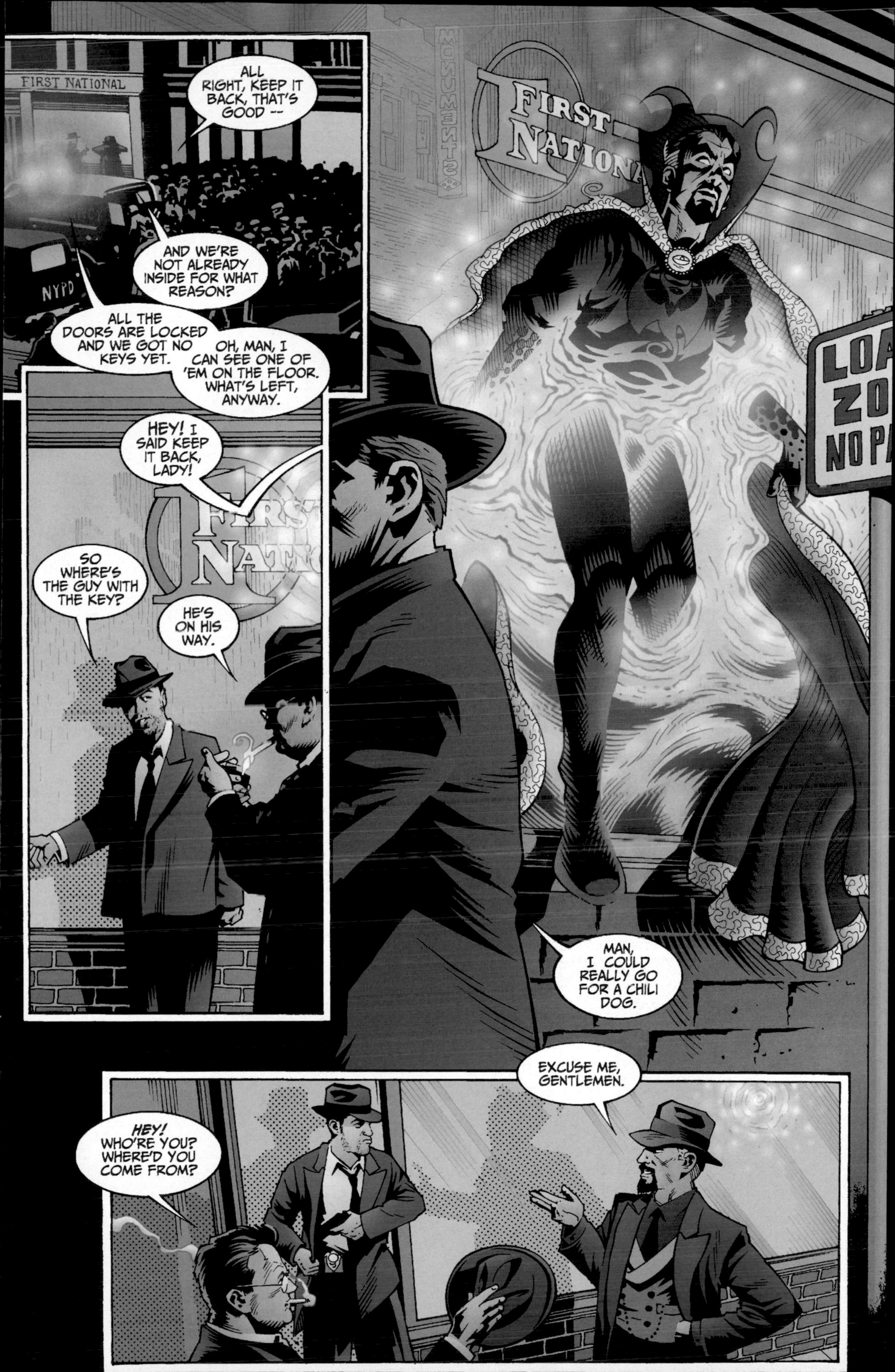
FIRST NATIONAL
ALL RIGHT, KEEP IT BACK, THAT'S GOOD --
AND WE'RE NOT ALREADY INSIDE FOR WHAT REASON?
NYPD
ALL THE DOORS ARE LOCKED AND WE GOT NO KEYS YET.
OH, MAN, I CAN SEE ONE OF 'EM ON THE FLOOR. WHAT'S LEFT, ANYWAY.
MONUMENTS
FIRST NATIONAL
HEY! I SAID KEEP IT BACK, LADY!
SO WHERE'S THE GUY WITH THE KEY?
HE'S ON HIS WAY.
MAN, I COULD REALLY GO FOR A CHILI DOG.
EXCUSE ME, GENTLEMEN.
HEY! WHO'RE YOU? WHERE'D YOU COME FROM?

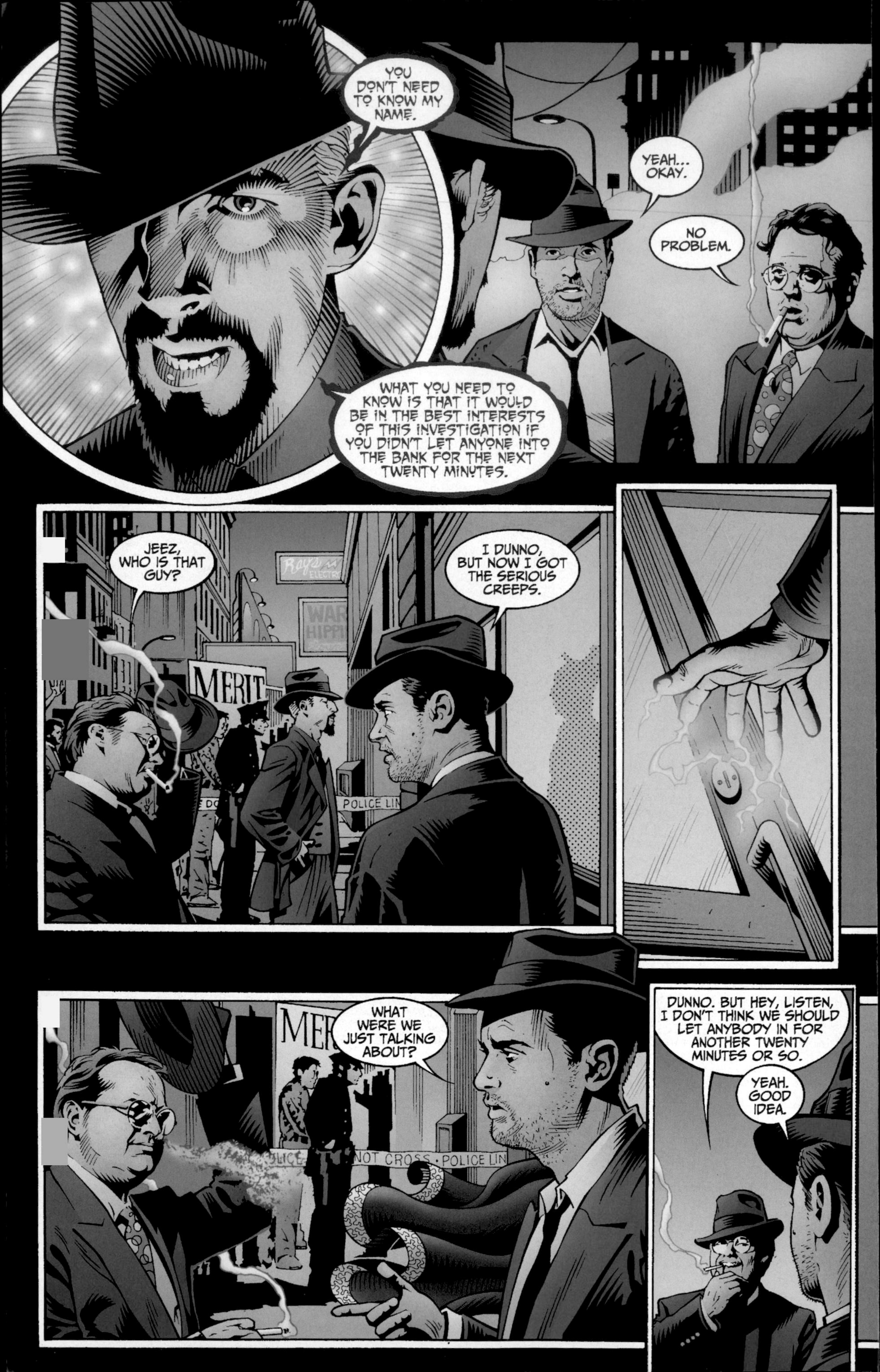
YOU DON'T NEED TO KNOW MY NAME.
YEAH... OKAY.
NO PROBLEM.
WHAT YOU NEED TO KNOW IS THAT IT WOULD BE IN THE BEST INTERESTS OF THIS INVESTIGATION IF YOU DIDN'T LET ANYONE INTO THE BANK FOR THE NEXT TWENTY MINUTES.
JEEZ, WHO IS THAT GUY?
I DUNNO, BUT NOW I GOT THE SERIOUS CREEPS.
MERIT
POLICE LIN
WHAT WERE WE JUST TALKING ABOUT?
NOT CROSS · POLICE LIN
DUNNO. BUT HEY, LISTEN, I DON'T THINK WE SHOULD LET ANYBODY IN FOR ANOTHER TWENTY MINUTES OR SO.
YEAH. GOOD IDEA.

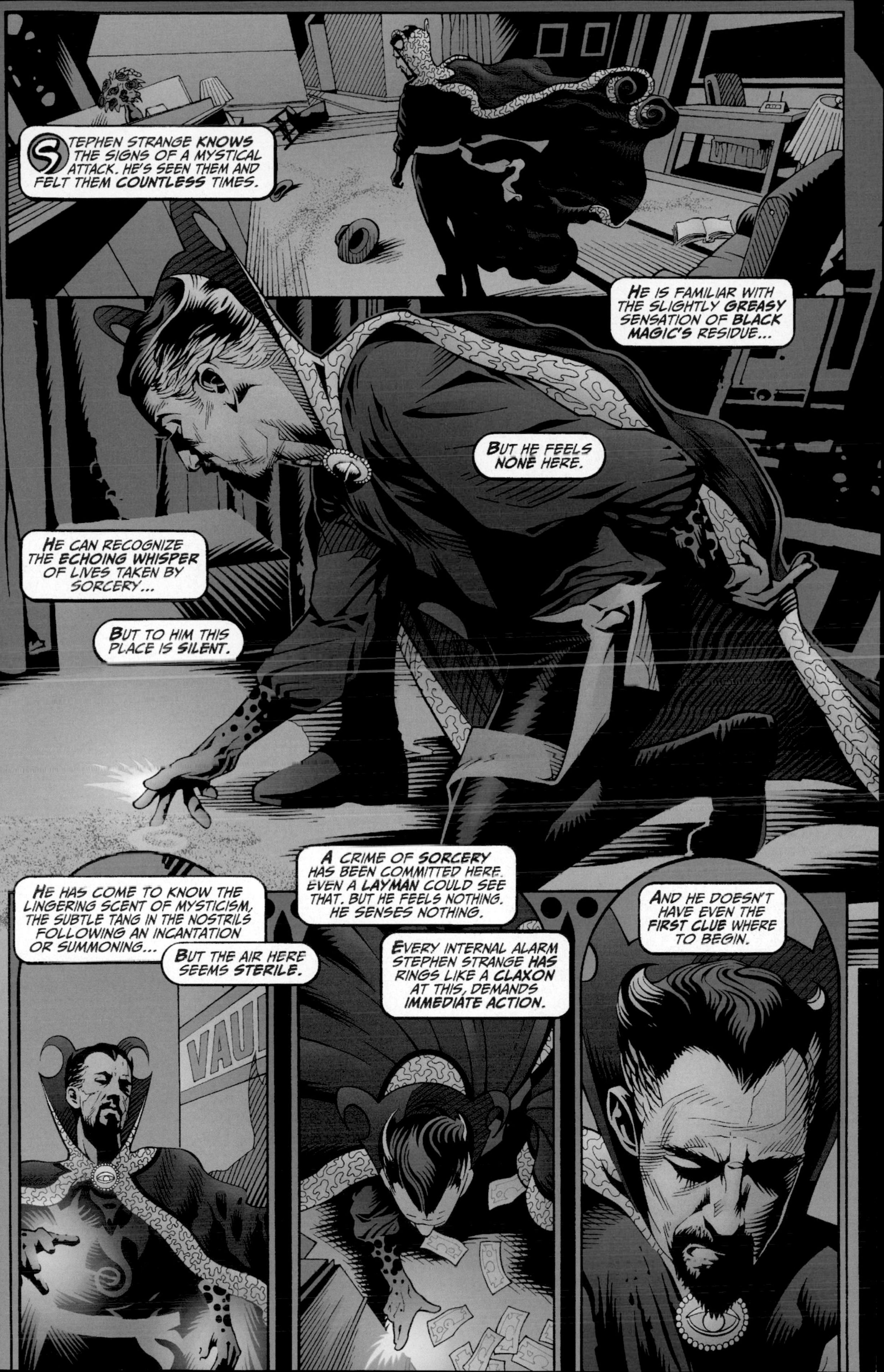
STEPHEN STRANGE KNOWS THE SIGNS OF A MYSTICAL ATTACK. HE'S SEEN THEM AND FELT THEM COUNTLESS TIMES.
HE IS FAMILIAR WITH THE SLIGHTLY GREASY SENSATION OF BLACK MAGIC'S RESIDUE...
BUT HE FEELS NONE HERE.
HE CAN RECOGNIZE THE ECHOING WHISPER OF LIVES TAKEN BY SORCERY...
BUT TO HIM THIS PLACE IS SILENT.
HE HAS COME TO KNOW THE LINGERING SCENT OF MYSTICISM, THE SUBTLE TANG IN THE NOSTRILS FOLLOWING AN INCANTATION OR SUMMONING...
BUT THE AIR HERE SEEMS STERILE.
VAU
A CRIME OF SORCERY HAS BEEN COMMITTED HERE. EVEN A LAYMAN COULD SEE THAT. BUT HE FEELS NOTHING. HE SENSES NOTHING.
EVERY INTERNAL ALARM STEPHEN STRANGE HAS RINGS LIKE A CLAXON AT THIS, DEMANDS IMMEDIATE ACTION.
AND HE DOESN'T HAVE EVEN THE FIRST CLUE WHERE TO BEGIN.

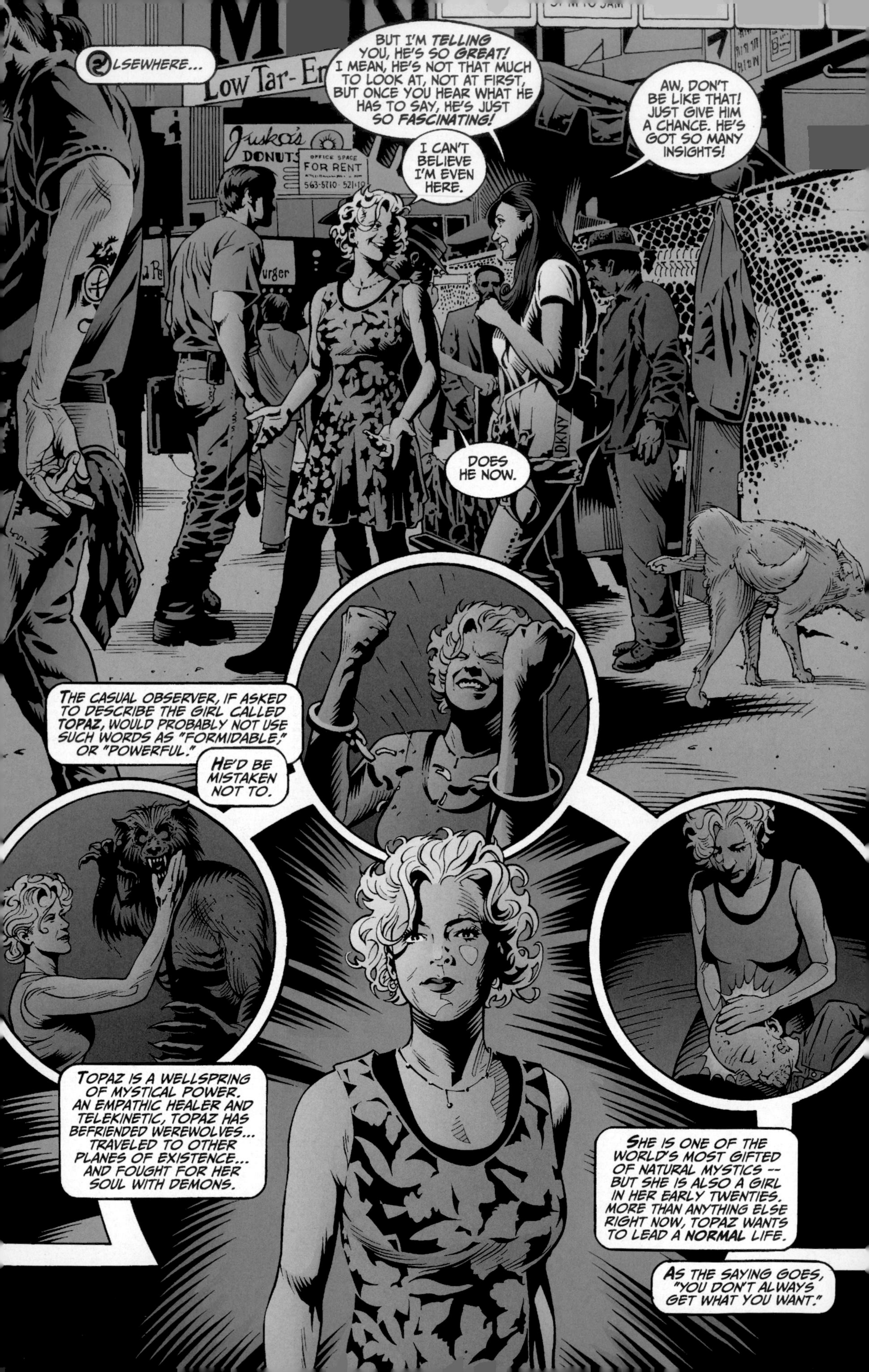
ELSEWHERE...
BUT I'M TELLING YOU, HE'S SO GREAT! I MEAN, HE'S NOT THAT MUCH TO LOOK AT, NOT AT FIRST, BUT ONCE YOU HEAR WHAT HE HAS TO SAY, HE'S JUST SO FASCINATING!
I CAN'T BELIEVE I'M EVEN HERE.
AW, DON'T BE LIKE THAT! JUST GIVE HIM A CHANCE. HE'S GOT SO MANY INSIGHTS!
DOES HE NOW.
Low Tar- En
Jusko's DONUTS
OFFICE SPACE FOR RENT 563-5710 · 521-18
urger
DKNY
THE CASUAL OBSERVER, IF ASKED TO DESCRIBE THE GIRL CALLED TOPAZ, WOULD PROBABLY NOT USE SUCH WORDS AS "FORMIDABLE," OR "POWERFUL."
HE'D BE MISTAKEN NOT TO.
TOPAZ IS A WELLSPRING OF MYSTICAL POWER. AN EMPATHIC HEALER AND TELEKINETIC, TOPAZ HAS BEFRIENDED WEREWOLVES... TRAVELED TO OTHER PLANES OF EXISTENCE... AND FOUGHT FOR HER SOUL WITH DEMONS.
SHE IS ONE OF THE WORLD'S MOST GIFTED OF NATURAL MYSTICS -- BUT SHE IS ALSO A GIRL IN HER EARLY TWENTIES. MORE THAN ANYTHING ELSE RIGHT NOW, TOPAZ WANTS TO LEAD A NORMAL LIFE.
AS THE SAYING GOES, "YOU DON'T ALWAYS GET WHAT YOU WANT."

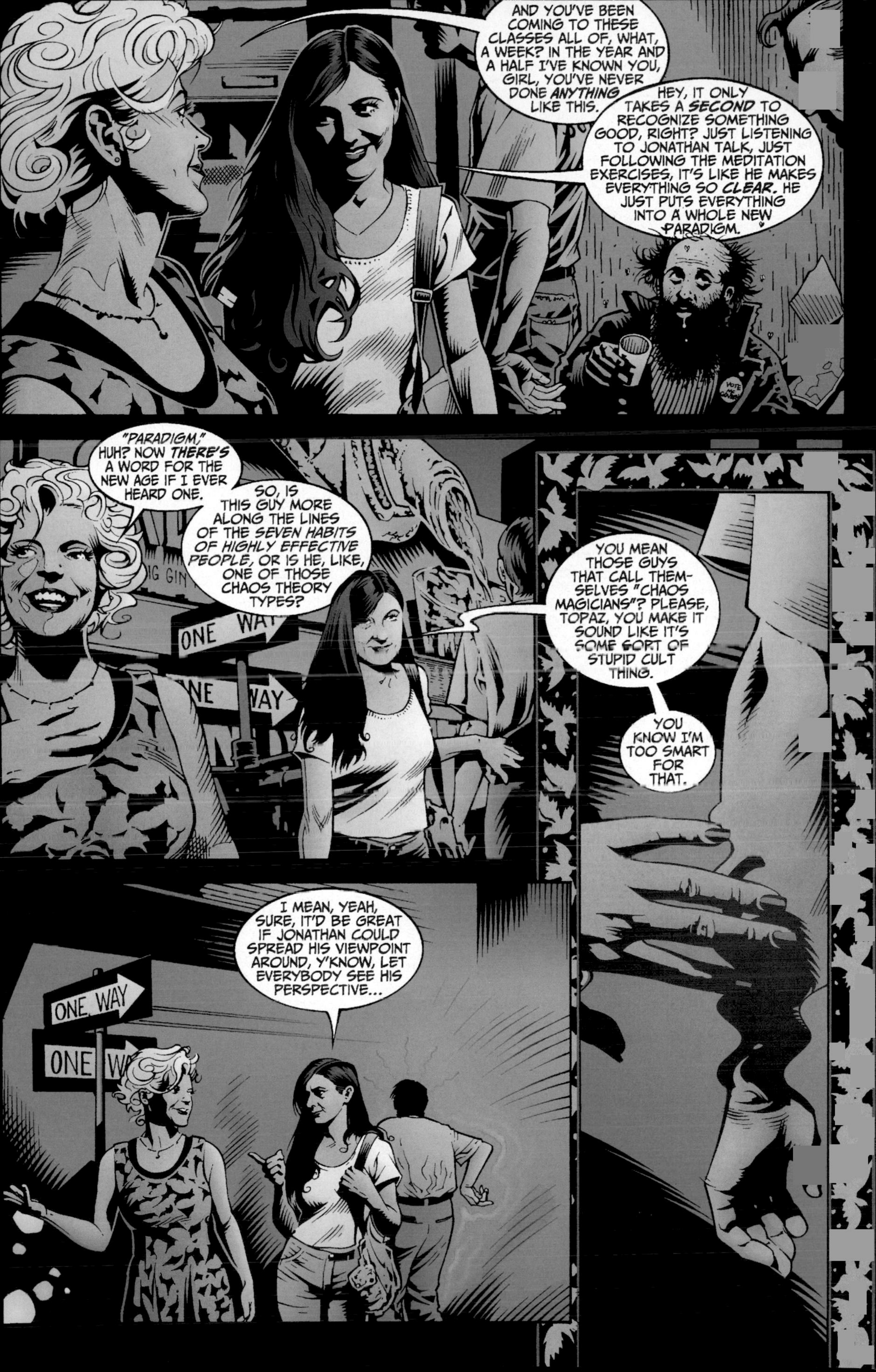
AND YOU'VE BEEN COMING TO THESE CLASSES ALL OF, WHAT, A WEEK? IN THE YEAR AND A HALF I'VE KNOWN YOU, GIRL, YOU'VE NEVER DONE *ANYTHING* LIKE THIS.
HEY, IT ONLY TAKES A *SECOND* TO RECOGNIZE SOMETHING GOOD, RIGHT? JUST LISTENING TO JONATHAN TALK, JUST FOLLOWING THE MEDITATION EXERCISES, IT'S LIKE HE MAKES EVERYTHING SO *CLEAR.* HE JUST PUTS EVERYTHING INTO A WHOLE NEW PARADIGM.
"PARADIGM," HUH? NOW *THERE'S* A WORD FOR THE NEW AGE IF I EVER HEARD ONE.
SO, IS THIS GUY MORE ALONG THE LINES OF THE *SEVEN HABITS OF HIGHLY EFFECTIVE PEOPLE,* OR IS HE, LIKE, ONE OF THOSE CHAOS THEORY TYPES?
ONE WAY
YOU MEAN THOSE GUYS THAT CALL THEMSELVES "CHAOS MAGICIANS"? PLEASE, TOPAZ, YOU MAKE IT SOUND LIKE IT'S SOME SORT OF STUPID CULT THING.
YOU KNOW I'M TOO SMART FOR THAT.
I MEAN, YEAH, SURE, IT'D BE GREAT IF JONATHAN COULD SPREAD HIS VIEWPOINT AROUND, Y'KNOW, LET EVERYBODY SEE HIS PERSPECTIVE...
ONE WAY

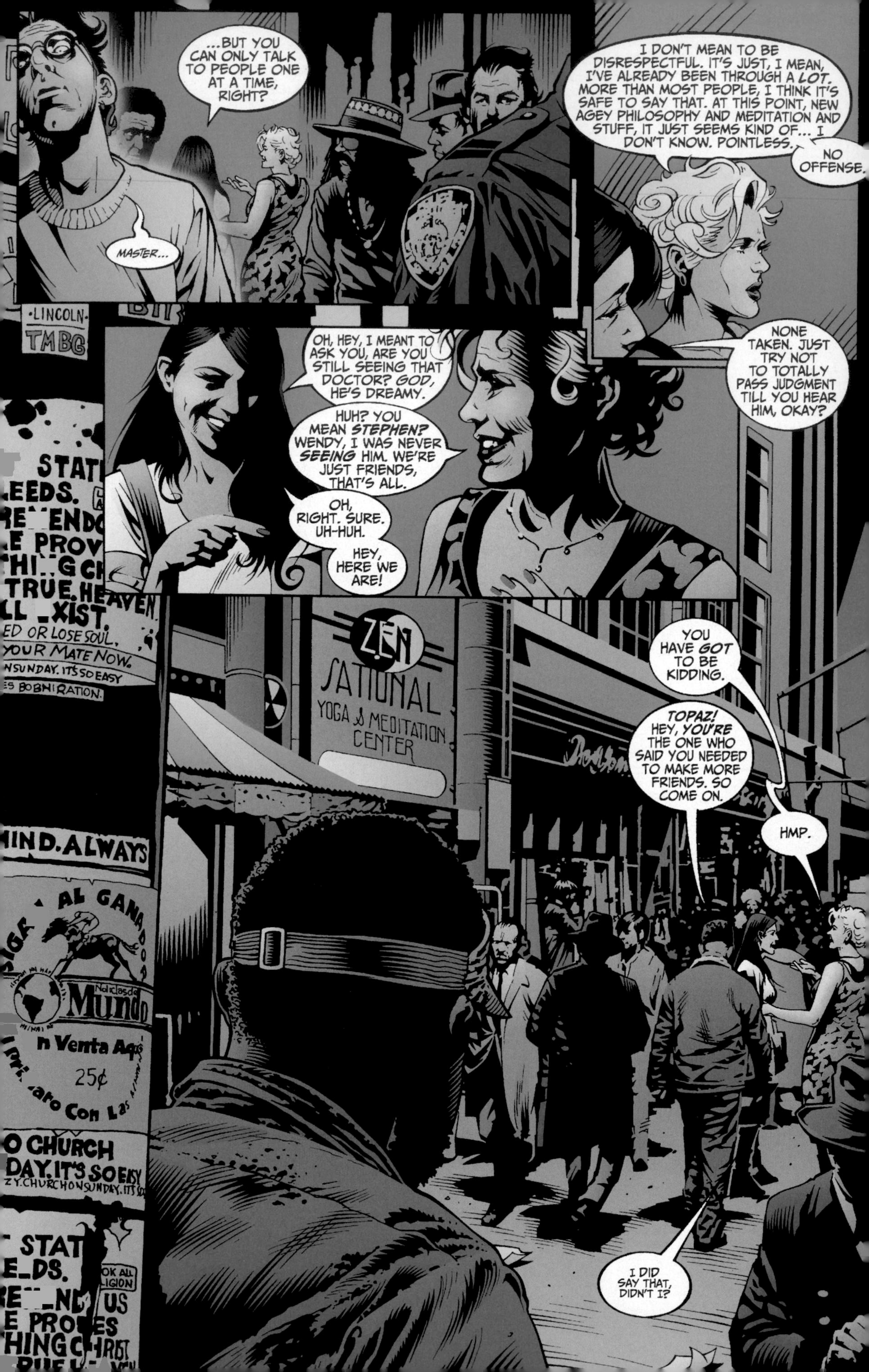

...BUT YOU CAN ONLY TALK TO PEOPLE ONE AT A TIME, RIGHT?
MASTER...
I DON'T MEAN TO BE DISRESPECTFUL. IT'S JUST, I MEAN, I'VE ALREADY BEEN THROUGH A LOT. MORE THAN MOST PEOPLE, I THINK IT'S SAFE TO SAY THAT. AT THIS POINT, NEW AGEY PHILOSOPHY AND MEDITATION AND STUFF, IT JUST SEEMS KIND OF... I DON'T KNOW. POINTLESS.
NO OFFENSE.
NONE TAKEN. JUST TRY NOT TO TOTALLY PASS JUDGMENT TILL YOU HEAR HIM, OKAY?
OH, HEY, I MEANT TO ASK YOU, ARE YOU STILL SEEING THAT DOCTOR? GOD, HE'S DREAMY.
HUH? YOU MEAN STEPHEN? WENDY, I WAS NEVER SEEING HIM. WE'RE JUST FRIENDS, THAT'S ALL.
OH, RIGHT. SURE. UH-HUH.
HEY, HERE WE ARE!
ZEN SATIONAL YOGA & MEDITATION CENTER
YOU HAVE GOT TO BE KIDDING.
TOPAZ! HEY, YOU'RE THE ONE WHO SAID YOU NEEDED TO MAKE MORE FRIENDS. SO COME ON.
HMP.
I DID SAY THAT, DIDN'T I?

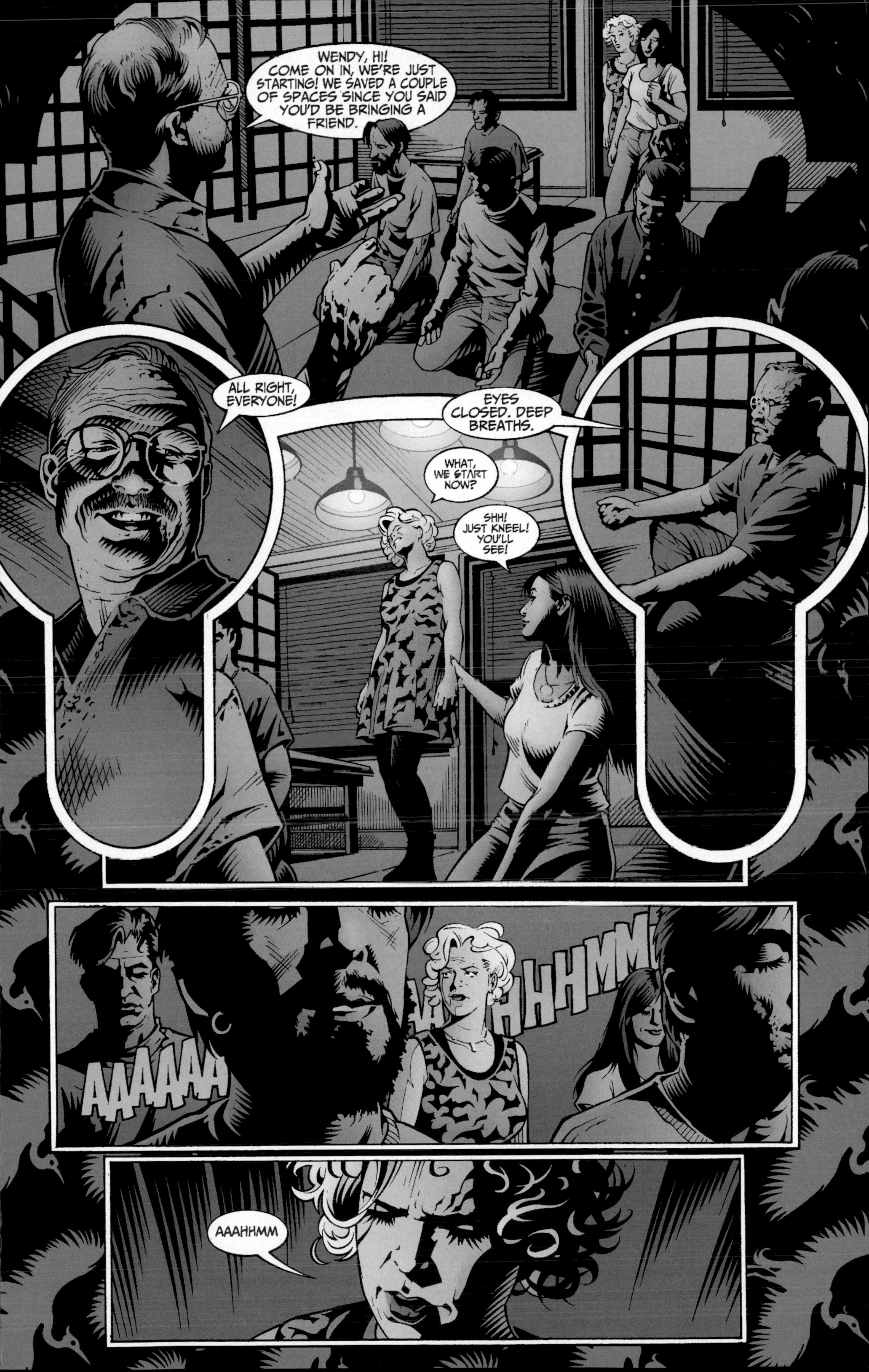

WENDY, HI! COME ON IN, WE'RE JUST STARTING! WE SAVED A COUPLE OF SPACES SINCE YOU SAID YOU'D BE BRINGING A FRIEND.
ALL RIGHT, EVERYONE!
EYES CLOSED. DEEP BREATHS.
WHAT, WE START NOW?
SHH! JUST KNEEL! YOU'LL SEE!
AAAAAA
HHHMM
AAAHHMM

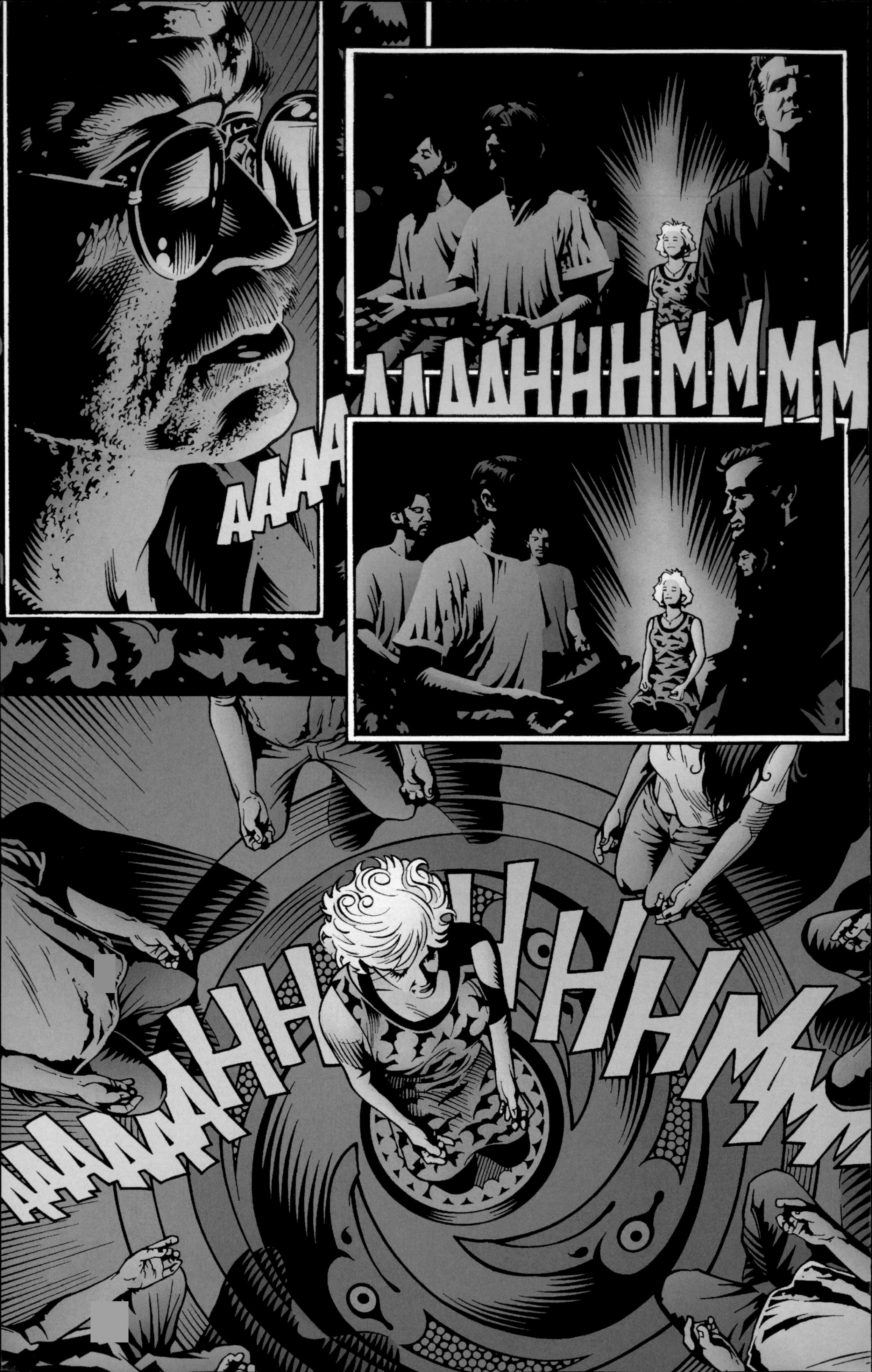

AAAAAAAHHHMMMMM
AAAAAHHHHHMM

AAA--
-- AAOOOUR
LORD AND
MASTER, HEAR
US, HEED US
GIVE TO US YOUR
MOURNFUL PAIN
OUR HEARTS FILLED
WITH LUST, YOU
FEED US
SUCCULENT, THE
CRIMSON STAIN

WILD AS TIGERS,
FINE AS COBWEBS
FLESH GROWN
SOFTER E'ER
WITH ROT COLD,
YOUR BREATH
FLOWS GENTLY
O'ER US BIND
OUR LIVES WITH
SILKEN KNOT

CHILD OF SPIDERS,
GOD OF VERMIN
SACRIFICE, NOW
COME TO SEE.
YOU WHO RUT IN
BLOODIED TORCHLIGHT
THREE OF ONE AND
ONE OF THREE

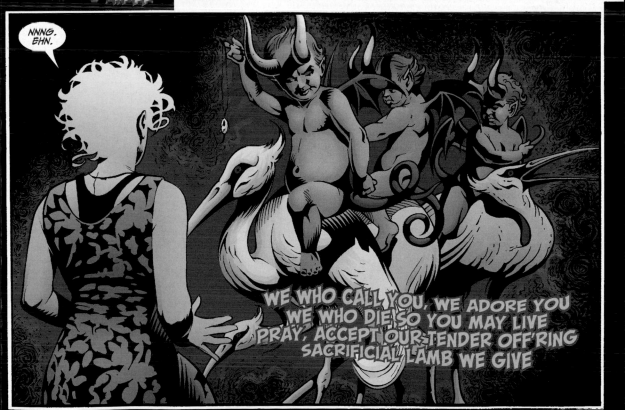

NNNG.
EHN.

WE WHO CALL YOU, WE ADORE YOU
WE WHO DIE SO YOU MAY LIVE
PRAY, ACCEPT OUR TENDER OFF'RING
SACRIFICIAL LAMB WE GIVE

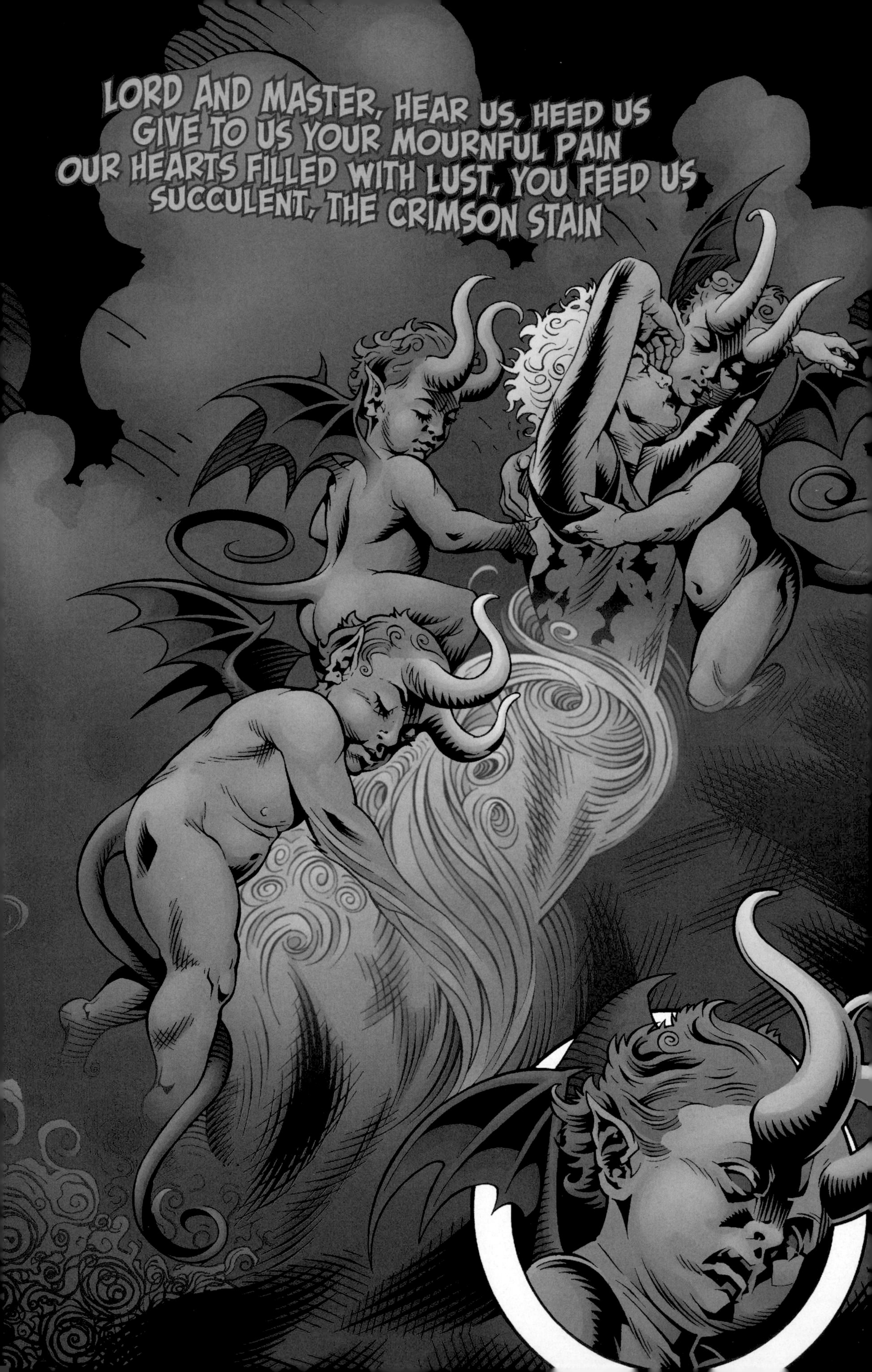
LORD AND MASTER, HEAR US, HEED US
GIVE TO US YOUR MOURNFUL PAIN
OUR HEARTS FILLED WITH LUST, YOU FEED US
SUCCULENT, THE CRIMSON STAIN

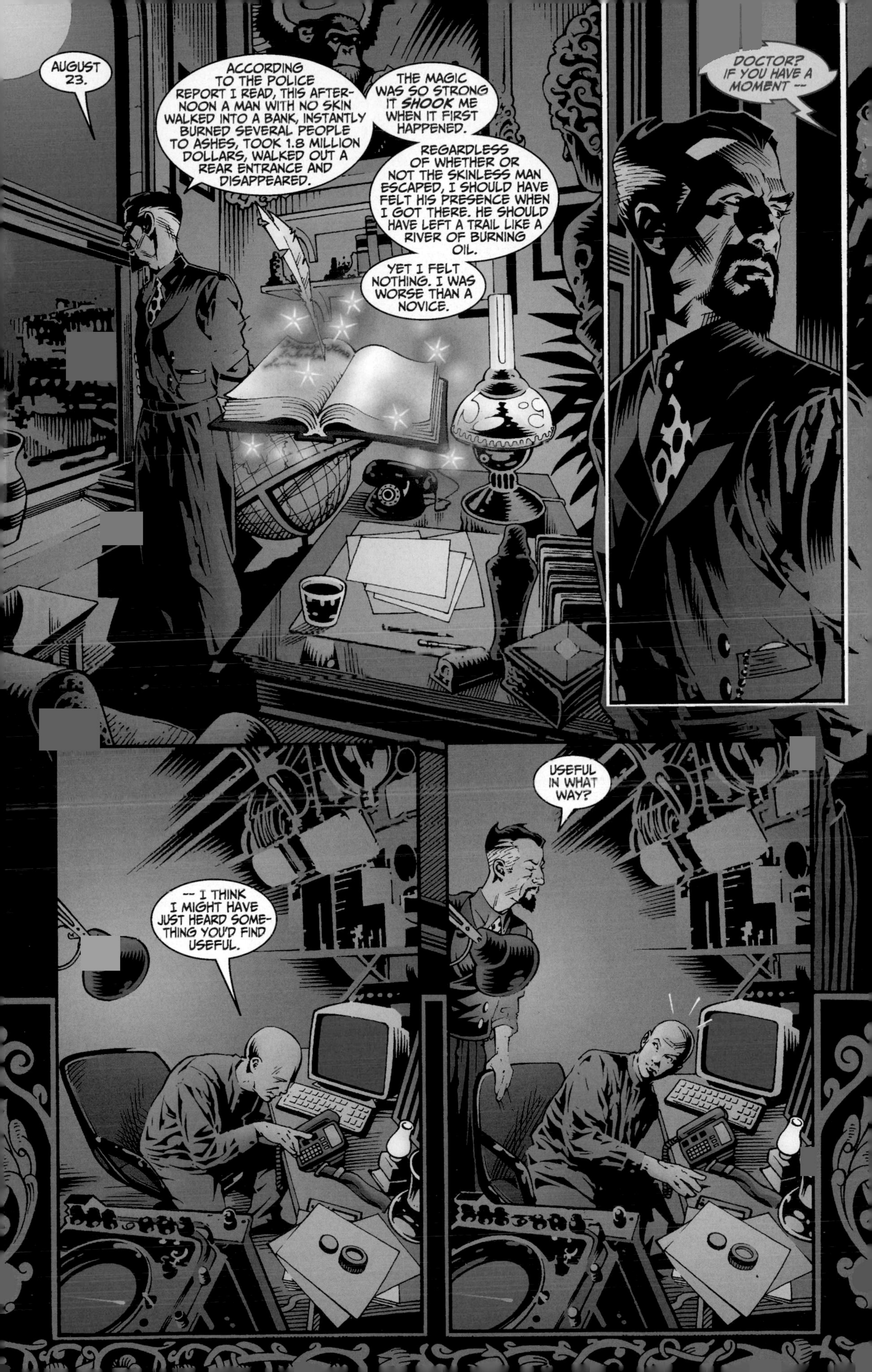
AUGUST 23.
ACCORDING TO THE POLICE REPORT I READ, THIS AFTERNOON A MAN WITH NO SKIN WALKED INTO A BANK, INSTANTLY BURNED SEVERAL PEOPLE TO ASHES, TOOK 1.8 MILLION DOLLARS, WALKED OUT A REAR ENTRANCE AND DISAPPEARED.
THE MAGIC WAS SO STRONG IT SHOOK ME WHEN IT FIRST HAPPENED.
REGARDLESS OF WHETHER OR NOT THE SKINLESS MAN ESCAPED, I SHOULD HAVE FELT HIS PRESENCE WHEN I GOT THERE. HE SHOULD HAVE LEFT A TRAIL LIKE A RIVER OF BURNING OIL.
YET I FELT NOTHING. I WAS WORSE THAN A NOVICE.
DOCTOR? IF YOU HAVE A MOMENT --
-- I THINK I MIGHT HAVE JUST HEARD SOMETHING YOU'D FIND USEFUL.
USEFUL IN WHAT WAY?

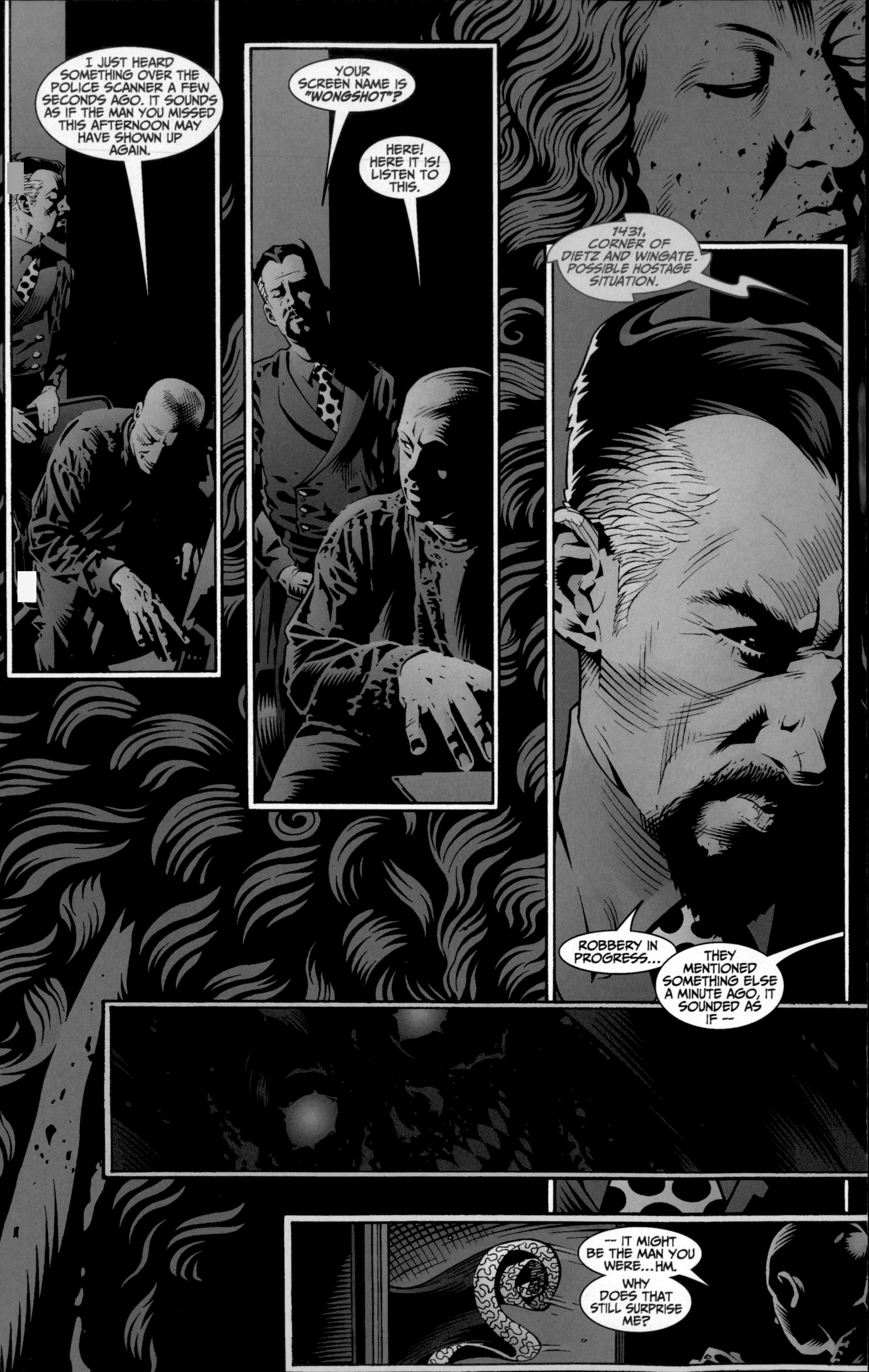
I JUST HEARD SOMETHING OVER THE POLICE SCANNER A FEW SECONDS AGO. IT SOUNDS AS IF THE MAN YOU MISSED THIS AFTERNOON MAY HAVE SHOWN UP AGAIN.
YOUR SCREEN NAME IS "WONGSHOT"?
HERE! HERE IT IS! LISTEN TO THIS.
1431. CORNER OF DIETZ AND WINGATE. POSSIBLE HOSTAGE SITUATION.
ROBBERY IN PROGRESS...
THEY MENTIONED SOMETHING ELSE A MINUTE AGO, IT SOUNDED AS IF --
-- IT MIGHT BE THE MAN YOU WERE...HM.
WHY DOES THAT STILL SURPRISE ME?

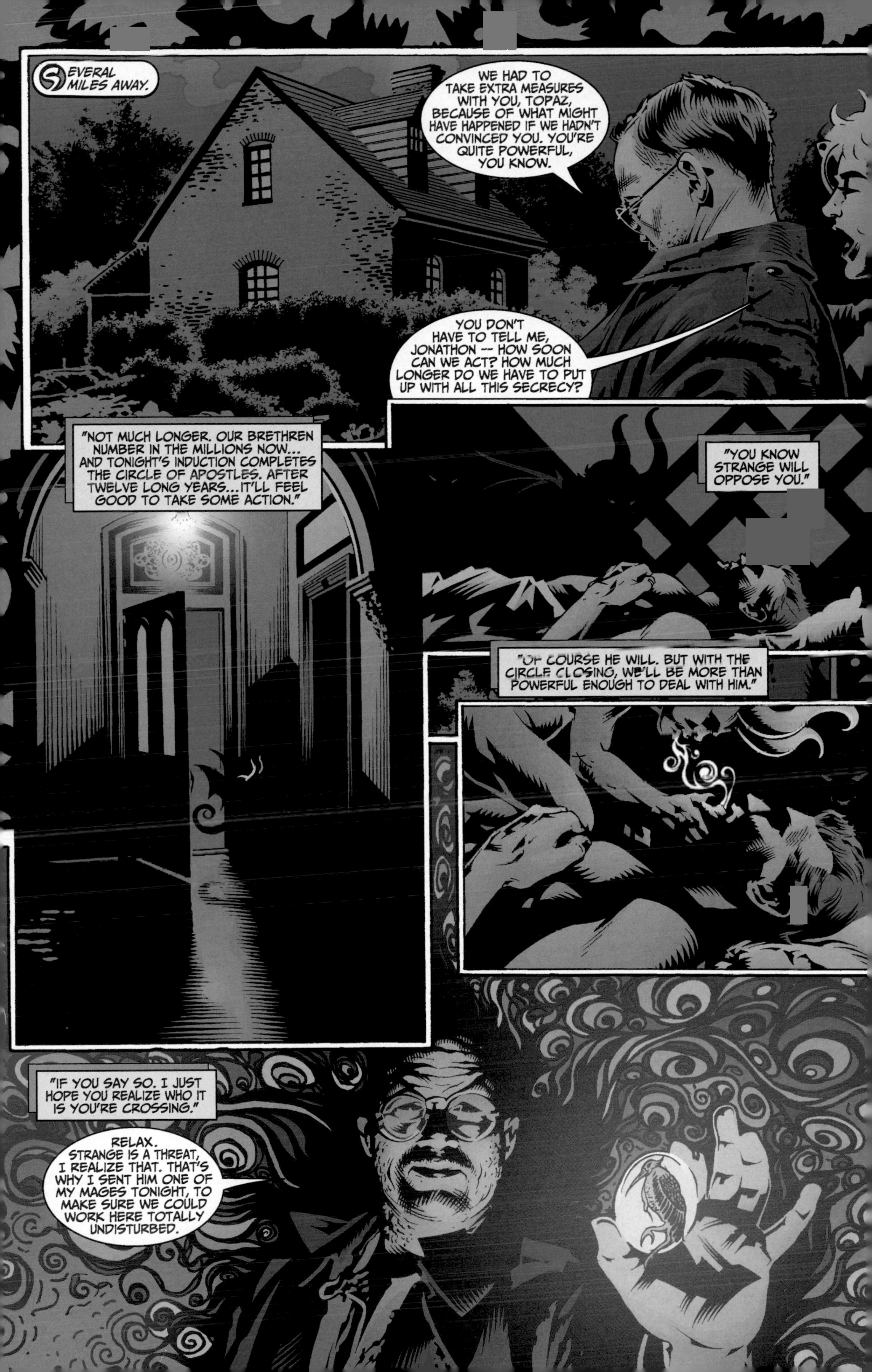
SEVERAL MILES AWAY.
WE HAD TO TAKE EXTRA MEASURES WITH YOU, TOPAZ, BECAUSE OF WHAT MIGHT HAVE HAPPENED IF WE HADN'T CONVINCED YOU. YOU'RE QUITE POWERFUL, YOU KNOW.
YOU DON'T HAVE TO TELL ME, JONATHON -- HOW SOON CAN WE ACT? HOW MUCH LONGER DO WE HAVE TO PUT UP WITH ALL THIS SECRECY?
"NOT MUCH LONGER. OUR BRETHREN NUMBER IN THE MILLIONS NOW... AND TONIGHT'S INDUCTION COMPLETES THE CIRCLE OF APOSTLES. AFTER TWELVE LONG YEARS...IT'LL FEEL GOOD TO TAKE SOME ACTION."
"YOU KNOW STRANGE WILL OPPOSE YOU."
"OF COURSE HE WILL. BUT WITH THE CIRCLE CLOSING, WE'LL BE MORE THAN POWERFUL ENOUGH TO DEAL WITH HIM."
"IF YOU SAY SO. I JUST HOPE YOU REALIZE WHO IT IS YOU'RE CROSSING."
RELAX. STRANGE IS A THREAT, I REALIZE THAT. THAT'S WHY I SENT HIM ONE OF MY MAGES TONIGHT, TO MAKE SURE WE COULD WORK HERE TOTALLY UNDISTURBED.

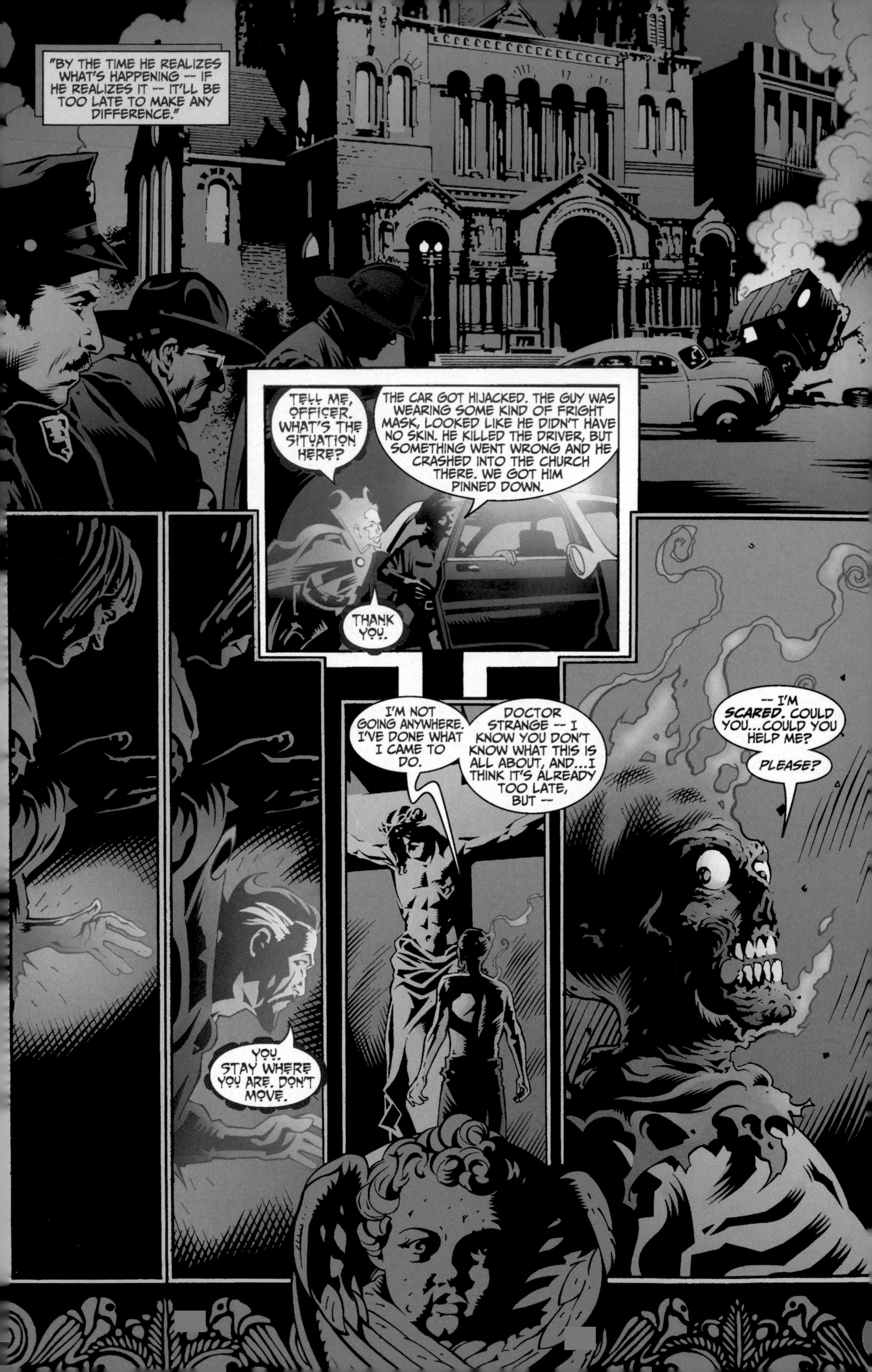
"BY THE TIME HE REALIZES WHAT'S HAPPENING -- IF HE REALIZES IT -- IT'LL BE TOO LATE TO MAKE ANY DIFFERENCE."
TELL ME, OFFICER. WHAT'S THE SITUATION HERE?
THE CAR GOT HIJACKED. THE GUY WAS WEARING SOME KIND OF FRIGHT MASK, LOOKED LIKE HE DIDN'T HAVE NO SKIN. HE KILLED THE DRIVER, BUT SOMETHING WENT WRONG AND HE CRASHED INTO THE CHURCH THERE. WE GOT HIM PINNED DOWN.
THANK YOU.
YOU. STAY WHERE YOU ARE. DON'T MOVE.
I'M NOT GOING ANYWHERE. I'VE DONE WHAT I CAME TO DO.
DOCTOR STRANGE -- I KNOW YOU DON'T KNOW WHAT THIS IS ALL ABOUT, AND...I THINK IT'S ALREADY TOO LATE, BUT --
-- I'M SCARED. COULD YOU...COULD YOU HELP ME?
PLEASE?

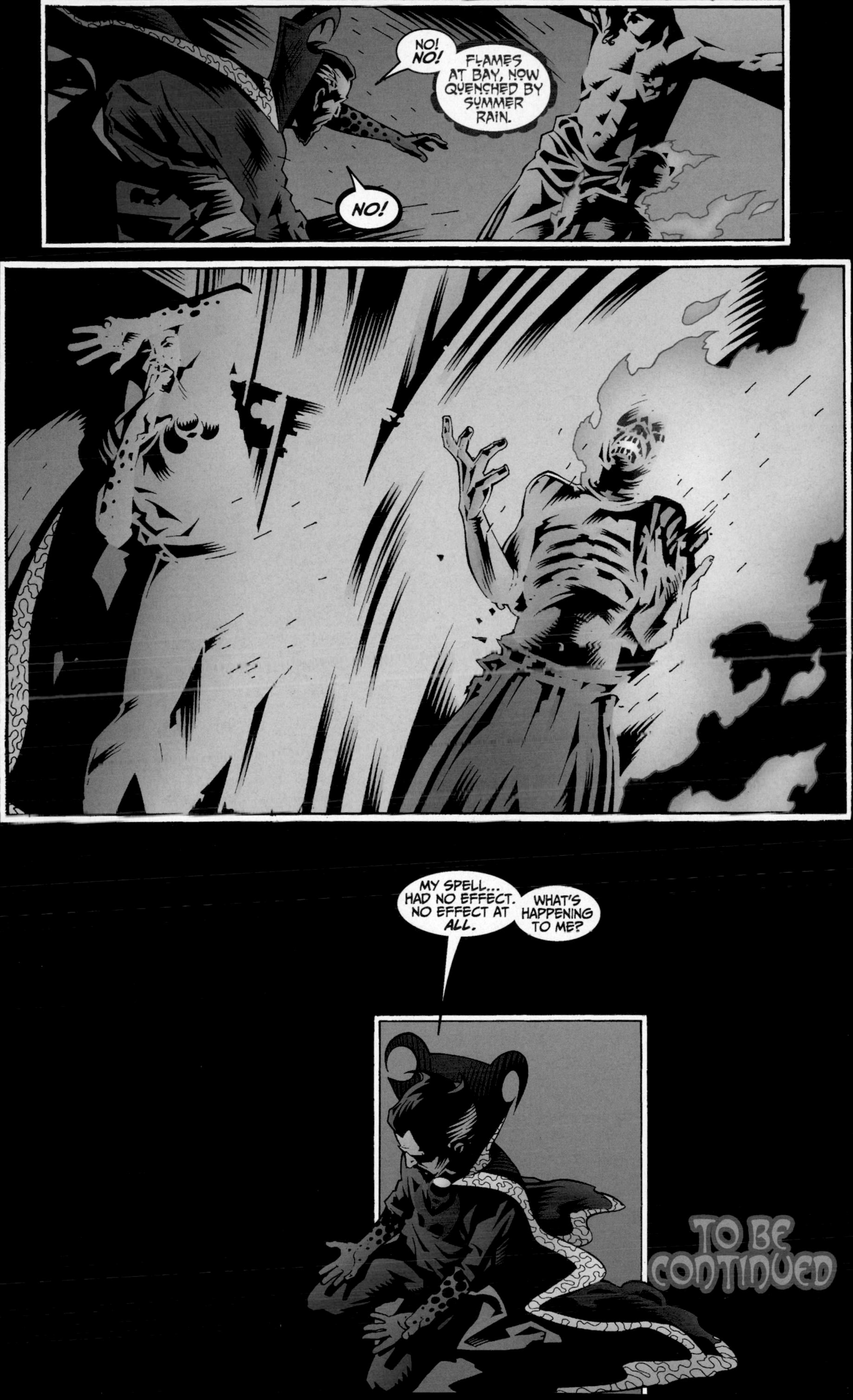
NO! NO!
FLAMES AT BAY, NOW QUENCHED BY SUMMER RAIN.
NO!
MY SPELL... HAD NO EFFECT. NO EFFECT AT ALL.
WHAT'S HAPPENING TO ME?
TO BE CONTINUED

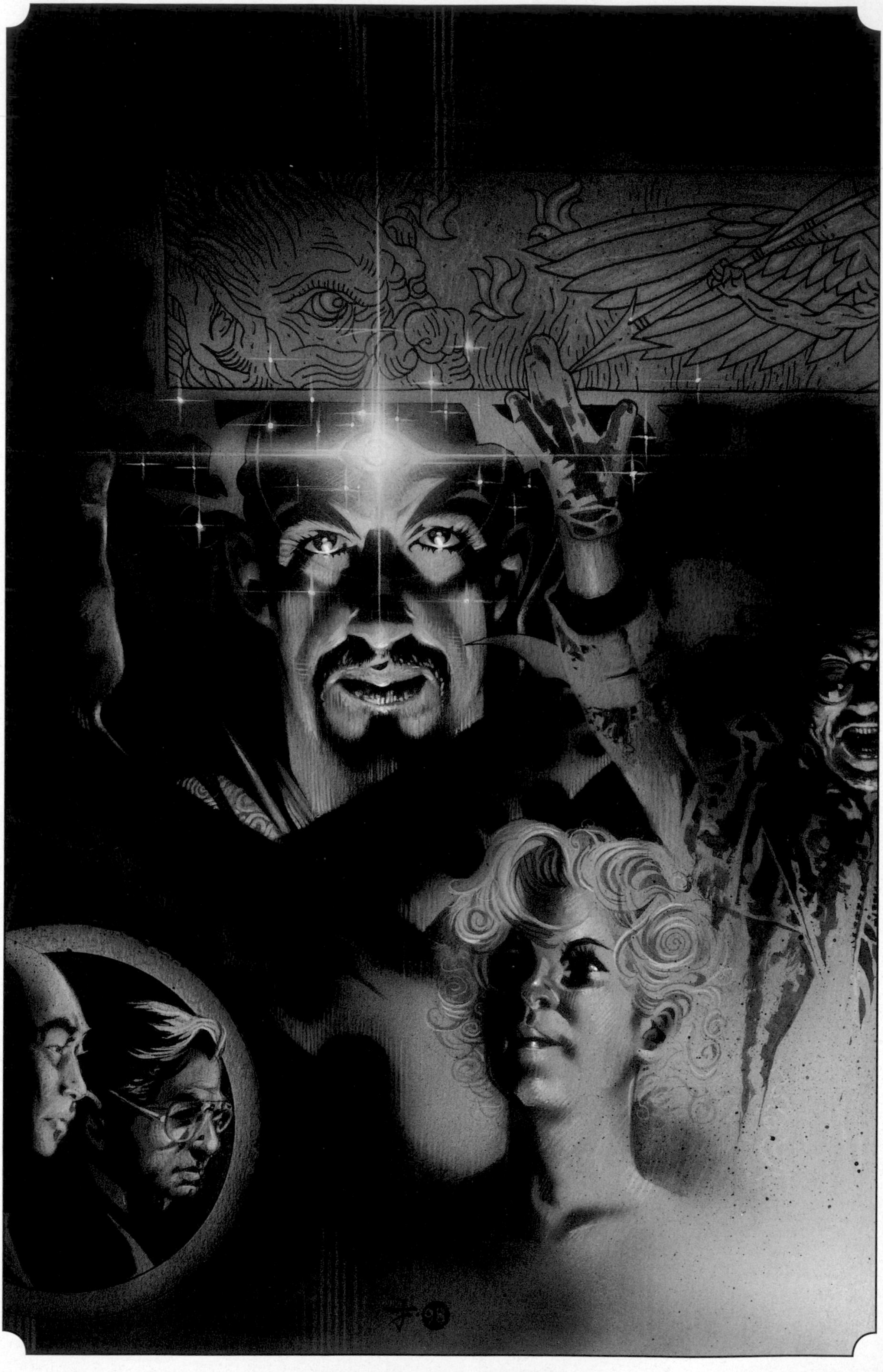

DOCTOR STRANGE #2

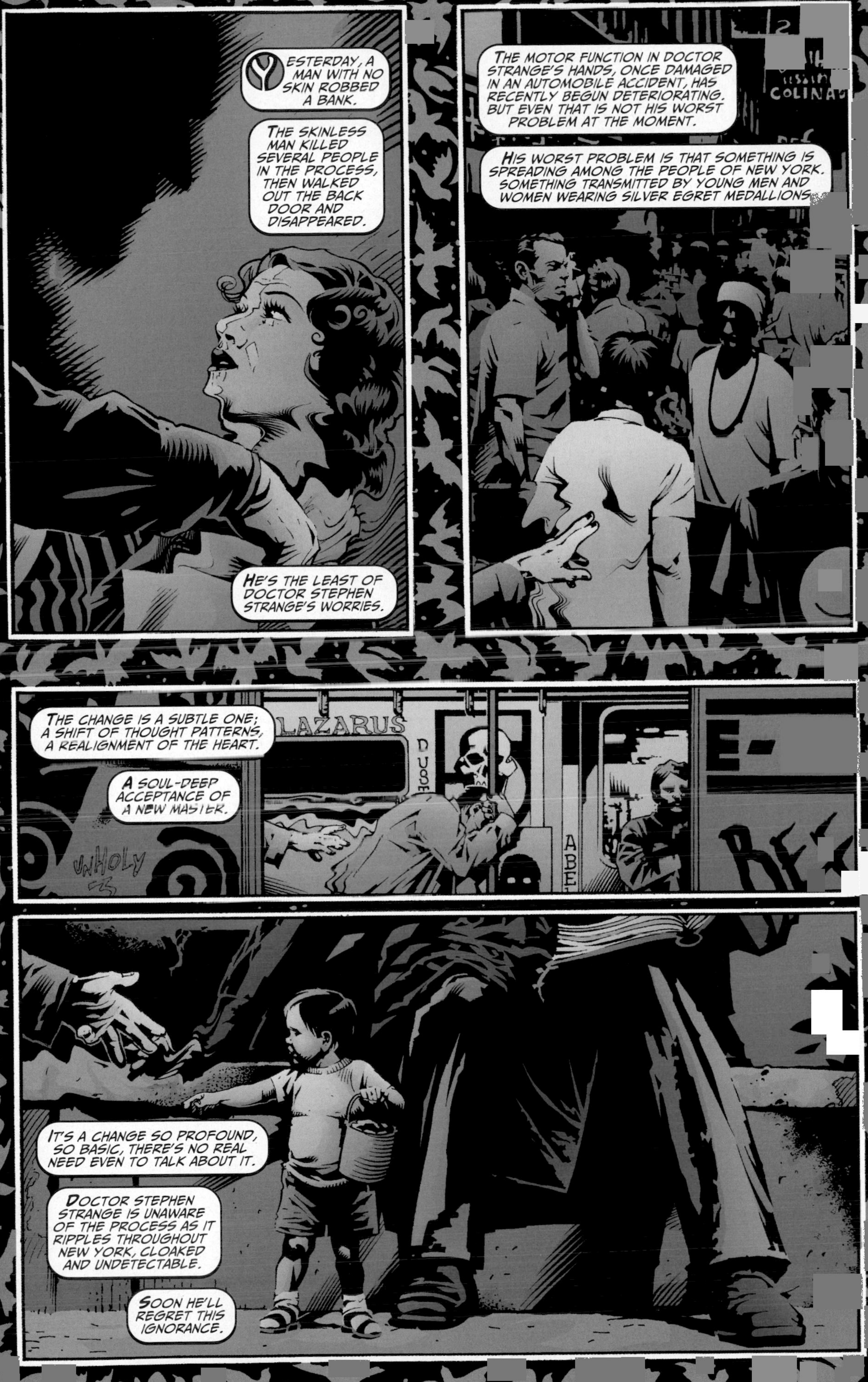

YESTERDAY, A MAN WITH NO SKIN ROBBED A BANK.
THE SKINLESS MAN KILLED SEVERAL PEOPLE IN THE PROCESS, THEN WALKED OUT THE BACK DOOR AND DISAPPEARED.
HE'S THE LEAST OF DOCTOR STEPHEN STRANGE'S WORRIES.
THE MOTOR FUNCTION IN DOCTOR STRANGE'S HANDS, ONCE DAMAGED IN AN AUTOMOBILE ACCIDENT, HAS RECENTLY BEGUN DETERIORATING. BUT EVEN THAT IS NOT HIS WORST PROBLEM AT THE MOMENT.
HIS WORST PROBLEM IS THAT SOMETHING IS SPREADING AMONG THE PEOPLE OF NEW YORK. SOMETHING TRANSMITTED BY YOUNG MEN AND WOMEN WEARING SILVER EGRET MEDALLIONS.
THE CHANGE IS A SUBTLE ONE; A SHIFT OF THOUGHT PATTERNS, A REALIGNMENT OF THE HEART.
A SOUL-DEEP ACCEPTANCE OF A NEW MASTER.
LAZARUS
IT'S A CHANGE SO PROFOUND, SO BASIC, THERE'S NO REAL NEED EVEN TO TALK ABOUT IT.
DOCTOR STEPHEN STRANGE IS UNAWARE OF THE PROCESS AS IT RIPPLES THROUGHOUT NEW YORK, CLOAKED AND UNDETECTABLE.
SOON HE'LL REGRET THIS IGNORANCE.

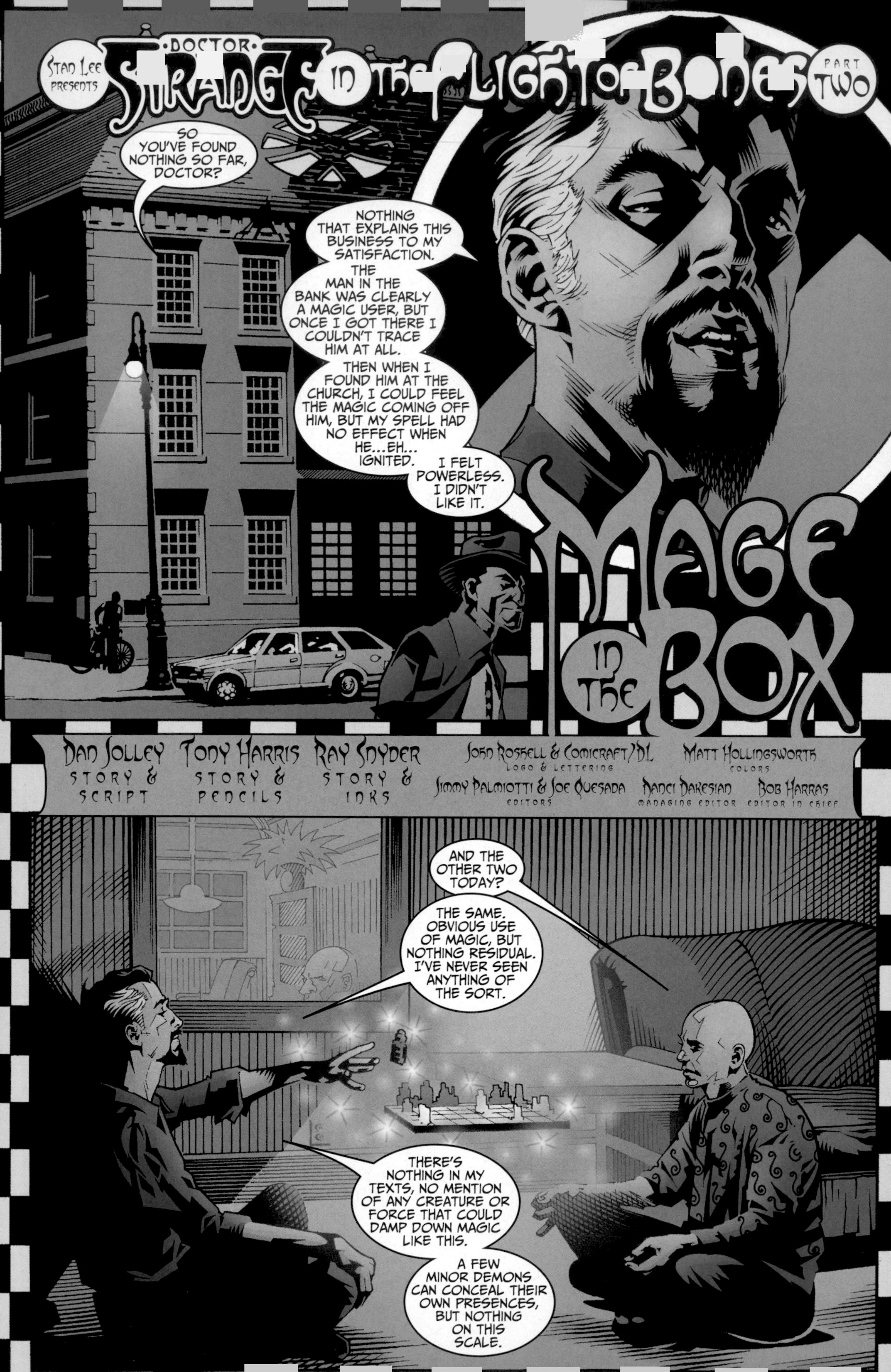
STAN LEE PRESENTS
DOCTOR
PART TWO
SO YOU'VE FOUND NOTHING SO FAR, DOCTOR?
NOTHING THAT EXPLAINS THIS BUSINESS TO MY SATISFACTION.
THE MAN IN THE BANK WAS CLEARLY A MAGIC USER, BUT ONCE I GOT THERE I COULDN'T TRACE HIM AT ALL.
THEN WHEN I FOUND HIM AT THE CHURCH, I COULD FEEL THE MAGIC COMING OFF HIM, BUT MY SPELL HAD NO EFFECT WHEN HE...EH... IGNITED.
I FELT POWERLESS. I DIDN'T LIKE IT.
MAGE IN THE BOX
DAN JOLLEY STORY & SCRIPT
TONY HARRIS STORY & PENCILS
RAY SNYDER STORY & INKS
JOHN ROSHELL & COMICRAFT/DL LOGO & LETTERING
MATT HOLLINGSWORTH COLORS
JIMMY PALMIOTTI & JOE QUESADA EDITORS
NANCI DAKESIAN MANAGING EDITOR
BOB HARRAS EDITOR IN CHIEF
AND THE OTHER TWO TODAY?
THE SAME. OBVIOUS USE OF MAGIC, BUT NOTHING RESIDUAL. I'VE NEVER SEEN ANYTHING OF THE SORT.
THERE'S NOTHING IN MY TEXTS, NO MENTION OF ANY CREATURE OR FORCE THAT COULD DAMP DOWN MAGIC LIKE THIS.
A FEW MINOR DEMONS CAN CONCEAL THEIR OWN PRESENCES, BUT NOTHING ON THIS SCALE.

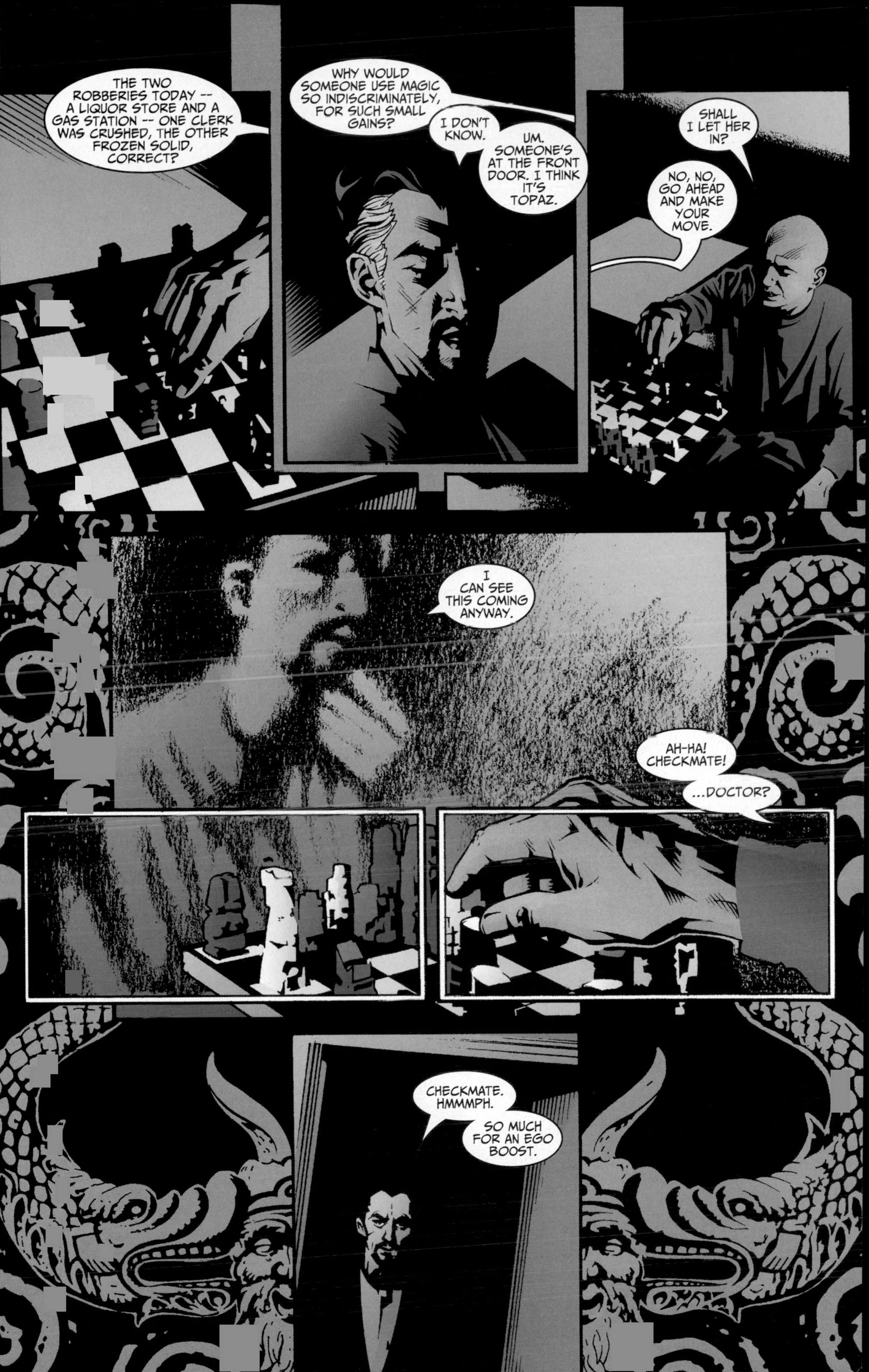
THE TWO ROBBERIES TODAY -- A LIQUOR STORE AND A GAS STATION -- ONE CLERK WAS CRUSHED, THE OTHER FROZEN SOLID, CORRECT?
WHY WOULD SOMEONE USE MAGIC SO INDISCRIMINATELY, FOR SUCH SMALL GAINS?
I DON'T KNOW.
UM. SOMEONE'S AT THE FRONT DOOR. I THINK IT'S TOPAZ.
SHALL I LET HER IN?
NO, NO, GO AHEAD AND MAKE YOUR MOVE.
I CAN SEE THIS COMING ANYWAY.
AH-HA! CHECKMATE!
...DOCTOR?
CHECKMATE. HMMMPH.
SO MUCH FOR AN EGO BOOST.

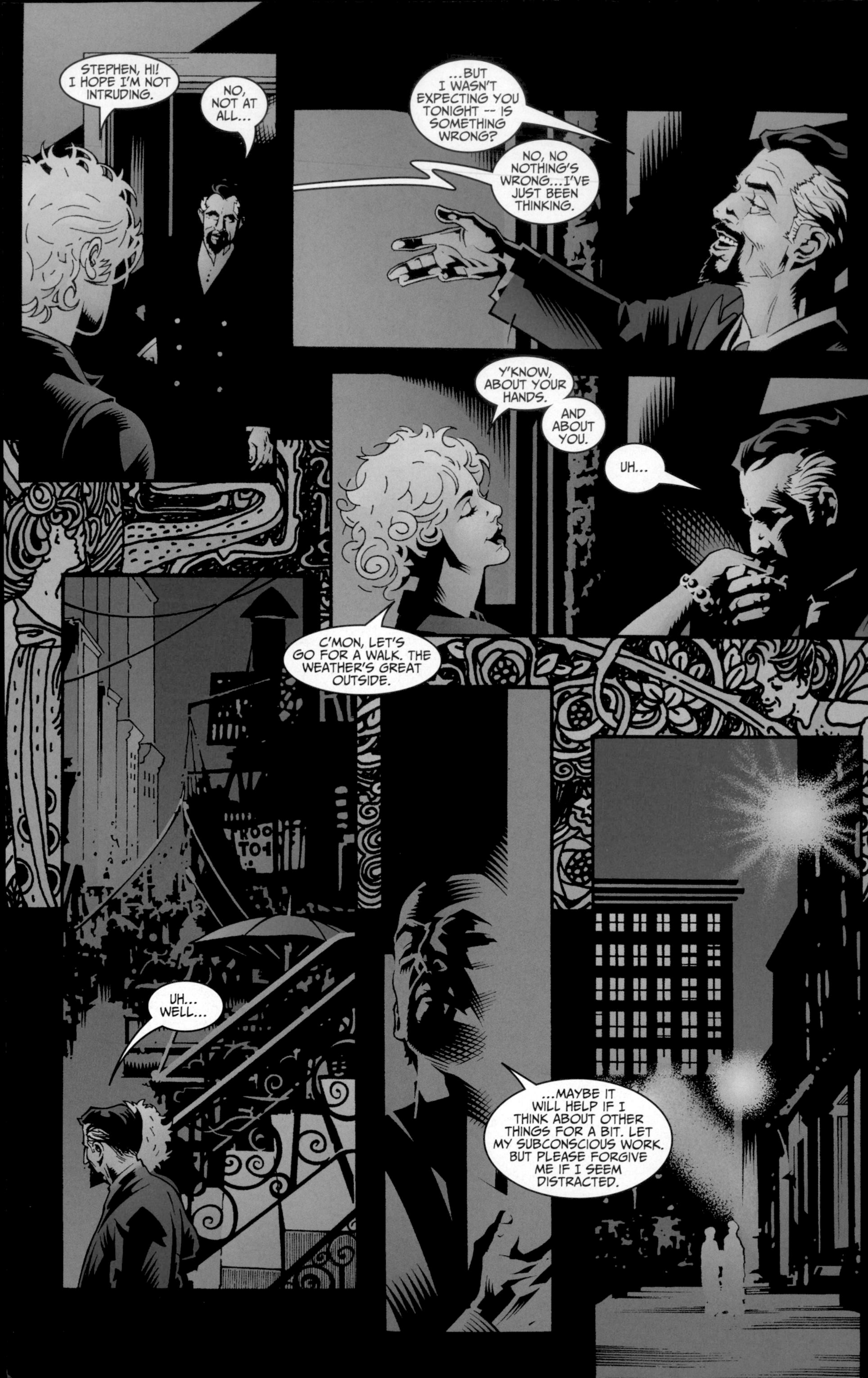
STEPHEN, HI! I HOPE I'M NOT INTRUDING.
NO, NOT AT ALL...
...BUT I WASN'T EXPECTING YOU TONIGHT -- IS SOMETHING WRONG?
NO, NO NOTHING'S WRONG...I'VE JUST BEEN THINKING.
Y'KNOW, ABOUT YOUR HANDS.
AND ABOUT YOU.
UH...
C'MON, LET'S GO FOR A WALK. THE WEATHER'S GREAT OUTSIDE.
UH... WELL...
...MAYBE IT WILL HELP IF I THINK ABOUT OTHER THINGS FOR A BIT. LET MY SUBCONSCIOUS WORK. BUT PLEASE FORGIVE ME IF I SEEM DISTRACTED.

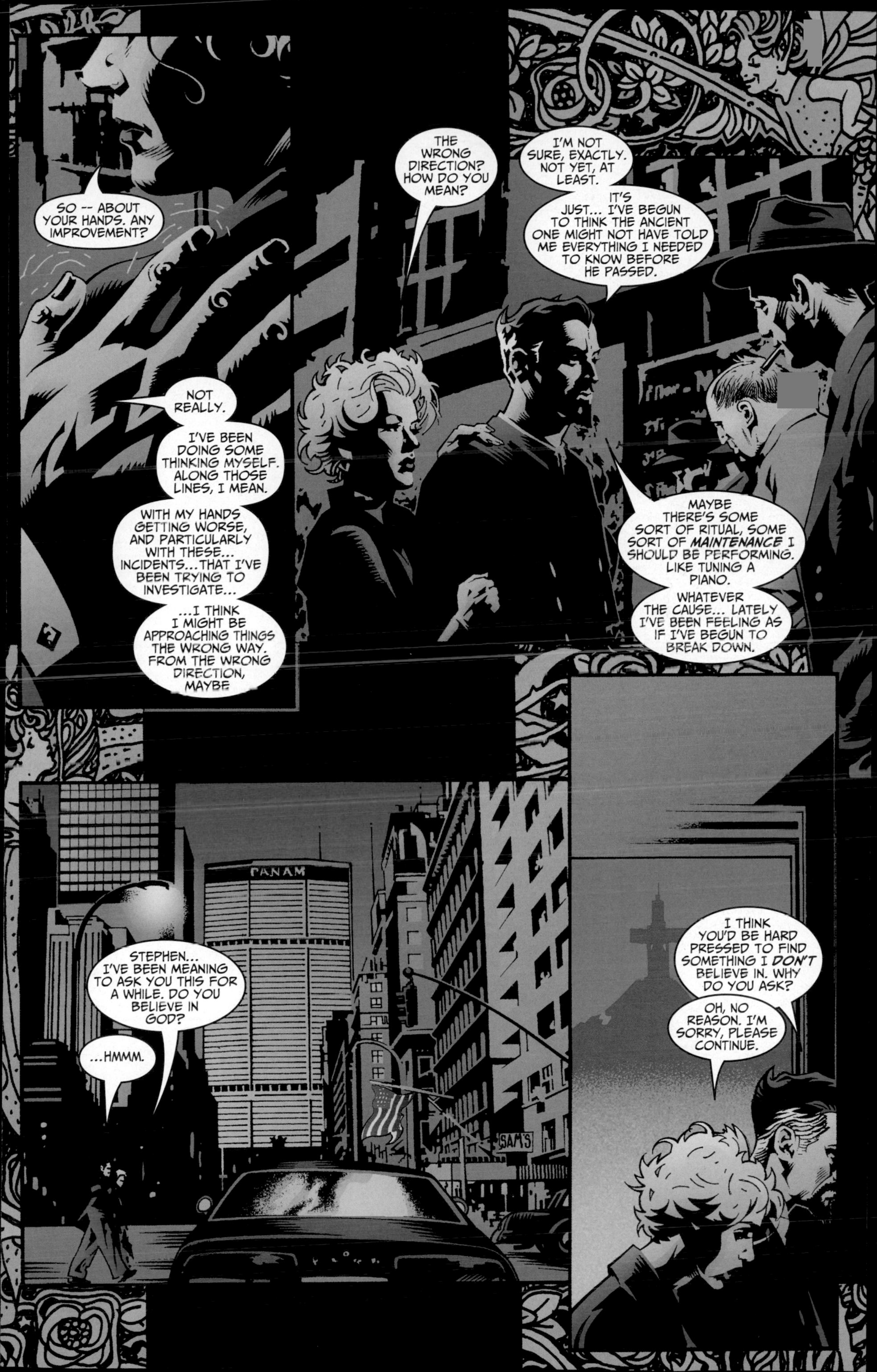
SO -- ABOUT YOUR HANDS. ANY IMPROVEMENT?
NOT REALLY.
I'VE BEEN DOING SOME THINKING MYSELF. ALONG THOSE LINES, I MEAN.
WITH MY HANDS GETTING WORSE, AND PARTICULARLY WITH THESE... INCIDENTS...THAT I'VE BEEN TRYING TO INVESTIGATE...
...I THINK I MIGHT BE APPROACHING THINGS THE WRONG WAY. FROM THE WRONG DIRECTION, MAYBE
THE WRONG DIRECTION? HOW DO YOU MEAN?
I'M NOT SURE, EXACTLY. NOT YET, AT LEAST.
IT'S JUST... I'VE BEGUN TO THINK THE ANCIENT ONE MIGHT NOT HAVE TOLD ME EVERYTHING I NEEDED TO KNOW BEFORE HE PASSED.
MAYBE THERE'S SOME SORT OF RITUAL, SOME SORT OF MAINTENANCE I SHOULD BE PERFORMING. LIKE TUNING A PIANO.
WHATEVER THE CAUSE... LATELY I'VE BEEN FEELING AS IF I'VE BEGUN TO BREAK DOWN.
PANAM
SAM'S
STEPHEN... I'VE BEEN MEANING TO ASK YOU THIS FOR A WHILE. DO YOU BELIEVE IN GOD?
...HMMM.
I THINK YOU'D BE HARD PRESSED TO FIND SOMETHING I DON'T BELIEVE IN. WHY DO YOU ASK?
OH, NO REASON. I'M SORRY, PLEASE CONTINUE.

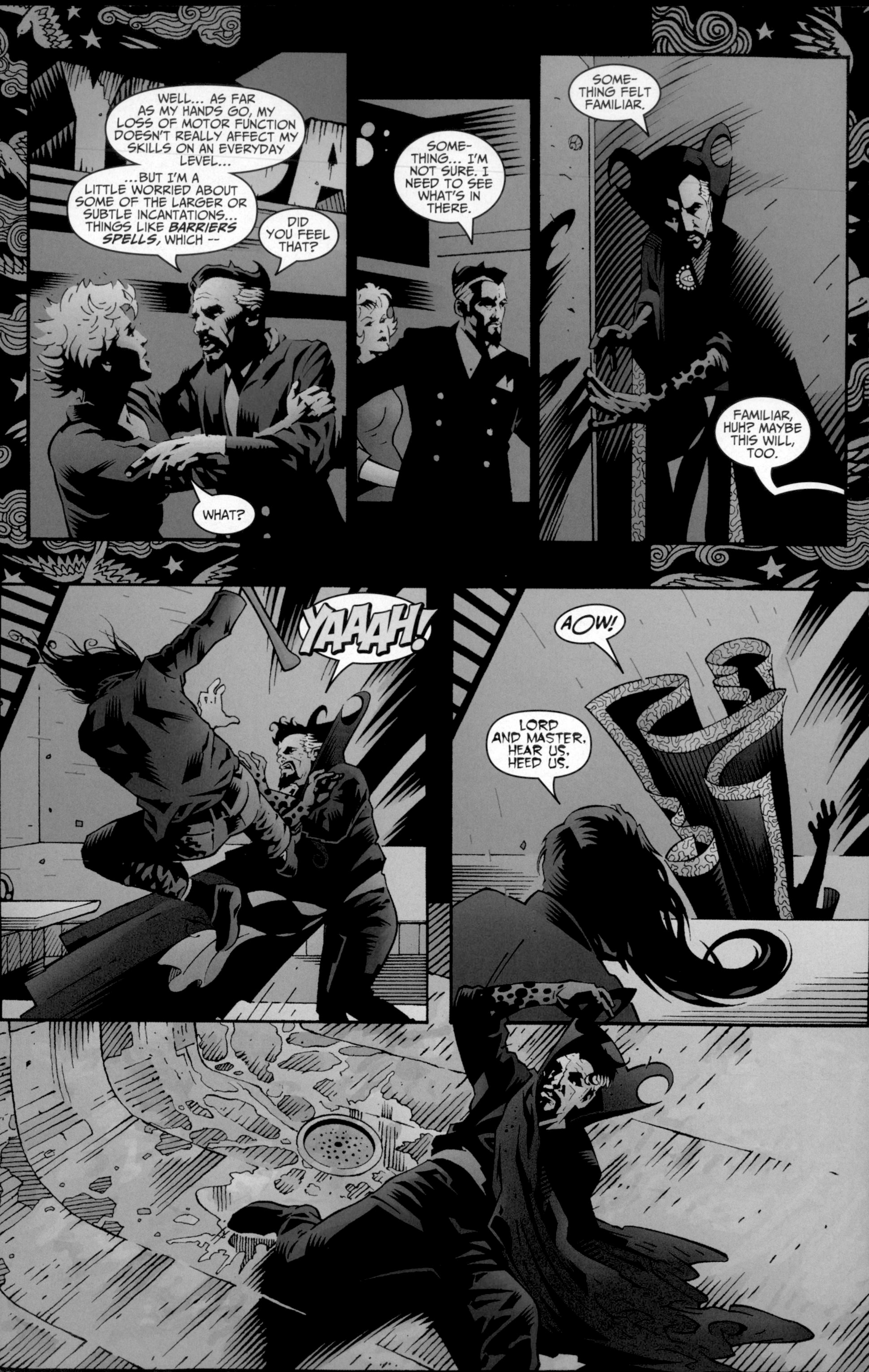
WELL... AS FAR AS MY HANDS GO, MY LOSS OF MOTOR FUNCTION DOESN'T REALLY AFFECT MY SKILLS ON AN EVERYDAY LEVEL...
...BUT I'M A LITTLE WORRIED ABOUT SOME OF THE LARGER OR SUBTLE INCANTATIONS... THINGS LIKE BARRIERS SPELLS, WHICH --
DID YOU FEEL THAT?
WHAT?
SOME-THING... I'M NOT SURE. I NEED TO SEE WHAT'S IN THERE.
SOME-THING FELT FAMILIAR.
FAMILIAR, HUH? MAYBE THIS WILL, TOO.
YAAAH!
AOW!
LORD AND MASTER, HEAR US. HEED US.

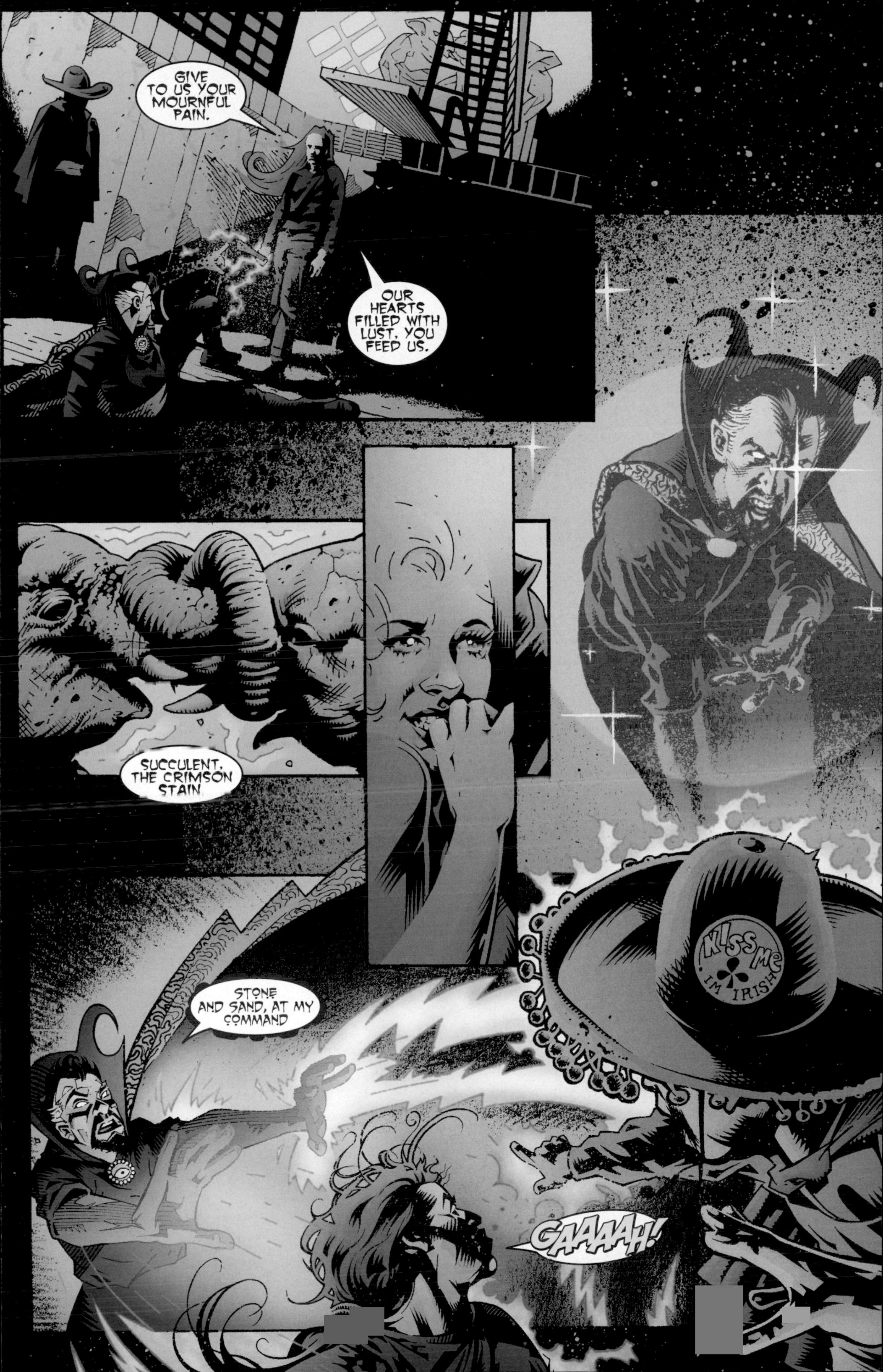
GIVE TO US YOUR MOURNFUL PAIN.
OUR HEARTS FILLED WITH LUST. YOU FEED US.
SUCCULENT, THE CRIMSON STAIN.
STONE AND SAND, AT MY COMMAND
KISS ME IM IRISH
GAAAAH!

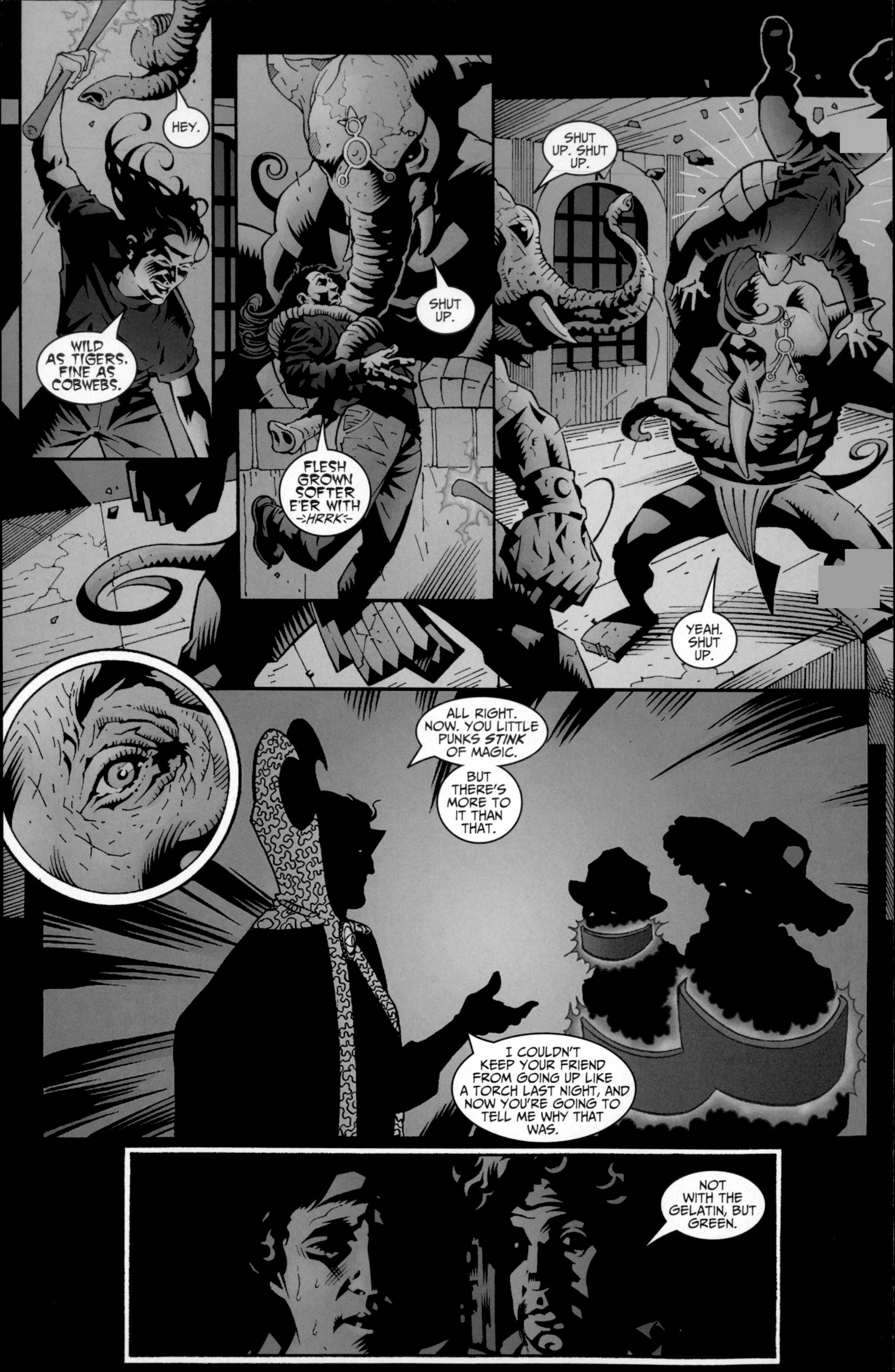
HEY.
WILD AS TIGERS. FINE AS COBWEBS.
SHUT UP.
FLESH GROWN SOFTER E'ER WITH -HRRK
SHUT UP. SHUT UP.
YEAH. SHUT UP.
ALL RIGHT. NOW. YOU LITTLE PUNKS STINK OF MAGIC.
BUT THERE'S MORE TO IT THAN THAT.
I COULDN'T KEEP YOUR FRIEND FROM GOING UP LIKE A TORCH LAST NIGHT, AND NOW YOU'RE GOING TO TELL ME WHY THAT WAS.
NOT WITH THE GELATIN, BUT GREEN.

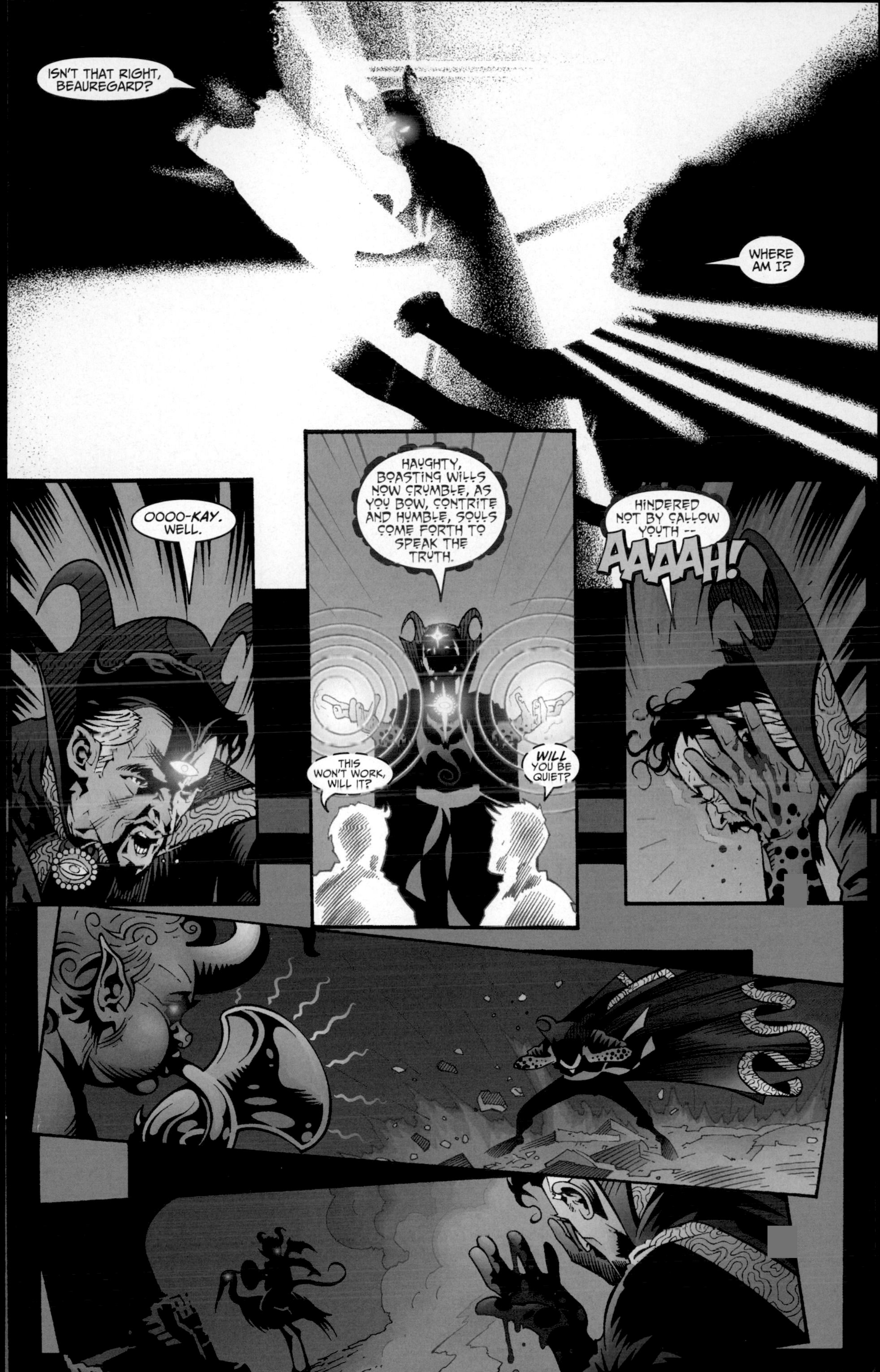
ISN'T THAT RIGHT, BEAUREGARD?
WHERE AM I?
OOOO-KAY. WELL.
HAUGHTY, BOASTING WILLS NOW CRUMBLE, AS YOU BOW, CONTRITE AND HUMBLE. SOULS COME FORTH TO SPEAK THE TRUTH.
THIS WON'T WORK, WILL IT?
WILL YOU BE QUIET?
HINDERED NOT BY CALLOW YOUTH --
AAAAH!

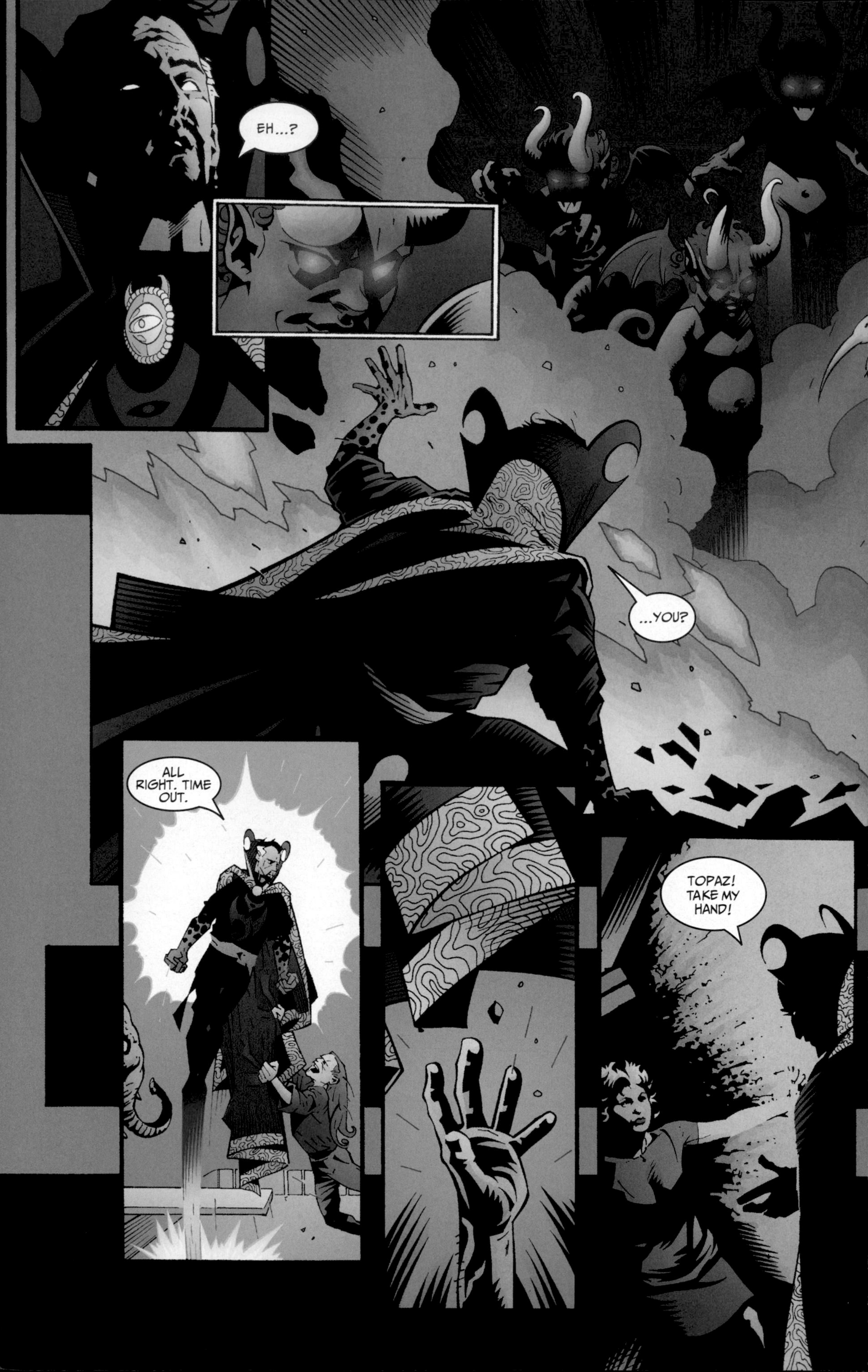
EH...?
...YOU?
ALL RIGHT. TIME OUT.
TOPAZ! TAKE MY HAND!

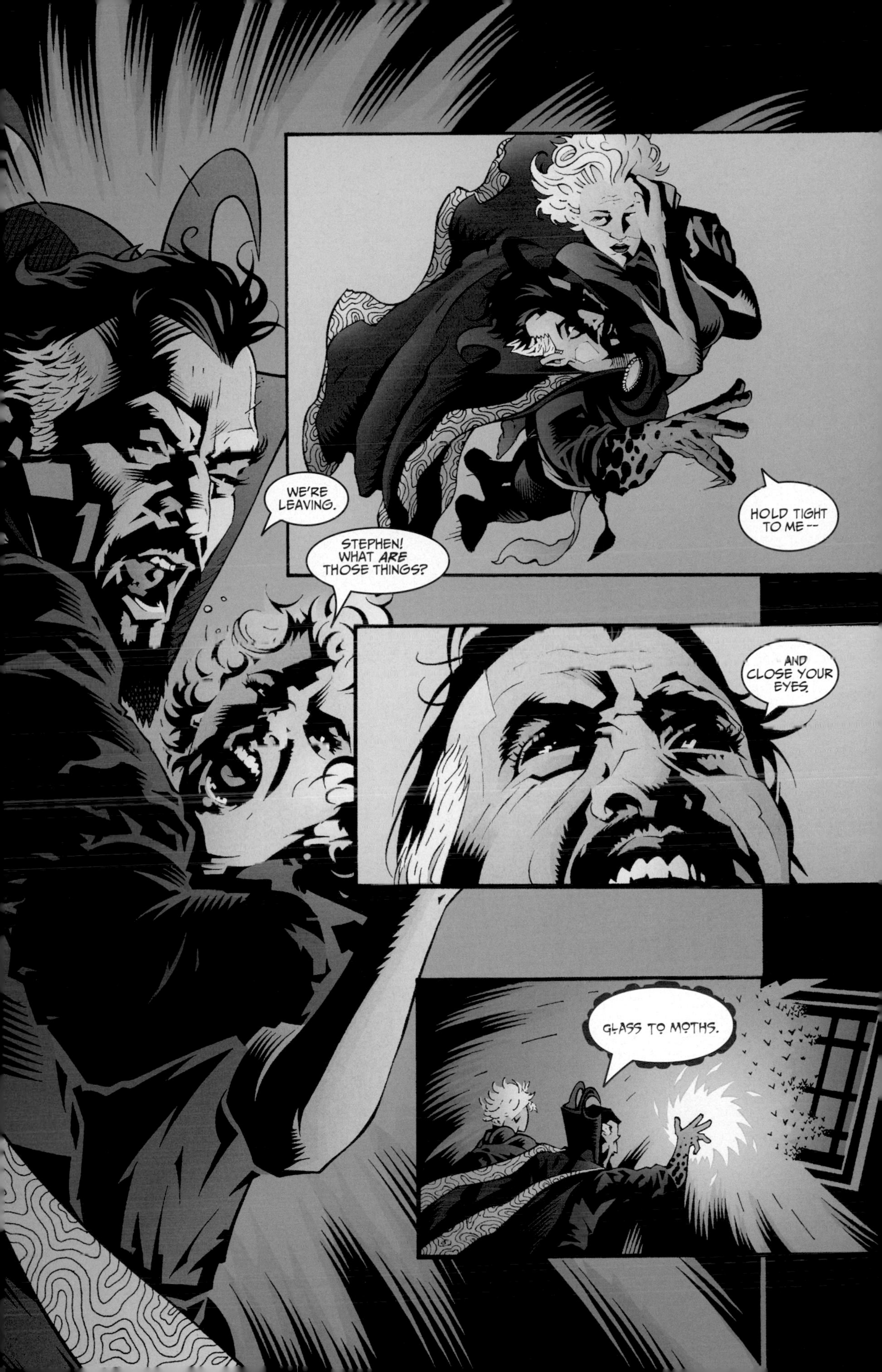
WE'RE LEAVING.
STEPHEN! WHAT ARE THOSE THINGS?
HOLD TIGHT TO ME --
AND CLOSE YOUR EYES.
GLASS TO MOTHS.

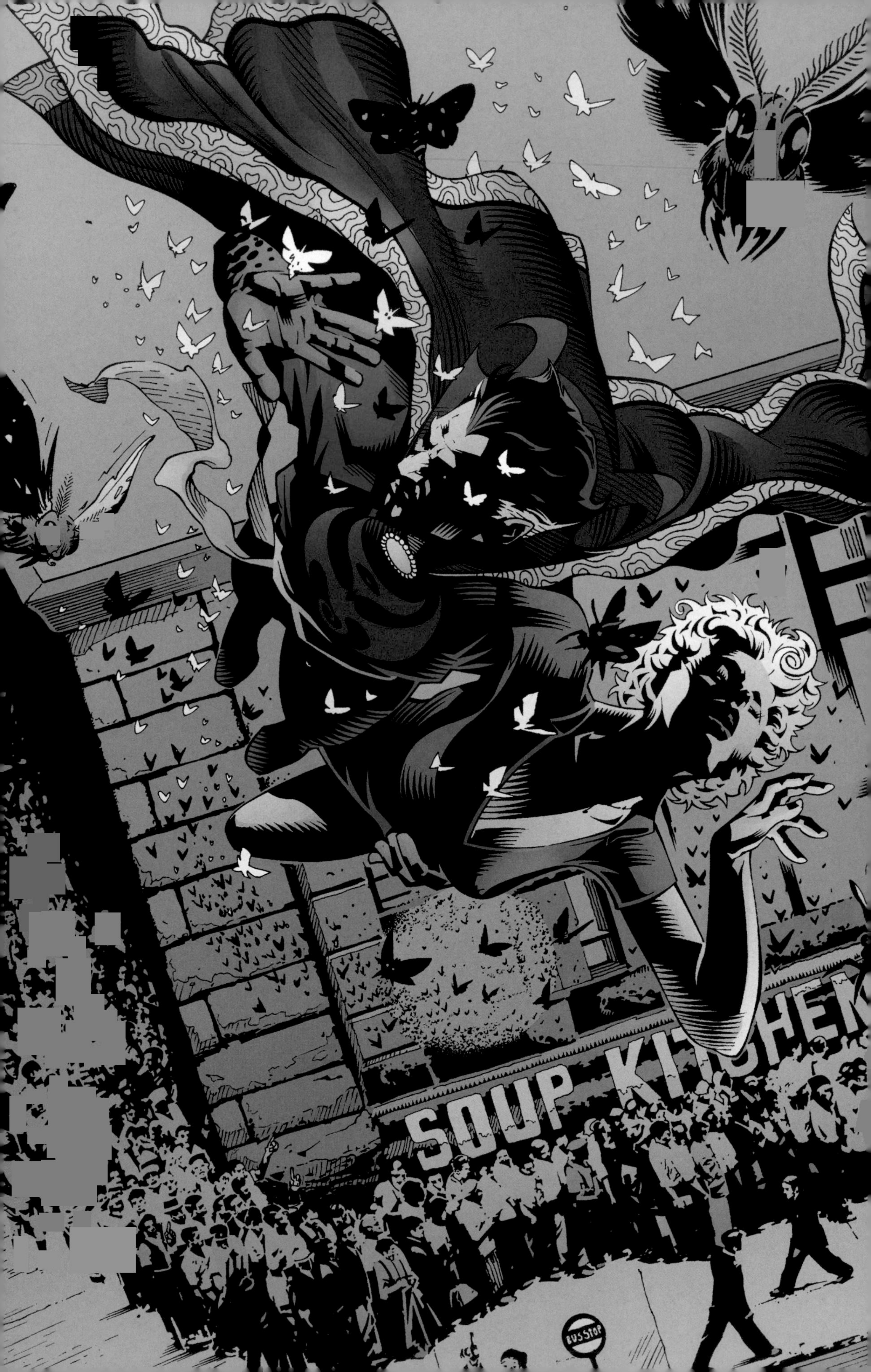
SOUP
BUS STOP

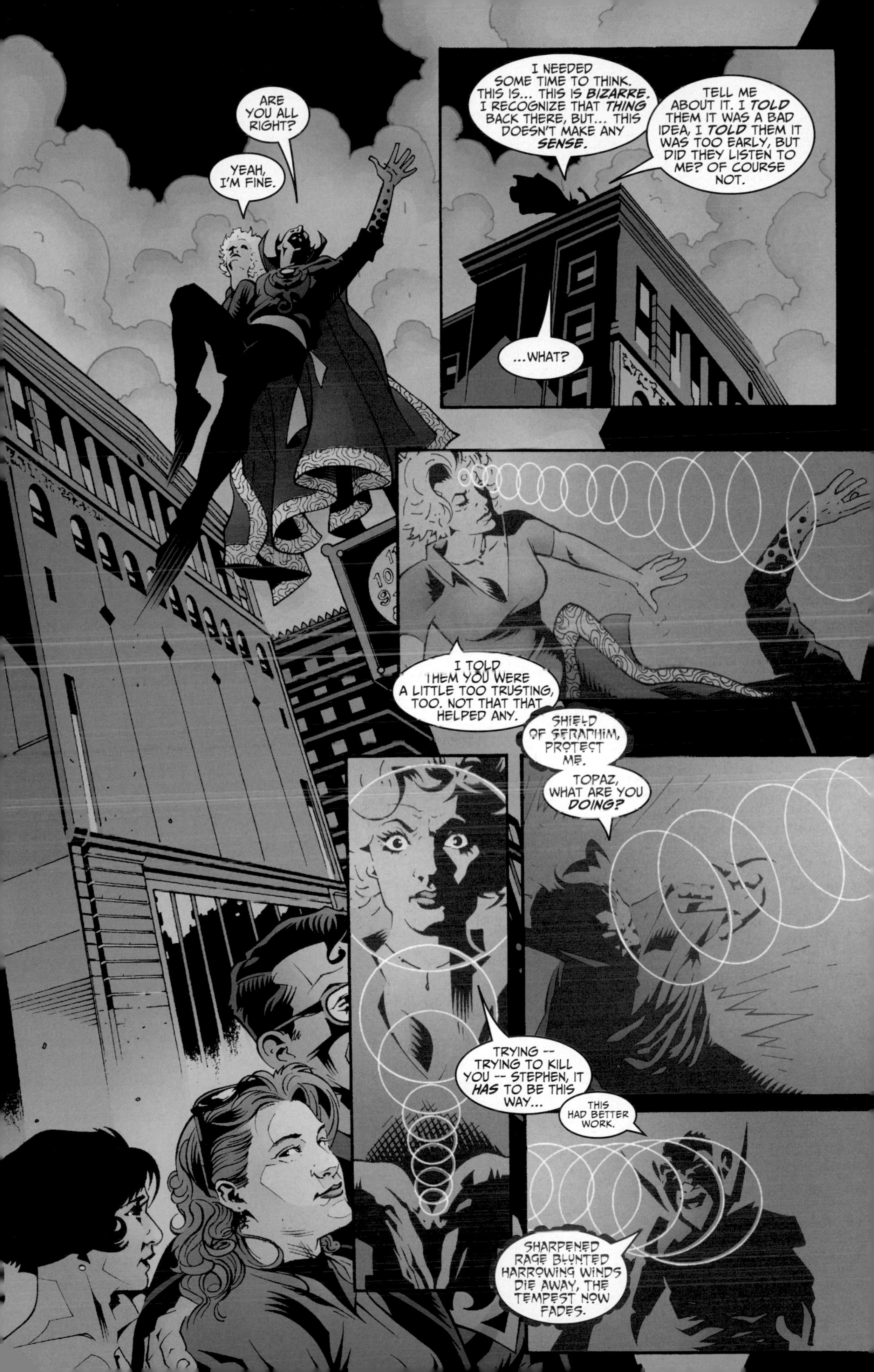
ARE YOU ALL RIGHT?
YEAH, I'M FINE.
I NEEDED SOME TIME TO THINK. THIS IS... THIS IS BIZARRE. I RECOGNIZE THAT THING BACK THERE, BUT... THIS DOESN'T MAKE ANY SENSE.
TELL ME ABOUT IT. I TOLD THEM IT WAS A BAD IDEA, I TOLD THEM IT WAS TOO EARLY, BUT DID THEY LISTEN TO ME? OF COURSE NOT.
...WHAT?
I TOLD THEM YOU WERE A LITTLE TOO TRUSTING, TOO. NOT THAT THAT HELPED ANY.
SHIELD OF SERAPHIM, PROTECT ME.
TOPAZ, WHAT ARE YOU DOING?
TRYING -- TRYING TO KILL YOU -- STEPHEN, IT HAS TO BE THIS WAY...
THIS HAD BETTER WORK.
SHARPENED RAGE BLUNTED HARROWING WINDS DIE AWAY, THE TEMPEST NOW FADES.

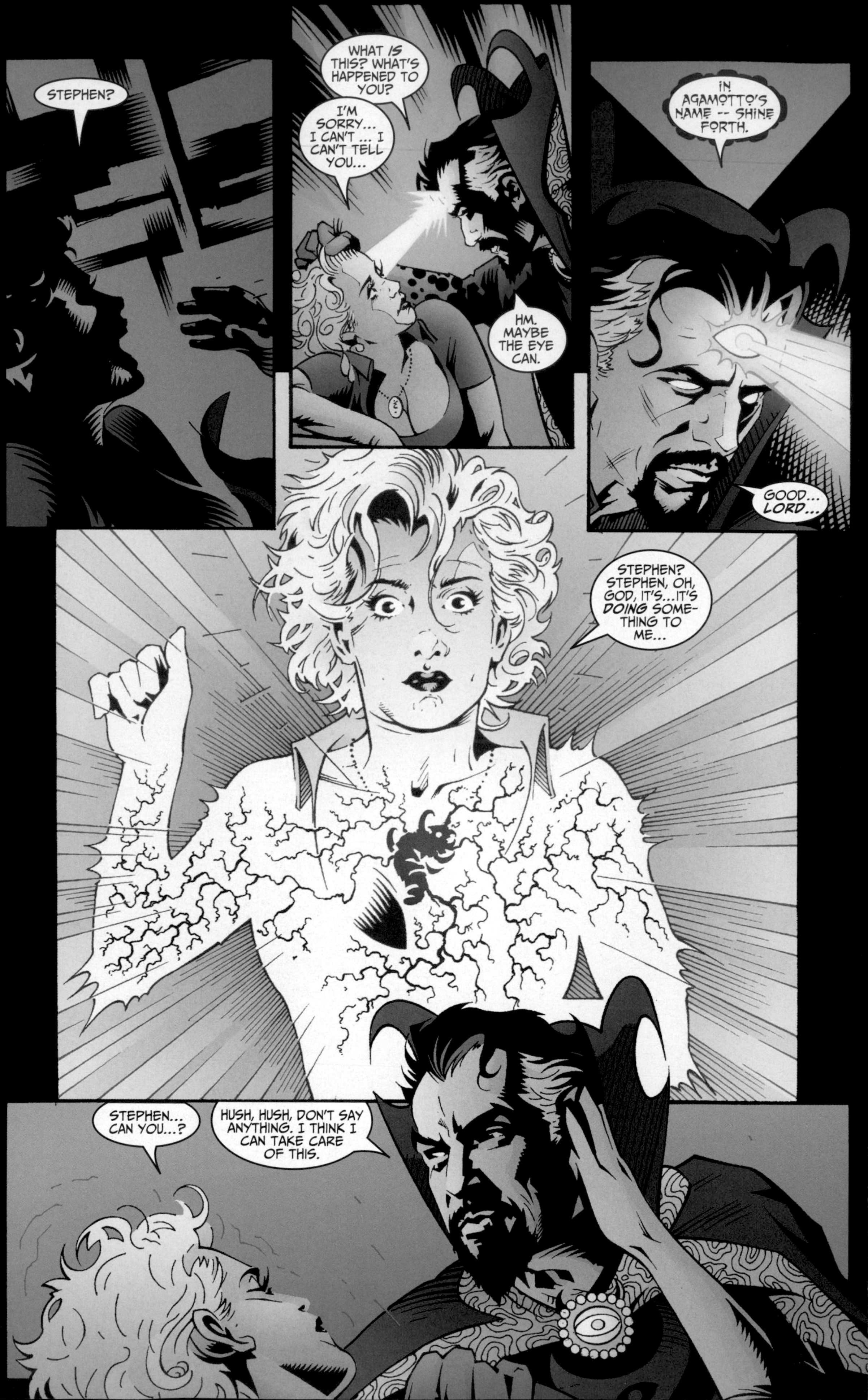
STEPHEN?
WHAT IS THIS? WHAT'S HAPPENED TO YOU?
I'M SORRY... I CAN'T ... I CAN'T TELL YOU...
HM. MAYBE THE EYE CAN.
IN AGAMOTTO'S NAME -- SHINE FORTH.
GOOD... LORD...
STEPHEN? STEPHEN, OH, GOD, IT'S...IT'S DOING SOME-THING TO ME...
STEPHEN... CAN YOU...?
HUSH, HUSH, DON'T SAY ANYTHING. I THINK I CAN TAKE CARE OF THIS.

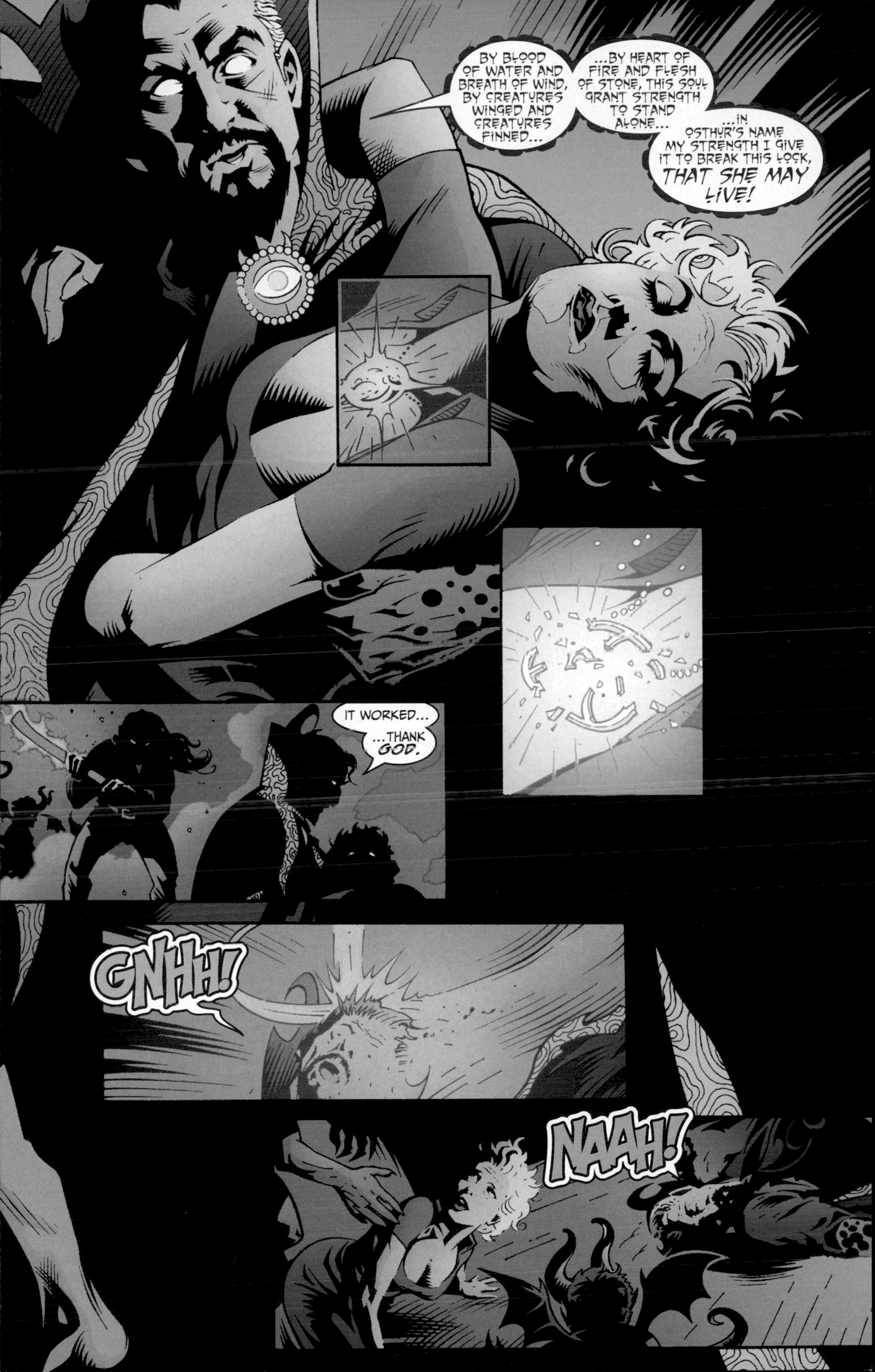

BY BLOOD OF WATER AND BREATH OF WIND, BY CREATURES WINGED AND CREATURES FINNED...
...BY HEART OF FIRE AND FLESH OF STONE, THIS SOUL GRANT STRENGTH TO STAND ALONE...
...IN OSTHUR'S NAME MY STRENGTH I GIVE IT TO BREAK THIS LOCK, THAT SHE MAY LIVE!
IT WORKED...
...THANK GOD.
GNHH!
NAAH!

IF YOU WERE SMART...

...YOU'D HAVE STAYED TO FINISH ME OFF.

BE STILL.

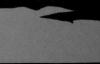

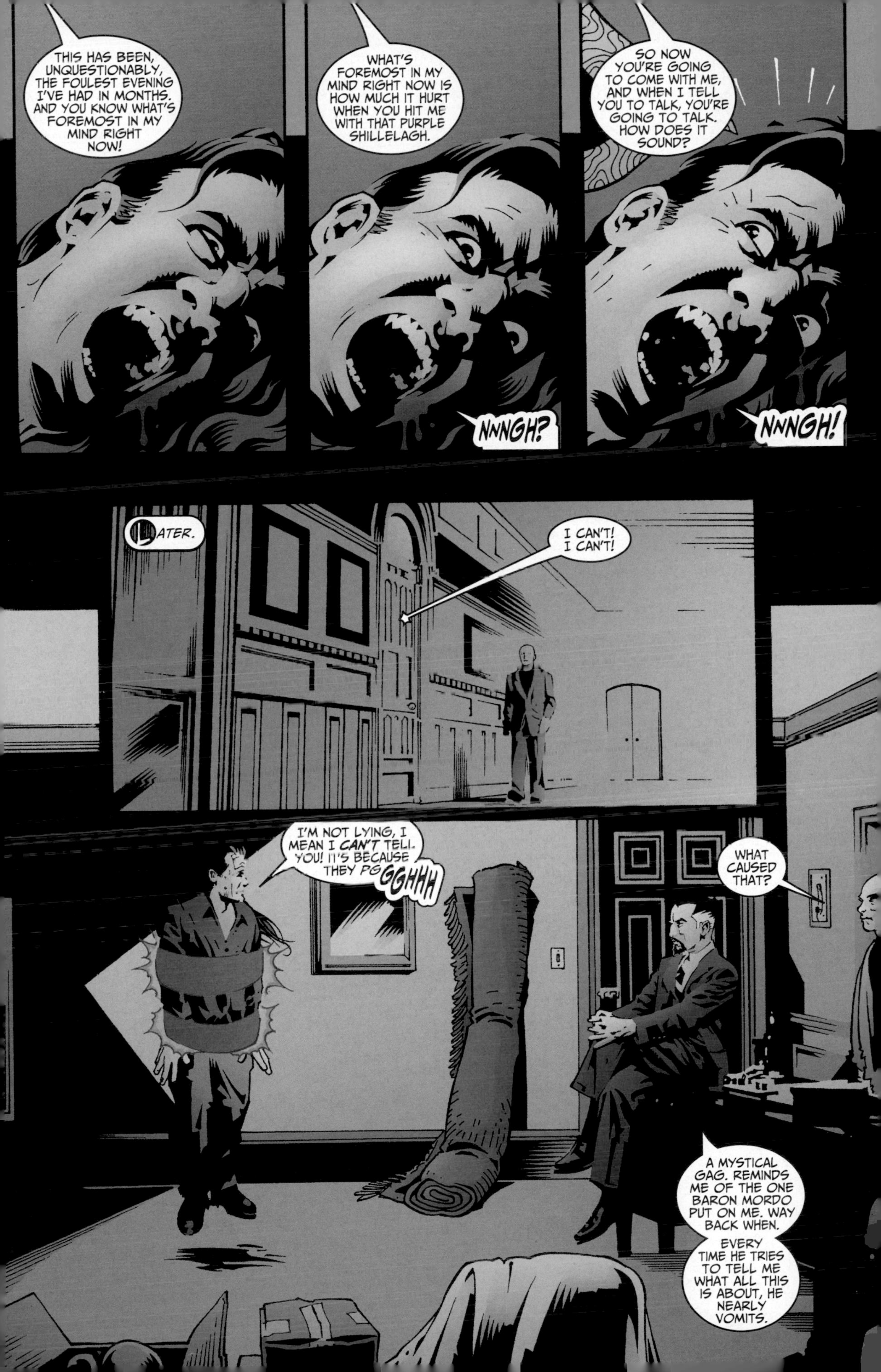
THIS HAS BEEN, UNQUESTIONABLY, THE FOULEST EVENING I'VE HAD IN MONTHS. AND YOU KNOW WHAT'S FOREMOST IN MY MIND RIGHT NOW!
WHAT'S FOREMOST IN MY MIND RIGHT NOW IS HOW MUCH IT HURT WHEN YOU HIT ME WITH THAT PURPLE SHILLELAGH.
NNNGH?
SO NOW YOU'RE GOING TO COME WITH ME, AND WHEN I TELL YOU TO TALK, YOU'RE GOING TO TALK. HOW DOES IT SOUND?
NNNGH!
LATER.
I CAN'T! I CAN'T!
I'M NOT LYING, I MEAN I *CAN'T* TELL YOU! IT'S BECAUSE THEY PG
GGHHH
WHAT CAUSED THAT?
A MYSTICAL GAG. REMINDS ME OF THE ONE BARON MORDO PUT ON ME. WAY BACK WHEN.
EVERY TIME HE TRIES TO TELL ME WHAT ALL THIS IS ABOUT, HE NEARLY VOMITS.

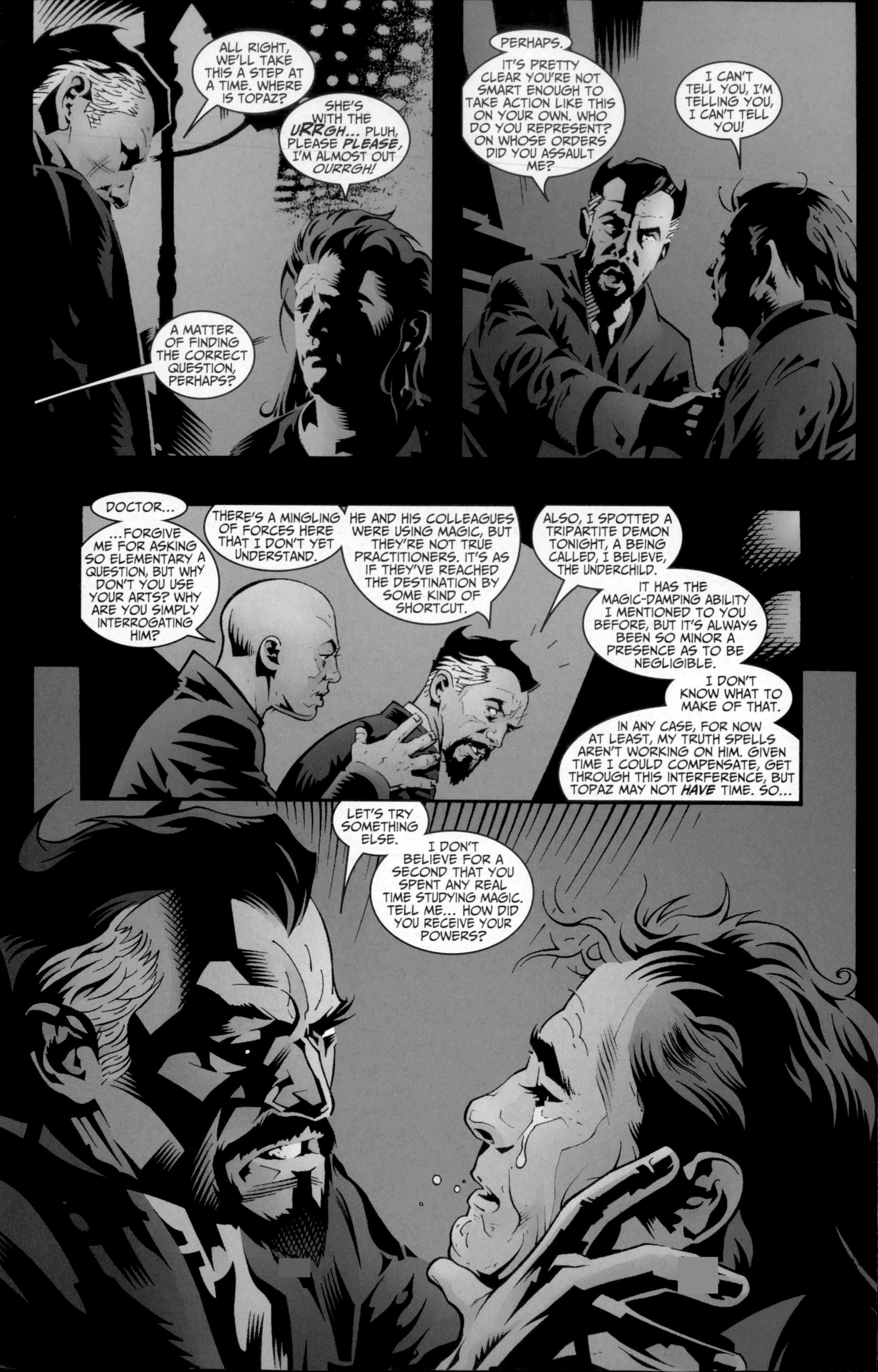
ALL RIGHT, WE'LL TAKE THIS A STEP AT A TIME. WHERE IS TOPAZ?
SHE'S WITH THE URRGH... PLUH, PLEASE PLEASE, I'M ALMOST OUT OURRGH!
A MATTER OF FINDING THE CORRECT QUESTION, PERHAPS?
PERHAPS.
IT'S PRETTY CLEAR YOU'RE NOT SMART ENOUGH TO TAKE ACTION LIKE THIS ON YOUR OWN. WHO DO YOU REPRESENT? ON WHOSE ORDERS DID YOU ASSAULT ME?
I CAN'T TELL YOU, I'M TELLING YOU, I CAN'T TELL YOU!
DOCTOR...
...FORGIVE ME FOR ASKING SO ELEMENTARY A QUESTION, BUT WHY DON'T YOU USE YOUR ARTS? WHY ARE YOU SIMPLY INTERROGATING HIM?
THERE'S A MINGLING OF FORCES HERE THAT I DON'T YET UNDERSTAND.
HE AND HIS COLLEAGUES WERE USING MAGIC, BUT THEY'RE NOT TRUE PRACTITIONERS. IT'S AS IF THEY'VE REACHED THE DESTINATION BY SOME KIND OF SHORTCUT.
ALSO, I SPOTTED A TRIPARTITE DEMON TONIGHT, A BEING CALLED, I BELIEVE, THE UNDERCHILD.
IT HAS THE MAGIC-DAMPING ABILITY I MENTIONED TO YOU BEFORE, BUT IT'S ALWAYS BEEN SO MINOR A PRESENCE AS TO BE NEGLIGIBLE.
I DON'T KNOW WHAT TO MAKE OF THAT.
IN ANY CASE, FOR NOW AT LEAST, MY TRUTH SPELLS AREN'T WORKING ON HIM. GIVEN TIME I COULD COMPENSATE, GET THROUGH THIS INTERFERENCE, BUT TOPAZ MAY NOT HAVE TIME. SO...
LET'S TRY SOMETHING ELSE.
I DON'T BELIEVE FOR A SECOND THAT YOU SPENT ANY REAL TIME STUDYING MAGIC. TELL ME... HOW DID YOU RECEIVE YOUR POWERS?

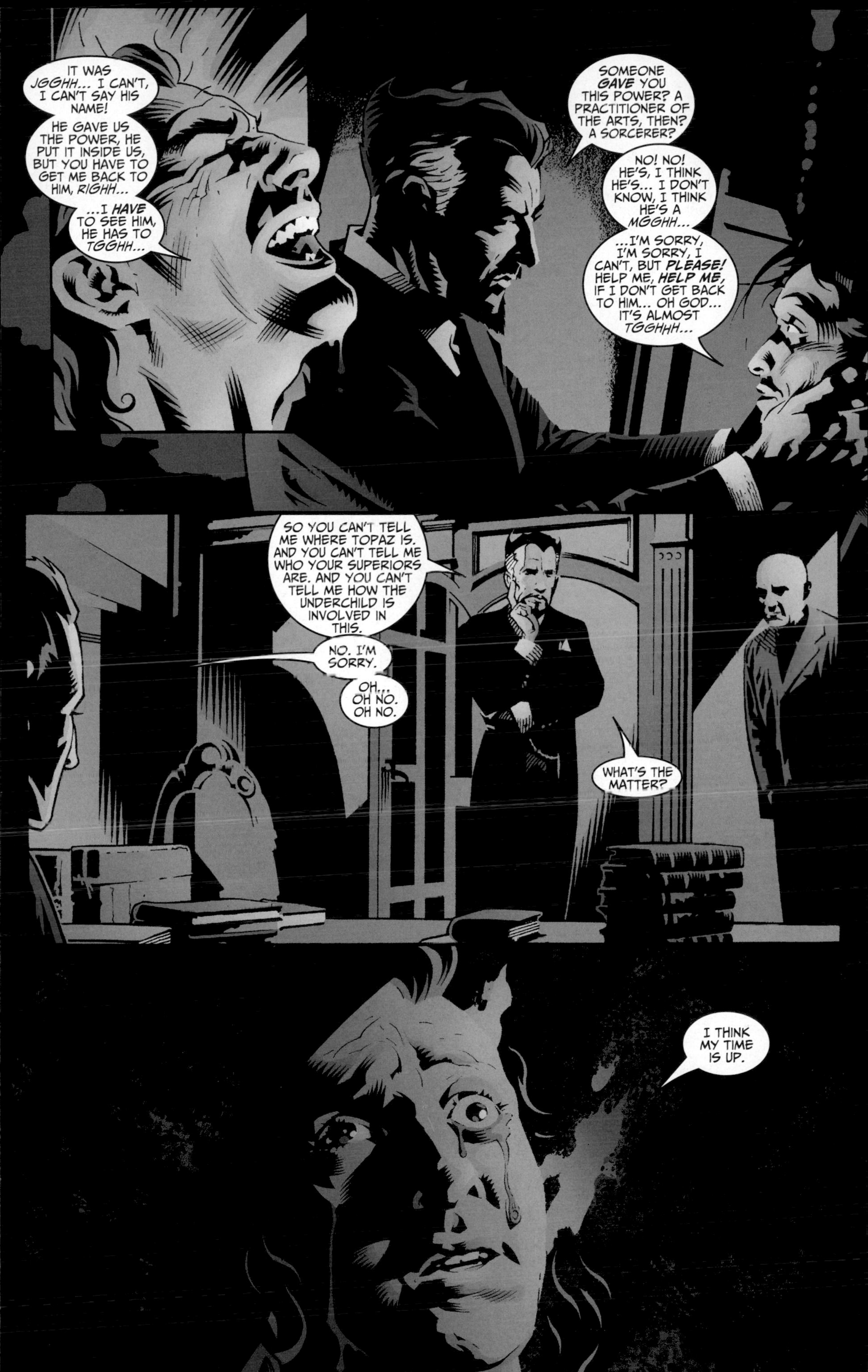
IT WAS JGGHH... I CAN'T, I CAN'T SAY HIS NAME!
HE GAVE US THE POWER, HE PUT IT INSIDE US, BUT YOU HAVE TO GET ME BACK TO HIM, RIGHH...
...I HAVE TO SEE HIM, HE HAS TO TGGHH...
SOMEONE GAVE YOU THIS POWER? A PRACTITIONER OF THE ARTS, THEN? A SORCERER?
NO! NO! HE'S, I THINK HE'S... I DON'T KNOW, I THINK HE'S A MGGHH...
...I'M SORRY, I'M SORRY, I CAN'T, BUT PLEASE! HELP ME, HELP ME, IF I DON'T GET BACK TO HIM... OH GOD... IT'S ALMOST TGGHHH...
SO YOU CAN'T TELL ME WHERE TOPAZ IS. AND YOU CAN'T TELL ME WHO YOUR SUPERIORS ARE. AND YOU CAN'T TELL ME HOW THE UNDERCHILD IS INVOLVED IN THIS.
NO. I'M SORRY.
OH... OH NO. OH NO.
WHAT'S THE MATTER?
I THINK MY TIME IS UP.

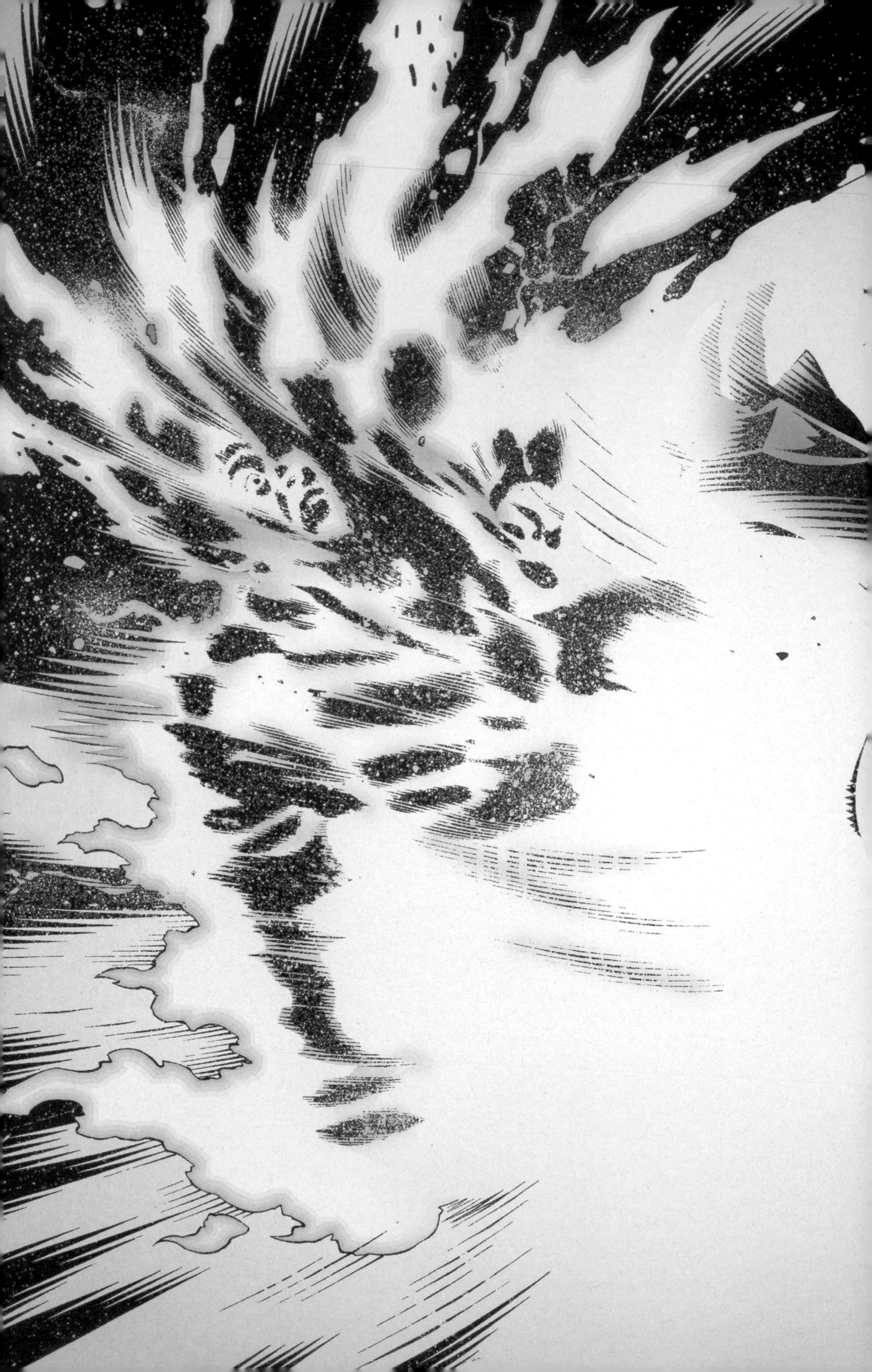

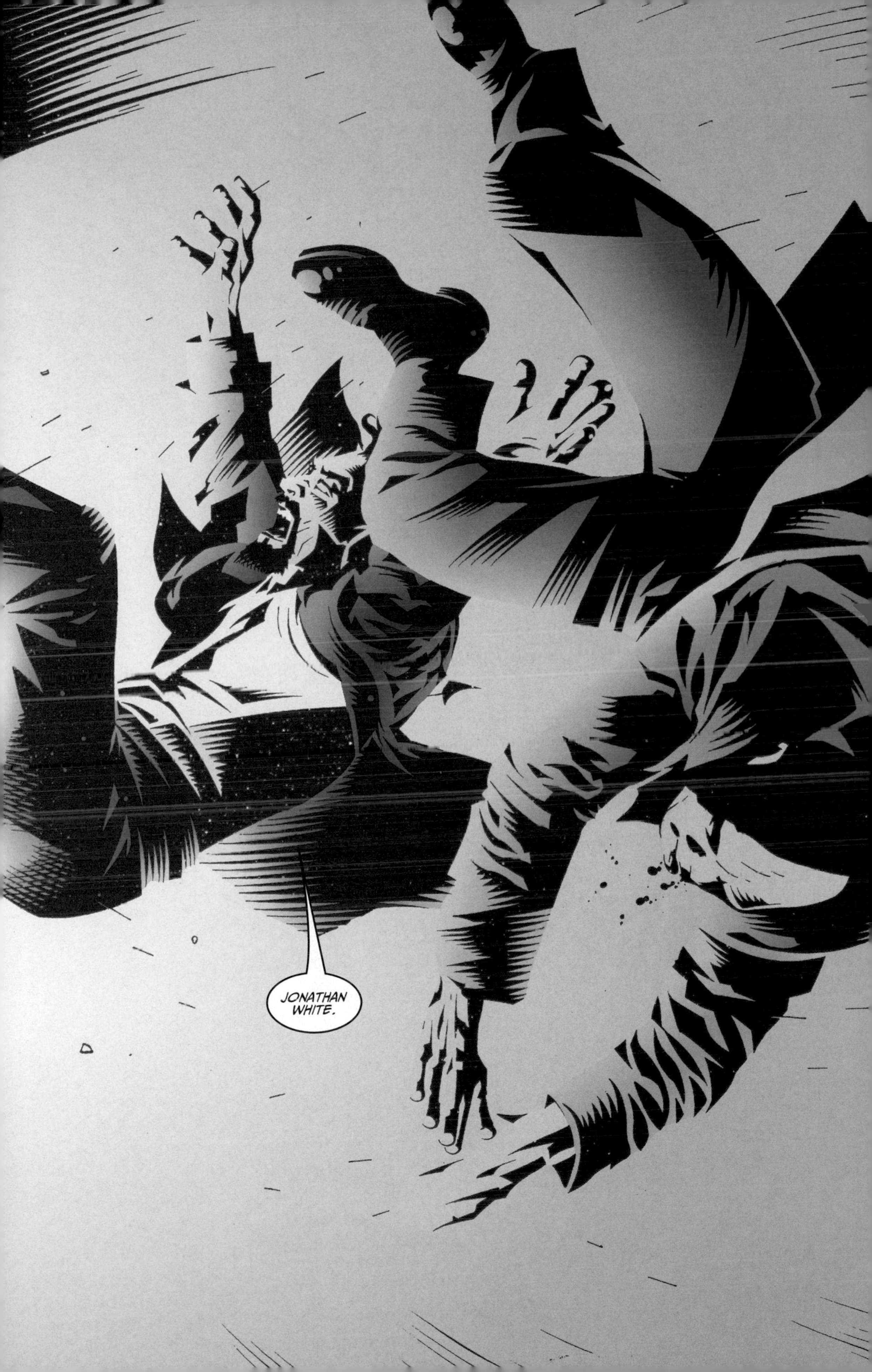
JONATHAN WHITE.

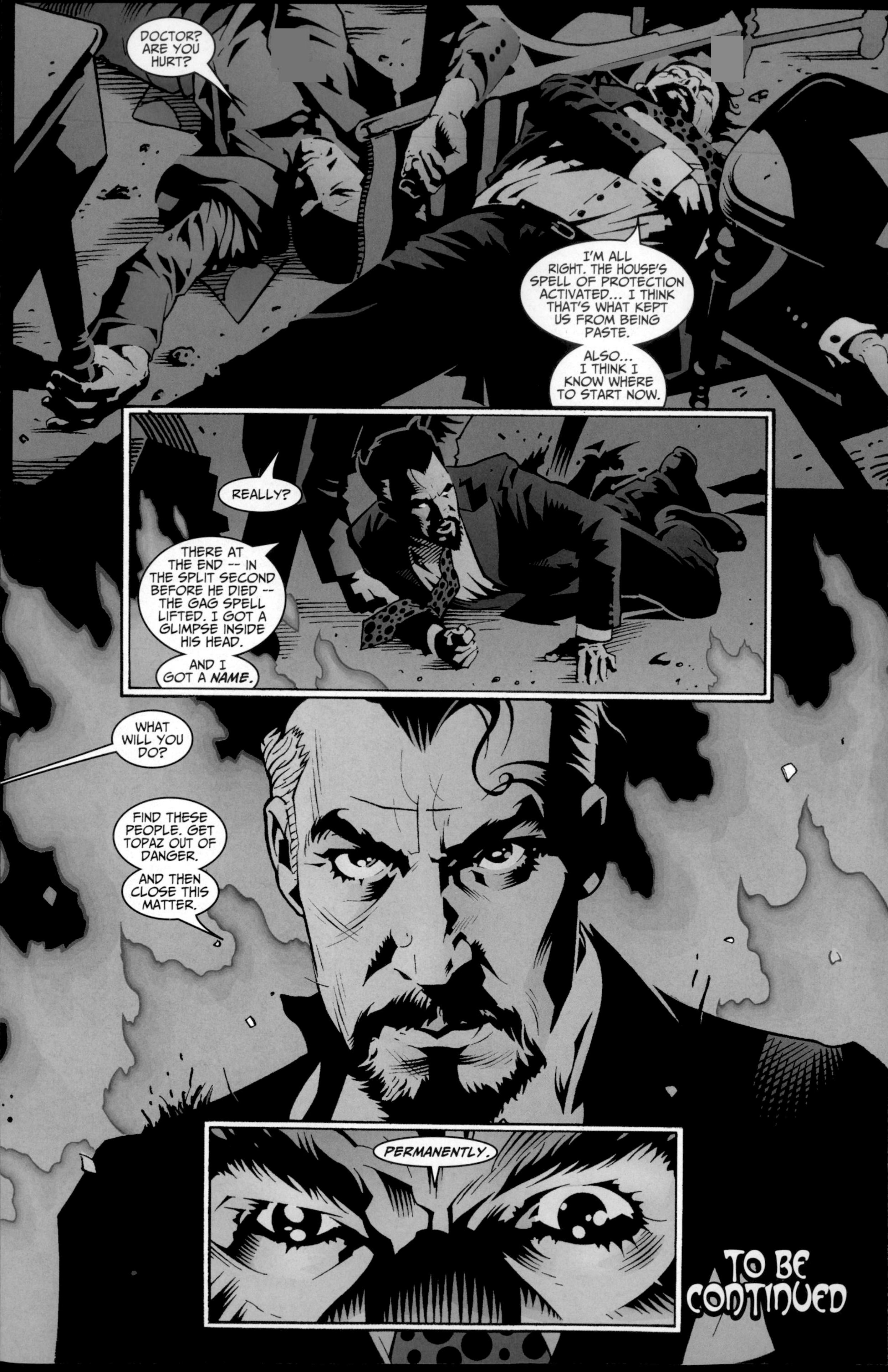
DOCTOR? ARE YOU HURT?
I'M ALL RIGHT. THE HOUSE'S SPELL OF PROTECTION ACTIVATED... I THINK THAT'S WHAT KEPT US FROM BEING PASTE.
ALSO... I THINK I KNOW WHERE TO START NOW.
REALLY?
THERE AT THE END -- IN THE SPLIT SECOND BEFORE HE DIED -- THE GAG SPELL LIFTED. I GOT A GLIMPSE INSIDE HIS HEAD.
AND I GOT A *NAME*.
WHAT WILL YOU DO?
FIND THESE PEOPLE. GET TOPAZ OUT OF DANGER.
AND THEN CLOSE THIS MATTER.
PERMANENTLY.
TO BE CONTINUED

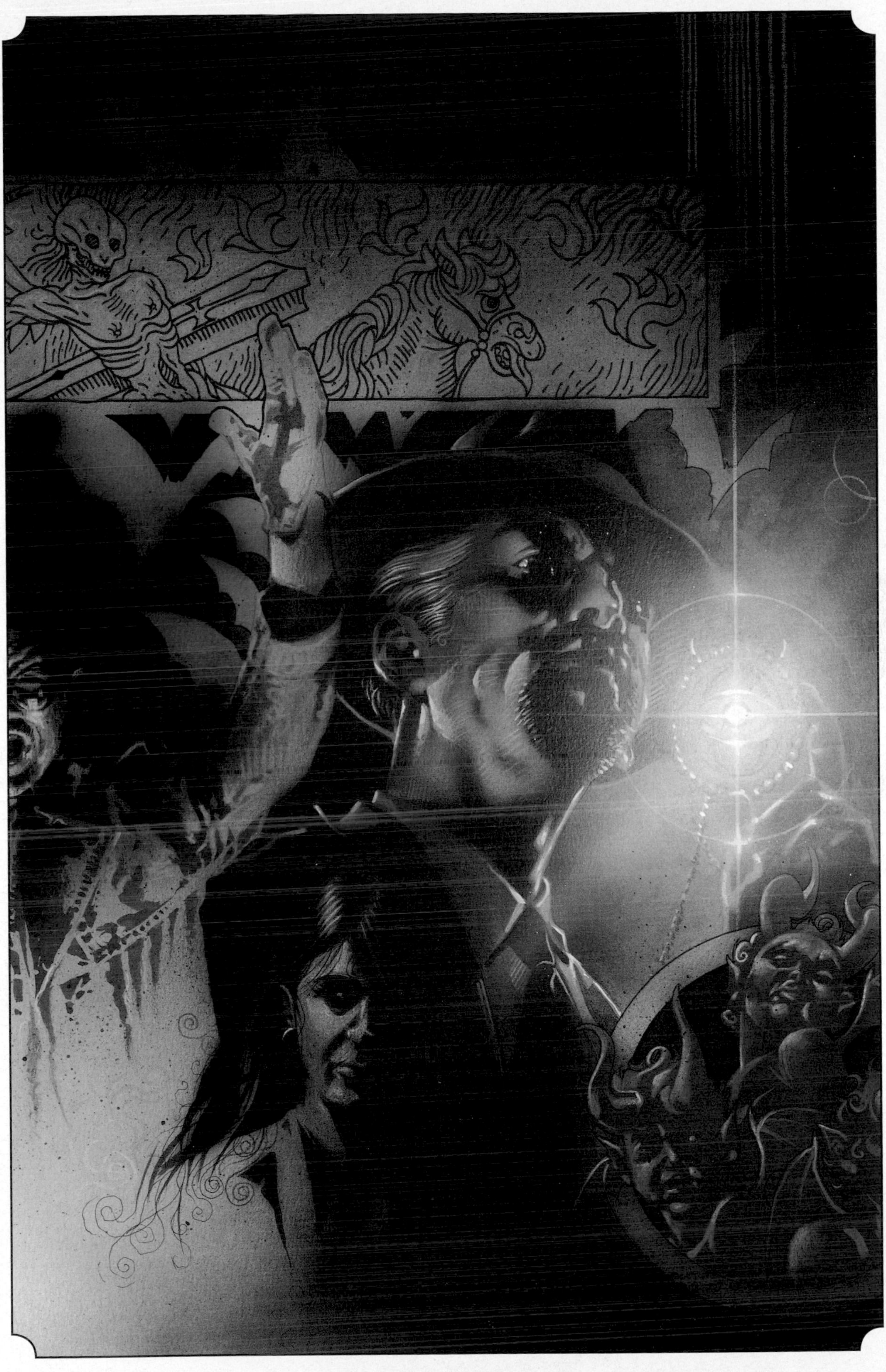

DOCTOR STRANGE #3

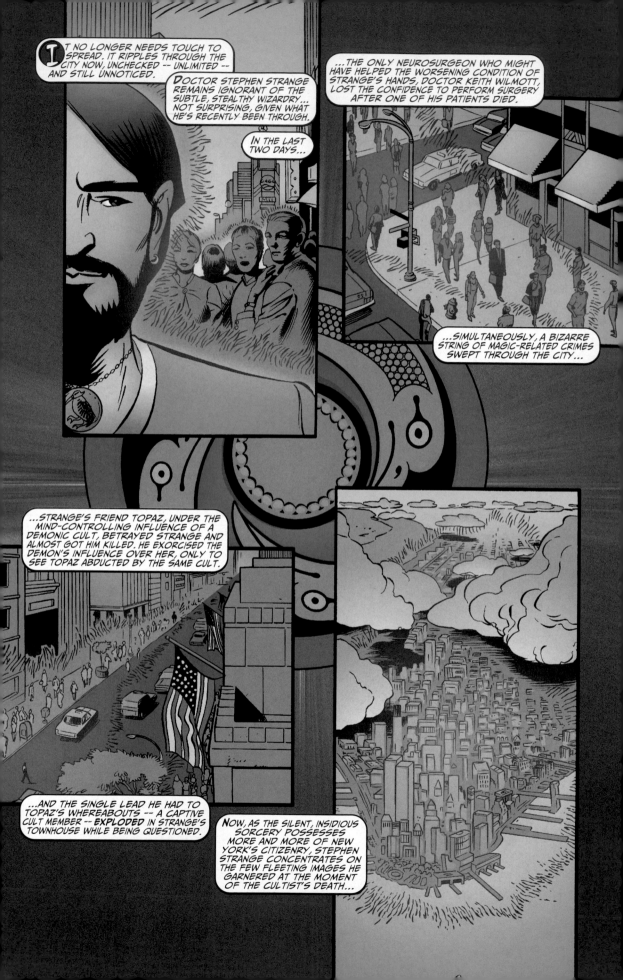

IT NO LONGER NEEDS TOUCH TO SPREAD. IT RIPPLES THROUGH THE CITY NOW, UNCHECKED -- UNLIMITED -- AND STILL UNNOTICED.

DOCTOR STEPHEN STRANGE REMAINS IGNORANT OF THE SUBTLE, STEALTHY WIZARDRY... NOT SURPRISING, GIVEN WHAT HE'S RECENTLY BEEN THROUGH.

IN THE LAST TWO DAYS...

...THE ONLY NEUROSURGEON WHO MIGHT HAVE HELPED THE WORSENING CONDITION OF STRANGE'S HANDS, DOCTOR KEITH WILMOTT, LOST THE CONFIDENCE TO PERFORM SURGERY AFTER ONE OF HIS PATIENTS DIED.

...SIMULTANEOUSLY, A BIZARRE STRING OF MAGIC-RELATED CRIMES SWEPT THROUGH THE CITY...

...STRANGE'S FRIEND TOPAZ, UNDER THE MIND-CONTROLLING INFLUENCE OF A DEMONIC CULT, BETRAYED STRANGE AND ALMOST GOT HIM KILLED. HE EXORCISED THE DEMON'S INFLUENCE OVER HER, ONLY TO SEE TOPAZ ABDUCTED BY THE SAME CULT.

...AND THE SINGLE LEAD HE HAD TO TOPAZ'S WHEREABOUTS -- A CAPTIVE CULT MEMBER -- **EXPLODED** IN STRANGE'S TOWNHOUSE WHILE BEING QUESTIONED.

NOW, AS THE SILENT, INSIDIOUS SORCERY POSSESSES MORE AND MORE OF NEW YORK'S CITIZENRY, STEPHEN STRANGE CONCENTRATES ON THE FEW FLEETING IMAGES HE GARNERED AT THE MOMENT OF THE CULTIST'S DEATH...

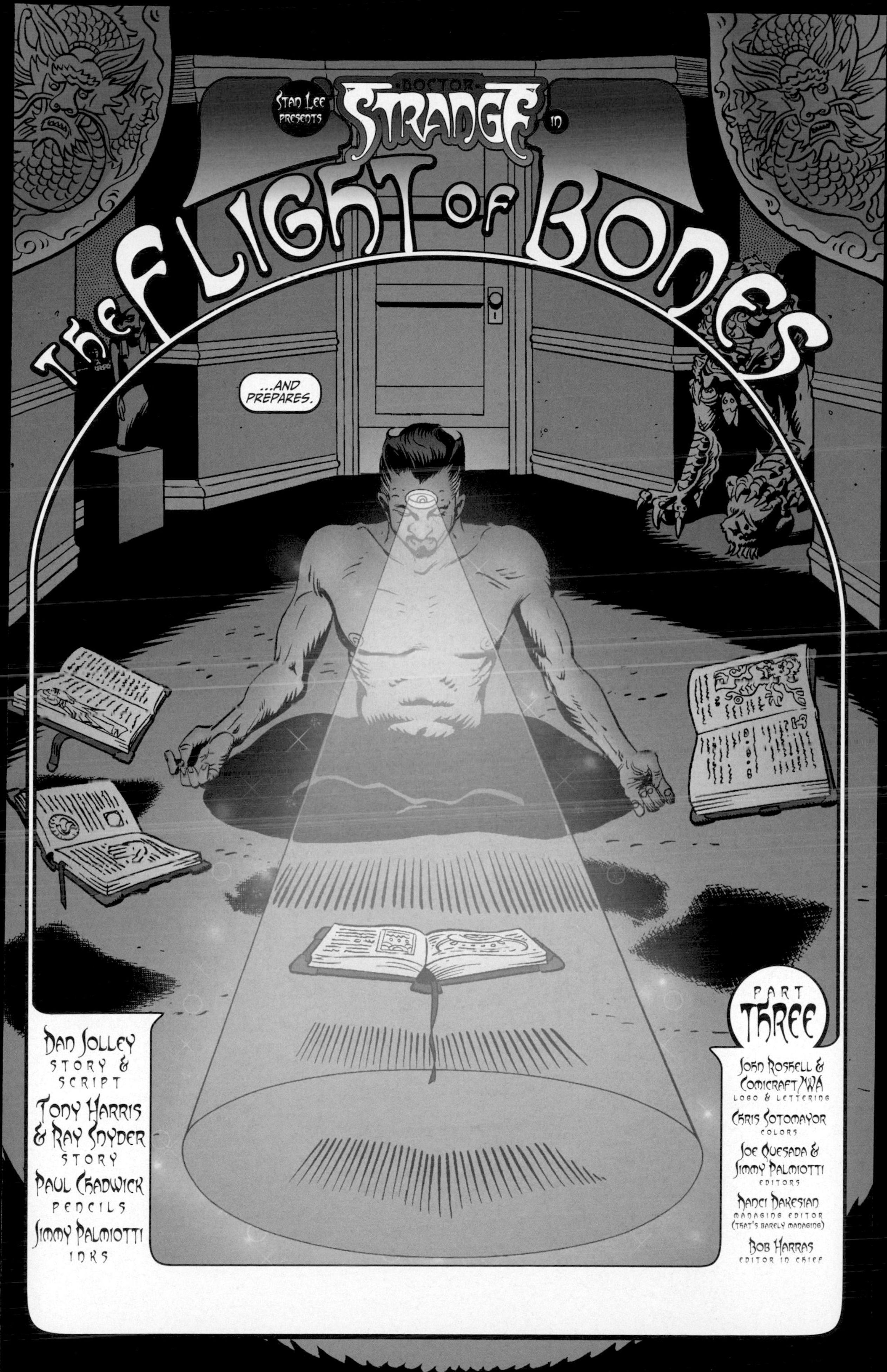

Stan Lee presents
Doctor Strange in
The Flight of Bones
...AND PREPARES.
Part Three
Dan Jolley story & script
Tony Harris & Ray Snyder story
Paul Chadwick pencils
Jimmy Palmiotti inks
John Roshell & Comicraft/WA logo & lettering
Chris Sotomayor colors
Joe Quesada & Jimmy Palmiotti editors
Nanci Dakesian managing editor (that's barely managing)
Bob Harras editor in chief

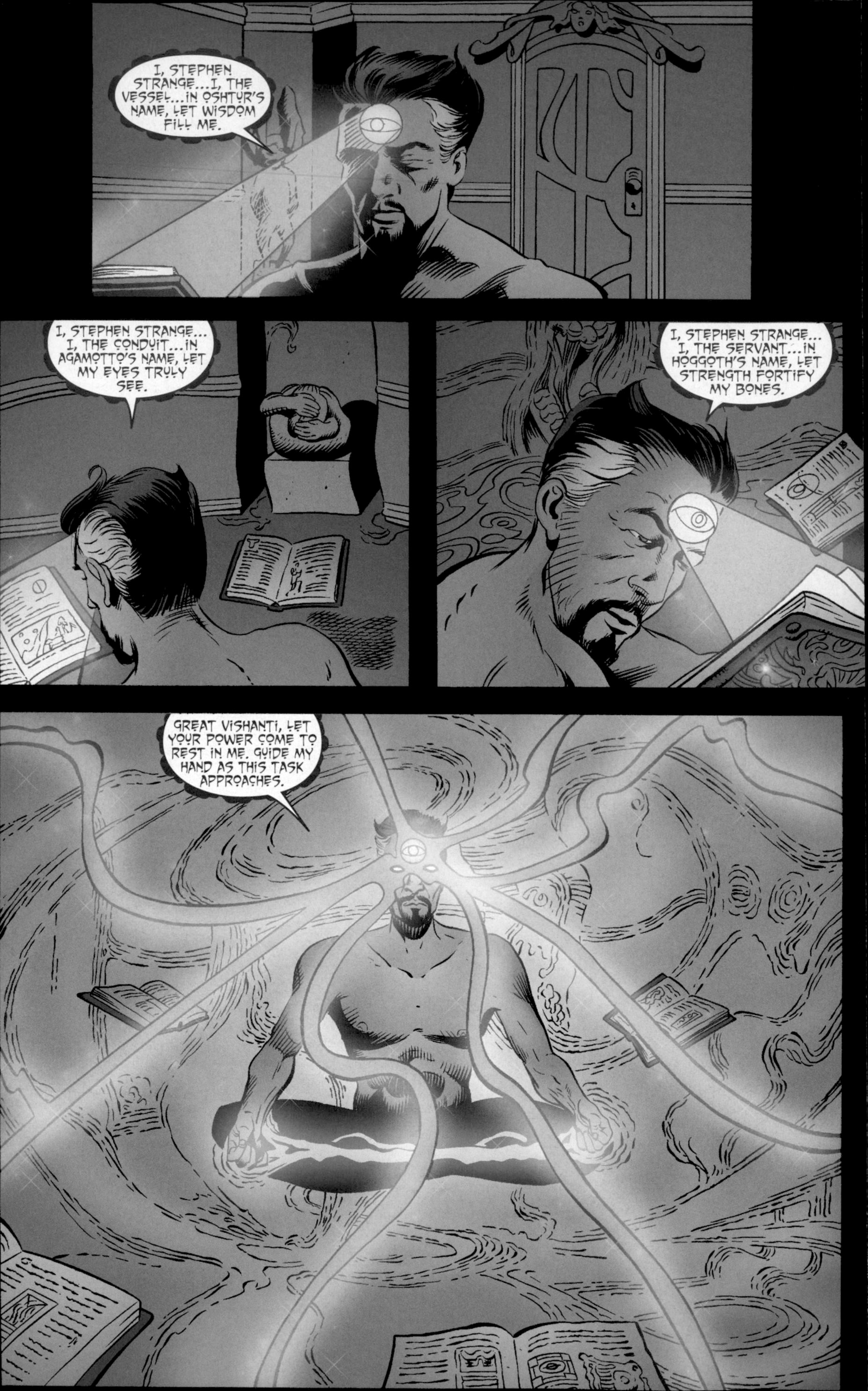
I, STEPHEN STRANGE...I, THE VESSEL...IN OSHTUR'S NAME, LET WISDOM FILL ME.
I, STEPHEN STRANGE... I, THE CONDUIT...IN AGAMOTTO'S NAME, LET MY EYES TRULY SEE.
I, STEPHEN STRANGE... I, THE SERVANT...IN HOGGOTH'S NAME, LET STRENGTH FORTIFY MY BONES.
GREAT VISHANTI, LET YOUR POWER COME TO REST IN ME. GUIDE MY HAND AS THIS TASK APPROACHES.

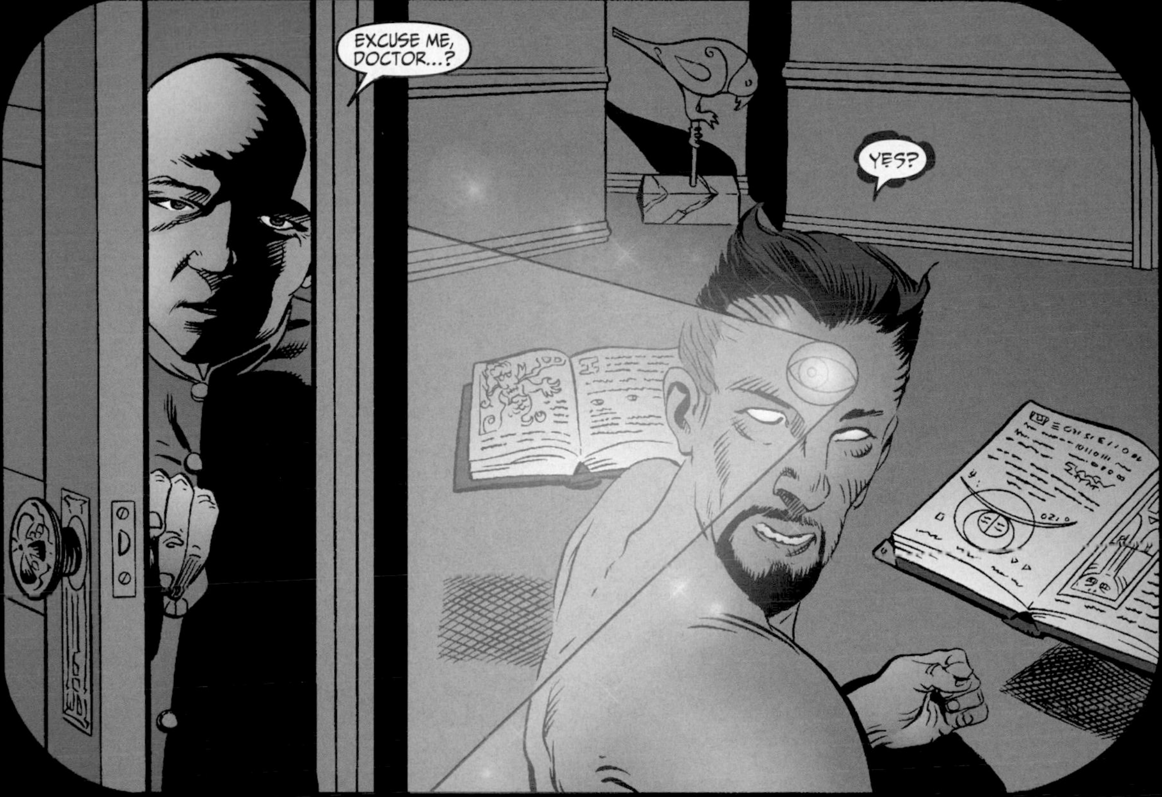
EXCUSE ME, DOCTOR...?
YES?

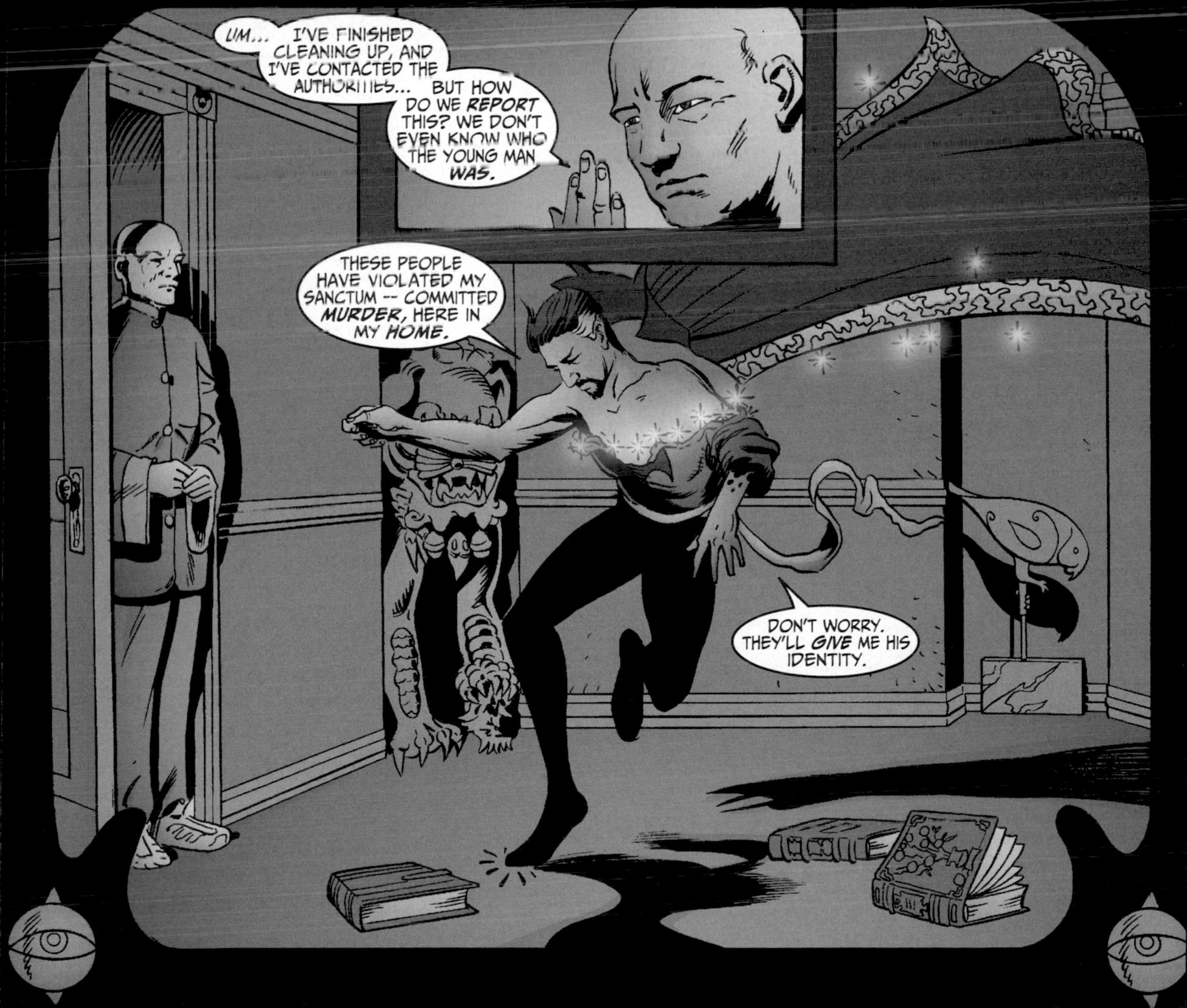
UM... I'VE FINISHED CLEANING UP, AND I'VE CONTACTED THE AUTHORITIES... BUT HOW DO WE REPORT THIS? WE DON'T EVEN KNOW WHO THE YOUNG MAN WAS.
THESE PEOPLE HAVE VIOLATED MY SANCTUM -- COMMITTED MURDER, HERE IN MY HOME.
DON'T WORRY. THEY'LL GIVE ME HIS IDENTITY.

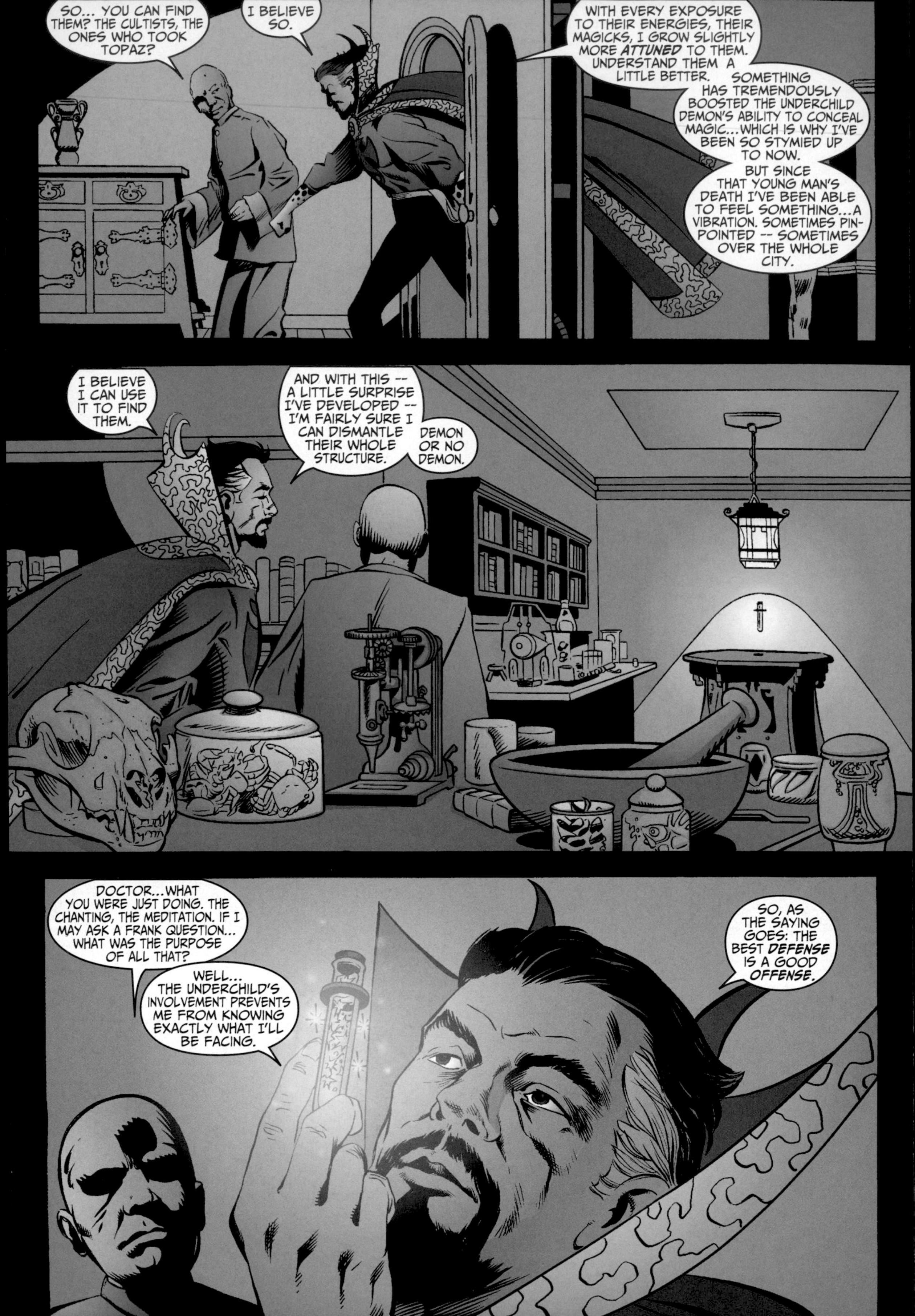

SO... YOU CAN FIND THEM? THE CULTISTS, THE ONES WHO TOOK TOPAZ?
I BELIEVE SO.
WITH EVERY EXPOSURE TO THEIR ENERGIES, THEIR MAGICKS, I GROW SLIGHTLY MORE ATTUNED TO THEM. UNDERSTAND THEM A LITTLE BETTER.
SOMETHING HAS TREMENDOUSLY BOOSTED THE UNDERCHILD DEMON'S ABILITY TO CONCEAL MAGIC...WHICH IS WHY I'VE BEEN SO STYMIED UP TO NOW.
BUT SINCE THAT YOUNG MAN'S DEATH I'VE BEEN ABLE TO FEEL SOMETHING...A VIBRATION. SOMETIMES PIN-POINTED -- SOMETIMES OVER THE WHOLE CITY.
I BELIEVE I CAN USE IT TO FIND THEM.
AND WITH THIS -- A LITTLE SURPRISE I'VE DEVELOPED -- I'M FAIRLY SURE I CAN DISMANTLE THEIR WHOLE STRUCTURE.
DEMON OR NO DEMON.
DOCTOR...WHAT YOU WERE JUST DOING. THE CHANTING, THE MEDITATION. IF I MAY ASK A FRANK QUESTION... WHAT WAS THE PURPOSE OF ALL THAT?
WELL... THE UNDERCHILD'S INVOLVEMENT PREVENTS ME FROM KNOWING EXACTLY WHAT I'LL BE FACING.
SO, AS THE SAYING GOES: THE BEST DEFENSE IS A GOOD OFFENSE.

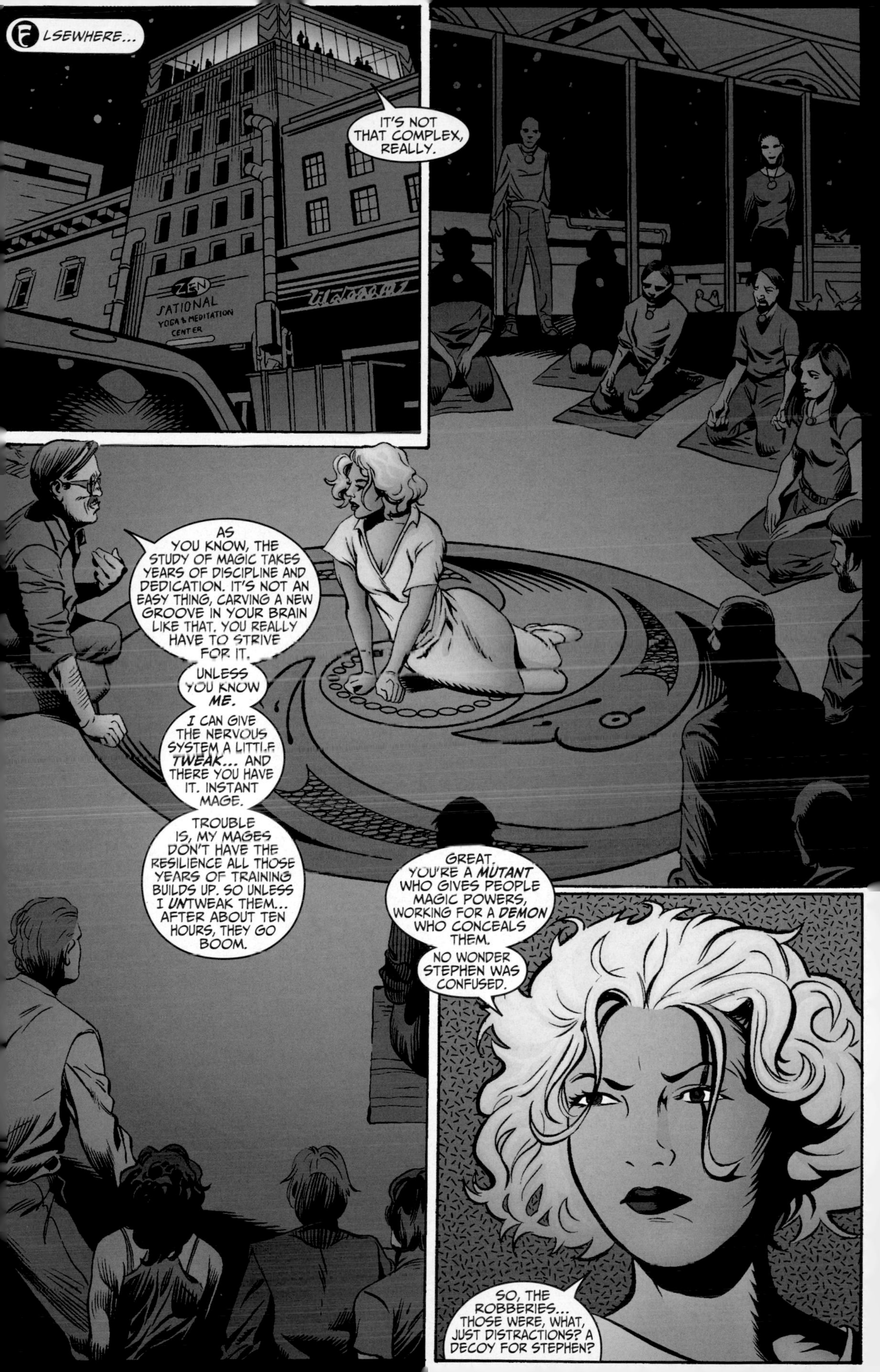
ELSEWHERE...
IT'S NOT THAT COMPLEX, REALLY.
ZEN SATIONAL YOGA & MEDITATION CENTER
AS YOU KNOW, THE STUDY OF MAGIC TAKES YEARS OF DISCIPLINE AND DEDICATION. IT'S NOT AN EASY THING, CARVING A NEW GROOVE IN YOUR BRAIN LIKE THAT. YOU REALLY HAVE TO STRIVE FOR IT.
UNLESS YOU KNOW ME.
I CAN GIVE THE NERVOUS SYSTEM A LITTLE TWEAK... AND THERE YOU HAVE IT. INSTANT MAGE.
TROUBLE IS, MY MAGES DON'T HAVE THE RESILIENCE ALL THOSE YEARS OF TRAINING BUILDS UP. SO UNLESS I UNTWEAK THEM... AFTER ABOUT TEN HOURS, THEY GO BOOM.
GREAT. YOU'RE A MUTANT WHO GIVES PEOPLE MAGIC POWERS, WORKING FOR A DEMON WHO CONCEALS THEM.
NO WONDER STEPHEN WAS CONFUSED.
SO, THE ROBBERIES... THOSE WERE, WHAT, JUST DISTRACTIONS? A DECOY FOR STEPHEN?

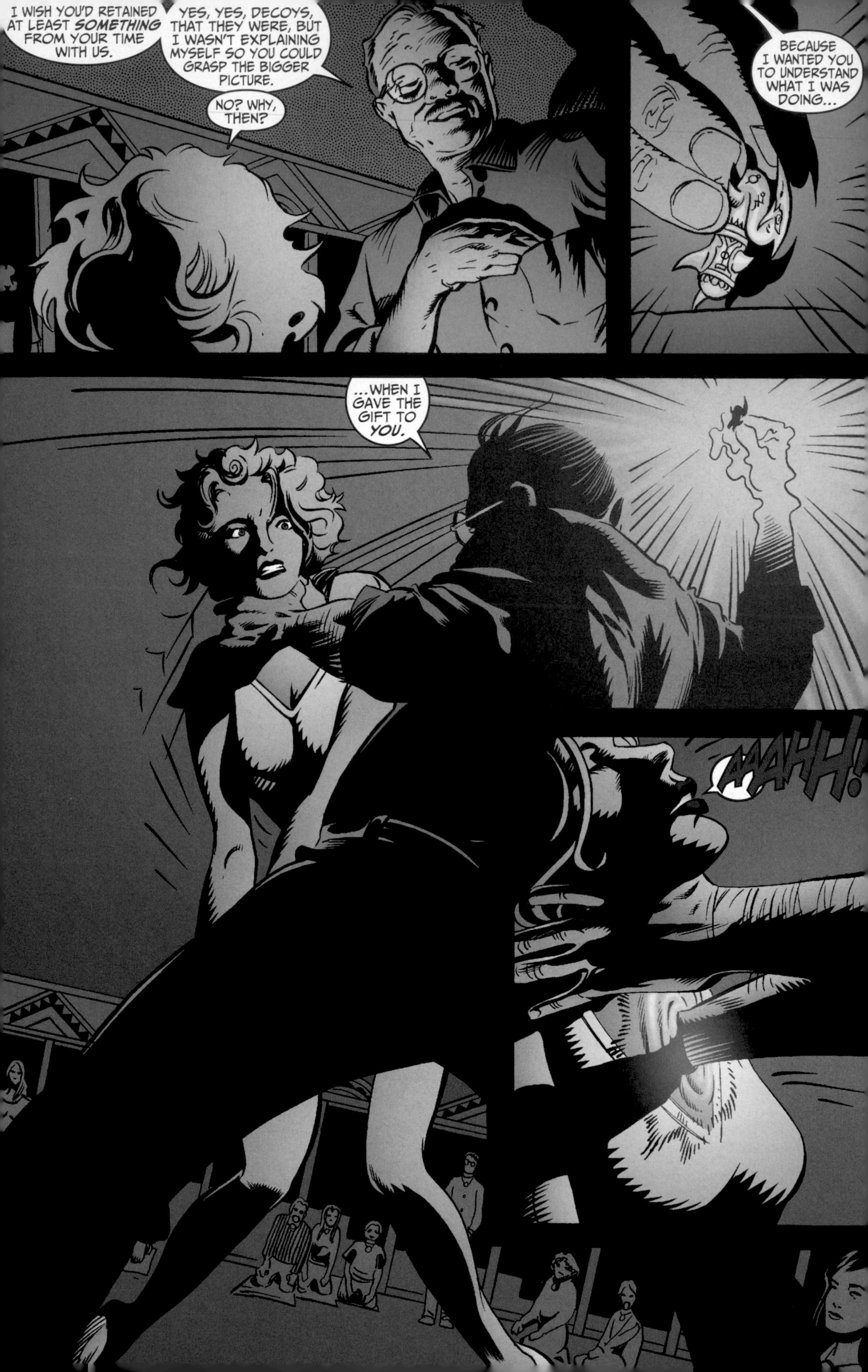
I WISH YOU'D RETAINED AT LEAST *SOMETHING* FROM YOUR TIME WITH US.
YES, YES, DECOYS, THAT THEY WERE, BUT I WASN'T EXPLAINING MYSELF SO YOU COULD GRASP THE BIGGER PICTURE.
NO? WHY, THEN?
BECAUSE I WANTED YOU TO UNDERSTAND WHAT I WAS DOING...
...WHEN I GAVE THE GIFT TO *YOU.*
AAAHH!

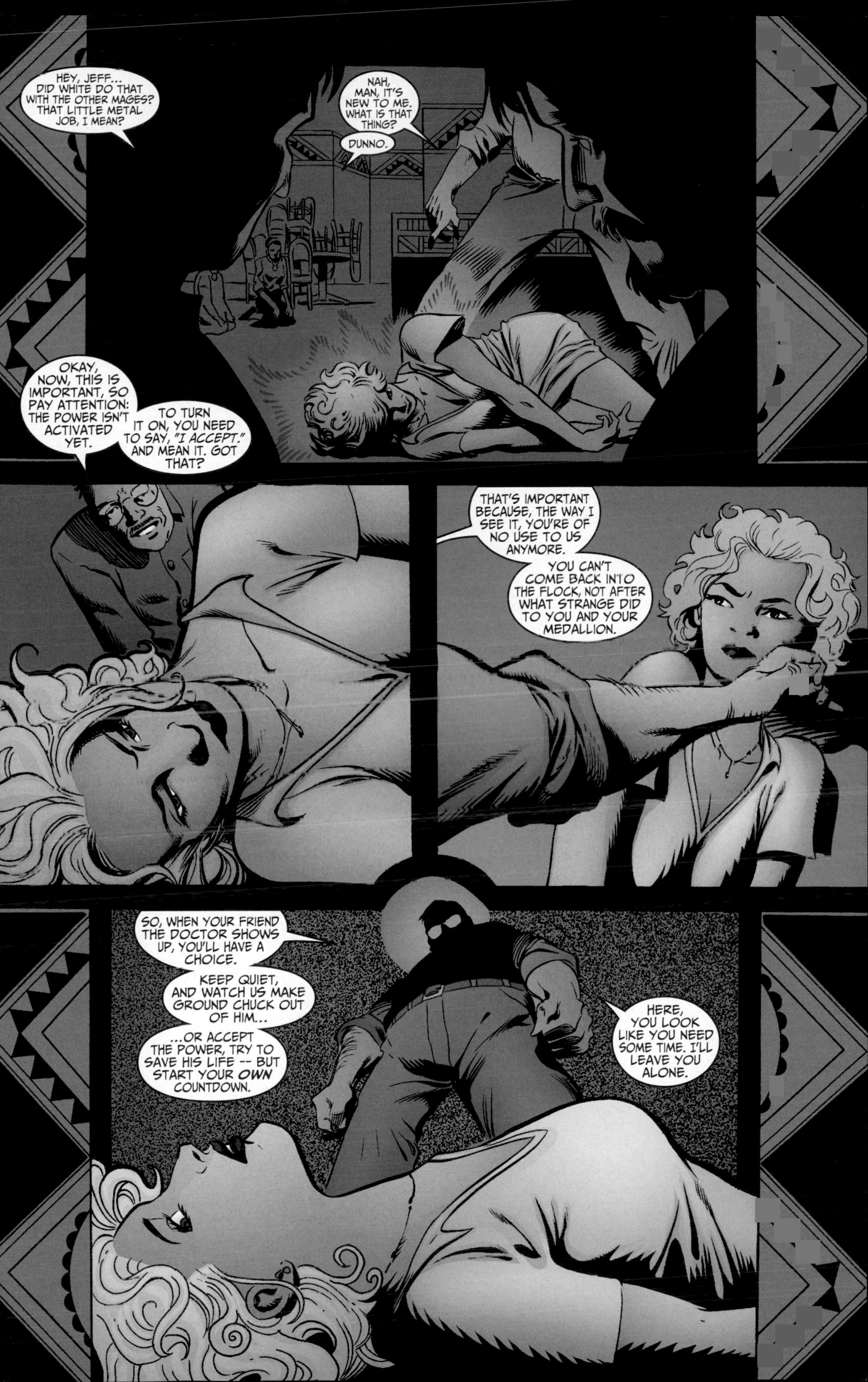
HEY, JEFF... DID WHITE DO THAT WITH THE OTHER MAGES? THAT LITTLE METAL JOB, I MEAN?
NAH, MAN, IT'S NEW TO ME. WHAT IS THAT THING?
DUNNO.
OKAY, NOW, THIS IS IMPORTANT, SO PAY ATTENTION: THE POWER ISN'T ACTIVATED YET.
TO TURN IT ON, YOU NEED TO SAY, "I ACCEPT." AND MEAN IT. GOT THAT?
THAT'S IMPORTANT BECAUSE, THE WAY I SEE IT, YOU'RE OF NO USE TO US ANYMORE.
YOU CAN'T COME BACK INTO THE FLOCK, NOT AFTER WHAT STRANGE DID TO YOU AND YOUR MEDALLION.
SO, WHEN YOUR FRIEND THE DOCTOR SHOWS UP, YOU'LL HAVE A CHOICE.
KEEP QUIET, AND WATCH US MAKE GROUND CHUCK OUT OF HIM...
...OR ACCEPT THE POWER, TRY TO SAVE HIS LIFE -- BUT START YOUR OWN COUNTDOWN.
HERE, YOU LOOK LIKE YOU NEED SOME TIME. I'LL LEAVE YOU ALONE.

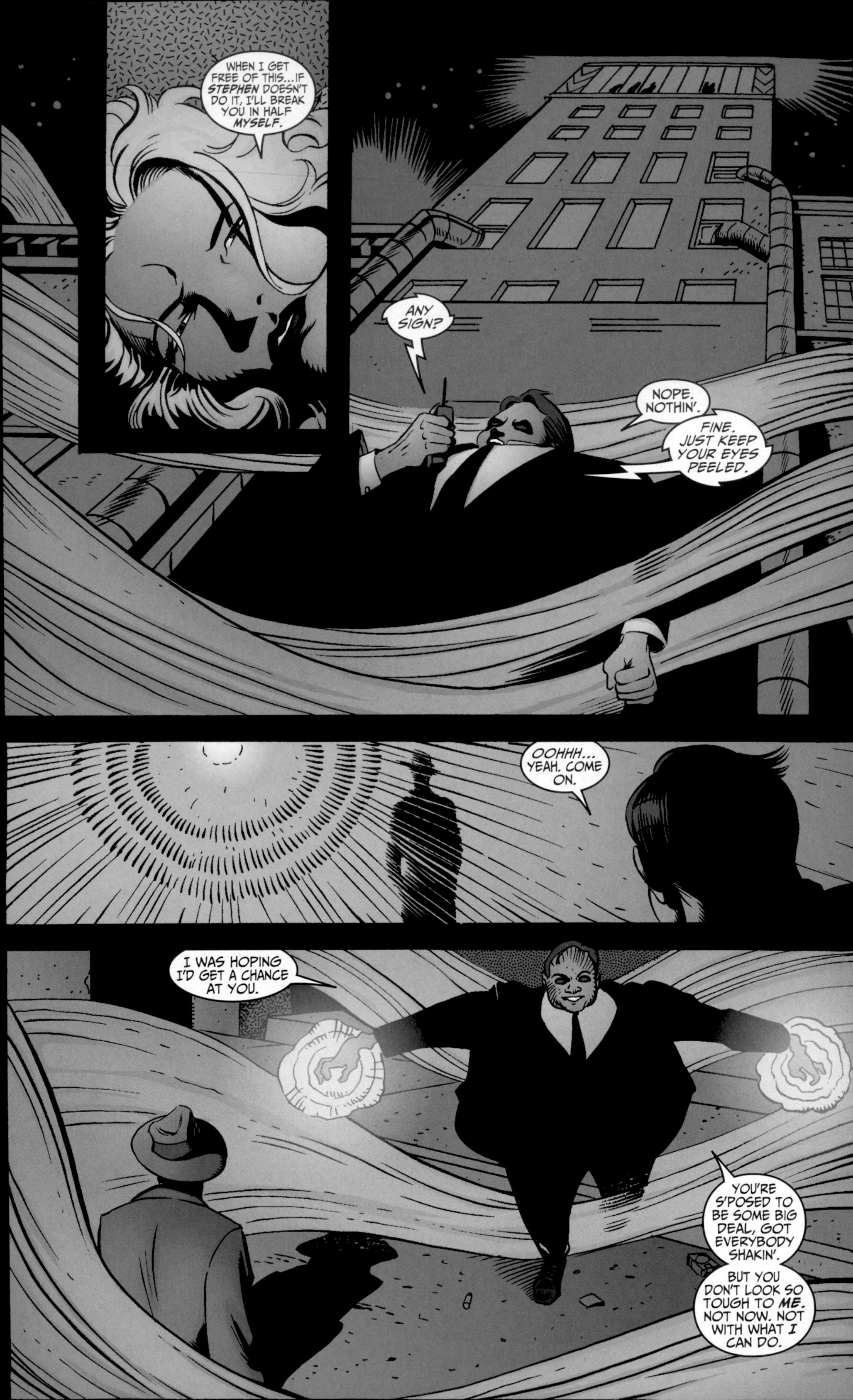
WHEN I GET FREE OF THIS...IF STEPHEN DOESN'T DO IT, I'LL BREAK YOU IN HALF MYSELF.
ANY SIGN?
NOPE. NOTHIN'.
FINE. JUST KEEP YOUR EYES PEELED.
OOHHH... YEAH. COME ON.
I WAS HOPING I'D GET A CHANCE AT YOU.
YOU'RE S'POSED TO BE SOME BIG DEAL, GOT EVERYBODY SHAKIN'.
BUT YOU DON'T LOOK SO TOUGH TO ME. NOT NOW. NOT WITH WHAT I CAN DO.

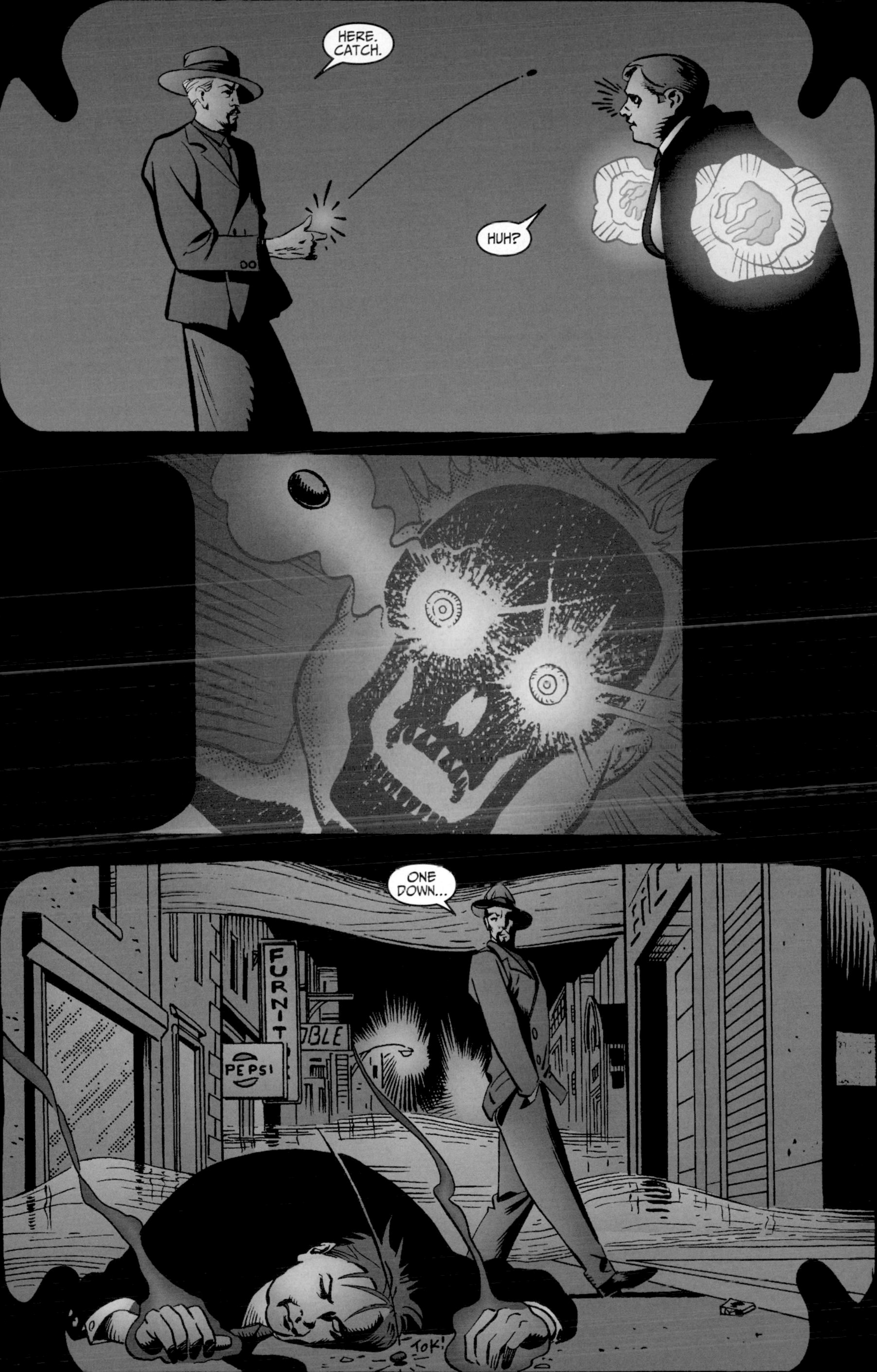
HERE. CATCH.
HUH?
ONE DOWN...
FURNIT
PEPSI
TOK!

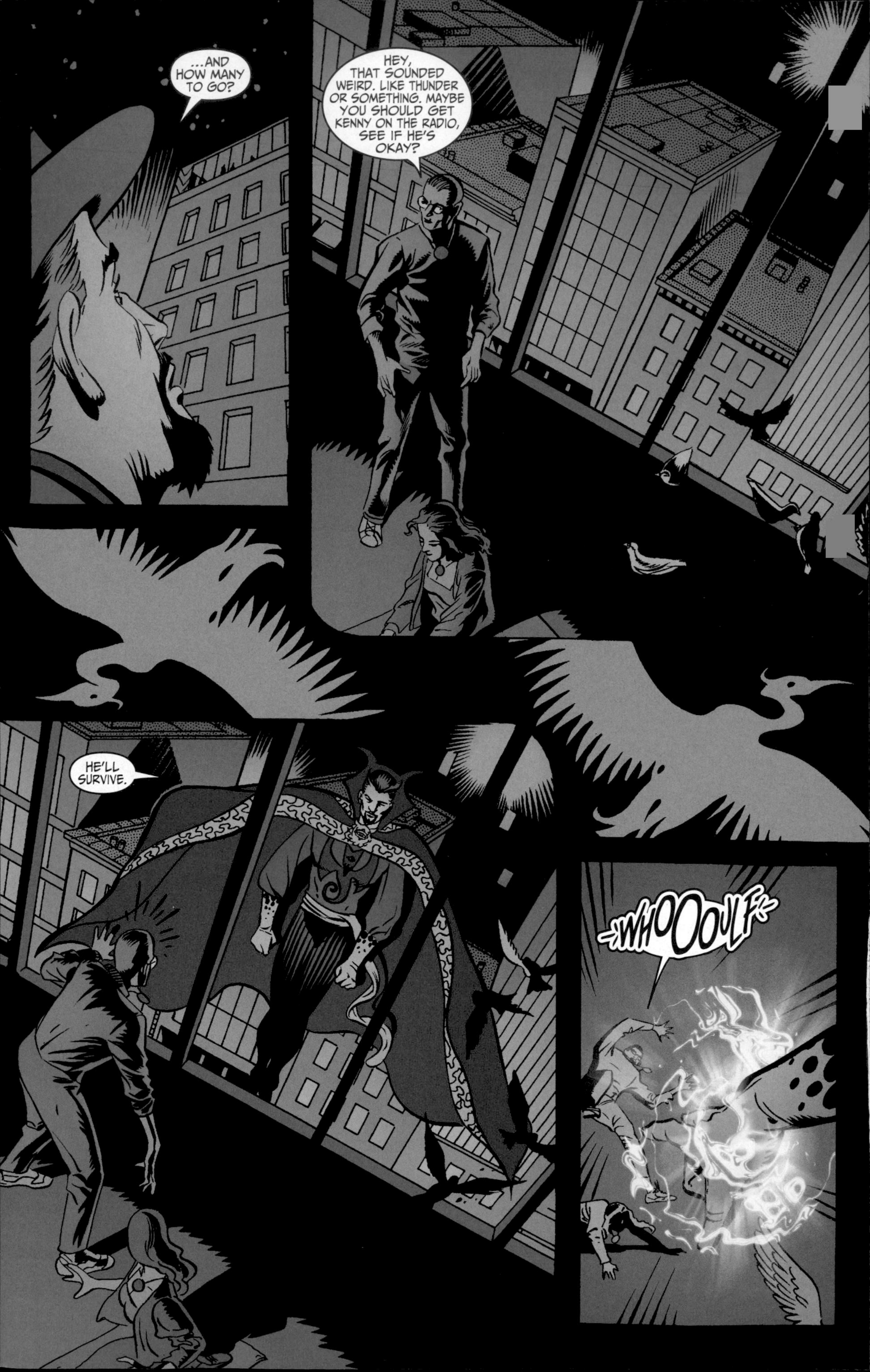
...AND HOW MANY TO GO?
HEY, THAT SOUNDED WEIRD. LIKE THUNDER OR SOMETHING. MAYBE YOU SHOULD GET KENNY ON THE RADIO, SEE IF HE'S OKAY?
HE'LL SURVIVE.
WHOOOULF

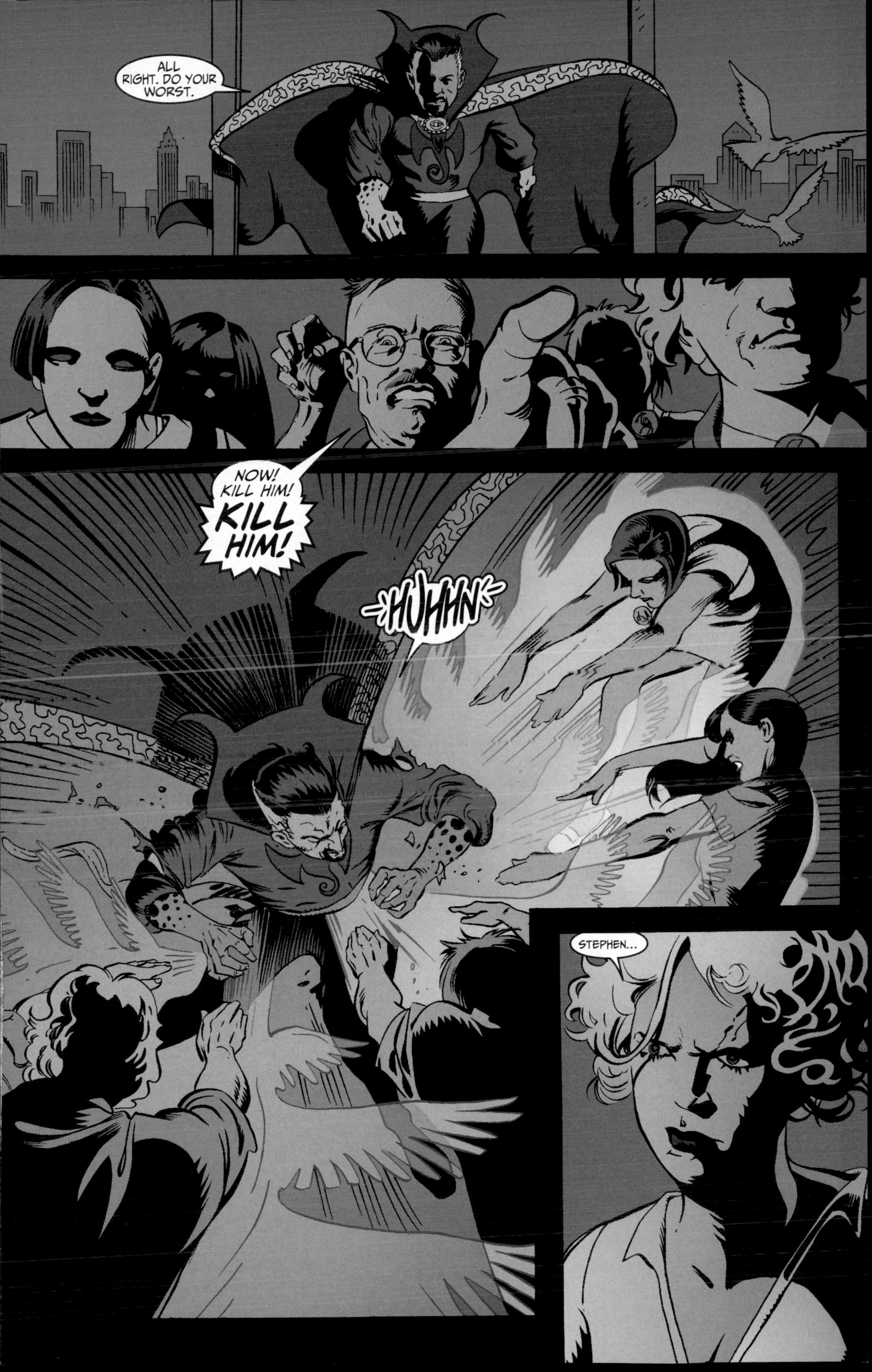
ALL RIGHT. DO YOUR WORST.
NOW! KILL HIM! KILL HIM!
HUHHN
STEPHEN...

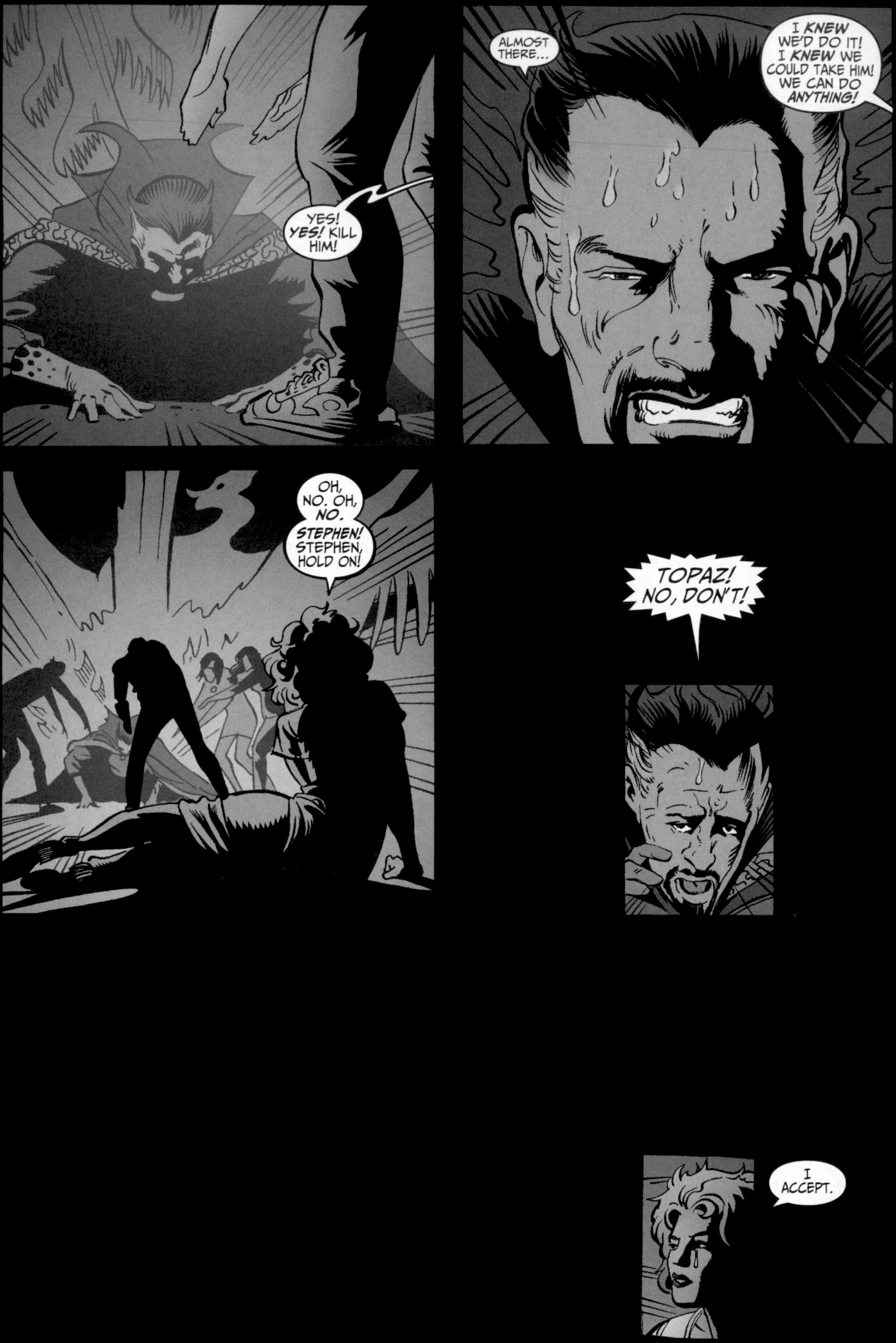
YES! YES! KILL HIM!
ALMOST THERE...
I KNEW WE'D DO IT! I KNEW WE COULD TAKE HIM! WE CAN DO ANYTHING!
OH, NO. OH, NO. STEPHEN! STEPHEN, HOLD ON!
TOPAZ! NO, DON'T!
I ACCEPT.

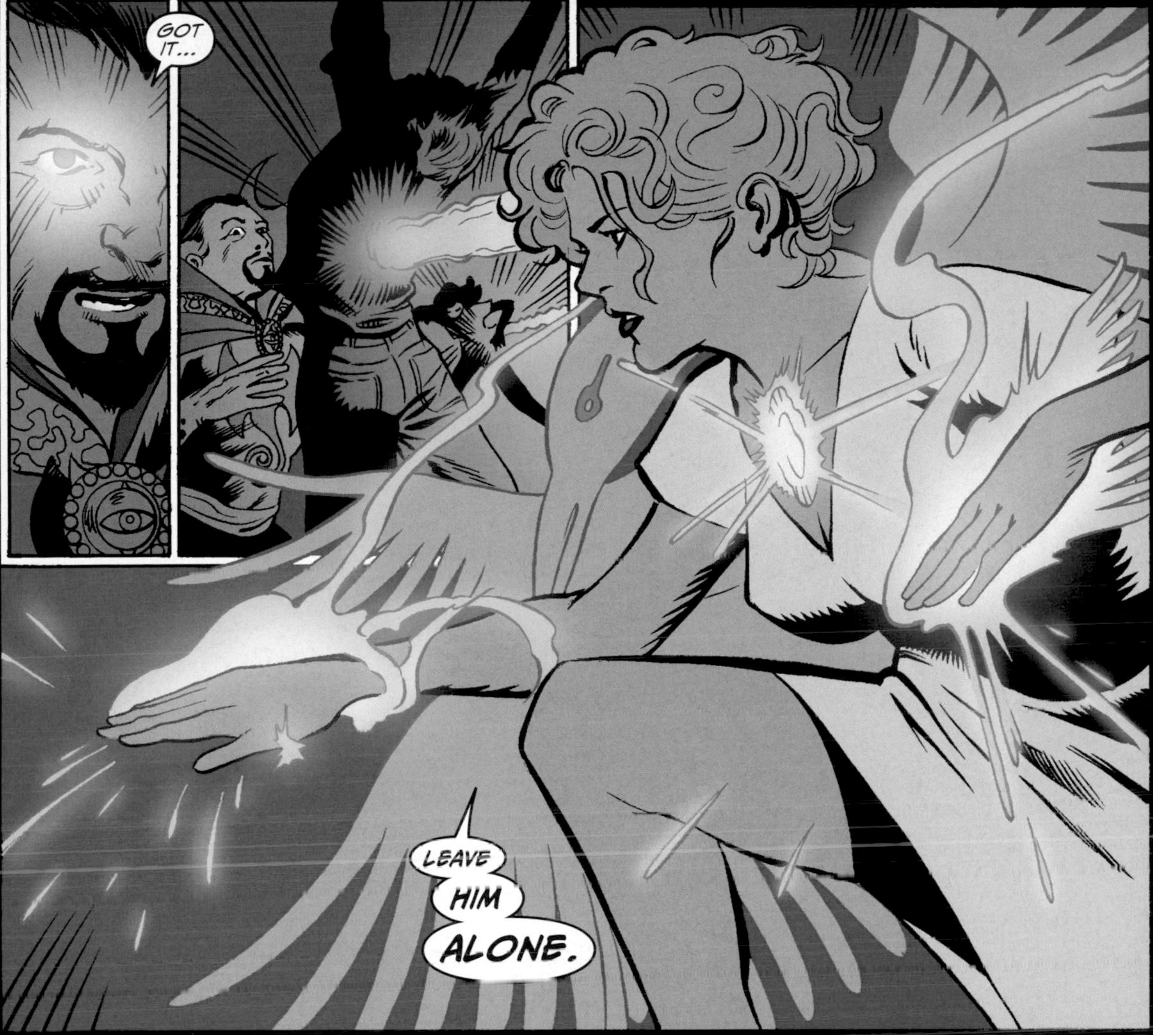
GOT IT...
LEAVE HIM ALONE.
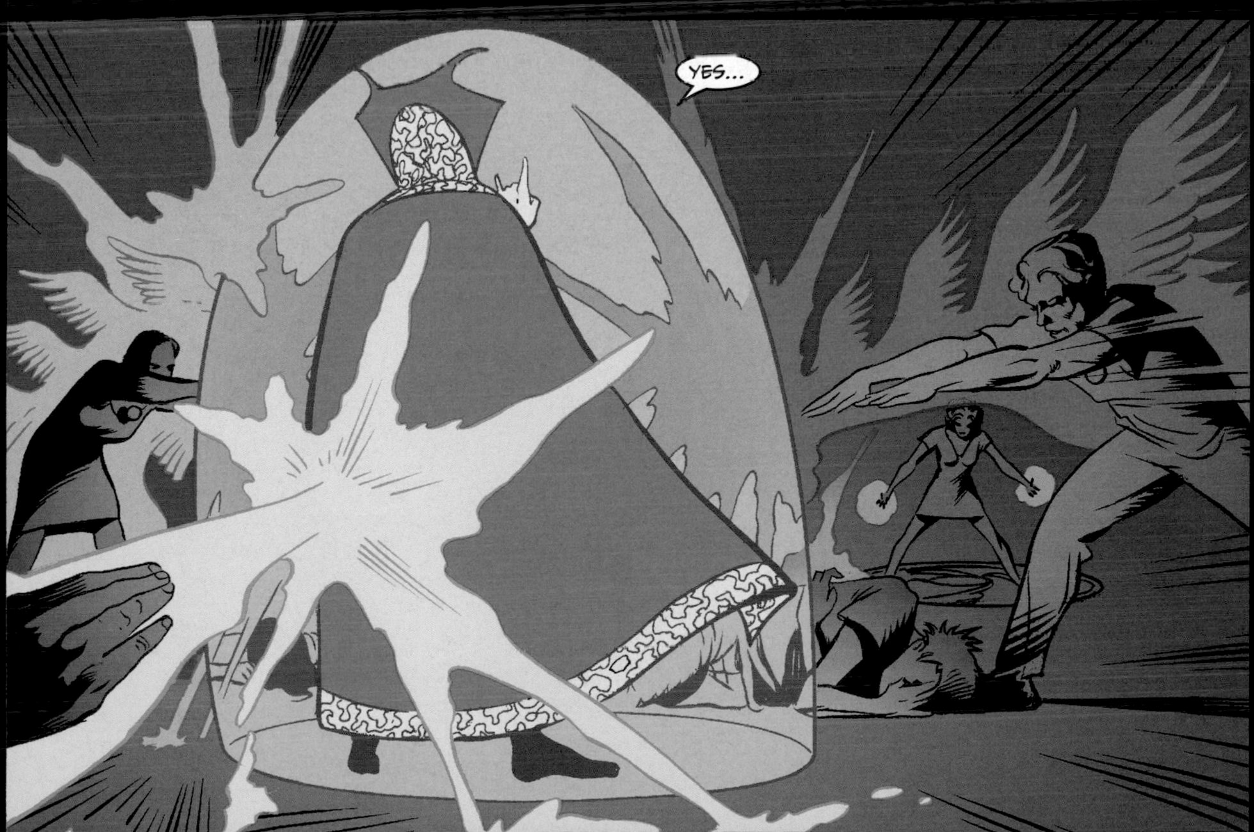
YES...

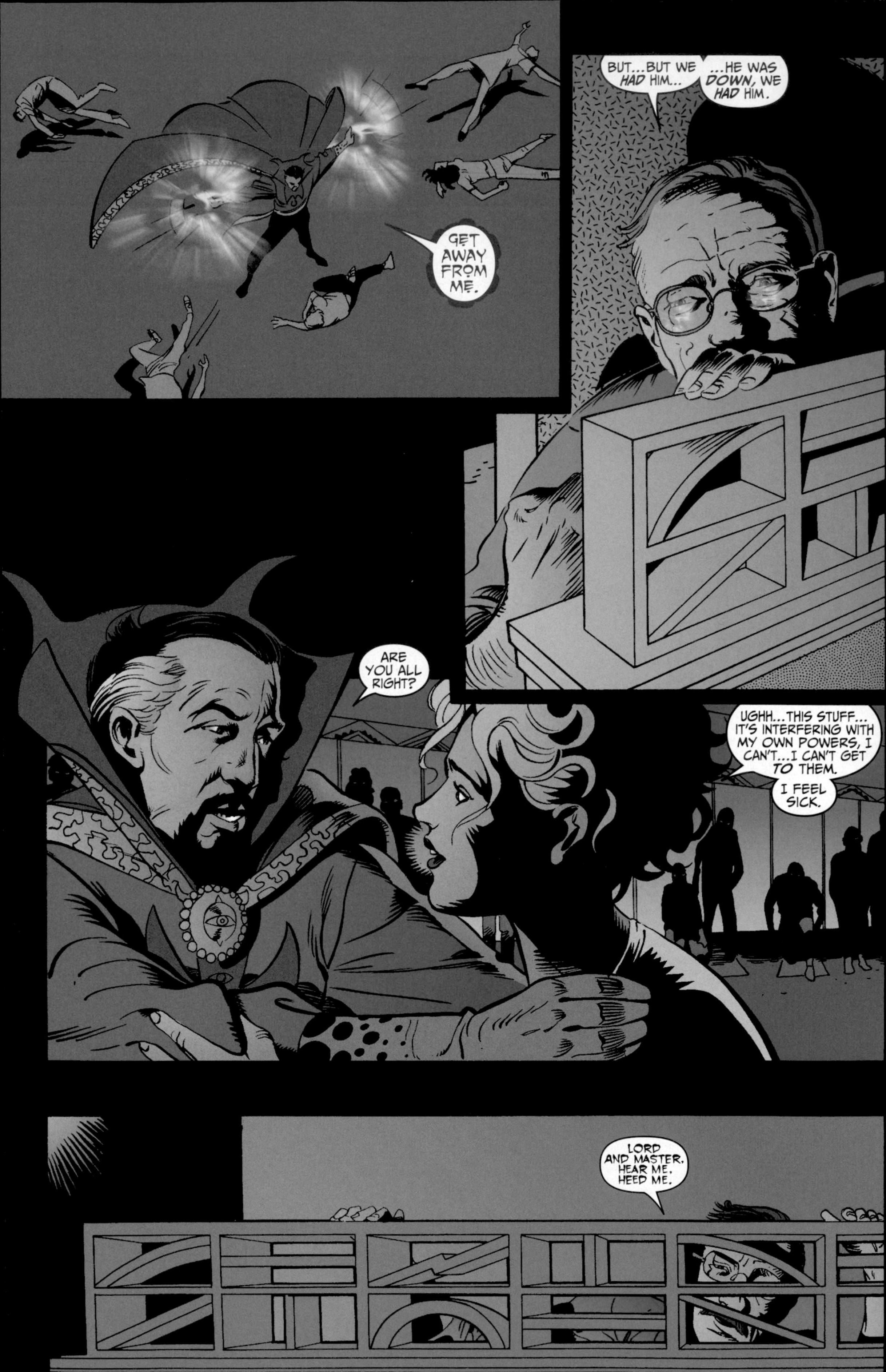
GET AWAY FROM ME.
BUT...BUT WE HAD HIM...
...HE WAS DOWN, WE HAD HIM.
ARE YOU ALL RIGHT?
UGHH...THIS STUFF... IT'S INTERFERING WITH MY OWN POWERS, I CAN'T...I CAN'T GET TO THEM.
I FEEL SICK.
LORD AND MASTER. HEAR ME. HEED ME.

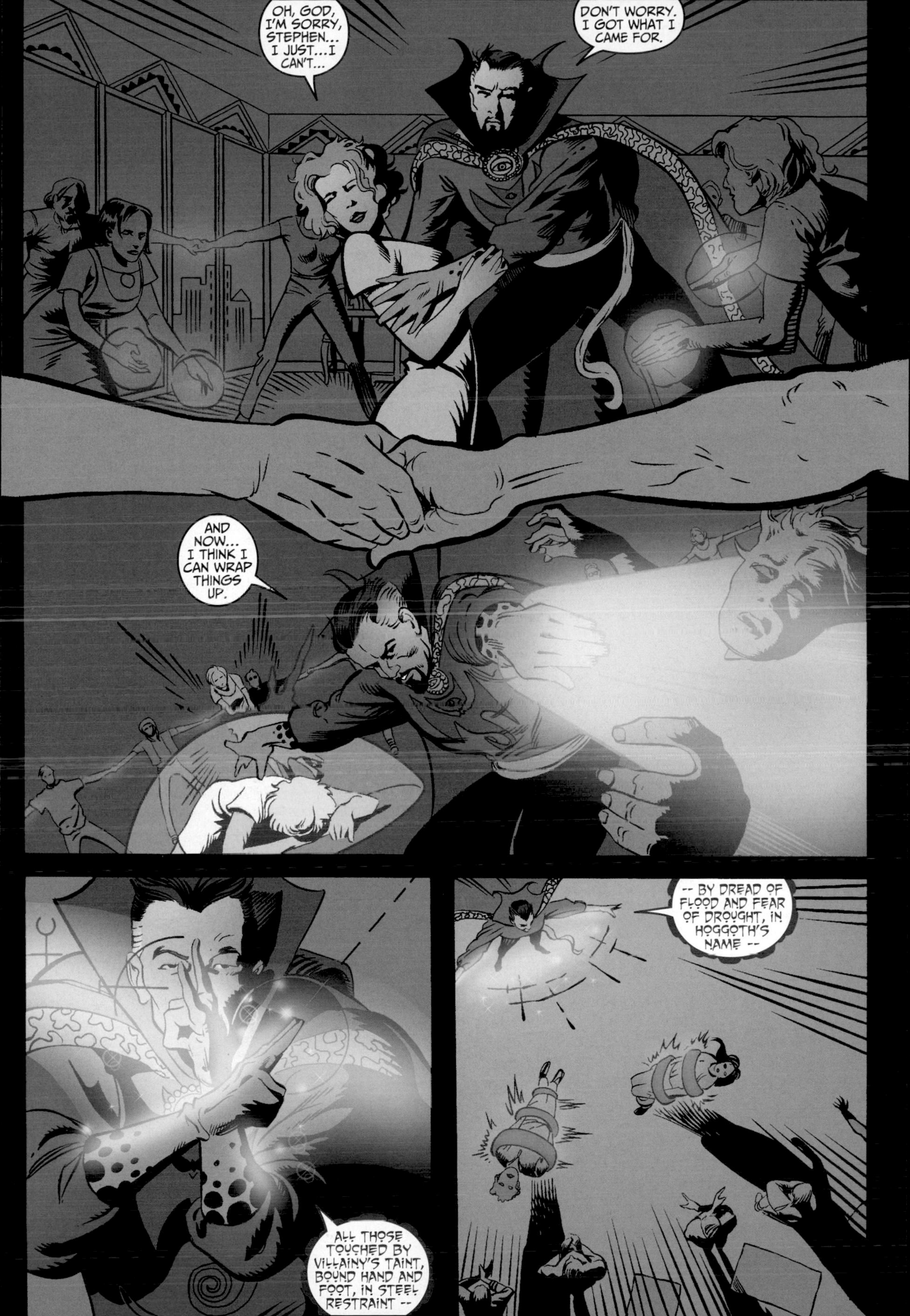

OH, GOD, I'M SORRY, STEPHEN... I JUST... I CAN'T...
DON'T WORRY. I GOT WHAT I CAME FOR.
AND NOW... I THINK I CAN WRAP THINGS UP.
ALL THOSE TOUCHED BY VILLAINY'S TAINT, BOUND HAND AND FOOT, IN STEEL RESTRAINT --
-- BY DREAD OF FLOOD AND FEAR OF DROUGHT, IN HOGGOTH'S NAME --

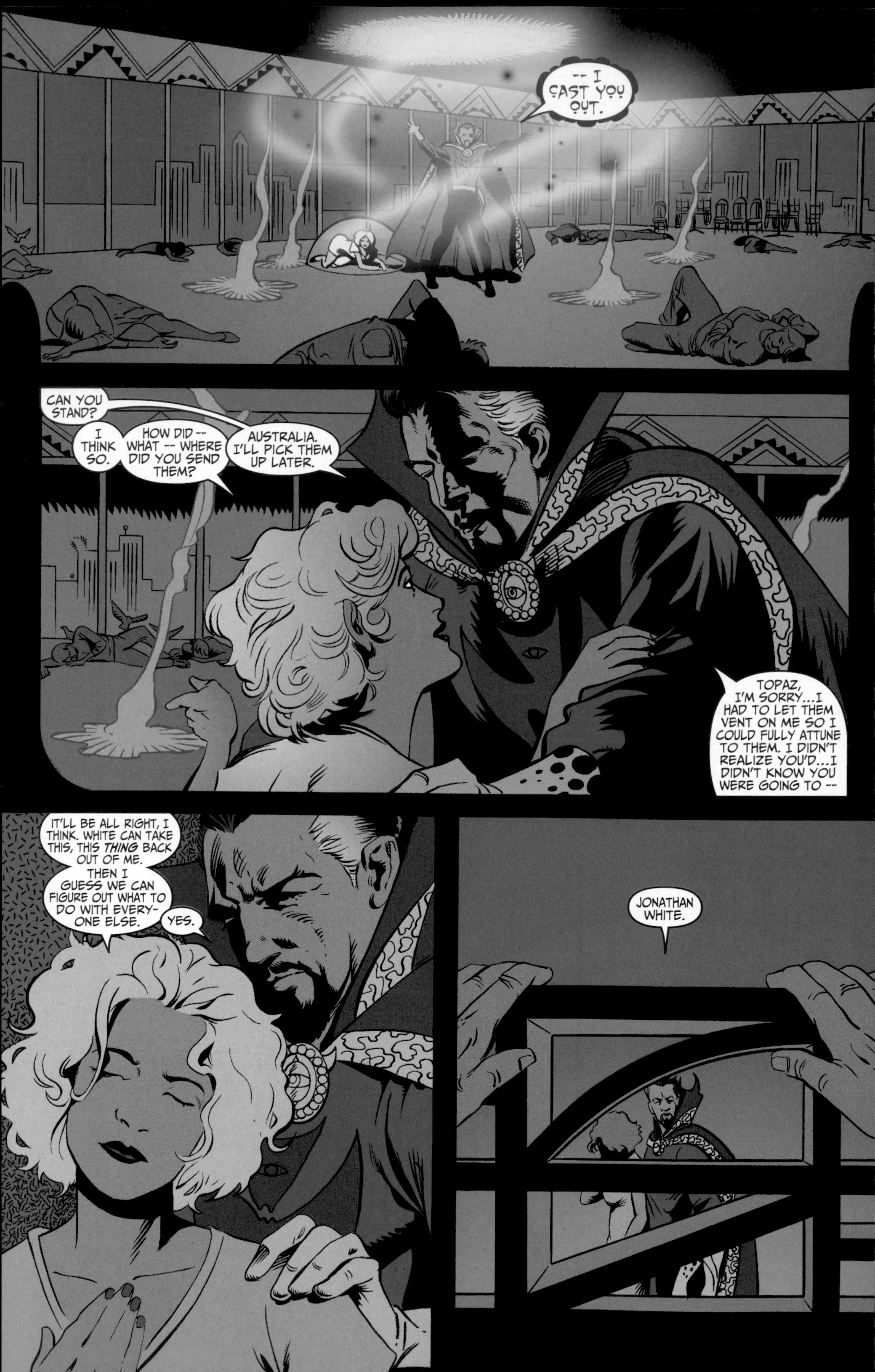
-- I CAST YOU OUT.
CAN YOU STAND?
I THINK SO.
HOW DID -- WHAT -- WHERE DID YOU SEND THEM?
AUSTRALIA. I'LL PICK THEM UP LATER.
TOPAZ, I'M SORRY...I HAD TO LET THEM VENT ON ME SO I COULD FULLY ATTUNE TO THEM. I DIDN'T REALIZE YOU'D...I DIDN'T KNOW YOU WERE GOING TO --
IT'LL BE ALL RIGHT, I THINK. WHITE CAN TAKE THIS, THIS THING BACK OUT OF ME.
THEN I GUESS WE CAN FIGURE OUT WHAT TO DO WITH EVERY-ONE ELSE.
YES.
JONATHAN WHITE.

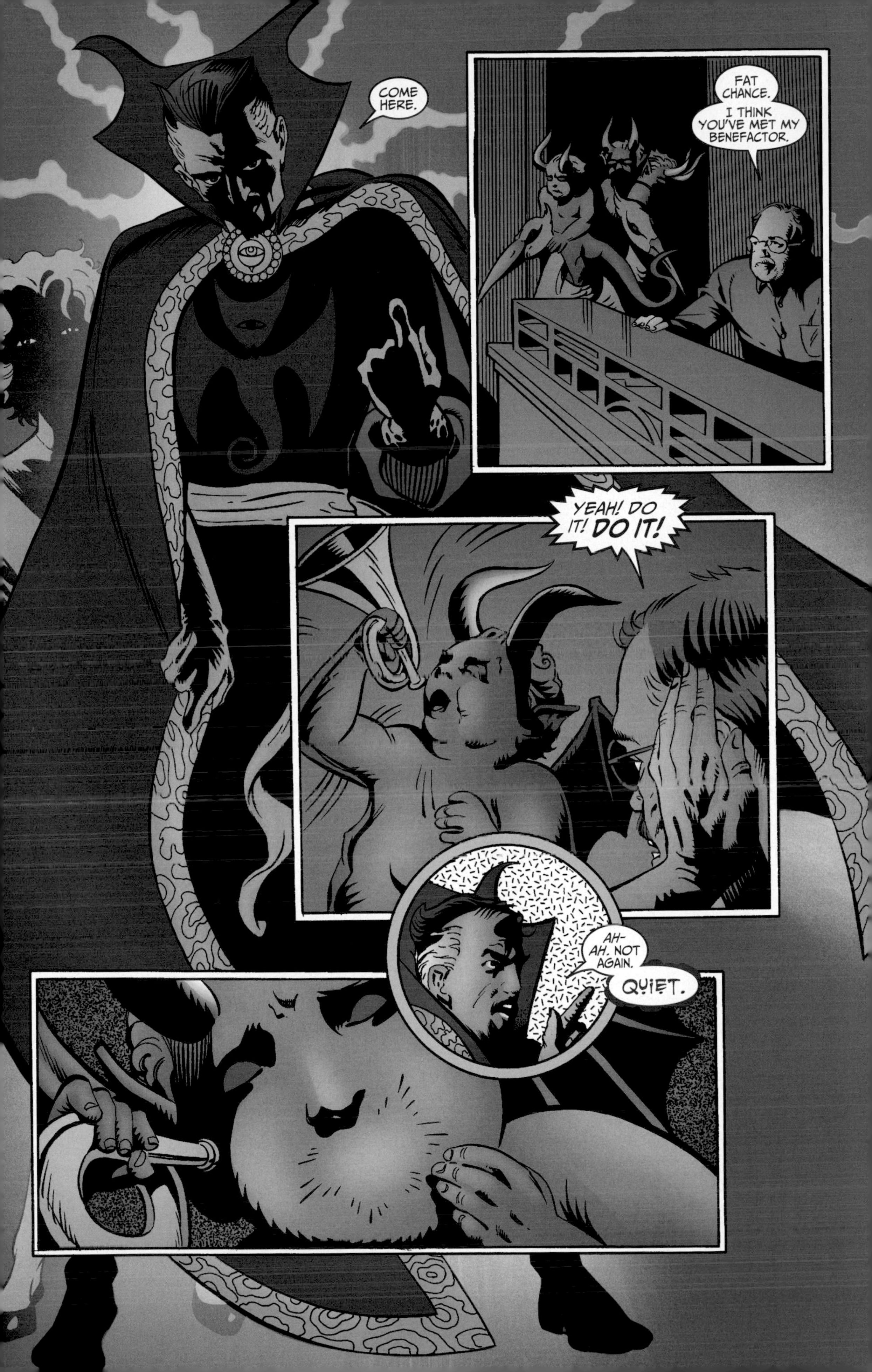
COME HERE.
FAT CHANCE.
I THINK YOU'VE MET MY BENEFACTOR.
YEAH! DO IT! DO IT!
AH-AH. NOT AGAIN.
QUIET.

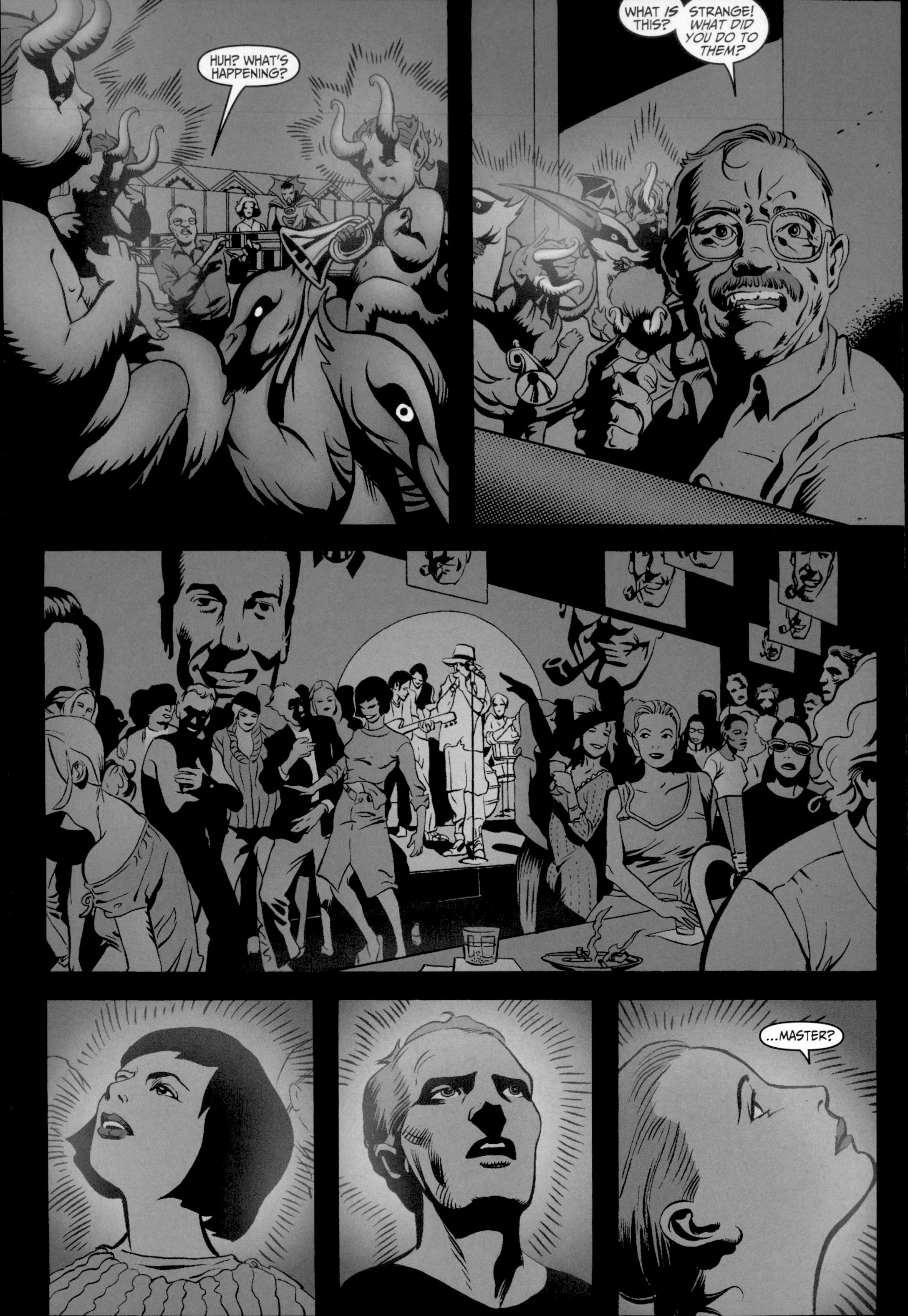
HUH? WHAT'S HAPPENING?
WHAT IS THIS?
STRANGE! WHAT DID YOU DO TO THEM?
...MASTER?

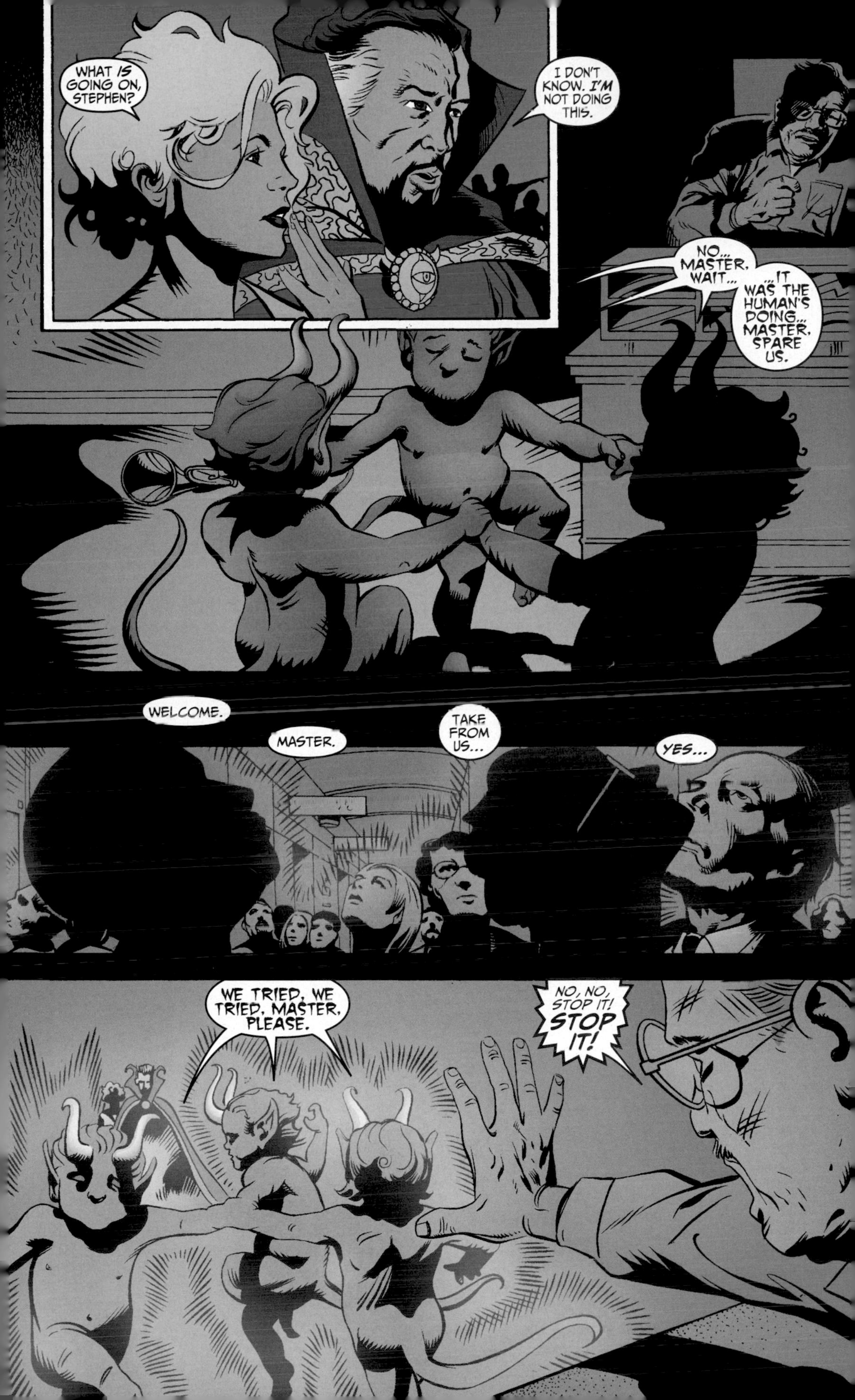
WHAT *IS* GOING ON, STEPHEN?
I DON'T KNOW. *I'M* NOT DOING THIS.
NO... MASTER. WAIT...
...IT WAS THE HUMAN'S DOING... MASTER. SPARE US.
WELCOME.
MASTER.
TAKE FROM US...
YES...
WE TRIED, WE TRIED, MASTER, PLEASE.
NO, NO, STOP IT! **STOP IT!**

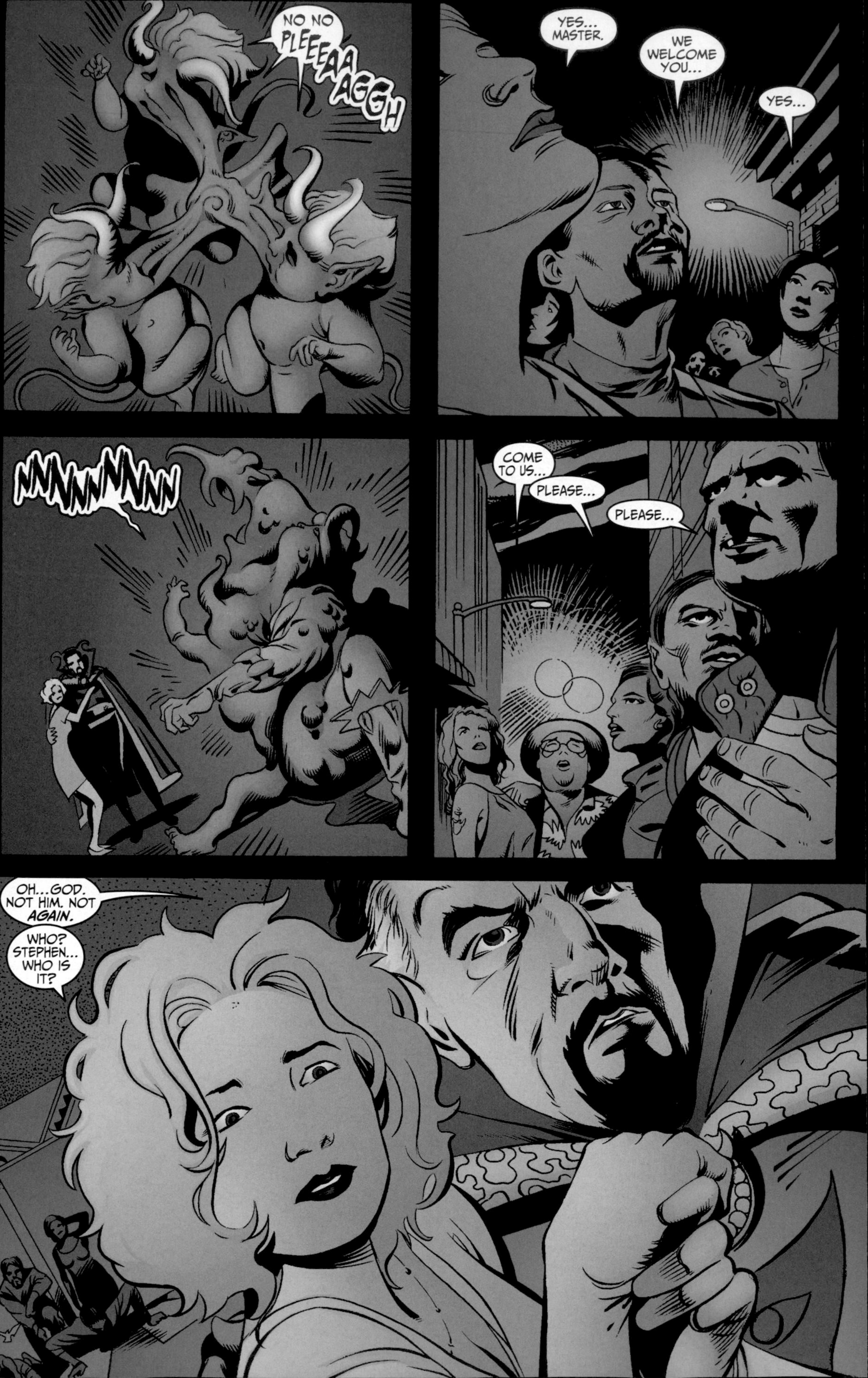
NO NO PLEEEAAAAGGH
YES... MASTER.
WE WELCOME YOU...
YES...
NNNNNNNNNN
COME TO US...
PLEASE...
PLEASE...
OH...GOD. NOT HIM. NOT AGAIN.
WHO? STEPHEN... WHO IS IT?

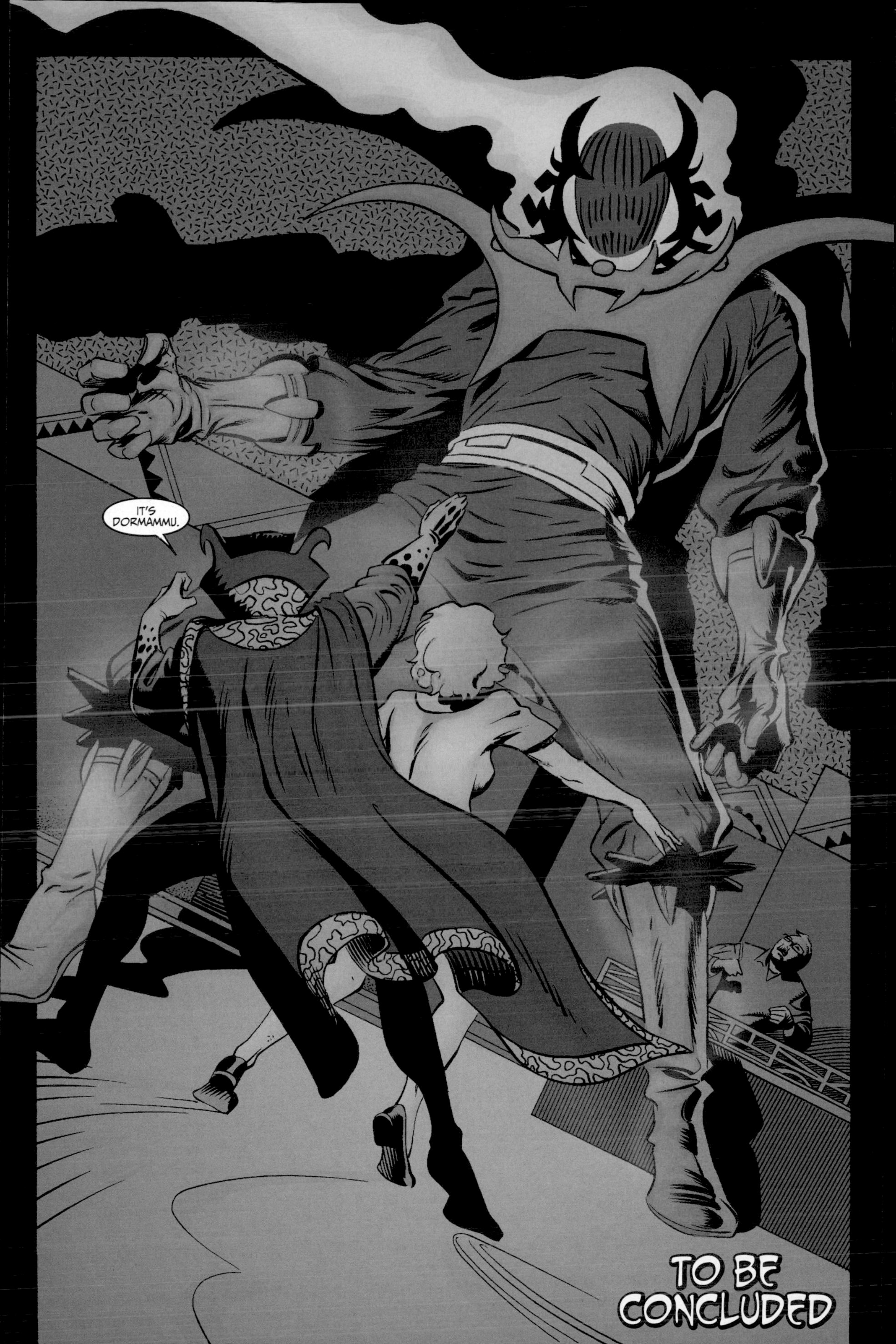
IT'S DORMAMMU.
TO BE CONCLUDED

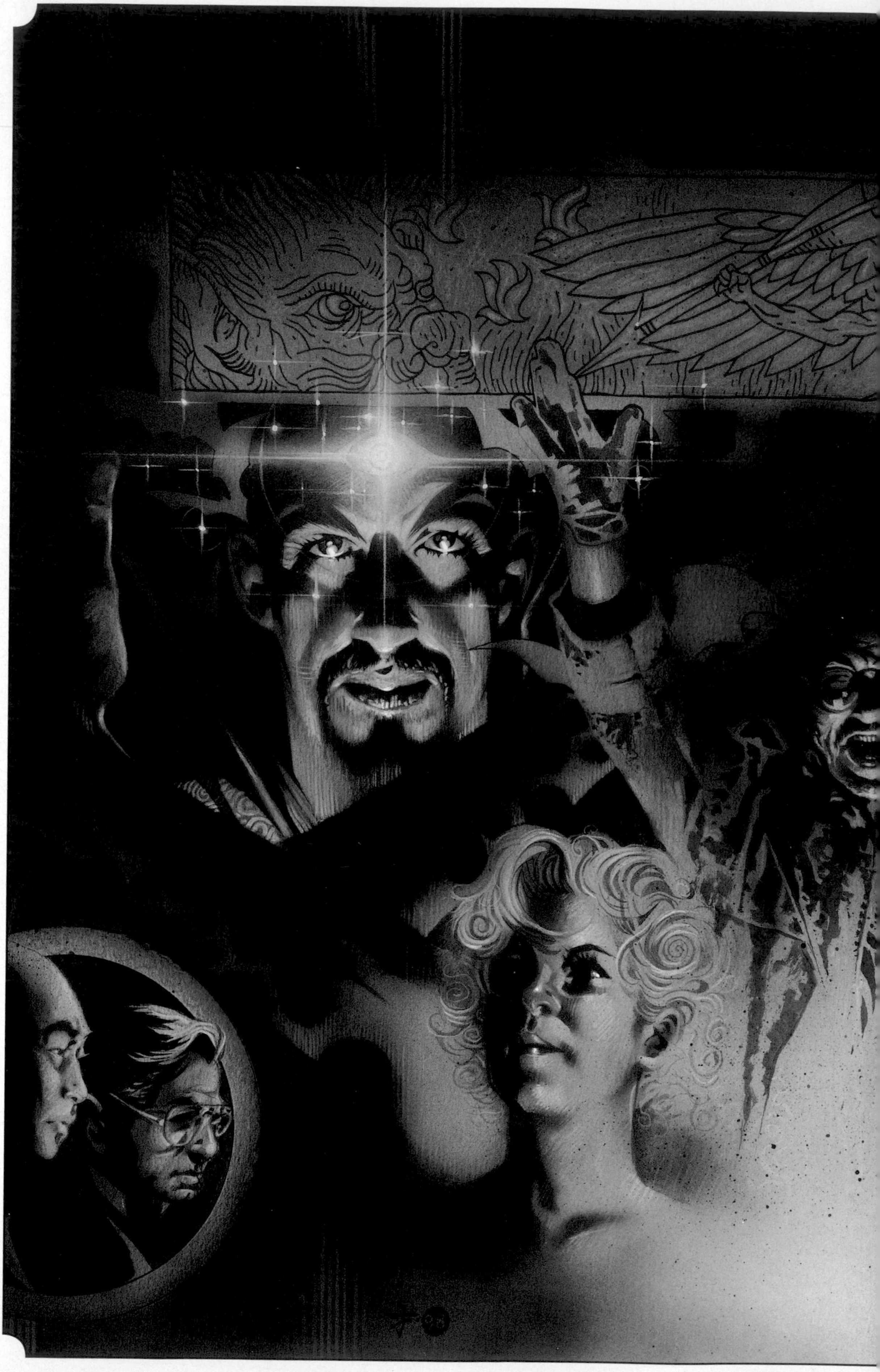

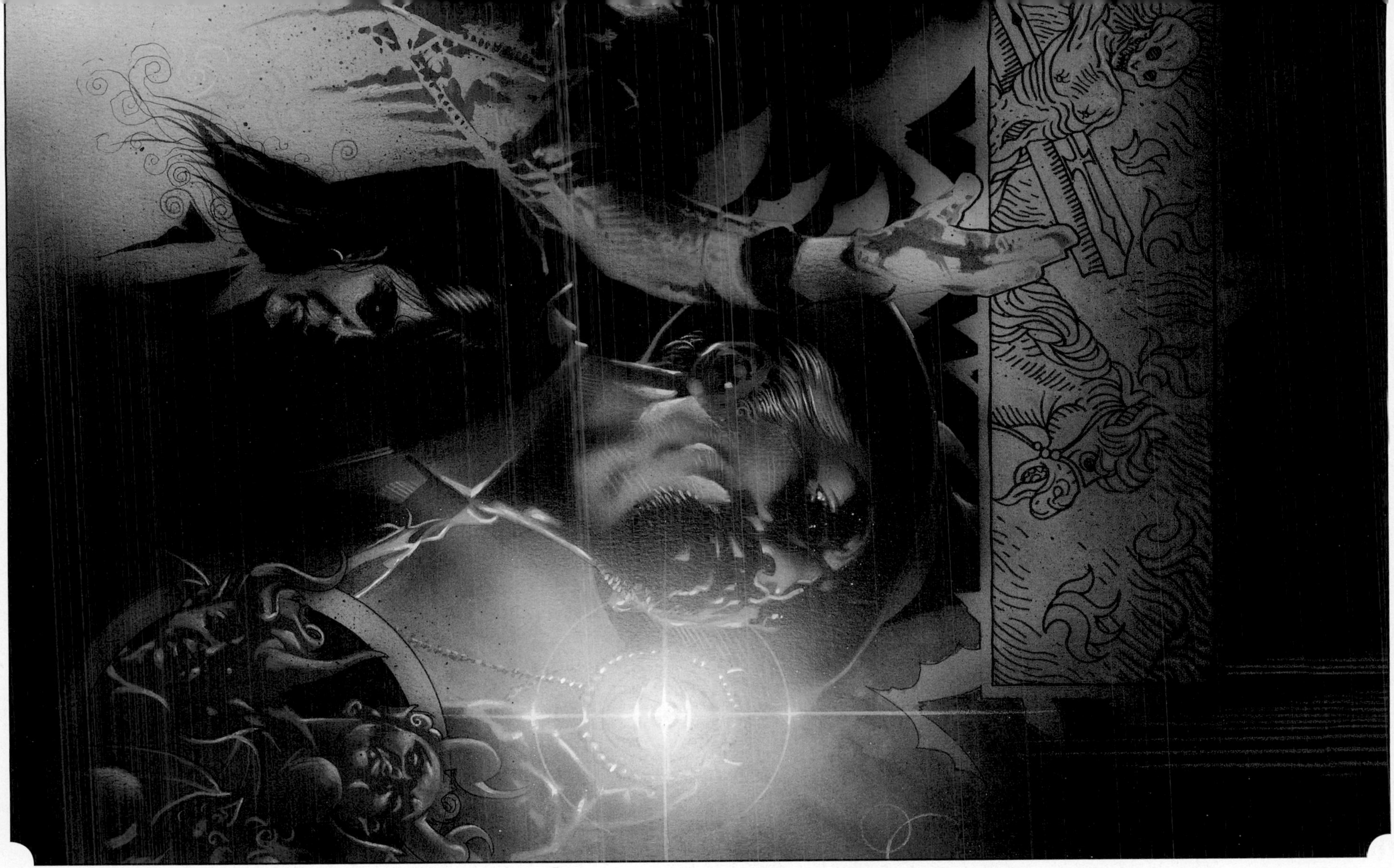

DOCTOR STRANGE #2-3'S COVERS COMBINE TO FORM ONE IMAGE. ART BY TONY HARRIS.

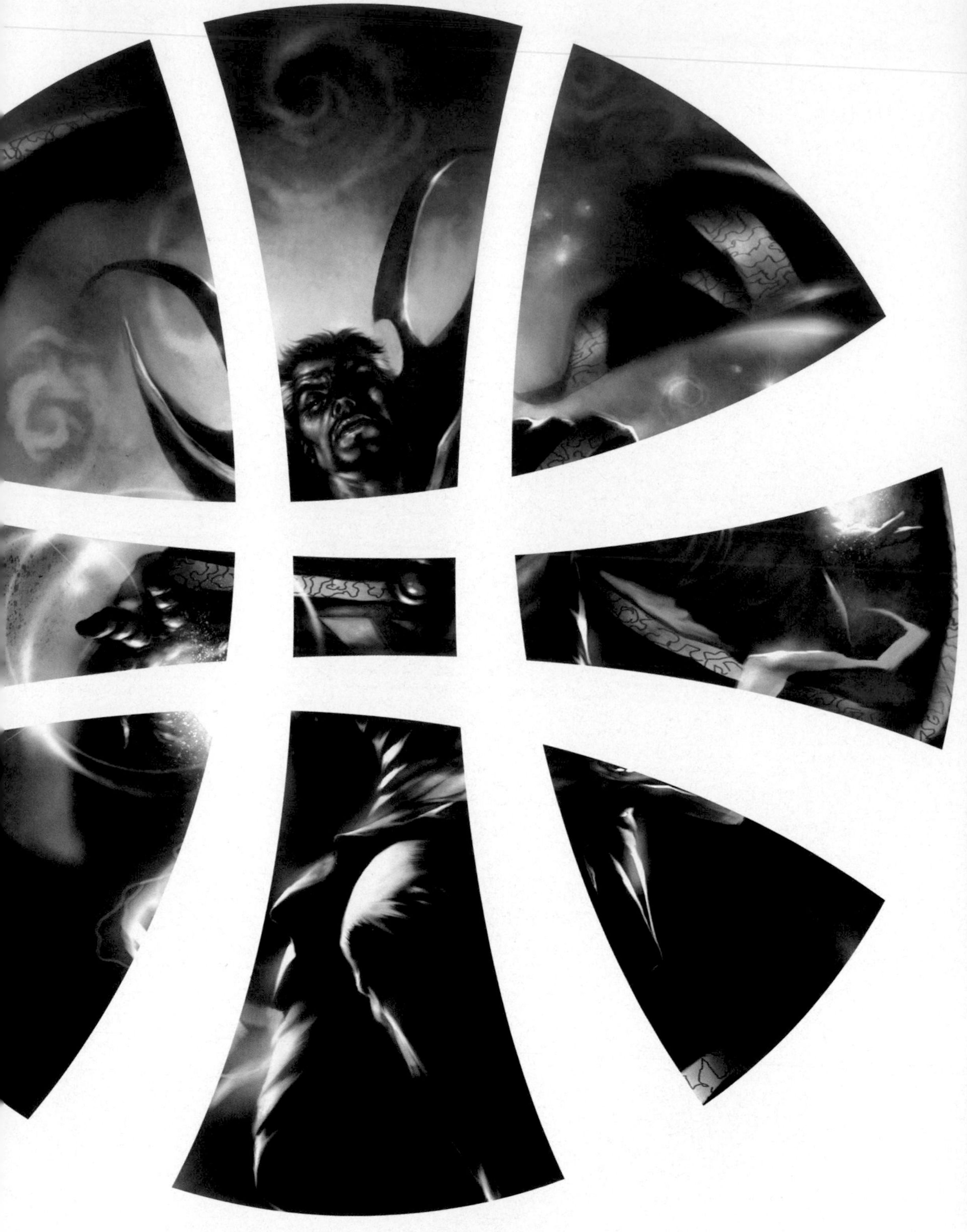

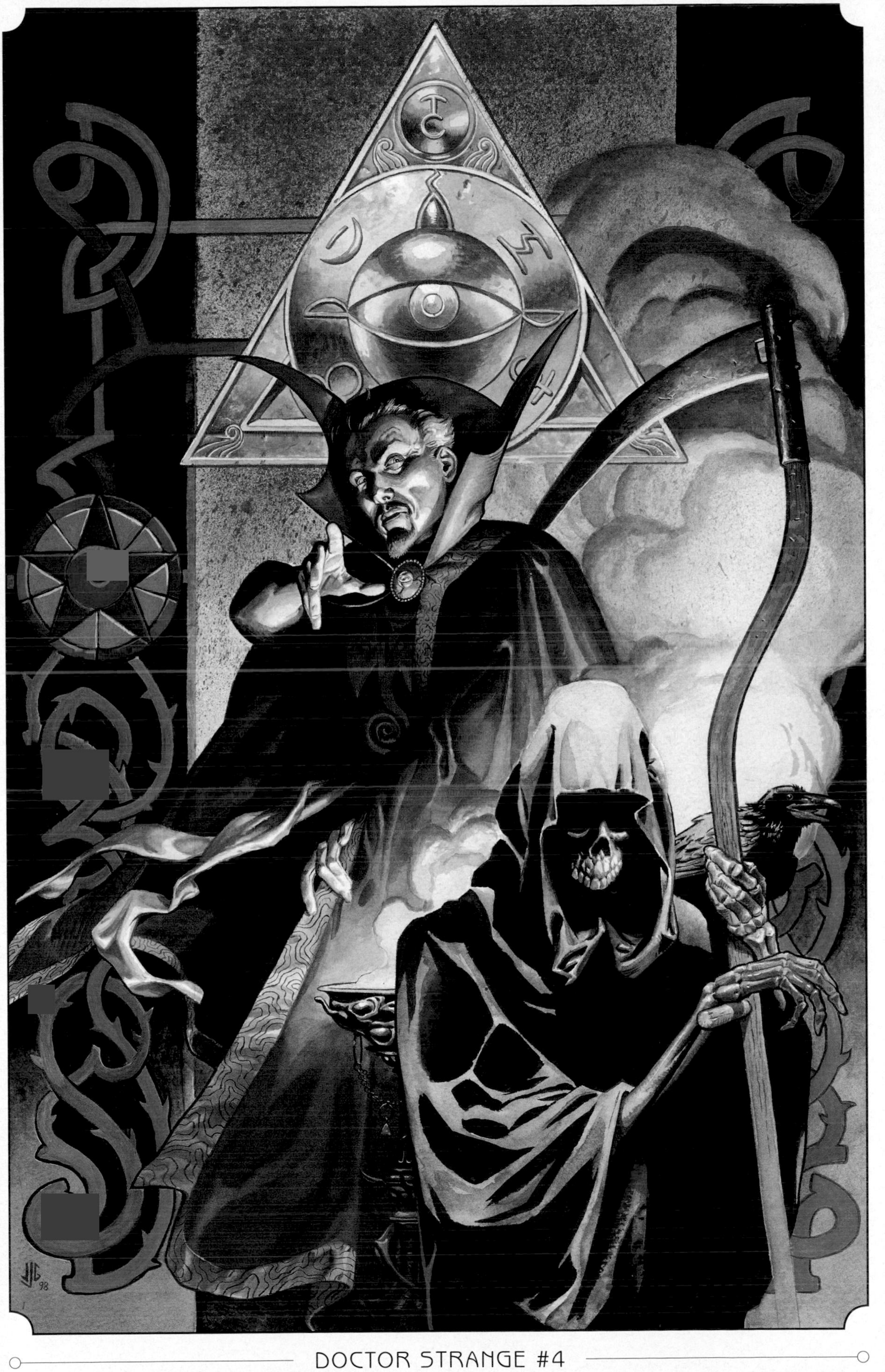

DOCTOR STRANGE #4

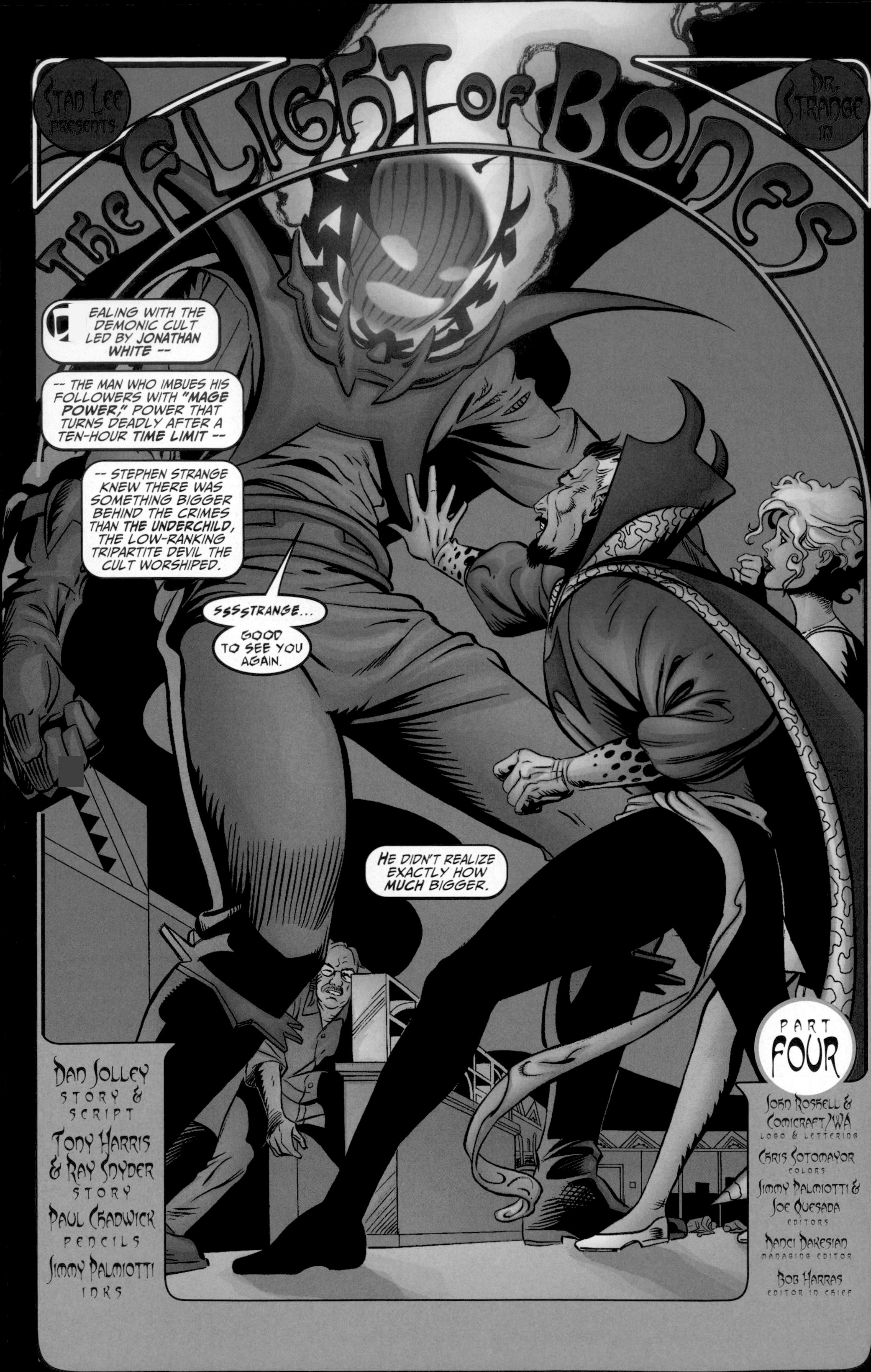
STAN LEE PRESENTS
DR. STRANGE IN
THE FLIGHT OF BONES
DEALING WITH THE DEMONIC CULT LED BY JONATHAN WHITE --
-- THE MAN WHO IMBUES HIS FOLLOWERS WITH "MAGE POWER," POWER THAT TURNS DEADLY AFTER A TEN-HOUR TIME LIMIT --
-- STEPHEN STRANGE KNEW THERE WAS SOMETHING BIGGER BEHIND THE CRIMES THAN THE UNDERCHILD, THE LOW-RANKING TRIPARTITE DEVIL THE CULT WORSHIPED.
SSSSTRANGE... GOOD TO SEE YOU AGAIN.
HE DIDN'T REALIZE EXACTLY HOW MUCH BIGGER.
PART FOUR
DAN JOLLEY STORY & SCRIPT
TONY HARRIS & RAY SNYDER STORY
PAUL CHADWICK PENCILS
JIMMY PALMIOTTI INKS
JOHN ROSHELL & COMICRAFT/WA LOGO & LETTERING
CHRIS SOTOMAYOR COLORS
JIMMY PALMIOTTI & JOE QUESADA EDITORS
NANCI DAKESIAN MANAGING EDITOR
BOB HARRAS EDITOR IN CHIEF

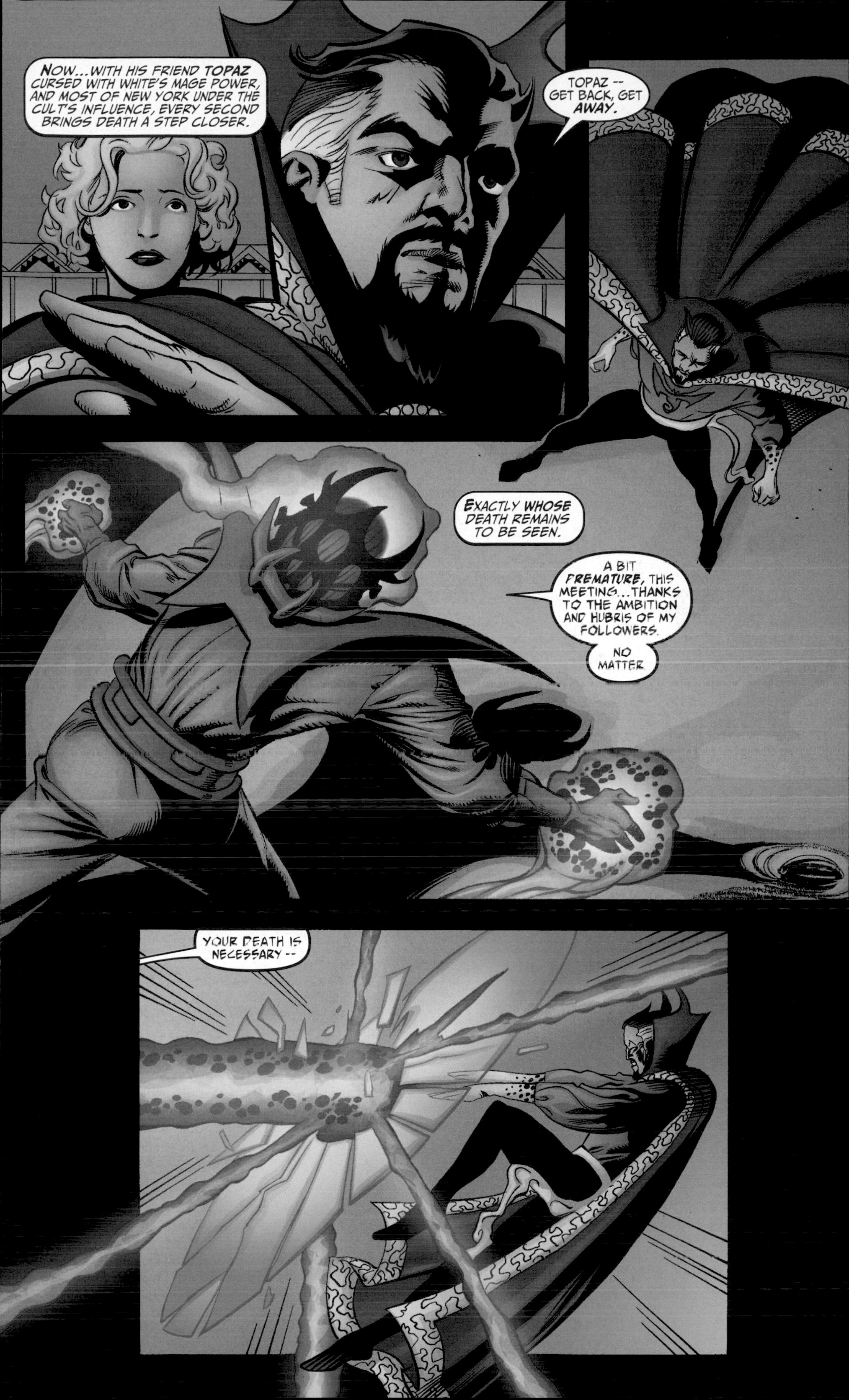
NOW... WITH HIS FRIEND TOPAZ CURSED WITH WHITE'S MAGE POWER, AND MOST OF NEW YORK UNDER THE CULT'S INFLUENCE, EVERY SECOND BRINGS DEATH A STEP CLOSER.
TOPAZ -- GET BACK, GET AWAY.
EXACTLY WHOSE DEATH REMAINS TO BE SEEN.
A BIT PREMATURE, THIS MEETING... THANKS TO THE AMBITION AND HUBRIS OF MY FOLLOWERS.
NO MATTER.
YOUR DEATH IS NECESSARY --

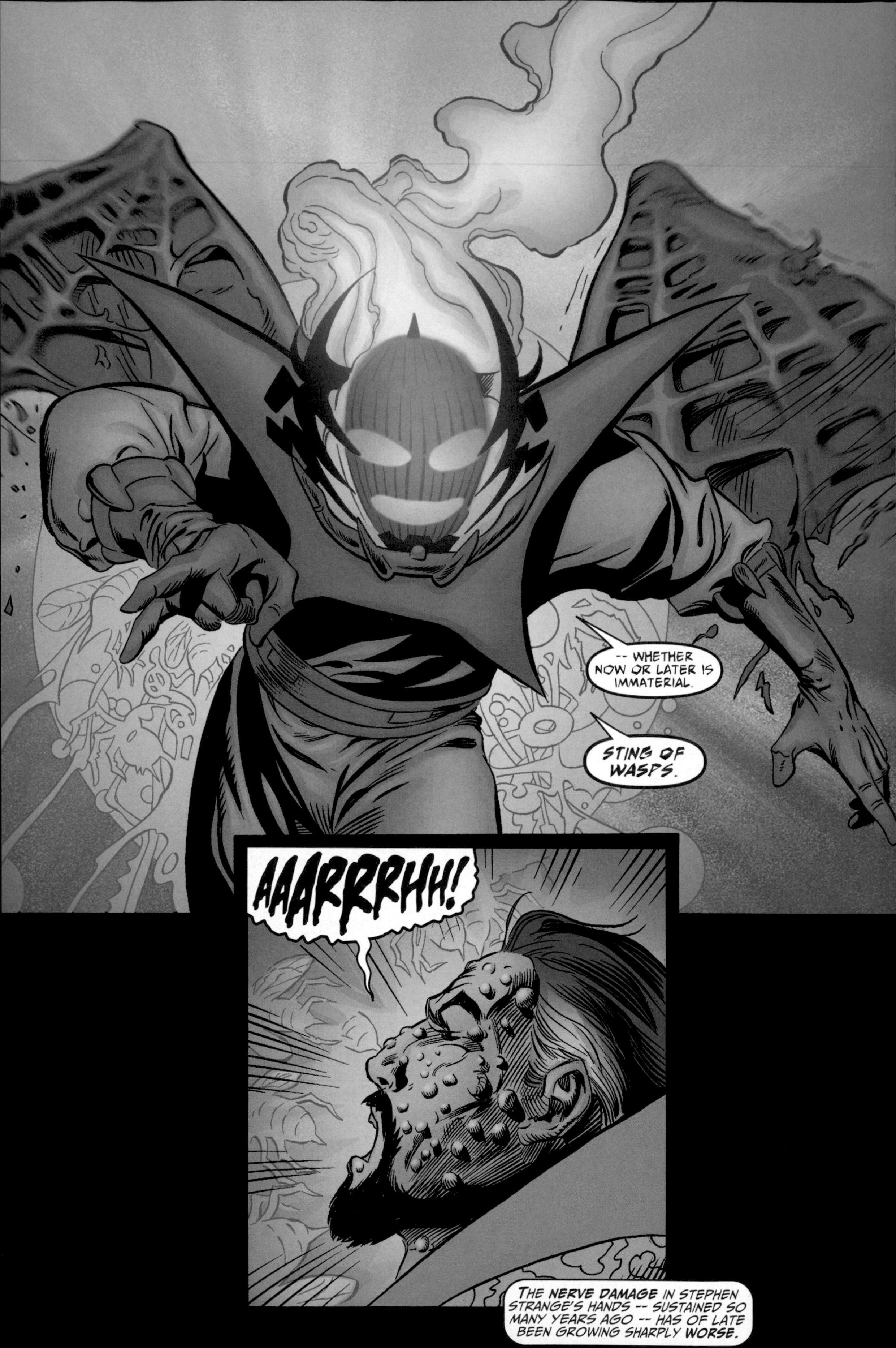
-- WHETHER NOW OR LATER IS IMMATERIAL.
STING OF WASPS.
AAARRRHH!
THE NERVE DAMAGE IN STEPHEN STRANGE'S HANDS -- SUSTAINED SO MANY YEARS AGO -- HAS OF LATE BEEN GROWING SHARPLY WORSE.

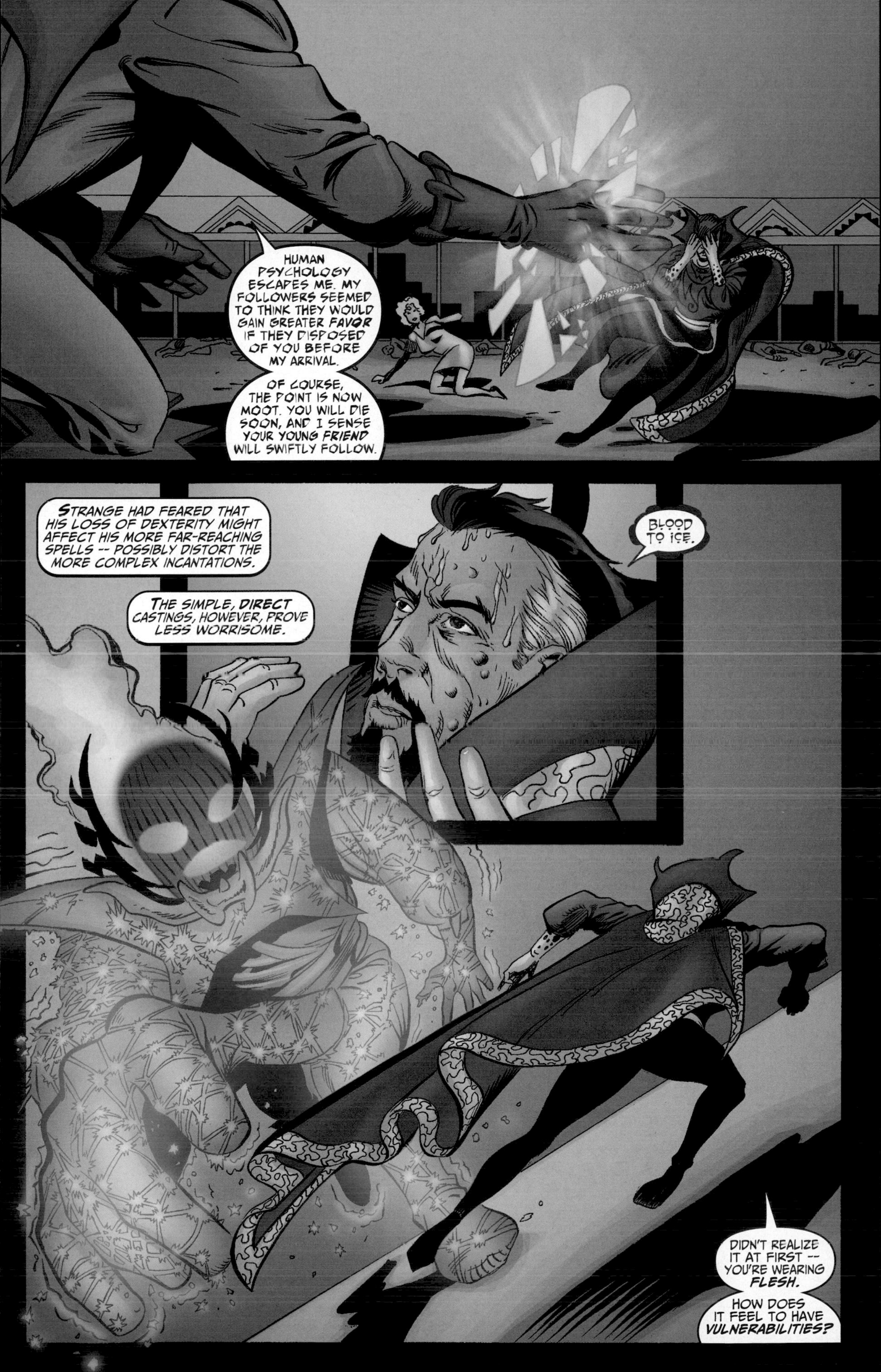
HUMAN PSYCHOLOGY ESCAPES ME. MY FOLLOWERS SEEMED TO THINK THEY WOULD GAIN GREATER FAVOR IF THEY DISPOSED OF YOU BEFORE MY ARRIVAL.
OF COURSE, THE POINT IS NOW MOOT. YOU WILL DIE SOON, AND I SENSE YOUR YOUNG FRIEND WILL SWIFTLY FOLLOW.
STRANGE HAD FEARED THAT HIS LOSS OF DEXTERITY MIGHT AFFECT HIS MORE FAR-REACHING SPELLS -- POSSIBLY DISTORT THE MORE COMPLEX INCANTATIONS.
THE SIMPLE, DIRECT CASTINGS, HOWEVER, PROVE LESS WORRISOME.
BLOOD TO ICE.
DIDN'T REALIZE IT AT FIRST -- YOU'RE WEARING FLESH.
HOW DOES IT FEEL TO HAVE VULNERABILITIES?

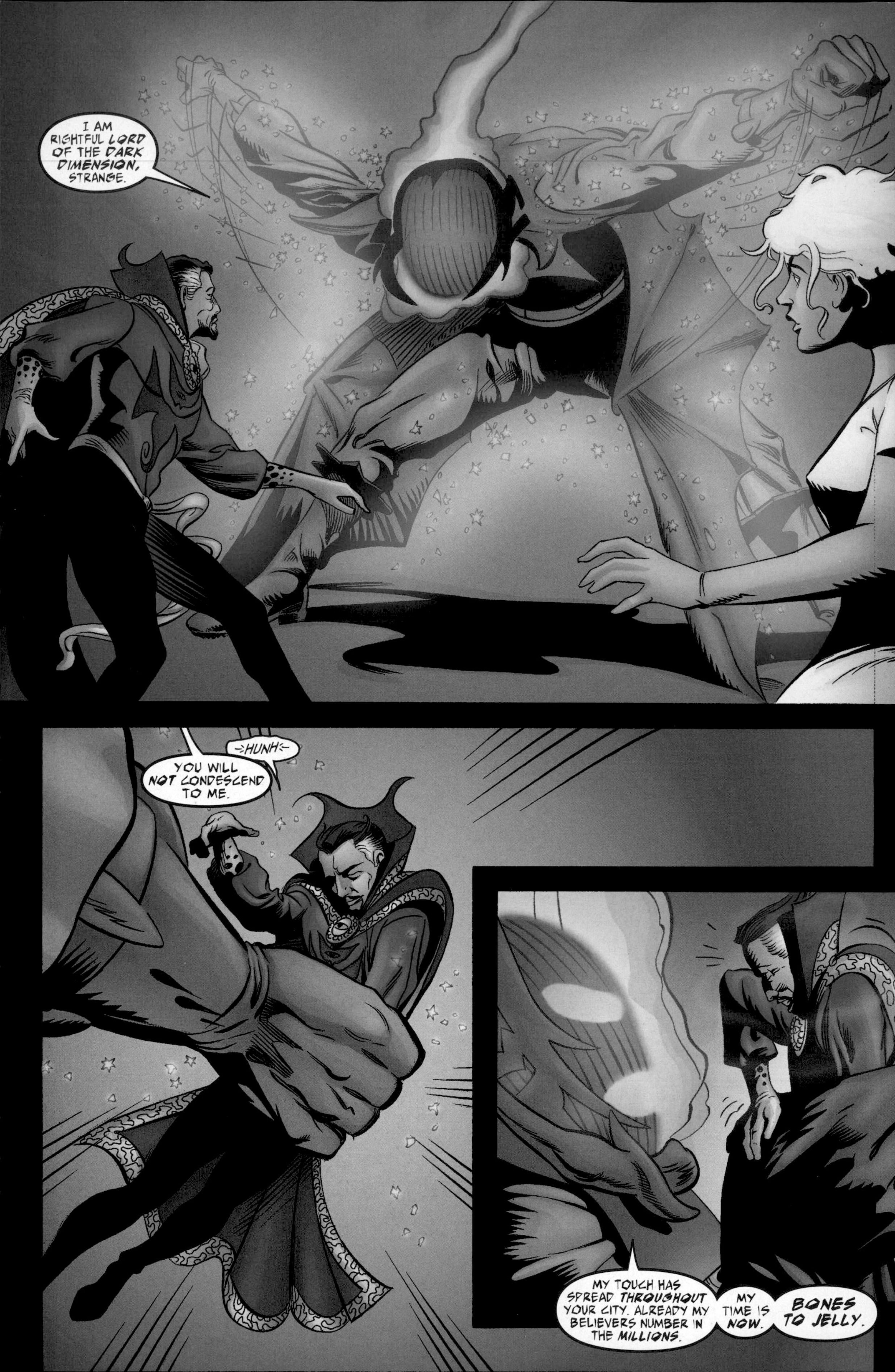
I AM RIGHTFUL LORD OF THE DARK DIMENSION, STRANGE.
YOU WILL NOT CONDESCEND TO ME.
-HUNH-
MY TOUCH HAS SPREAD THROUGHOUT YOUR CITY. ALREADY MY BELIEVERS NUMBER IN THE MILLIONS.
MY TIME IS NOW.
BONES TO JELLY.

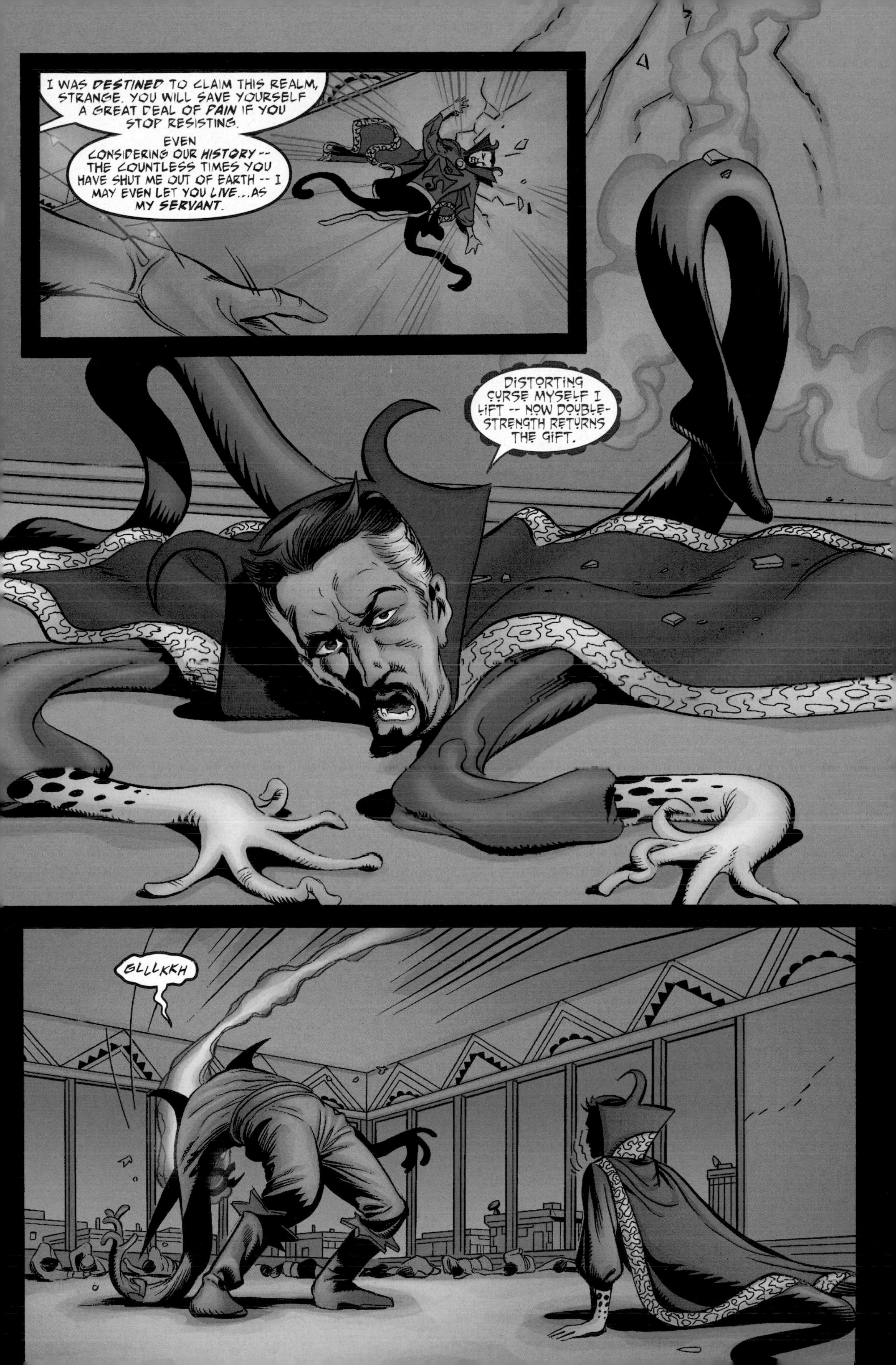
I WAS DESTINED TO CLAIM THIS REALM, STRANGE. YOU WILL SAVE YOURSELF A GREAT DEAL OF PAIN IF YOU STOP RESISTING.
EVEN CONSIDERING OUR HISTORY -- THE COUNTLESS TIMES YOU HAVE SHUT ME OUT OF EARTH -- I MAY EVEN LET YOU LIVE...AS MY SERVANT.
DISTORTING CURSE MYSELF I LIFT -- NOW DOUBLE-STRENGTH RETURNS THE GIFT.
GLLLKKH

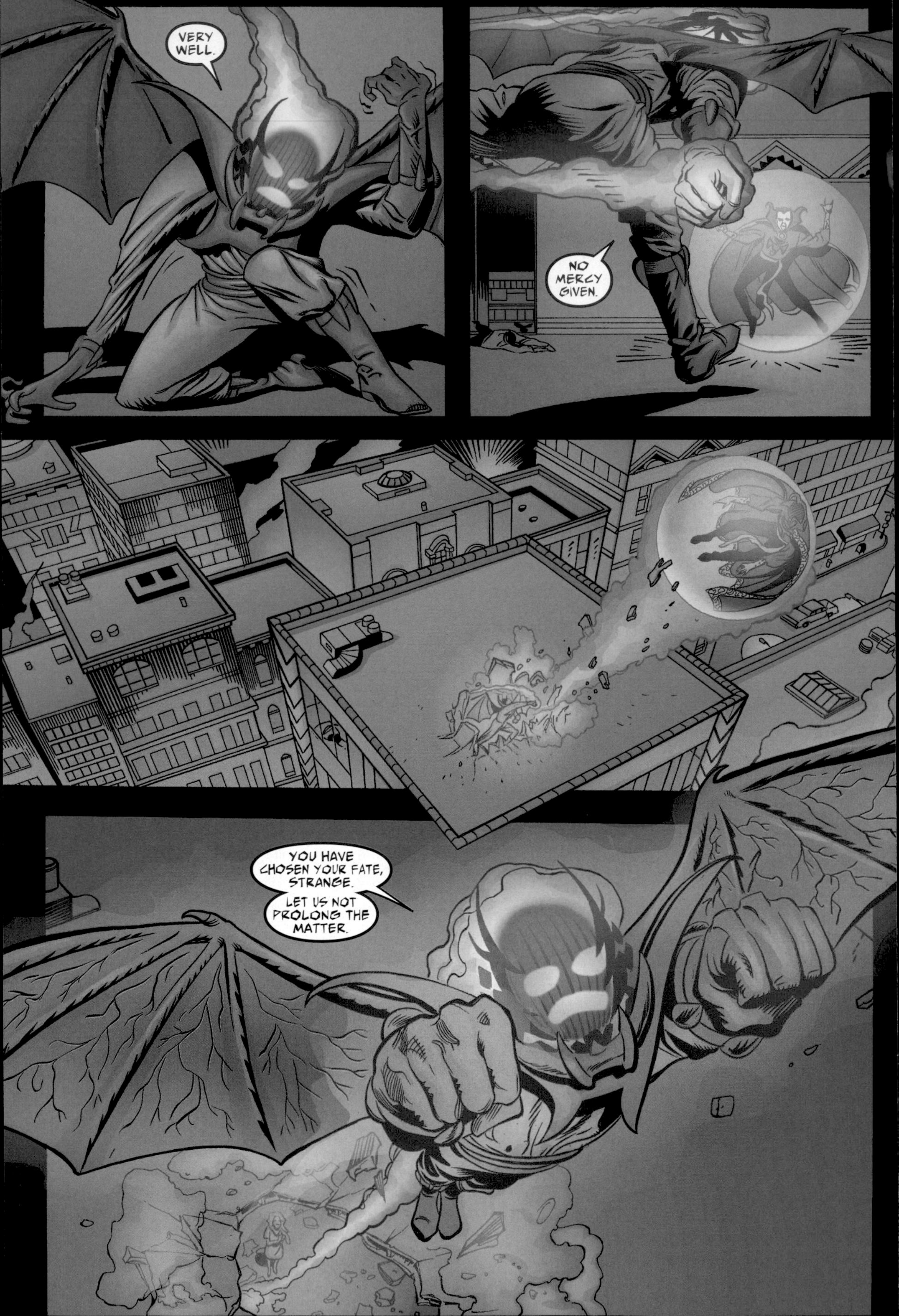
VERY WELL.
NO MERCY GIVEN.
YOU HAVE CHOSEN YOUR FATE, STRANGE.
LET US NOT PROLONG THE MATTER.

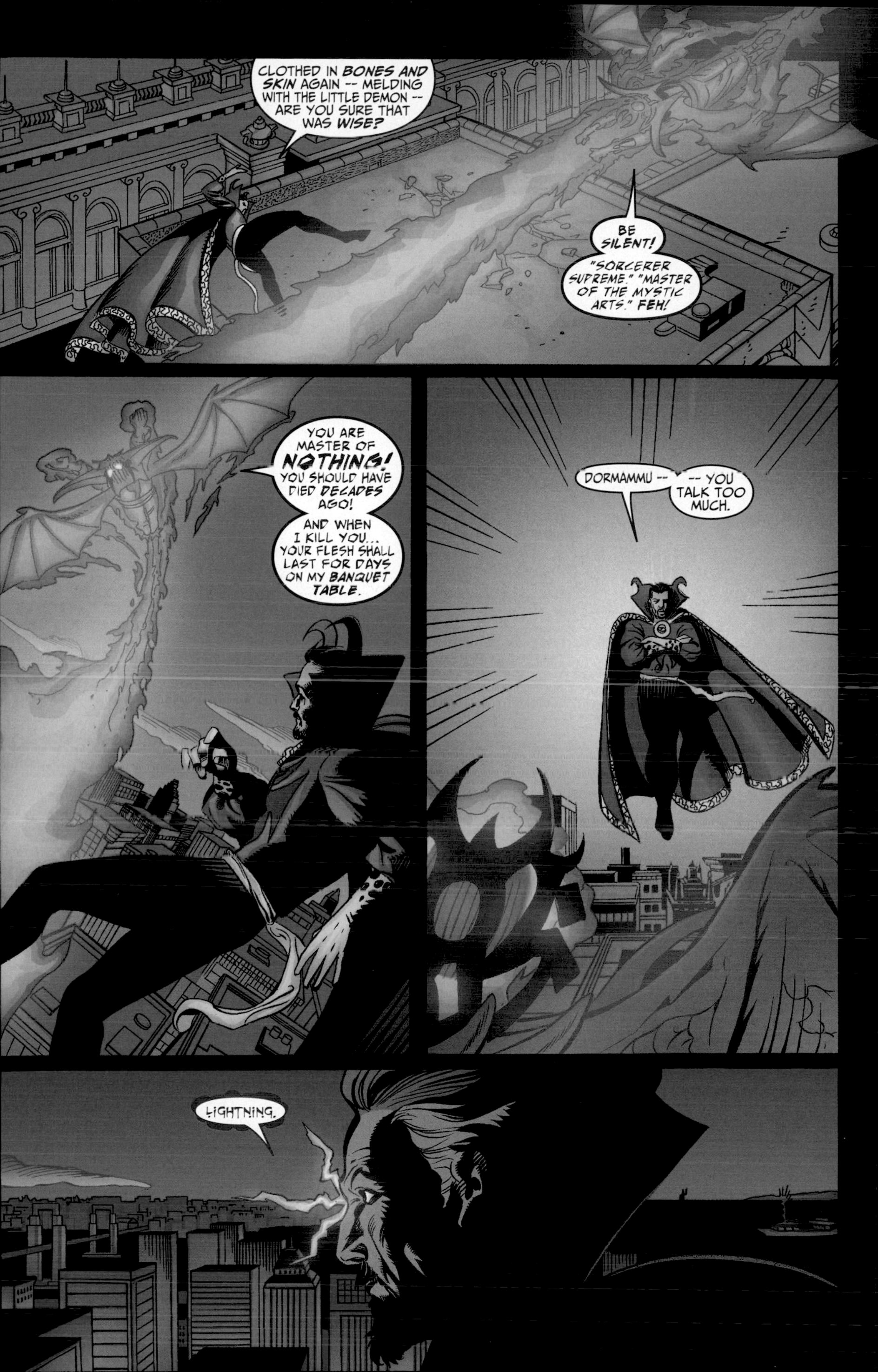
CLOTHED IN BONES AND SKIN AGAIN -- MELDING WITH THE LITTLE DEMON -- ARE YOU SURE THAT WAS WISE?
BE SILENT!
"SORCERER SUPREME." "MASTER OF THE MYSTIC ARTS." FEH!
YOU ARE MASTER OF NOTHING! YOU SHOULD HAVE DIED DECADES AGO!
AND WHEN I KILL YOU... YOUR FLESH SHALL LAST FOR DAYS ON MY BANQUET TABLE.
DORMAMMU --
-- YOU TALK TOO MUCH.
LIGHTNING.

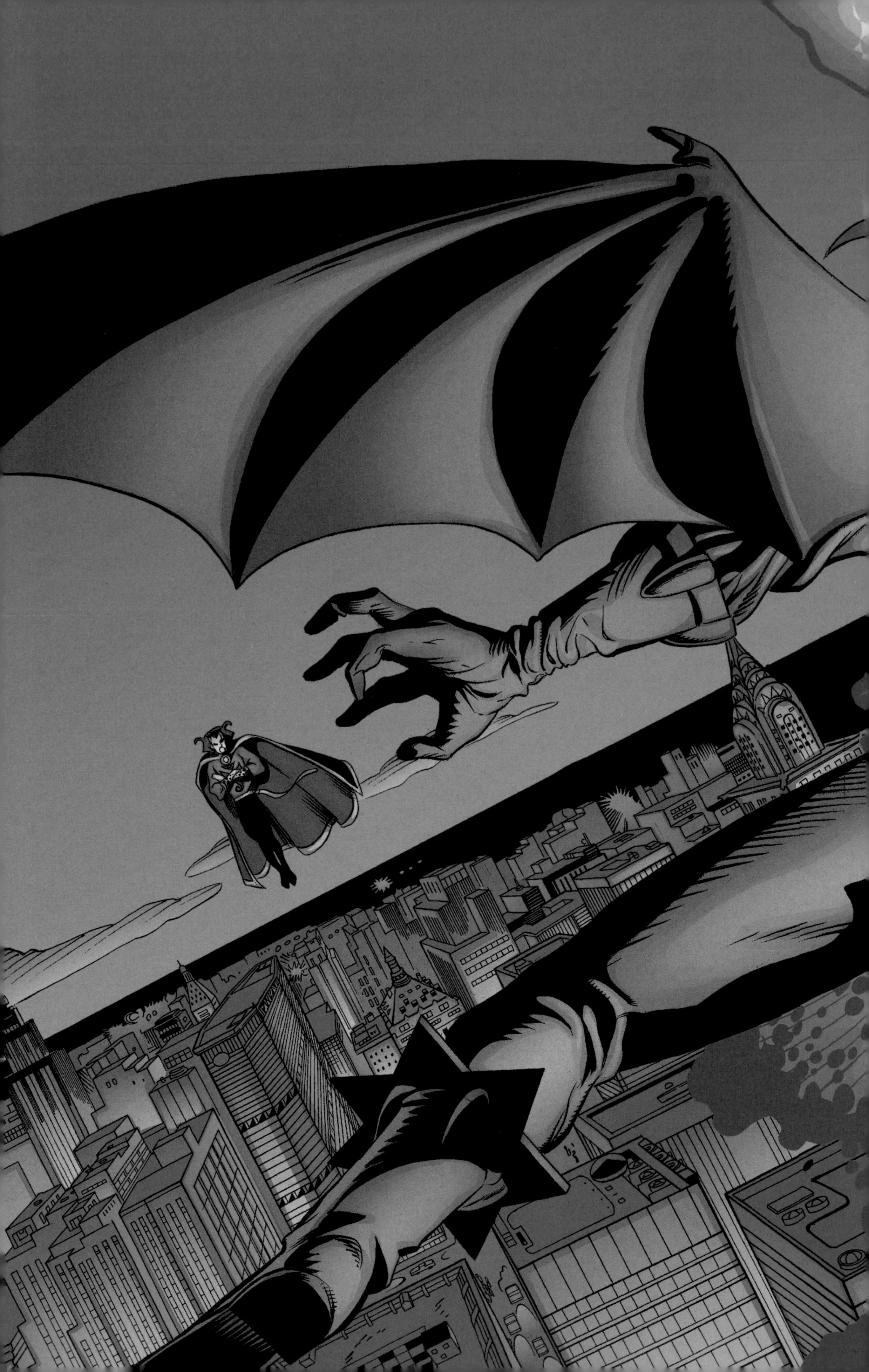

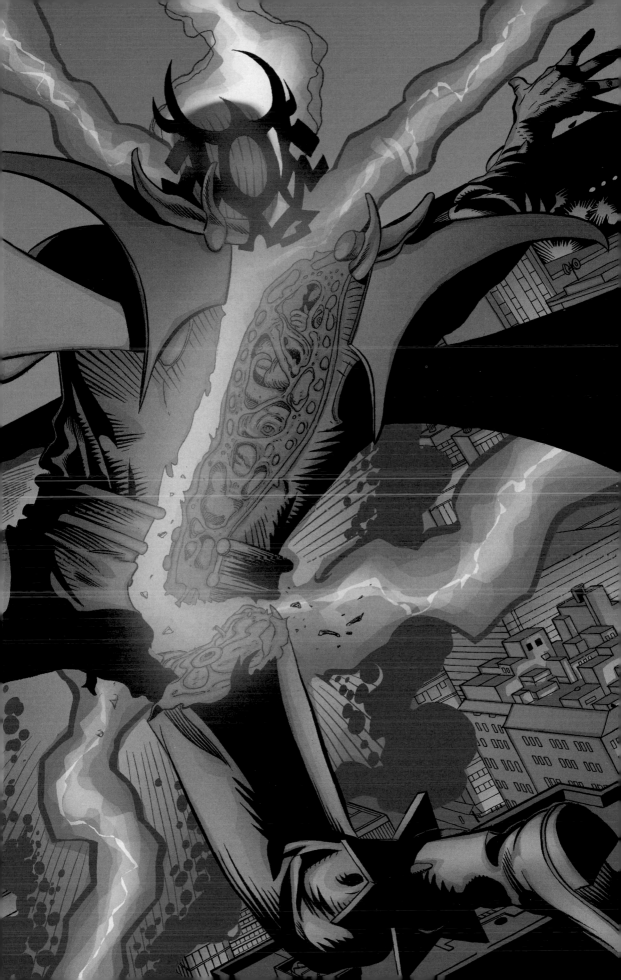

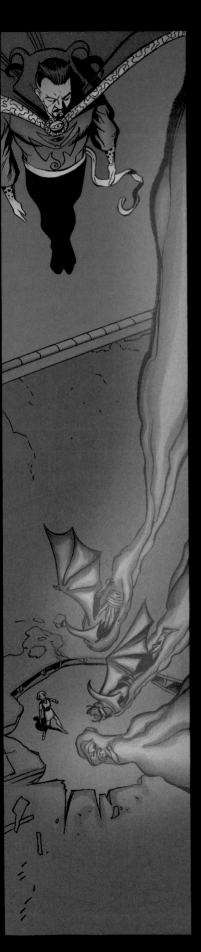

I'LL ADMIT, YOUR PRESENCE WAS A *SURPRISE* -- BUT IT ONLY DELAYED THE INEVITABLE.

YOU'RE TIED TO THE *UNDERCHILD*, DORMAMMU. I'M SURE STRIKING A DEAL LIKE THIS WAS VIRTUALLY THE ONLY AVENUE *LEFT* TO YOU, AS FAR AS GAINING ACCESS TO EARTH.

BUT ONCE I UNDERSTOOD THE *DEMON'S* ENERGY, CONTROLLING AND DEFEATING IT -- AND BY EXTENSION, *YOU* -- BECAME JUST A MATTER OF TIME.

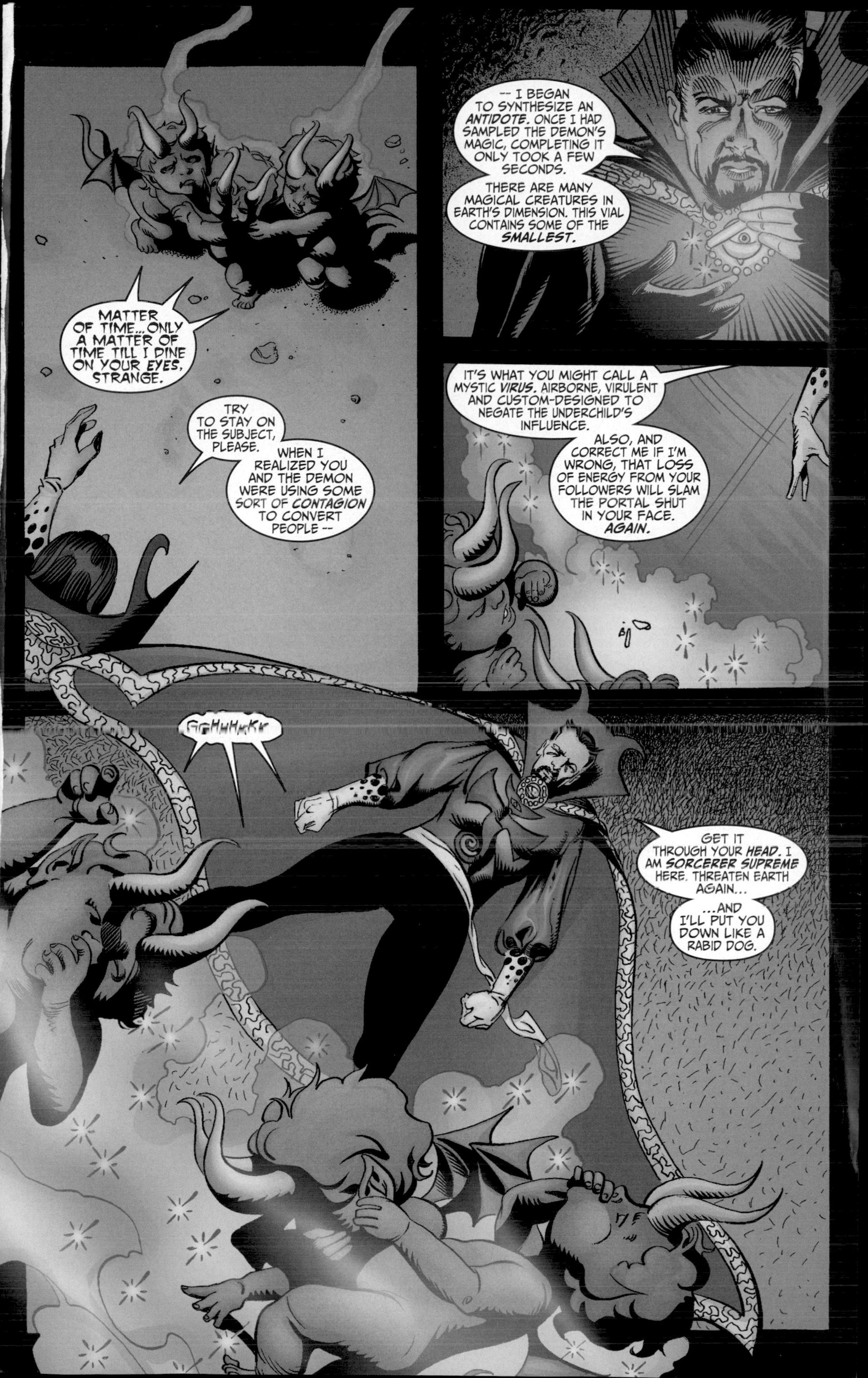
MATTER OF TIME...ONLY A MATTER OF TIME TILL I DINE ON YOUR EYES, STRANGE.
TRY TO STAY ON THE SUBJECT, PLEASE.
WHEN I REALIZED YOU AND THE DEMON WERE USING SOME SORT OF CONTAGION TO CONVERT PEOPLE --
-- I BEGAN TO SYNTHESIZE AN ANTIDOTE. ONCE I HAD SAMPLED THE DEMON'S MAGIC, COMPLETING IT ONLY TOOK A FEW SECONDS.
THERE ARE MANY MAGICAL CREATURES IN EARTH'S DIMENSION. THIS VIAL CONTAINS SOME OF THE SMALLEST.
IT'S WHAT YOU MIGHT CALL A MYSTIC VIRUS. AIRBORNE, VIRULENT AND CUSTOM-DESIGNED TO NEGATE THE UNDERCHILD'S INFLUENCE.
ALSO, AND CORRECT ME IF I'M WRONG, THAT LOSS OF ENERGY FROM YOUR FOLLOWERS WILL SLAM THE PORTAL SHUT IN YOUR FACE. AGAIN.
GRHHHKK
GET IT THROUGH YOUR HEAD. I AM SORCERER SUPREME HERE. THREATEN EARTH AGAIN...
...AND I'LL PUT YOU DOWN LIKE A RABID DOG.

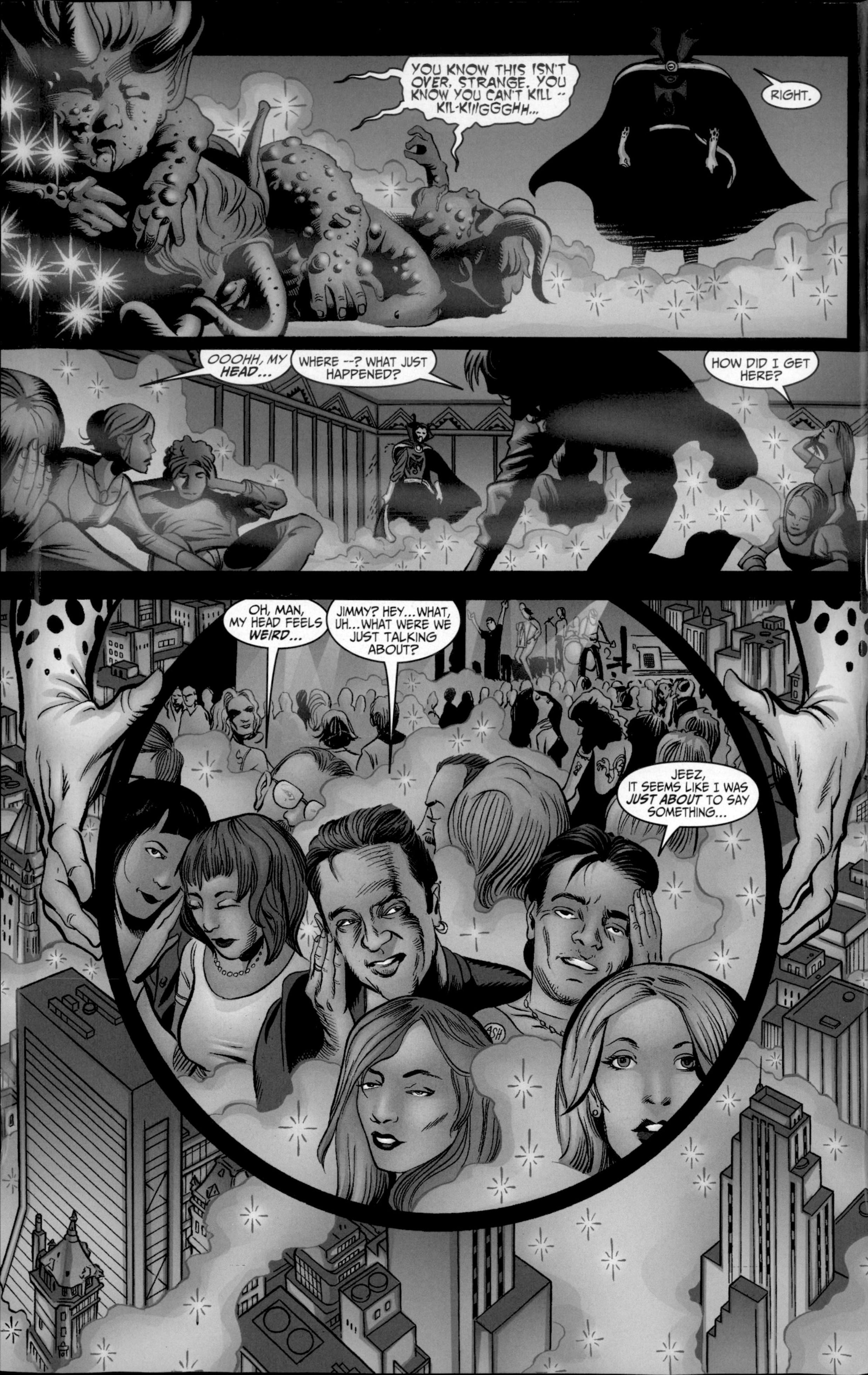
YOU KNOW THIS ISN'T OVER, STRANGE. YOU KNOW YOU CAN'T KILL -- KIL-KIIIGGGHH...
RIGHT.
OOOHH, MY HEAD...
WHERE --? WHAT JUST HAPPENED?
HOW DID I GET HERE?
OH, MAN, MY HEAD FEELS WEIRD...
JIMMY? HEY...WHAT, UH...WHAT WERE WE JUST TALKING ABOUT?
JEEZ, IT SEEMS LIKE I WAS JUST ABOUT TO SAY SOMETHING...

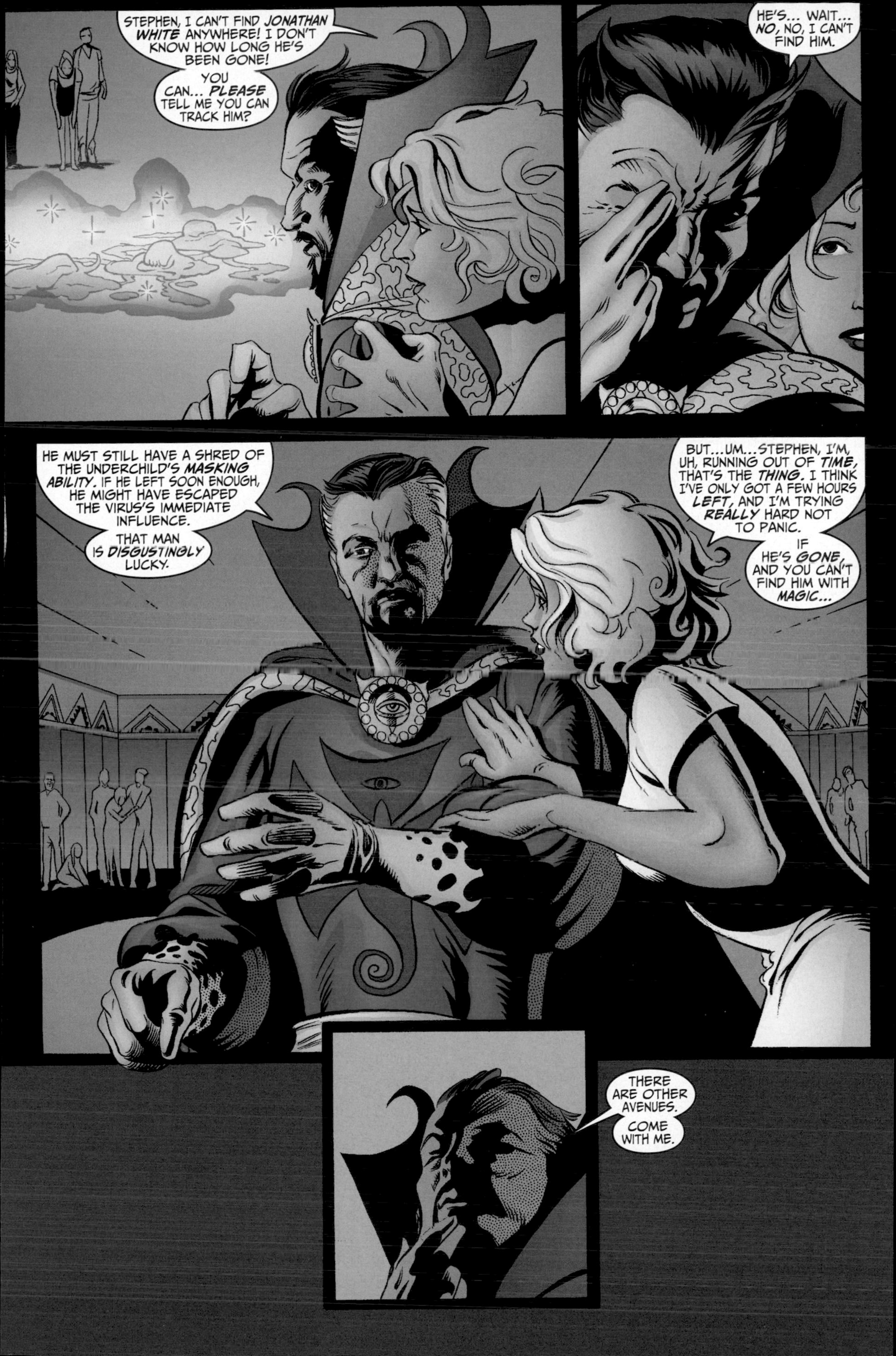
STEPHEN, I CAN'T FIND JONATHAN WHITE ANYWHERE! I DON'T KNOW HOW LONG HE'S BEEN GONE!
YOU CAN... PLEASE TELL ME YOU CAN TRACK HIM?
HE'S... WAIT... NO, NO, I CAN'T FIND HIM.
HE MUST STILL HAVE A SHRED OF THE UNDERCHILD'S MASKING ABILITY. IF HE LEFT SOON ENOUGH, HE MIGHT HAVE ESCAPED THE VIRUS'S IMMEDIATE INFLUENCE.
THAT MAN IS DISGUSTINGLY LUCKY.
BUT...UM...STEPHEN, I'M, UH, RUNNING OUT OF TIME, THAT'S THE THING. I THINK I'VE ONLY GOT A FEW HOURS LEFT, AND I'M TRYING REALLY HARD NOT TO PANIC.
IF HE'S GONE, AND YOU CAN'T FIND HIM WITH MAGIC...
THERE ARE OTHER AVENUES.
COME WITH ME.

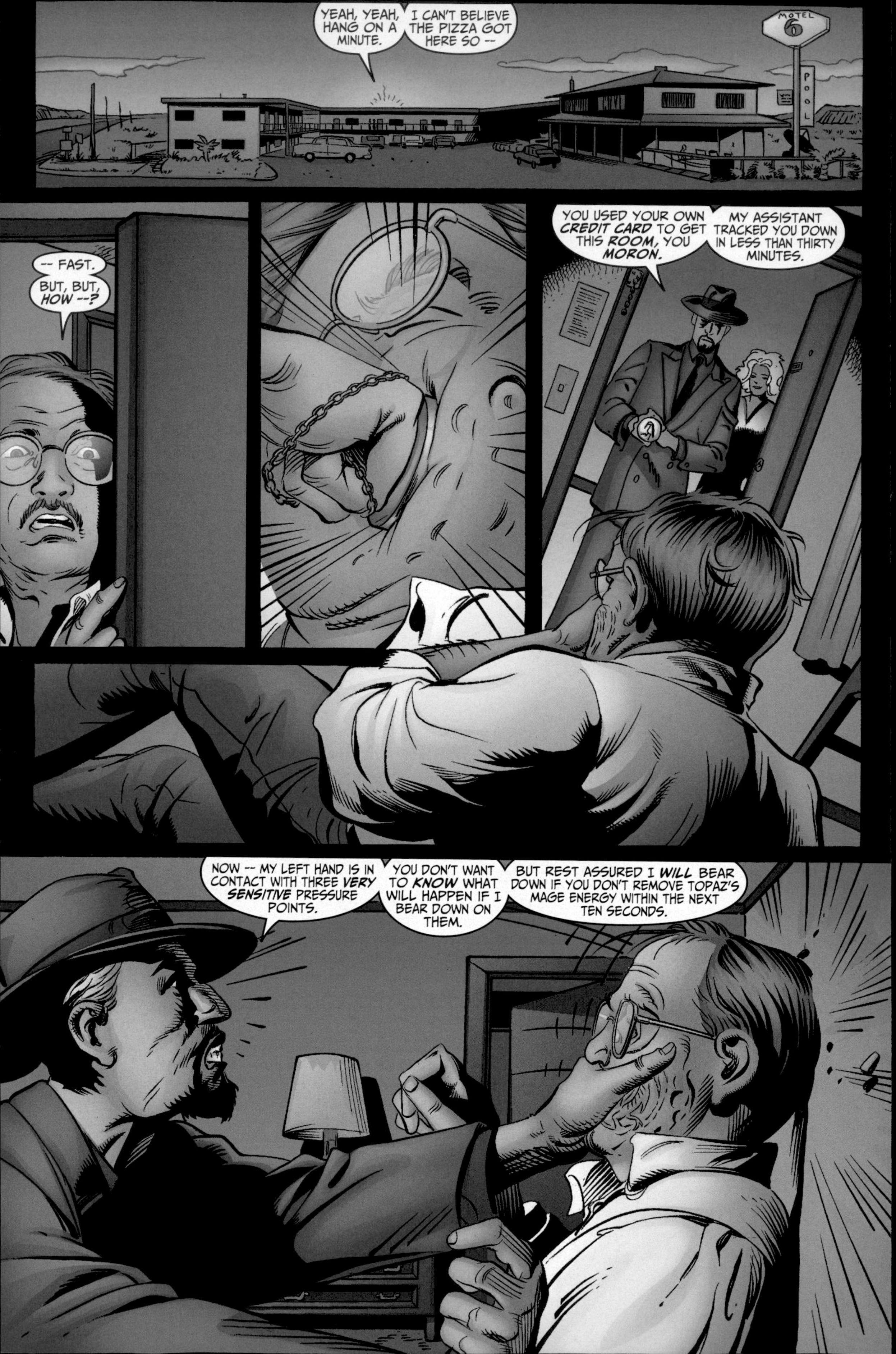

YEAH, YEAH, HANG ON A MINUTE.
I CAN'T BELIEVE THE PIZZA GOT HERE SO --
MOTEL 6
POOL
-- FAST.
BUT, BUT, HOW --?
YOU USED YOUR OWN CREDIT CARD TO GET THIS ROOM, YOU MORON.
MY ASSISTANT TRACKED YOU DOWN IN LESS THAN THIRTY MINUTES.
NOW -- MY LEFT HAND IS IN CONTACT WITH THREE VERY SENSITIVE PRESSURE POINTS.
YOU DON'T WANT TO KNOW WHAT WILL HAPPEN IF I BEAR DOWN ON THEM.
BUT REST ASSURED I WILL BEAR DOWN IF YOU DON'T REMOVE TOPAZ'S MAGE ENERGY WITHIN THE NEXT TEN SECONDS.

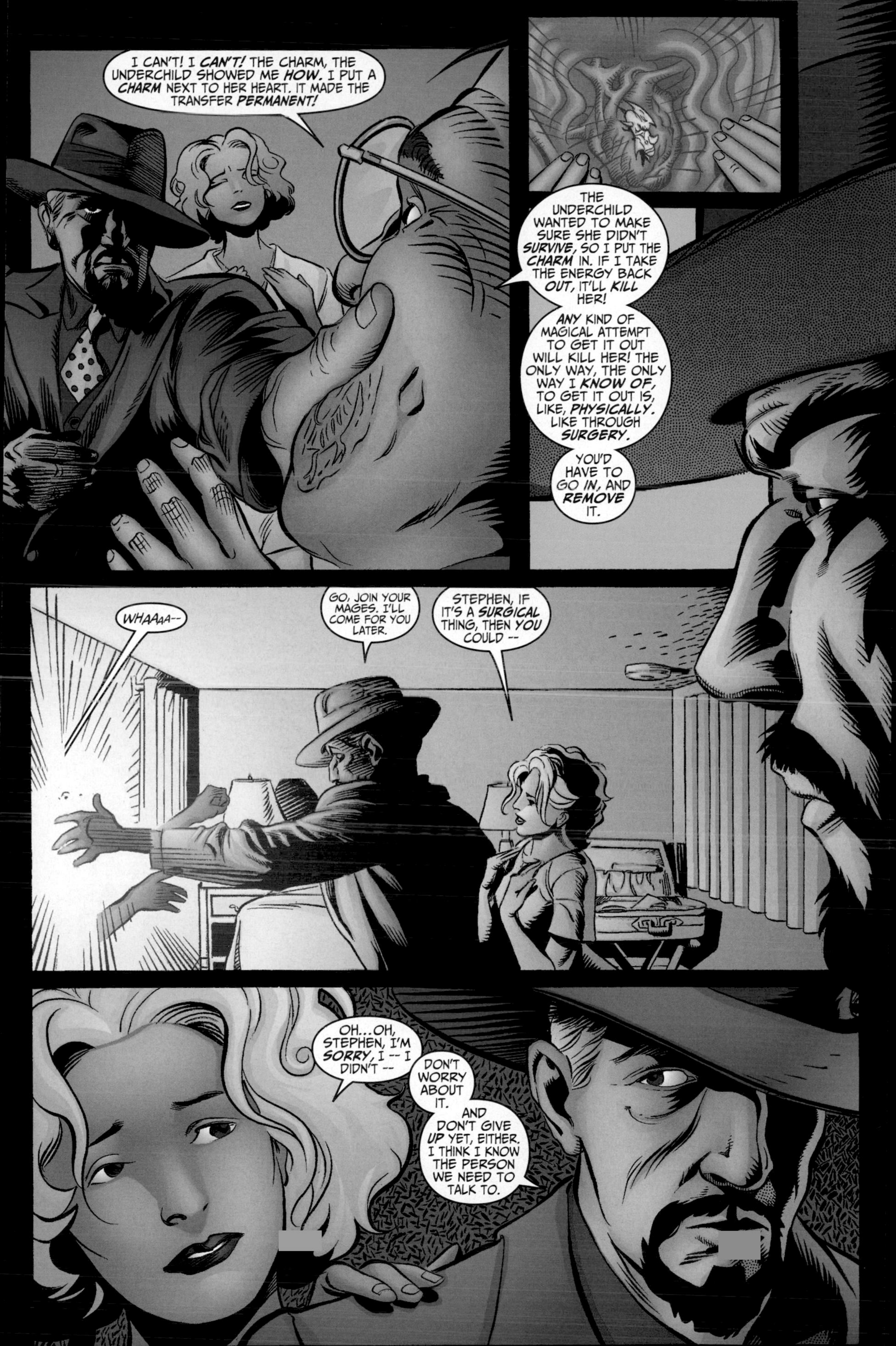

I CAN'T! I CAN'T! THE CHARM, THE UNDERCHILD SHOWED ME HOW. I PUT A CHARM NEXT TO HER HEART. IT MADE THE TRANSFER PERMANENT!
THE UNDERCHILD WANTED TO MAKE SURE SHE DIDN'T SURVIVE, SO I PUT THE CHARM IN. IF I TAKE THE ENERGY BACK OUT, IT'LL KILL HER!
ANY KIND OF MAGICAL ATTEMPT TO GET IT OUT WILL KILL HER! THE ONLY WAY, THE ONLY WAY I KNOW OF, TO GET IT OUT IS, LIKE, PHYSICALLY. LIKE THROUGH SURGERY.
YOU'D HAVE TO GO IN, AND REMOVE IT.
WHAAAA--
GO, JOIN YOUR MAGES. I'LL COME FOR YOU LATER.
STEPHEN, IF IT'S A SURGICAL THING, THEN YOU COULD --
OH...OH, STEPHEN, I'M SORRY, I -- I DIDN'T --
DON'T WORRY ABOUT IT.
AND DON'T GIVE UP YET, EITHER. I THINK I KNOW THE PERSON WE NEED TO TALK TO.

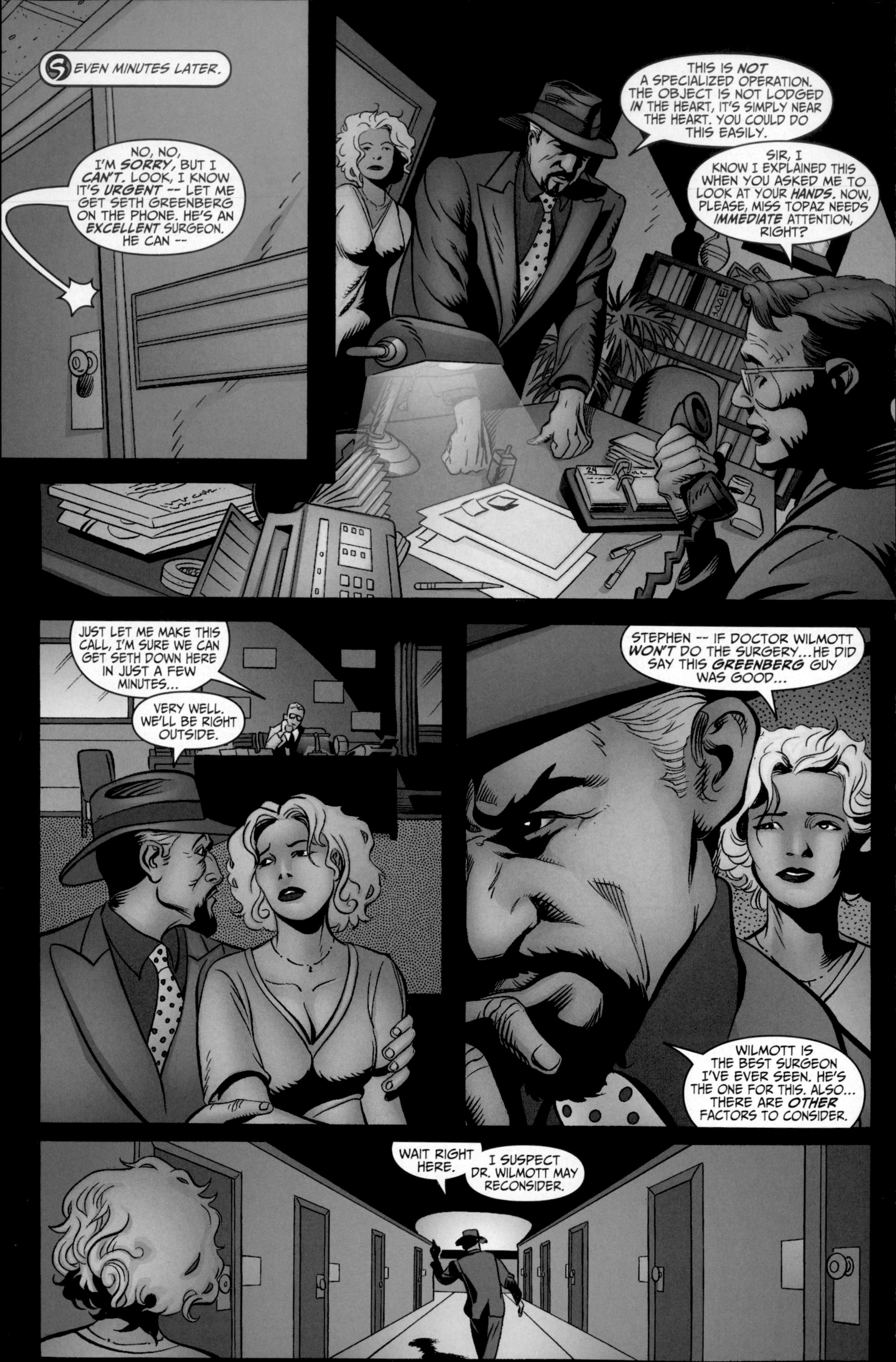
SEVEN MINUTES LATER.
NO, NO, I'M SORRY, BUT I CAN'T. LOOK, I KNOW IT'S URGENT -- LET ME GET SETH GREENBERG ON THE PHONE. HE'S AN EXCELLENT SURGEON. HE CAN --
THIS IS NOT A SPECIALIZED OPERATION. THE OBJECT IS NOT LODGED IN THE HEART, IT'S SIMPLY NEAR THE HEART. YOU COULD DO THIS EASILY.
SIR, I KNOW I EXPLAINED THIS WHEN YOU ASKED ME TO LOOK AT YOUR HANDS. NOW, PLEASE, MISS TOPAZ NEEDS IMMEDIATE ATTENTION, RIGHT?
JUST LET ME MAKE THIS CALL, I'M SURE WE CAN GET SETH DOWN HERE IN JUST A FEW MINUTES...
VERY WELL. WE'LL BE RIGHT OUTSIDE.
STEPHEN -- IF DOCTOR WILMOTT WON'T DO THE SURGERY... HE DID SAY THIS GREENBERG GUY WAS GOOD...
WILMOTT IS THE BEST SURGEON I'VE EVER SEEN. HE'S THE ONE FOR THIS. ALSO... THERE ARE OTHER FACTORS TO CONSIDER.
WAIT RIGHT HERE.
I SUSPECT DR. WILMOTT MAY RECONSIDER.

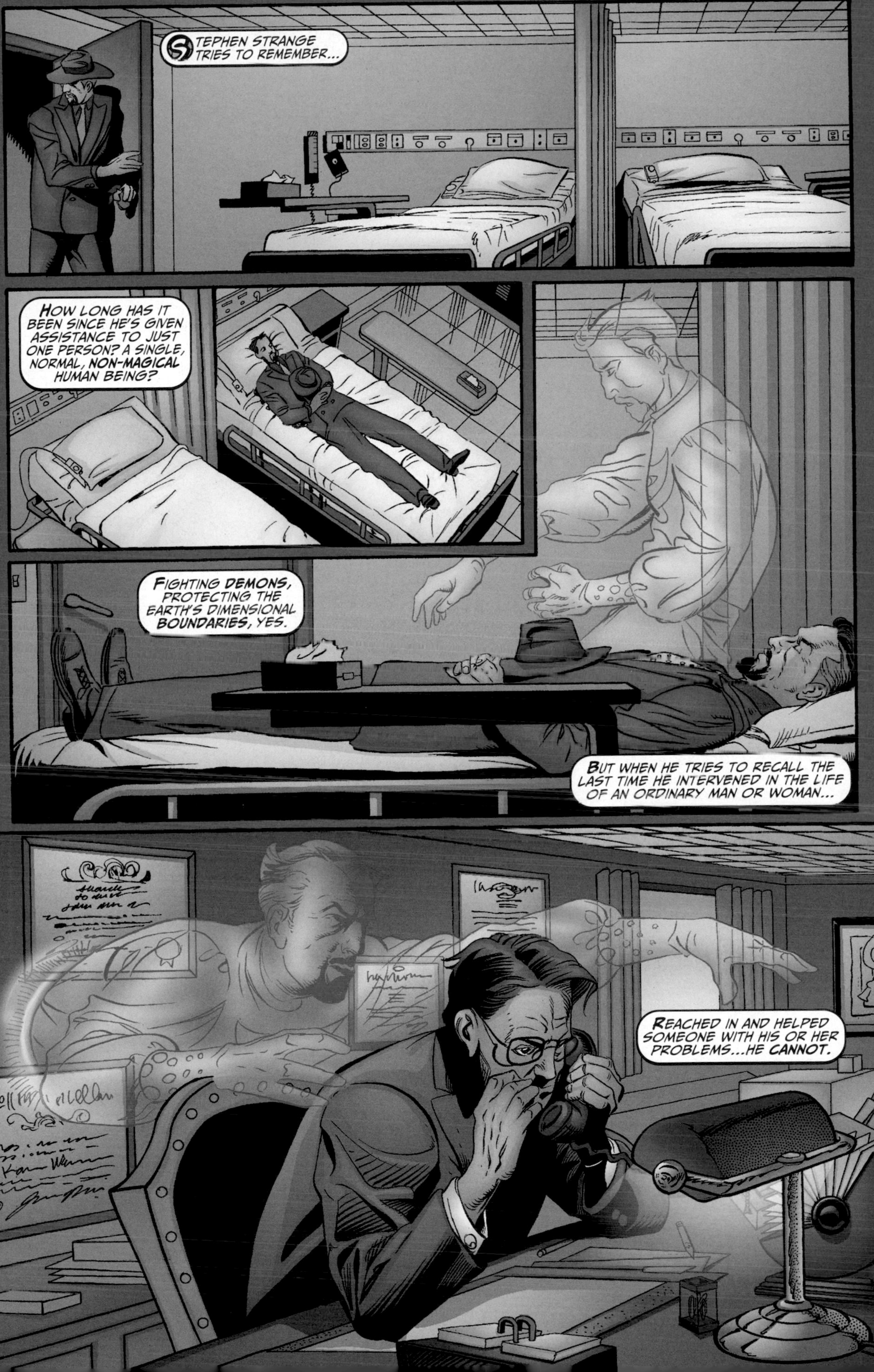
STEPHEN STRANGE TRIES TO REMEMBER...
HOW LONG HAS IT BEEN SINCE HE'S GIVEN ASSISTANCE TO JUST ONE PERSON? A SINGLE, NORMAL, NON-MAGICAL HUMAN BEING?
FIGHTING DEMONS, PROTECTING THE EARTH'S DIMENSIONAL BOUNDARIES, YES.
BUT WHEN HE TRIES TO RECALL THE LAST TIME HE INTERVENED IN THE LIFE OF AN ORDINARY MAN OR WOMAN...
REACHED IN AND HELPED SOMEONE WITH HIS OR HER PROBLEMS...HE CANNOT.

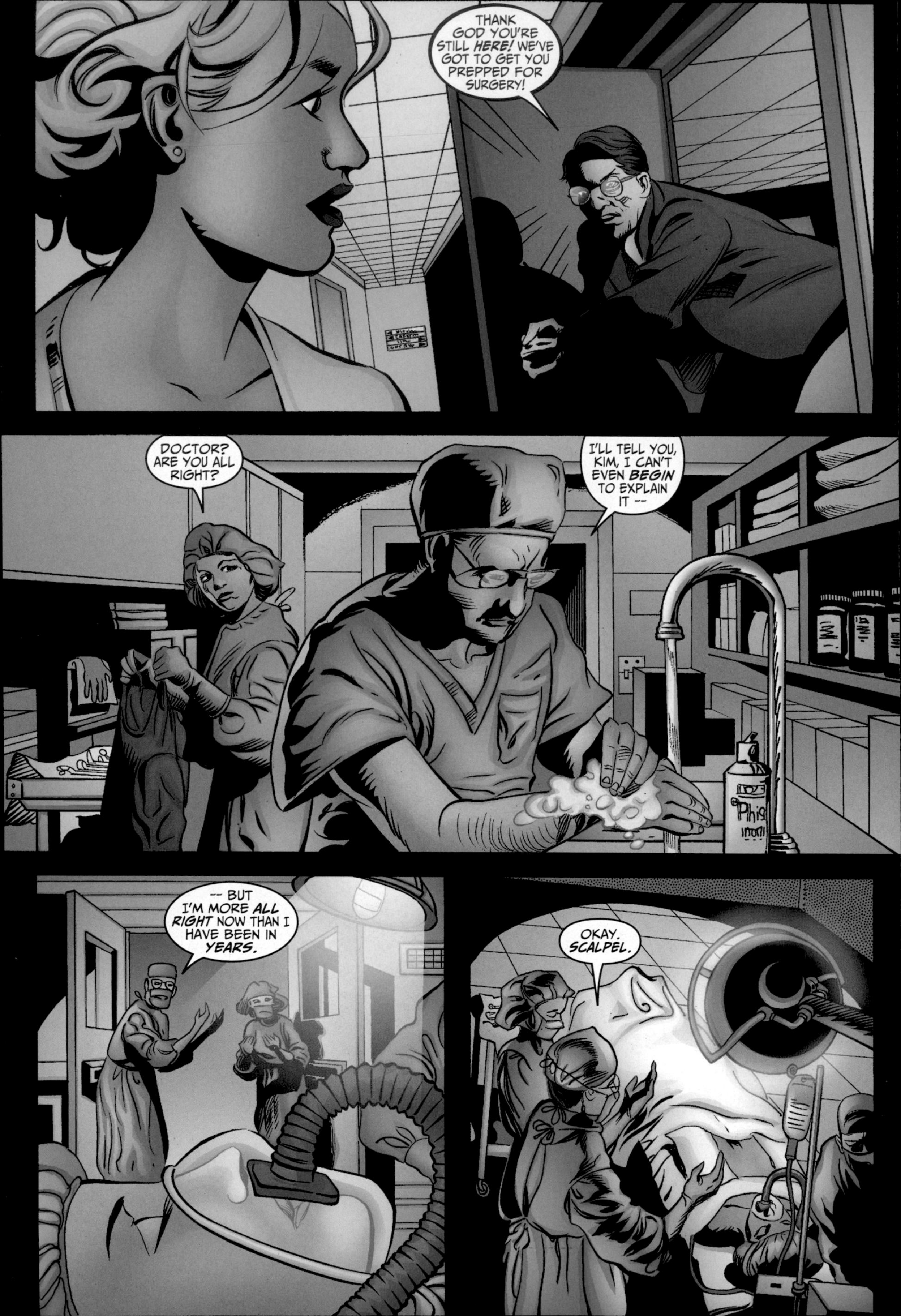
THANK GOD YOU'RE STILL HERE! WE'VE GOT TO GET YOU PREPPED FOR SURGERY!
DOCTOR? ARE YOU ALL RIGHT?
I'LL TELL YOU, KIM, I CAN'T EVEN BEGIN TO EXPLAIN IT --
-- BUT I'M MORE ALL RIGHT NOW THAN I HAVE BEEN IN YEARS.
OKAY. SCALPEL.

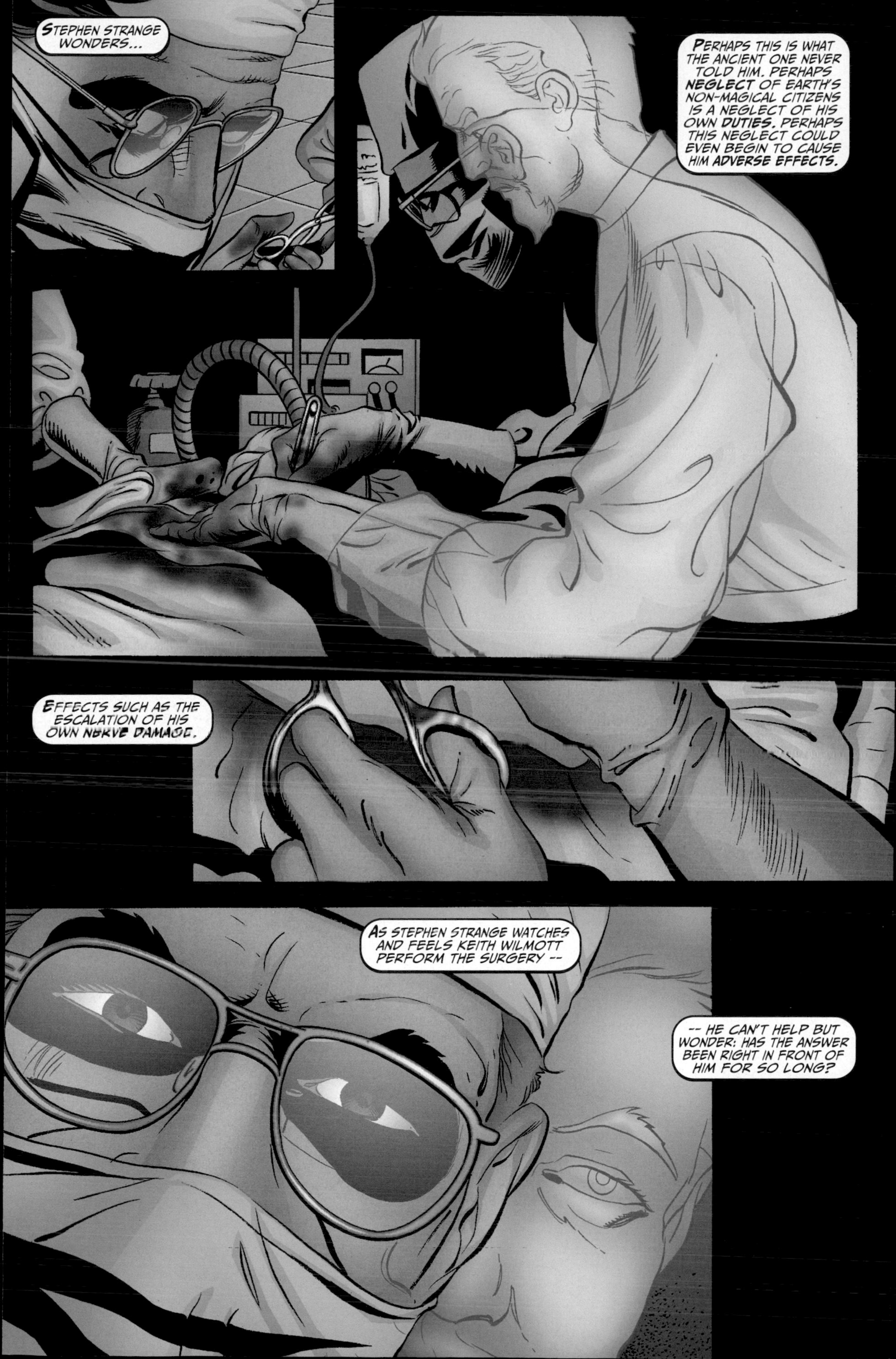
STEPHEN STRANGE WONDERS...
PERHAPS THIS IS WHAT THE ANCIENT ONE NEVER TOLD HIM. PERHAPS NEGLECT OF EARTH'S NON-MAGICAL CITIZENS IS A NEGLECT OF HIS OWN DUTIES. PERHAPS THIS NEGLECT COULD EVEN BEGIN TO CAUSE HIM ADVERSE EFFECTS.
EFFECTS SUCH AS THE ESCALATION OF HIS OWN NERVE DAMAGE.
AS STEPHEN STRANGE WATCHES AND FEELS KEITH WILMOTT PERFORM THE SURGERY --
-- HE CAN'T HELP BUT WONDER: HAS THE ANSWER BEEN RIGHT IN FRONT OF HIM FOR SO LONG?

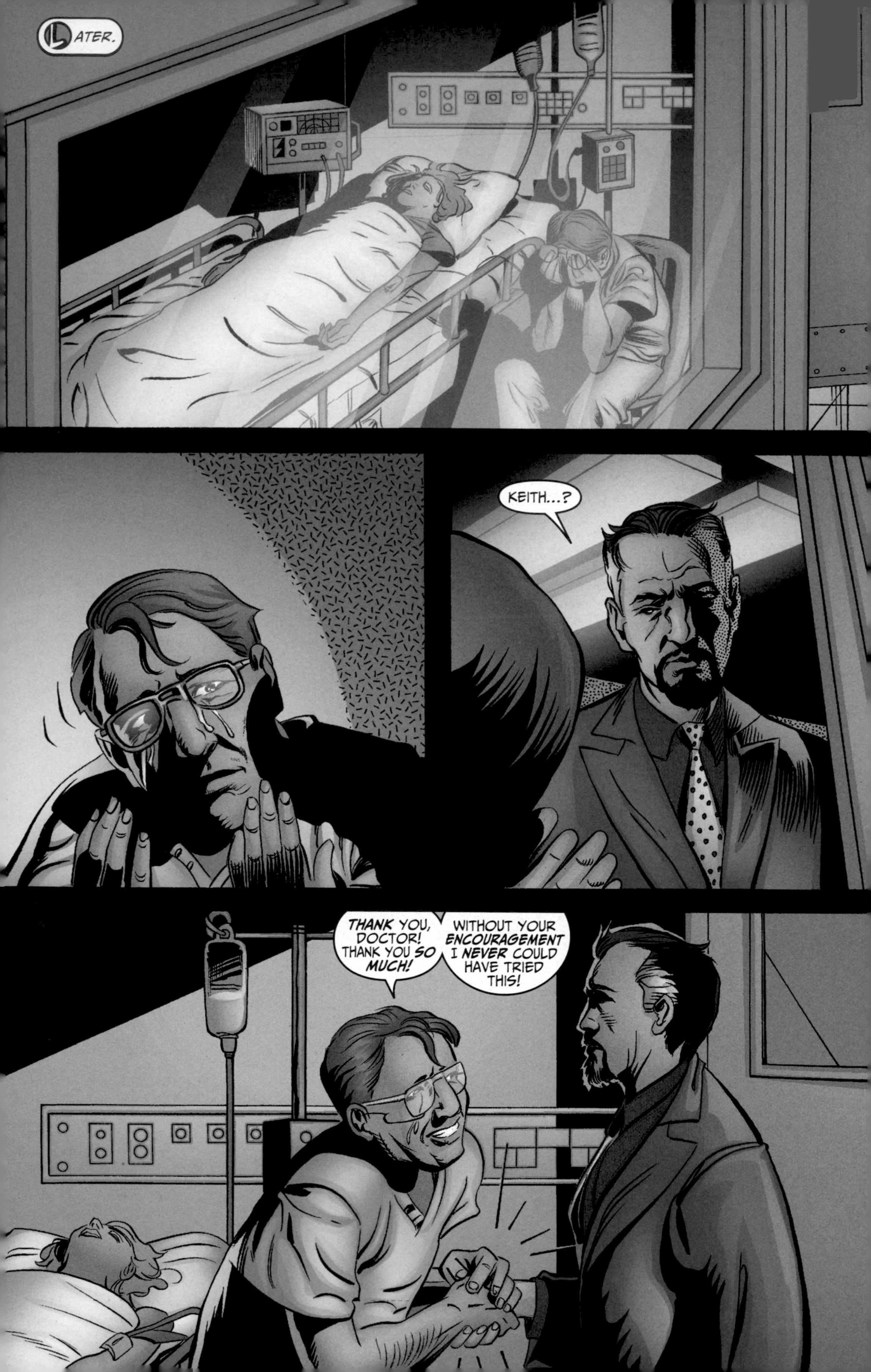
LATER.
KEITH...?
THANK YOU, DOCTOR! THANK YOU SO MUCH!
WITHOUT YOUR ENCOURAGEMENT I NEVER COULD HAVE TRIED THIS!

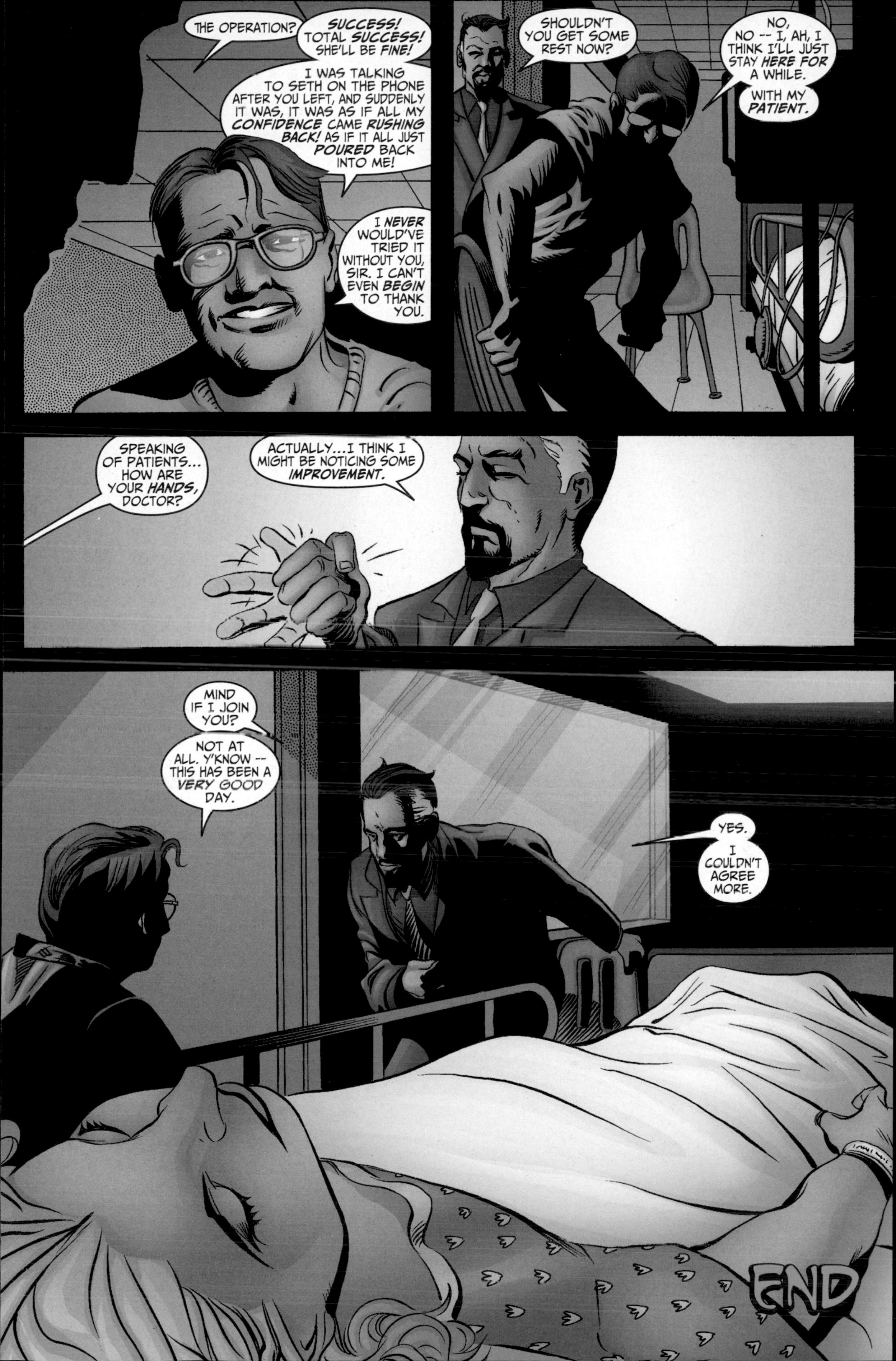
THE OPERATION?
SUCCESS! TOTAL SUCCESS! SHE'LL BE FINE!
I WAS TALKING TO SETH ON THE PHONE AFTER YOU LEFT, AND SUDDENLY IT WAS, IT WAS AS IF ALL MY CONFIDENCE CAME RUSHING BACK! AS IF IT ALL JUST POURED BACK INTO ME!
I NEVER WOULD'VE TRIED IT WITHOUT YOU, SIR. I CAN'T EVEN BEGIN TO THANK YOU.
SHOULDN'T YOU GET SOME REST NOW?
NO, NO -- I, AH, I THINK I'LL JUST STAY HERE FOR A WHILE.
WITH MY PATIENT.
SPEAKING OF PATIENTS... HOW ARE YOUR HANDS, DOCTOR?
ACTUALLY...I THINK I MIGHT BE NOTICING SOME IMPROVEMENT.
MIND IF I JOIN YOU?
NOT AT ALL. Y'KNOW -- THIS HAS BEEN A VERY GOOD DAY.
YES.
I COULDN'T AGREE MORE.
END

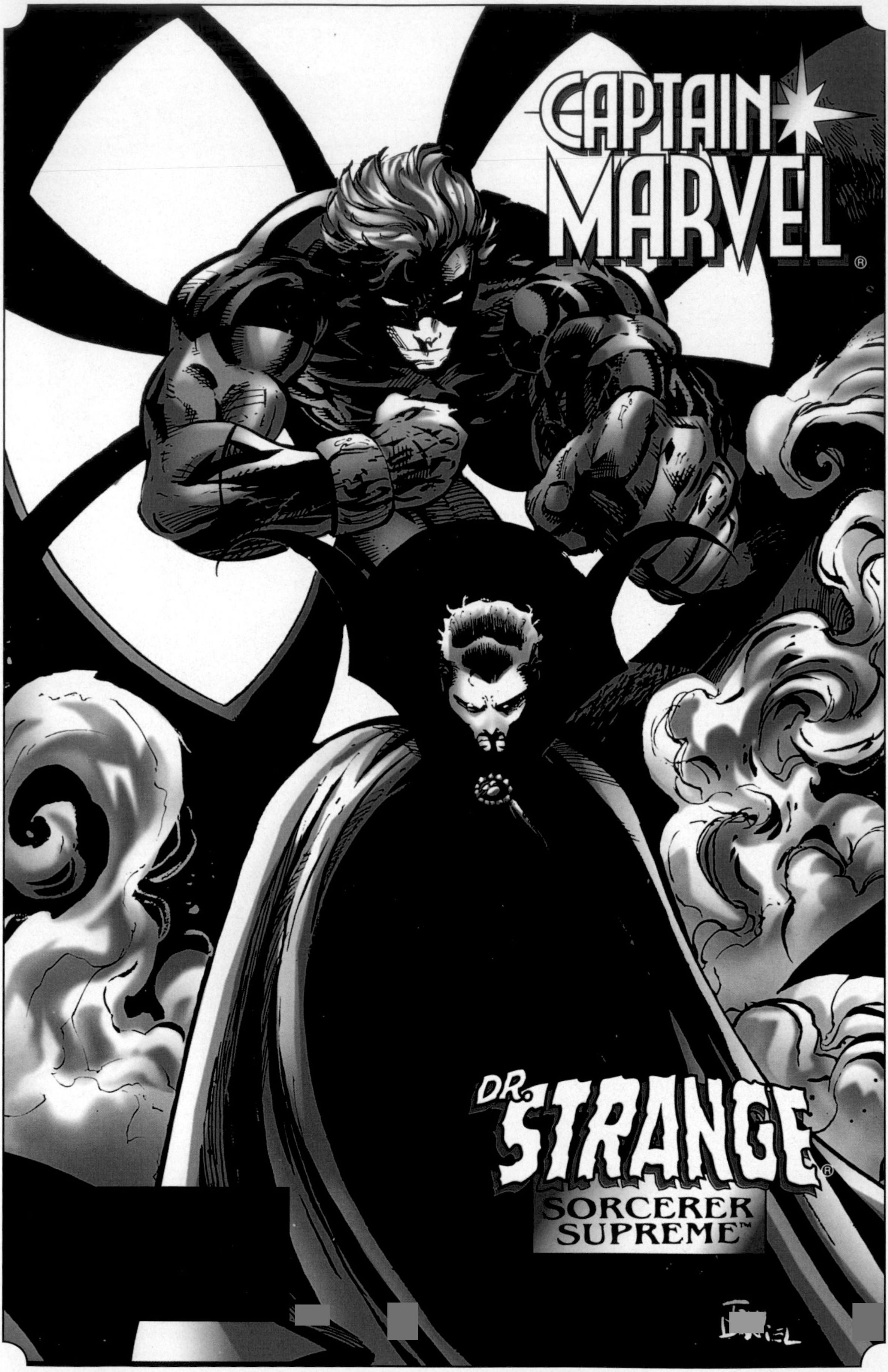
CAPTAIN MARVEL®
DR. STRANGE®
SORCERER SUPREME™

MARVEL SHADOWS AND LIGHT (1997) #1

STRANGE REFLECTIONS

BY MICHAEL GOLDEN WITH JOHN BEATTY, AL MILGROM & RICHARD STARKINGS' COMICRAFT

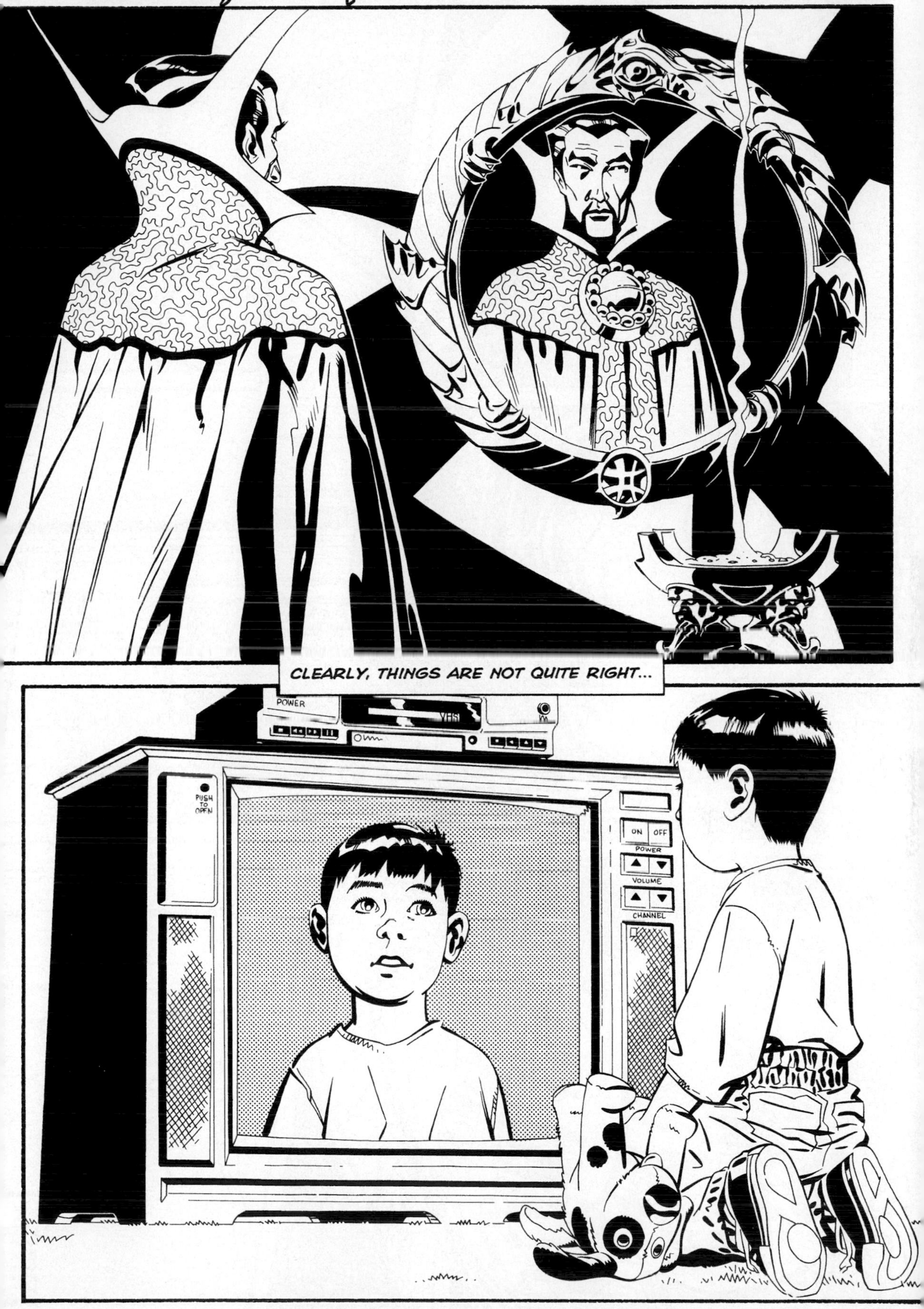
CLEARLY, THINGS ARE NOT QUITE RIGHT...
POWER
VHS
PUSH TO OPEN
ON OFF
POWER
VOLUME
CHANNEL

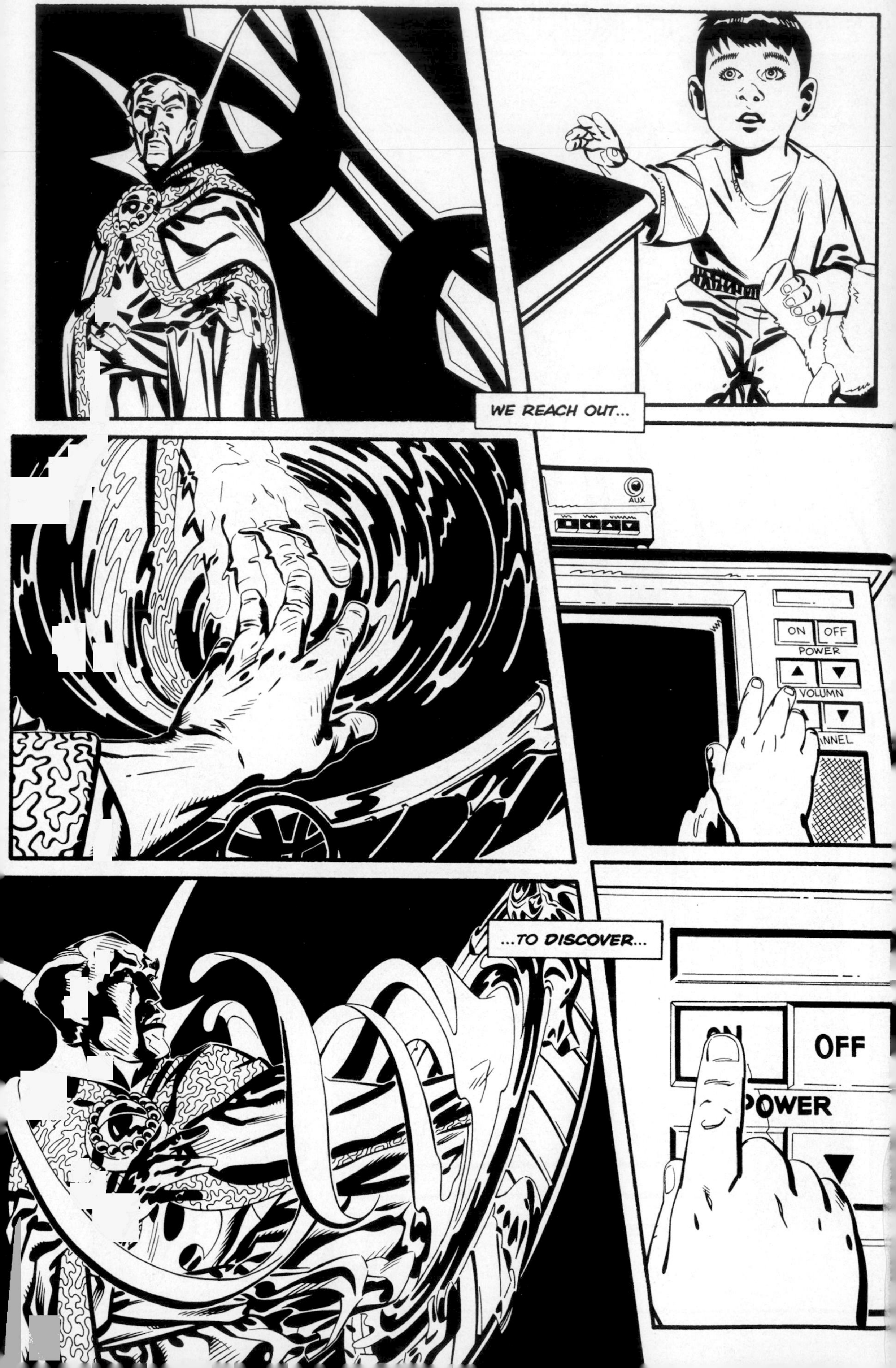
WE REACH OUT...
AUX
ON OFF
POWER
VOLUMN
...TO DISCOVER...
OFF

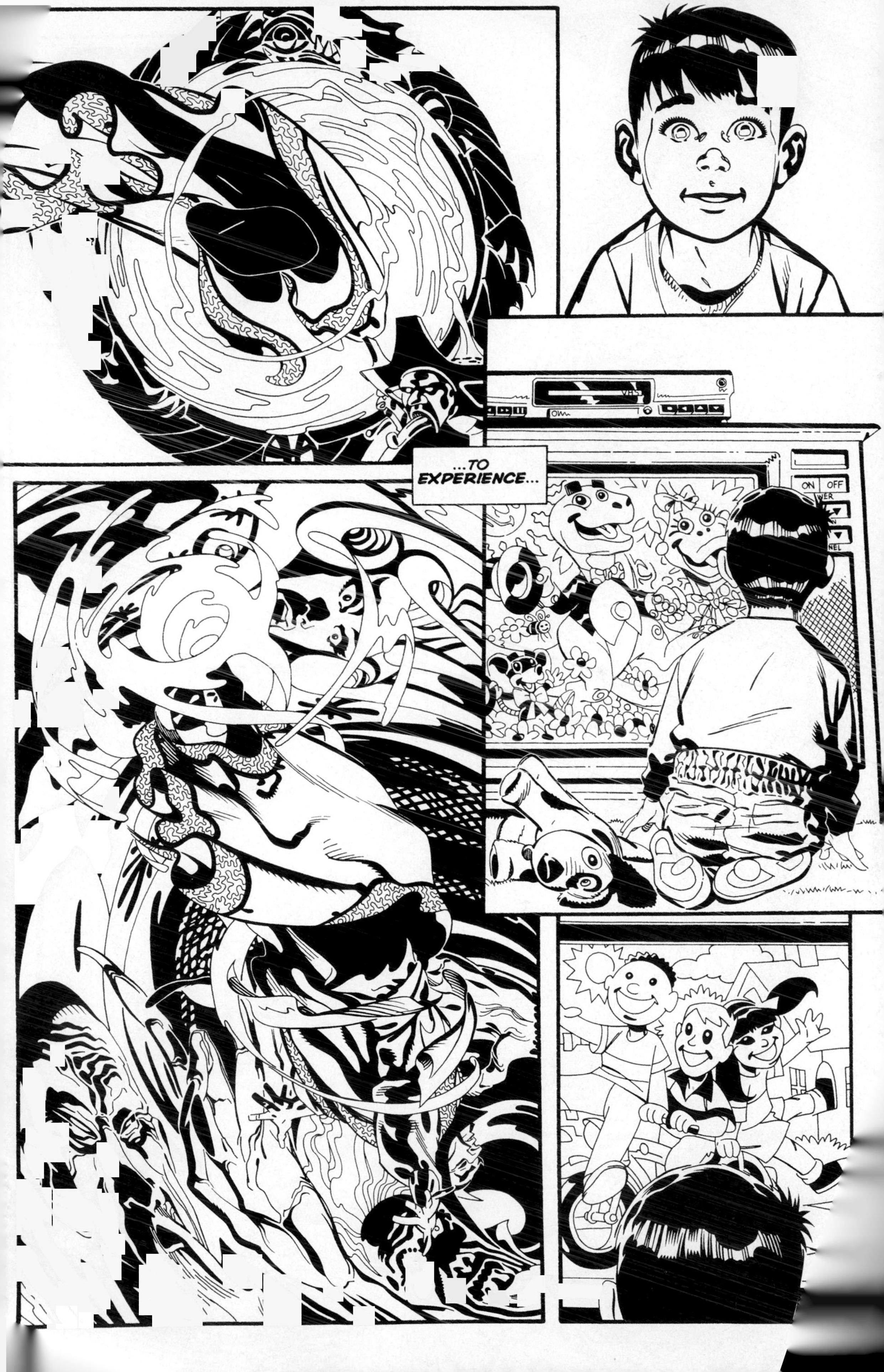
...TO EXPERIENCE...
ON OFF

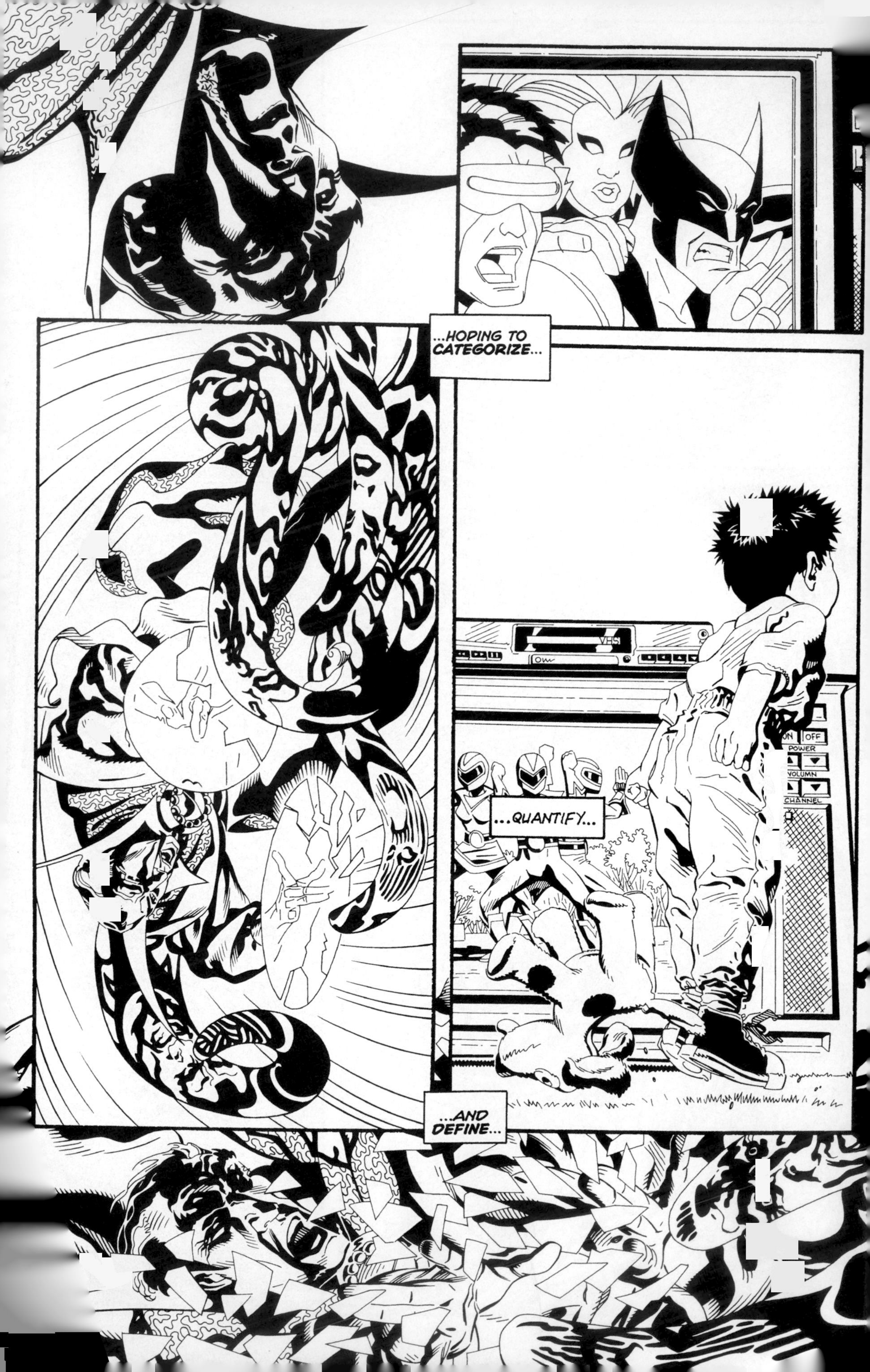
...HOPING TO CATEGORIZE...
VHS
ON OFF
POWER
VOLUMN
CHANNEL
...QUANTIFY...
...AND DEFINE...

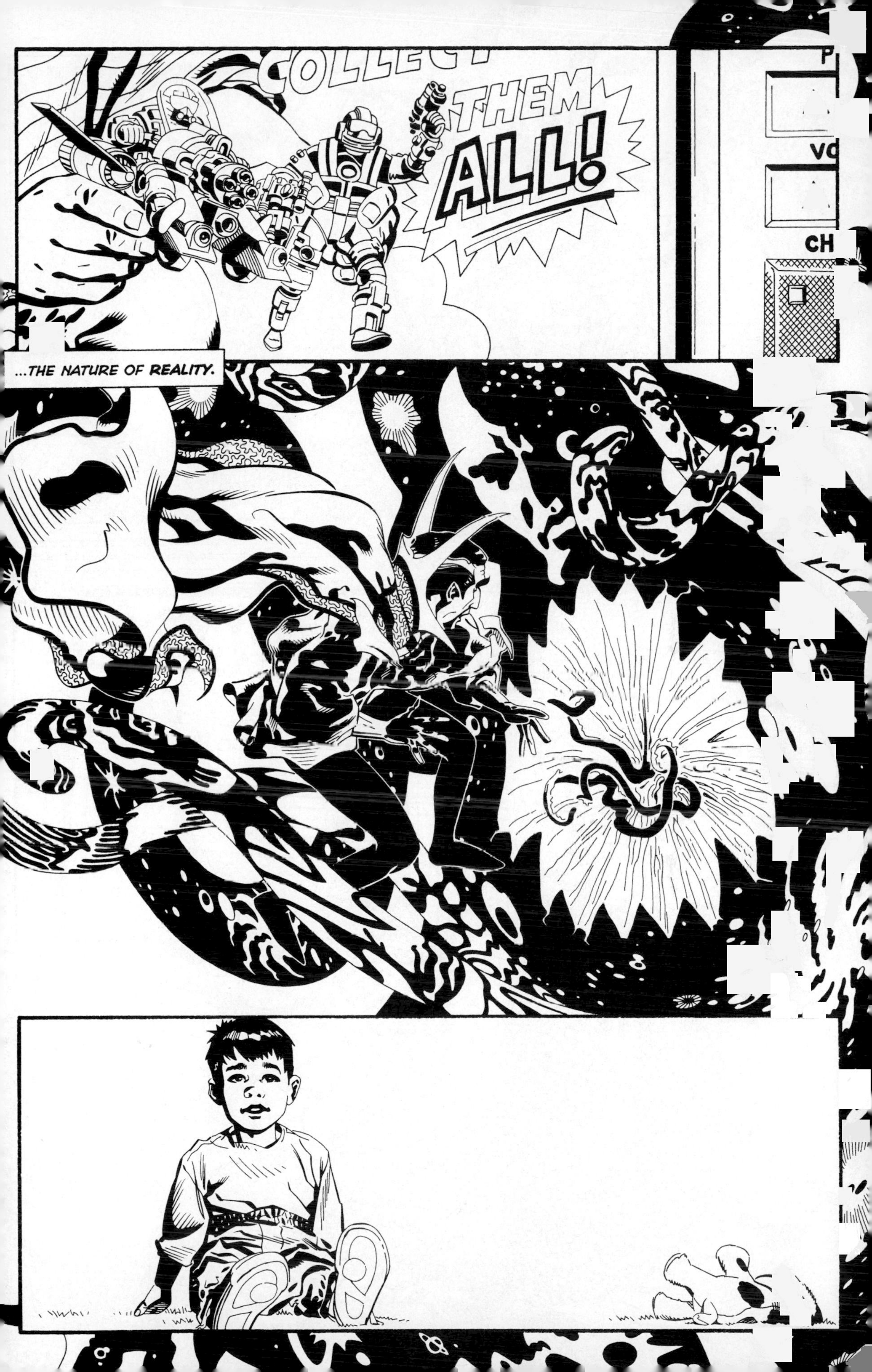
COLLECT THEM ALL!
...THE NATURE OF REALITY.

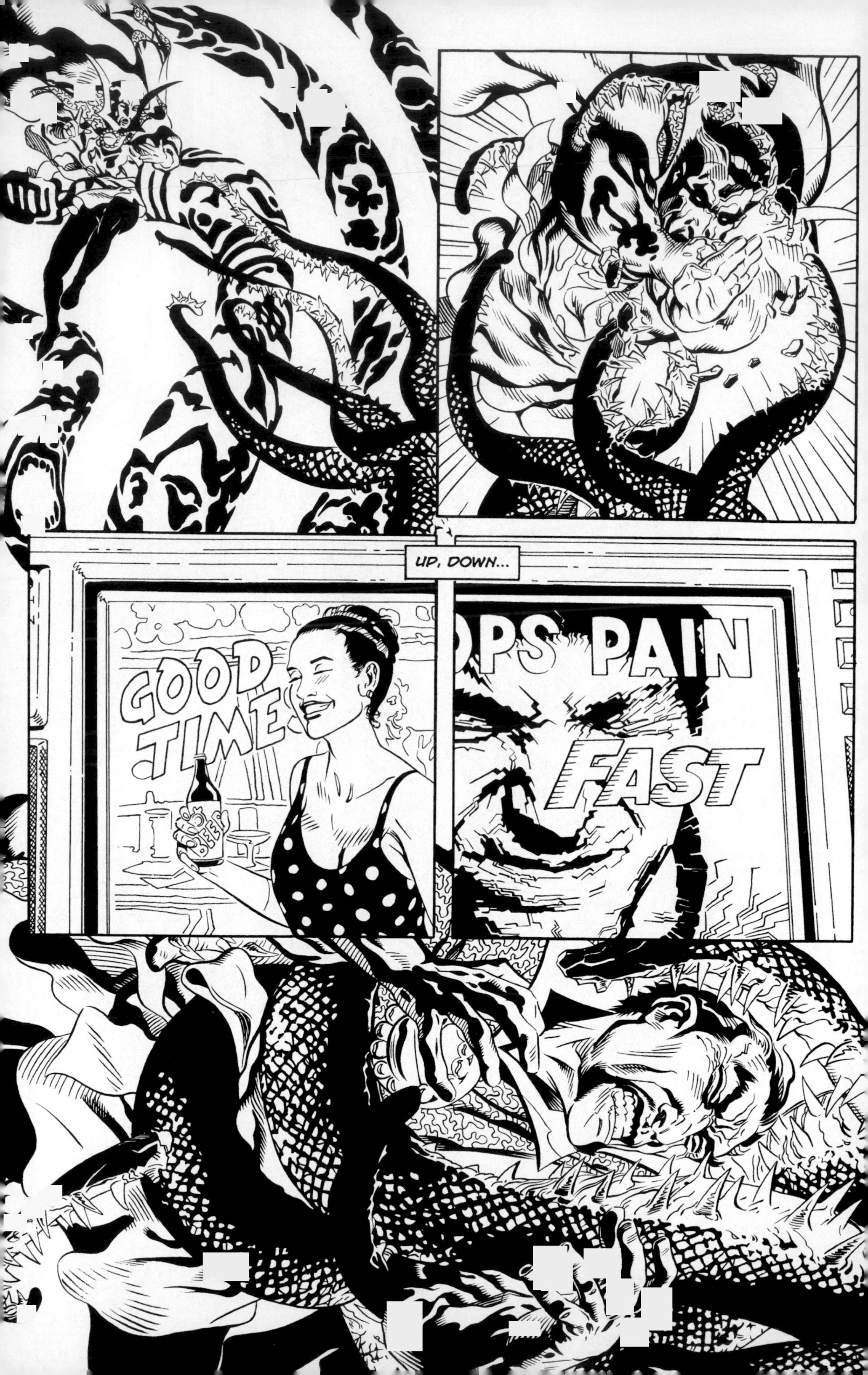
UP, DOWN...
GOOD TIME
OPS PAIN
FAST

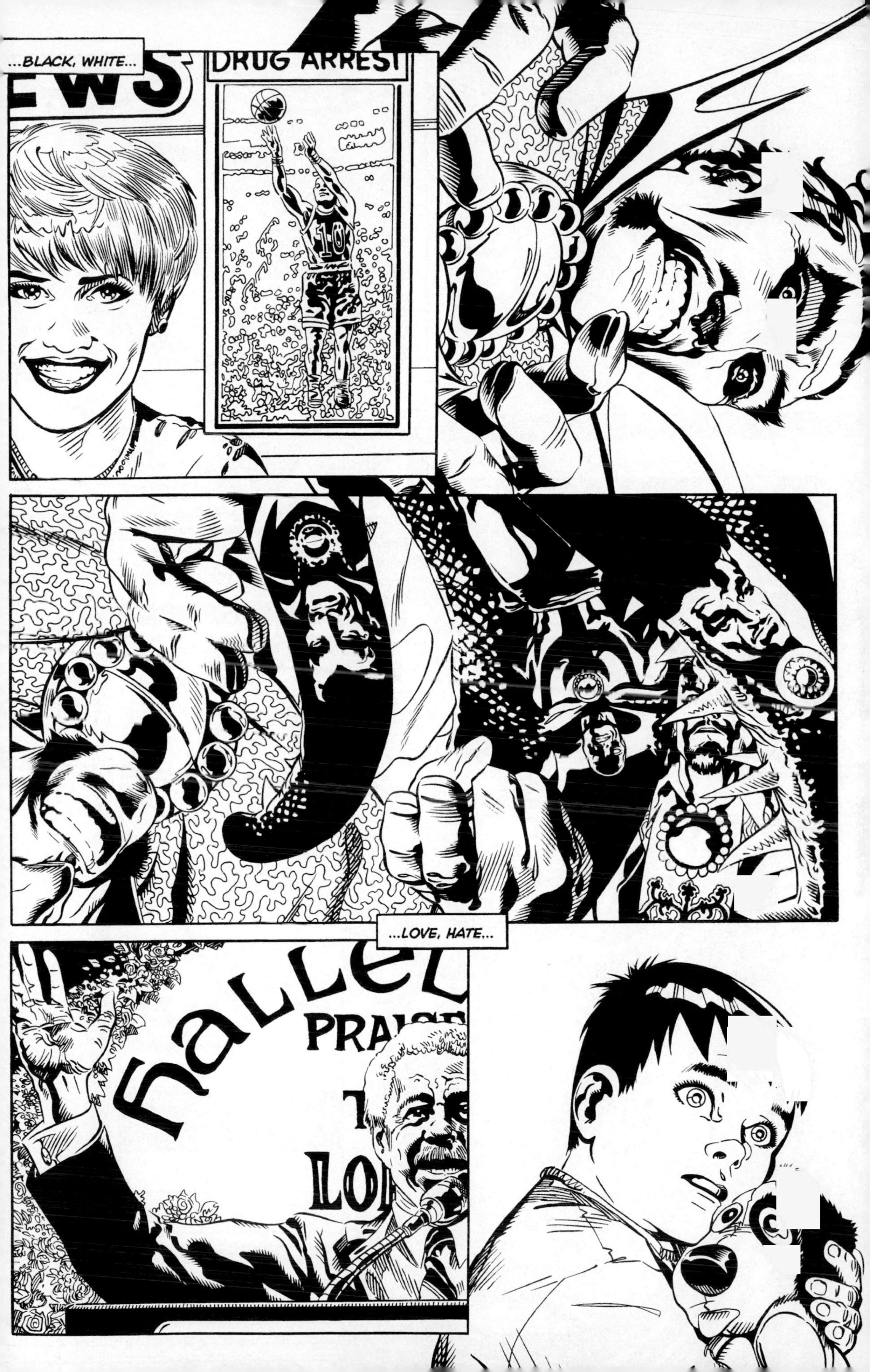
...BLACK, WHITE...
DRUG ARREST
...LOVE, HATE...
PRAIS

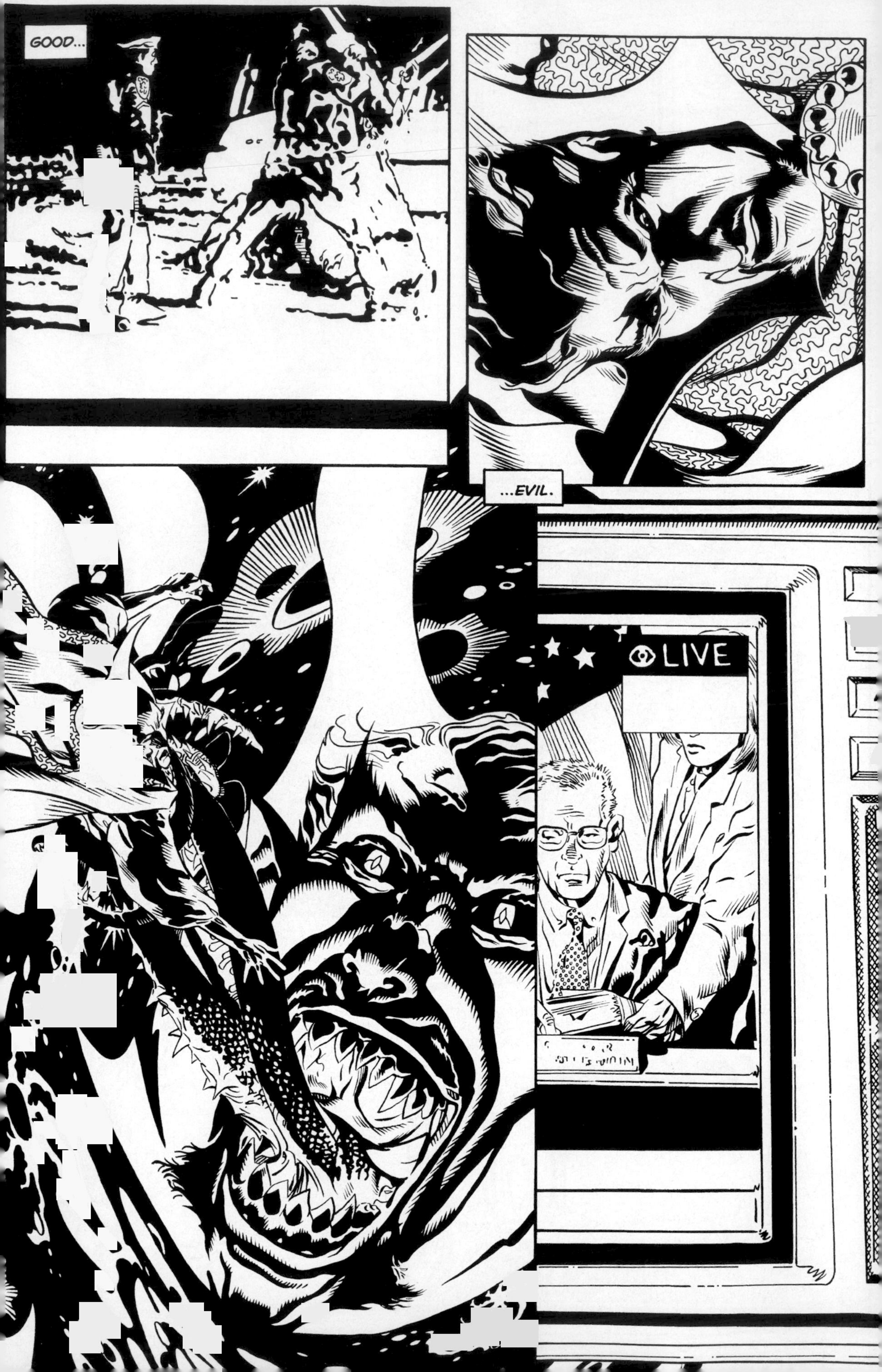
GOOD...
...EVIL.
LIVE

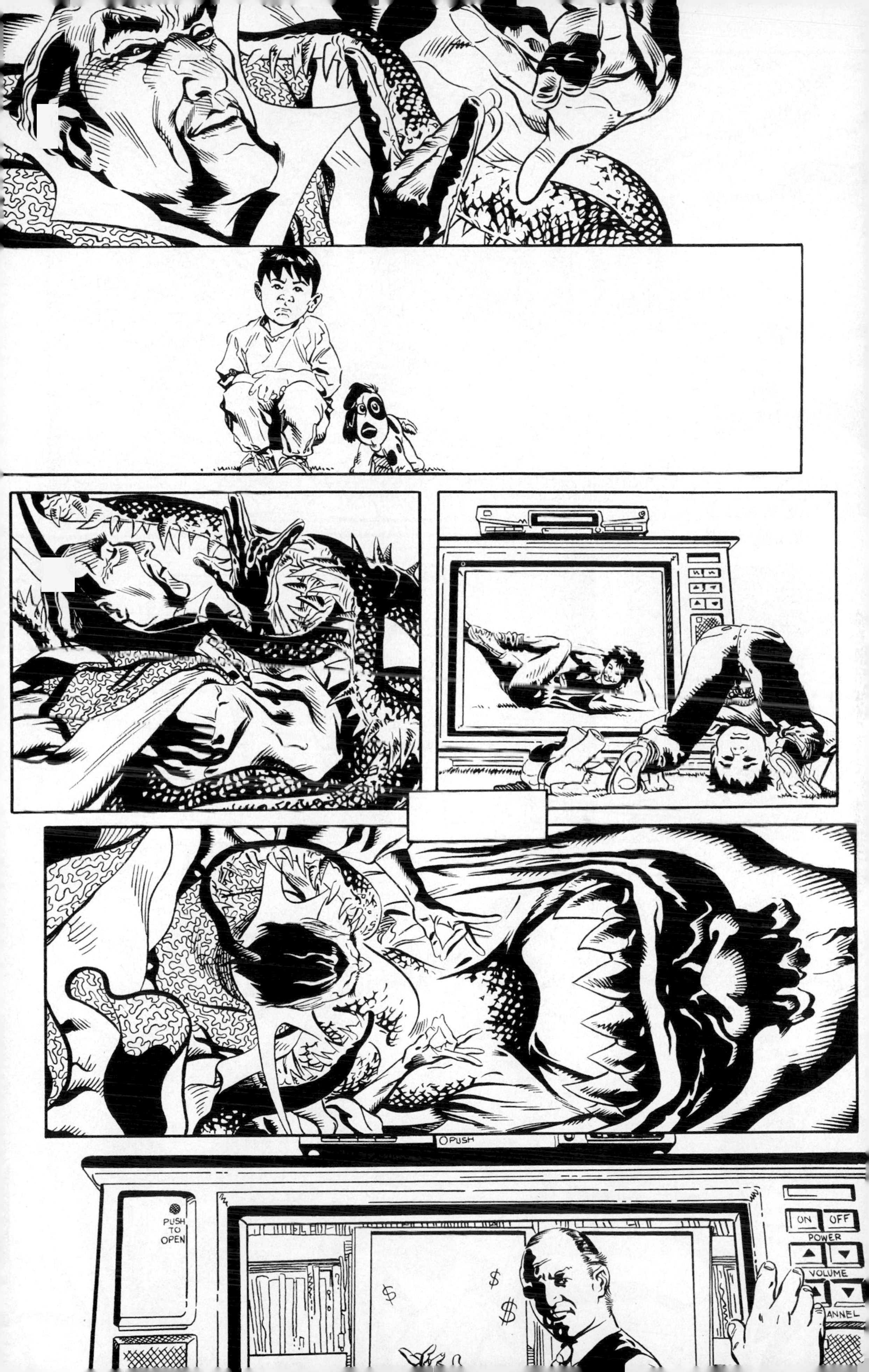
PUSH
PUSH TO OPEN
ON
OFF
POWER
VOLUME
ANNEL

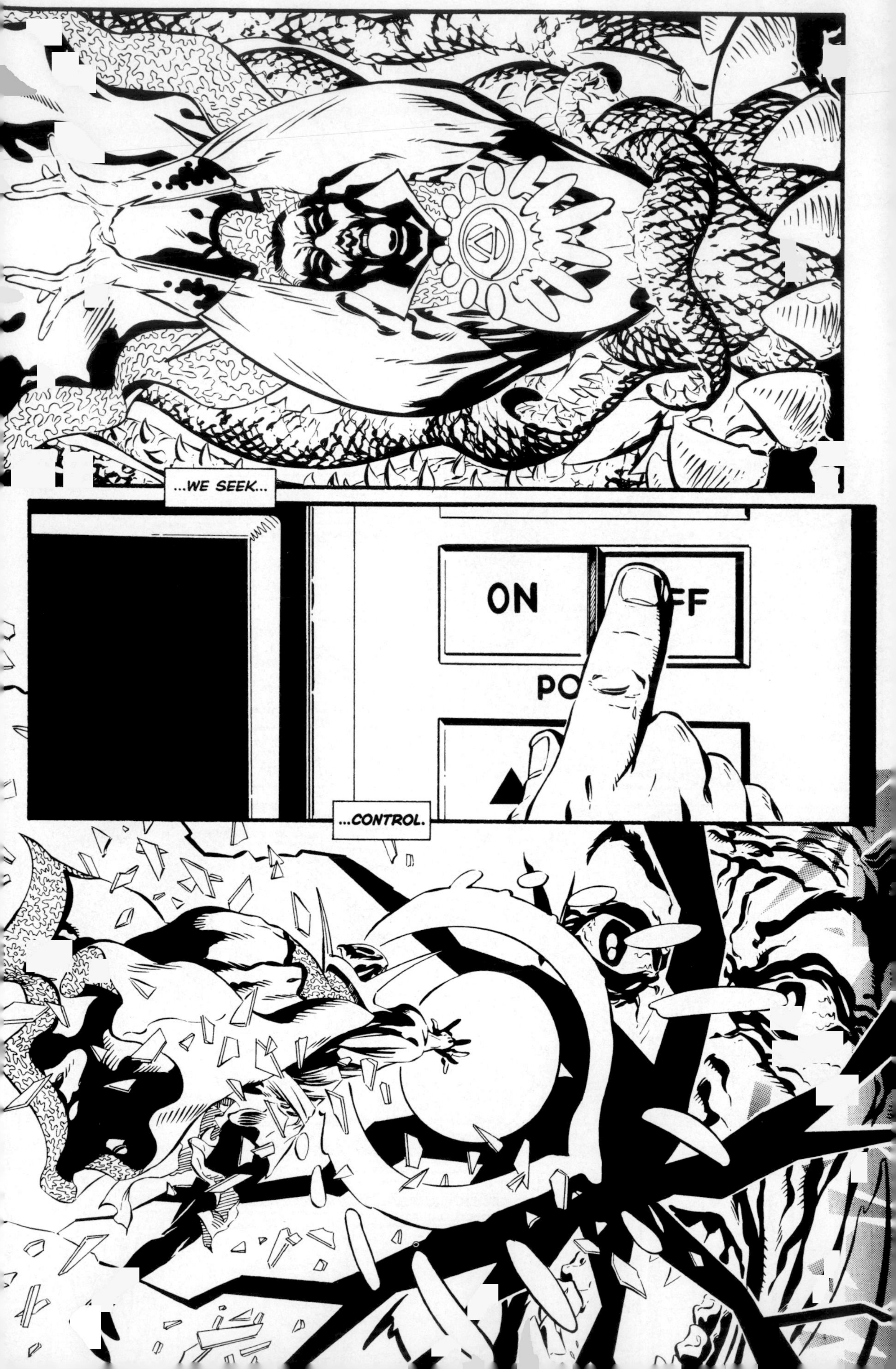
...WE SEEK...
ON
...CONTROL.

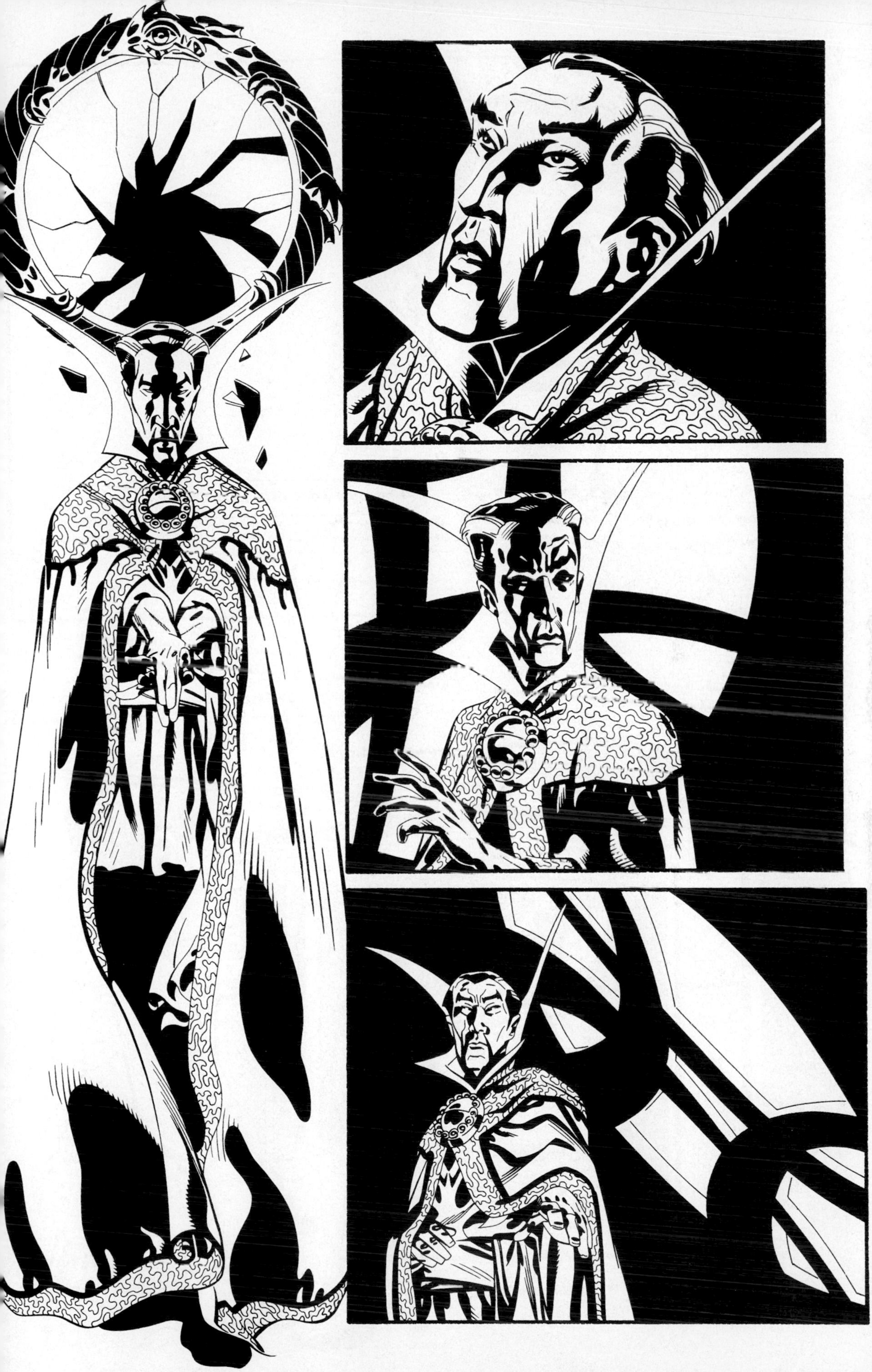

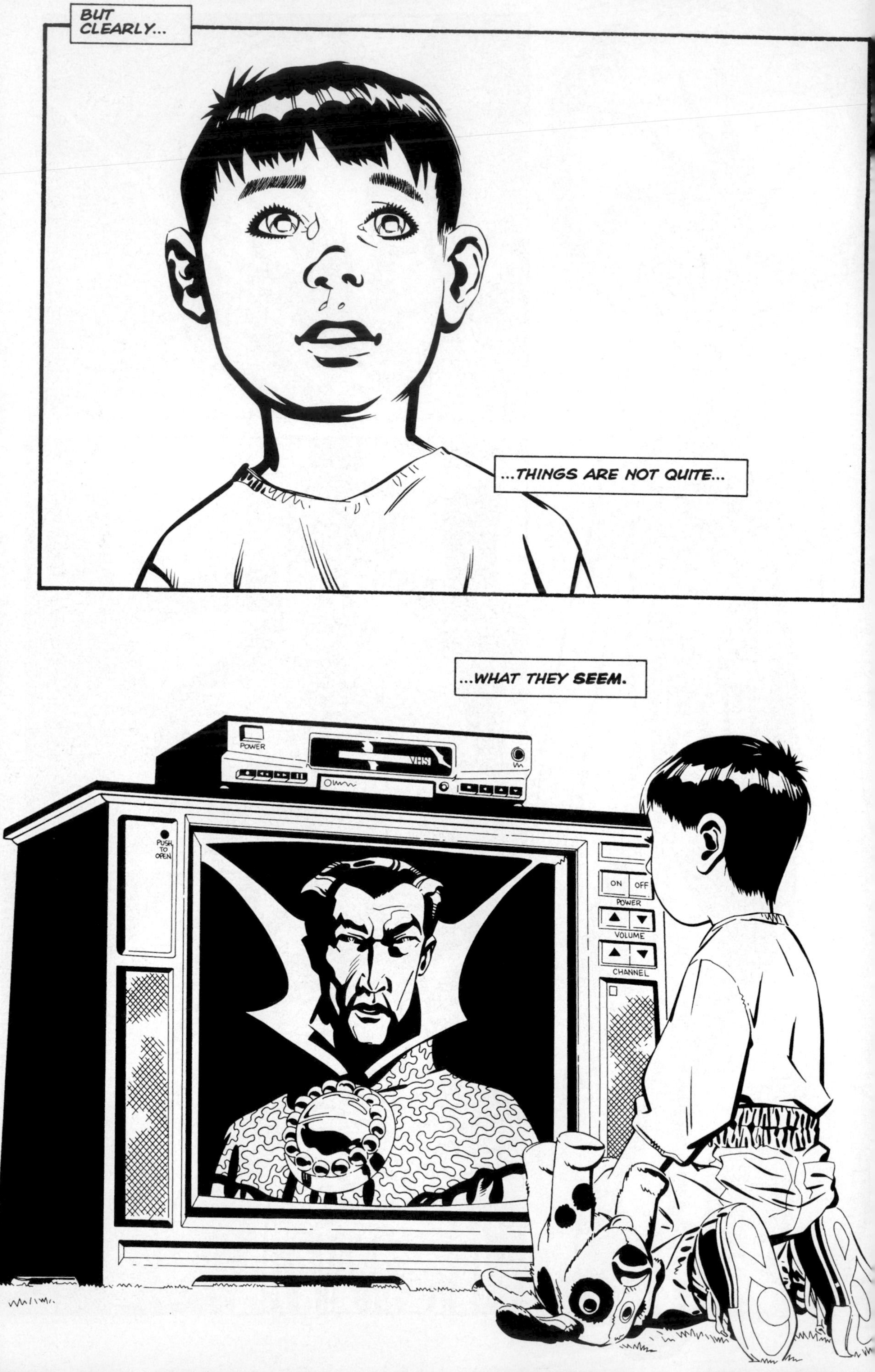
BUT CLEARLY...
...THINGS ARE NOT QUITE...
...WHAT THEY SEEM.
POWER
VHS
PUSH TO OPEN
ON
OFF
POWER
VOLUME
CHANNEL

JIM STARLIN

J im Starlin is a creator who has long been linked to the more cosmic-oriented heroes in the industry, even from his very beginnings. "My first project was IRON MAN #56, where I created the universe-conquering Thanos, perhaps the character people think of most when they hear my name. Then I did IRON MAN #57, but Stan (Lee) didn't like that issue too much, so I kind of got fired," laughs Starlin. Stan surely liked what came next, though. Starlin's take on two of Marvel's galaxy-trotting heroes, Captain Marvel and Adam Warlock was outstanding. Currently doing another space-faring comic for DC called HARDCORE STATION, Starlin is also quick to remind, "Sure I got the lock on the cosmic heroes, but let's not forget, I am the guy who killed Robin. That's always good enough to get me a free drink in Mexico or someplace."

T rading in supernovas for the supernatural, Starlin now tries his hand at a character that he feels has seen better days. "I don't care much for the way Dr. Strange has been used recently. It's funny, because DC's made the same mistakes with Dr. Fate, so I guess people don't know how to handle a mystical character." Starlin intends his handling of Strange to be more of a traditional approach. "There's nothing wrong with the classic (Steve) Ditko creation... that is, Strange as a man who's trying to redeem himself by battling evil in metaphysical terms. That's the way he should be written and that's the way I'll be writing him."

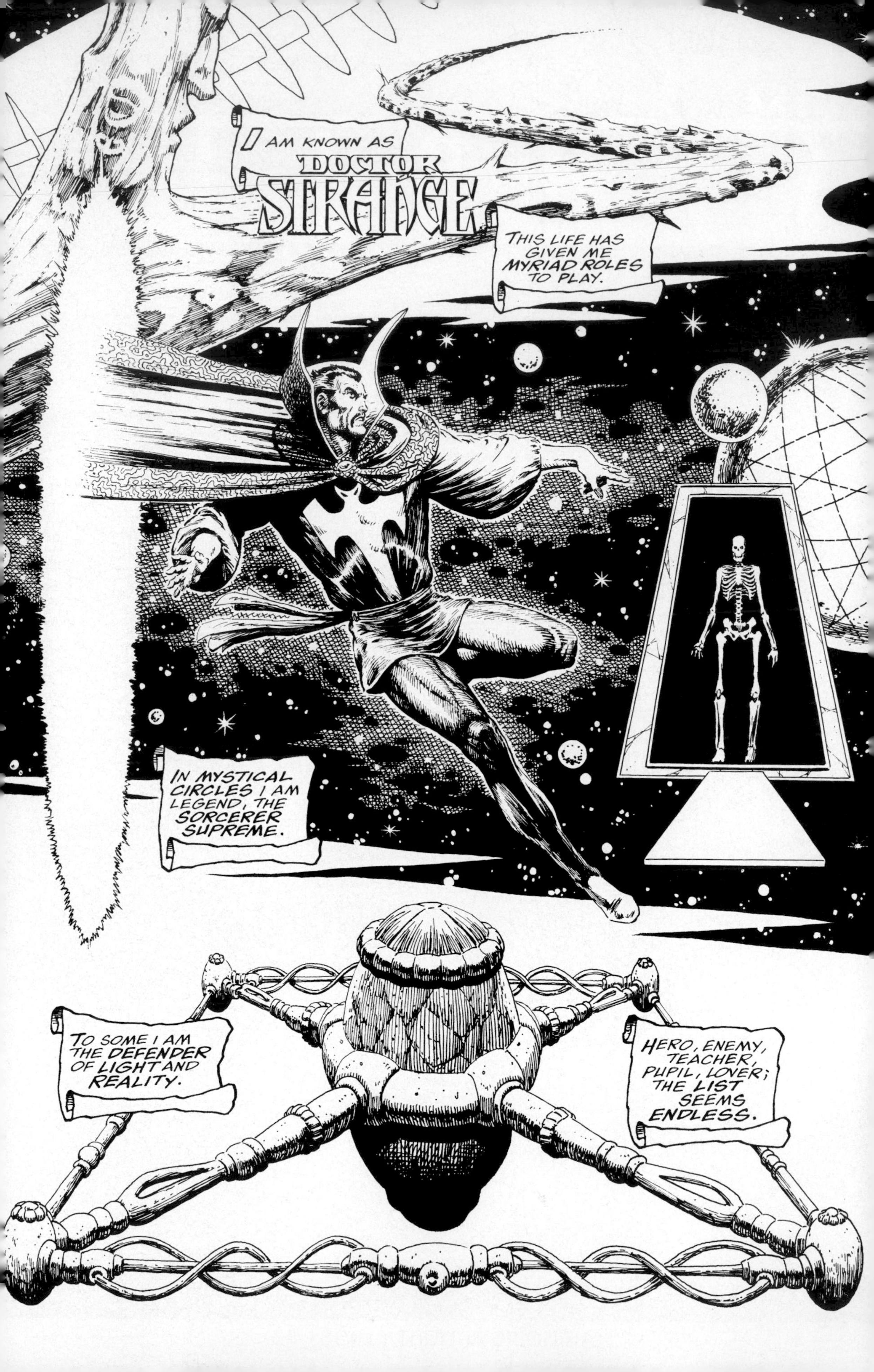
I AM KNOWN AS
DOCTOR
STRANGE
THIS LIFE HAS GIVEN ME MYRIAD ROLES TO PLAY.
IN MYSTICAL CIRCLES I AM LEGEND, THE SORCERER SUPREME.
TO SOME I AM THE DEFENDER OF LIGHT AND REALITY.
HERO, ENEMY, TEACHER, PUPIL, LOVER; THE LIST SEEMS ENDLESS.

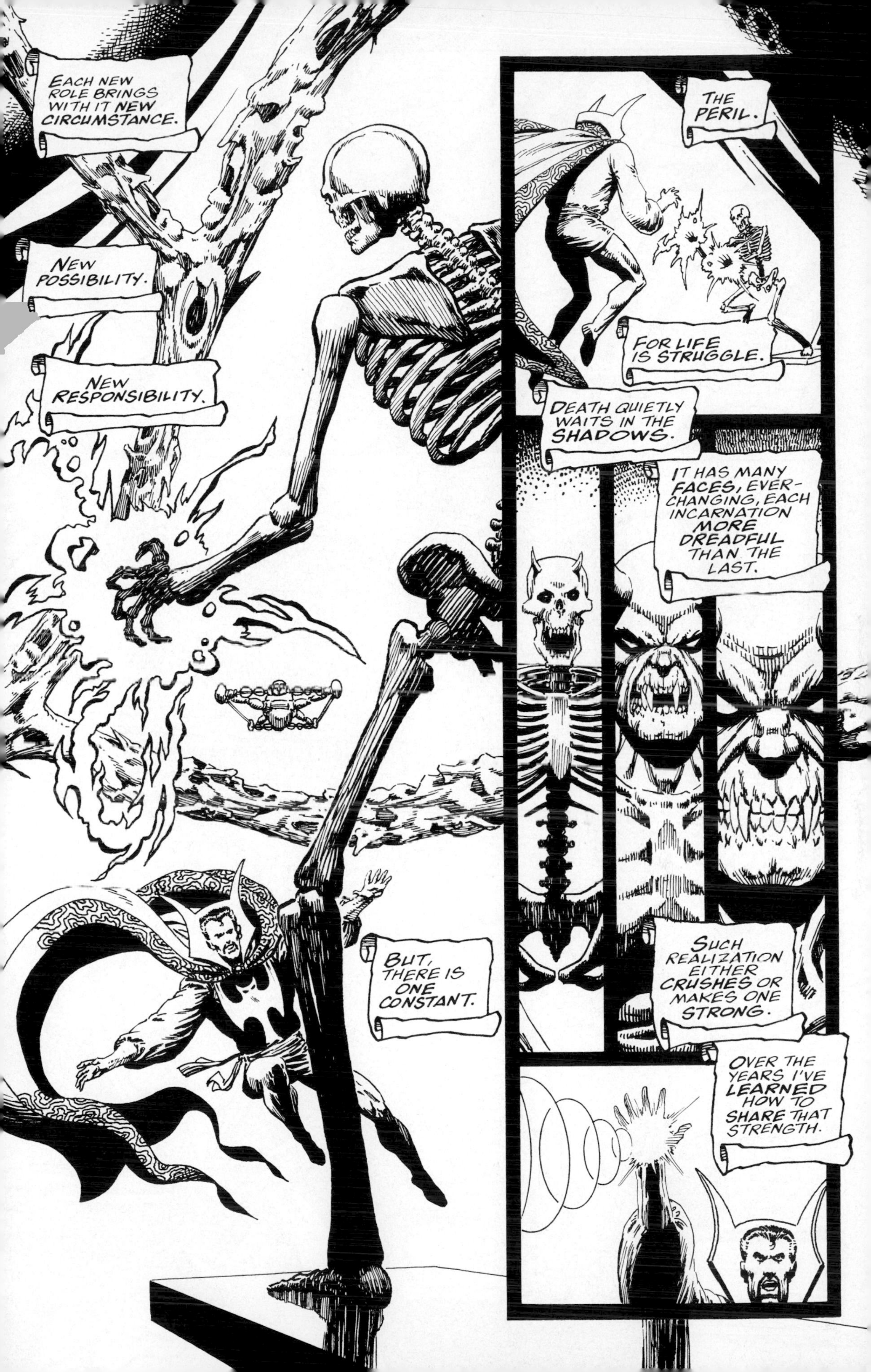
EACH NEW ROLE BRINGS WITH IT NEW CIRCUMSTANCE.
NEW POSSIBILITY.
NEW RESPONSIBILITY.
BUT, THERE IS ONE CONSTANT.
THE PERIL.
FOR LIFE IS STRUGGLE.
DEATH QUIETLY WAITS IN THE SHADOWS.
IT HAS MANY FACES, EVER-CHANGING, EACH INCARNATION MORE DREADFUL THAN THE LAST.
SUCH REALIZATION EITHER CRUSHES OR MAKES ONE STRONG.
OVER THE YEARS I'VE LEARNED HOW TO SHARE THAT STRENGTH.

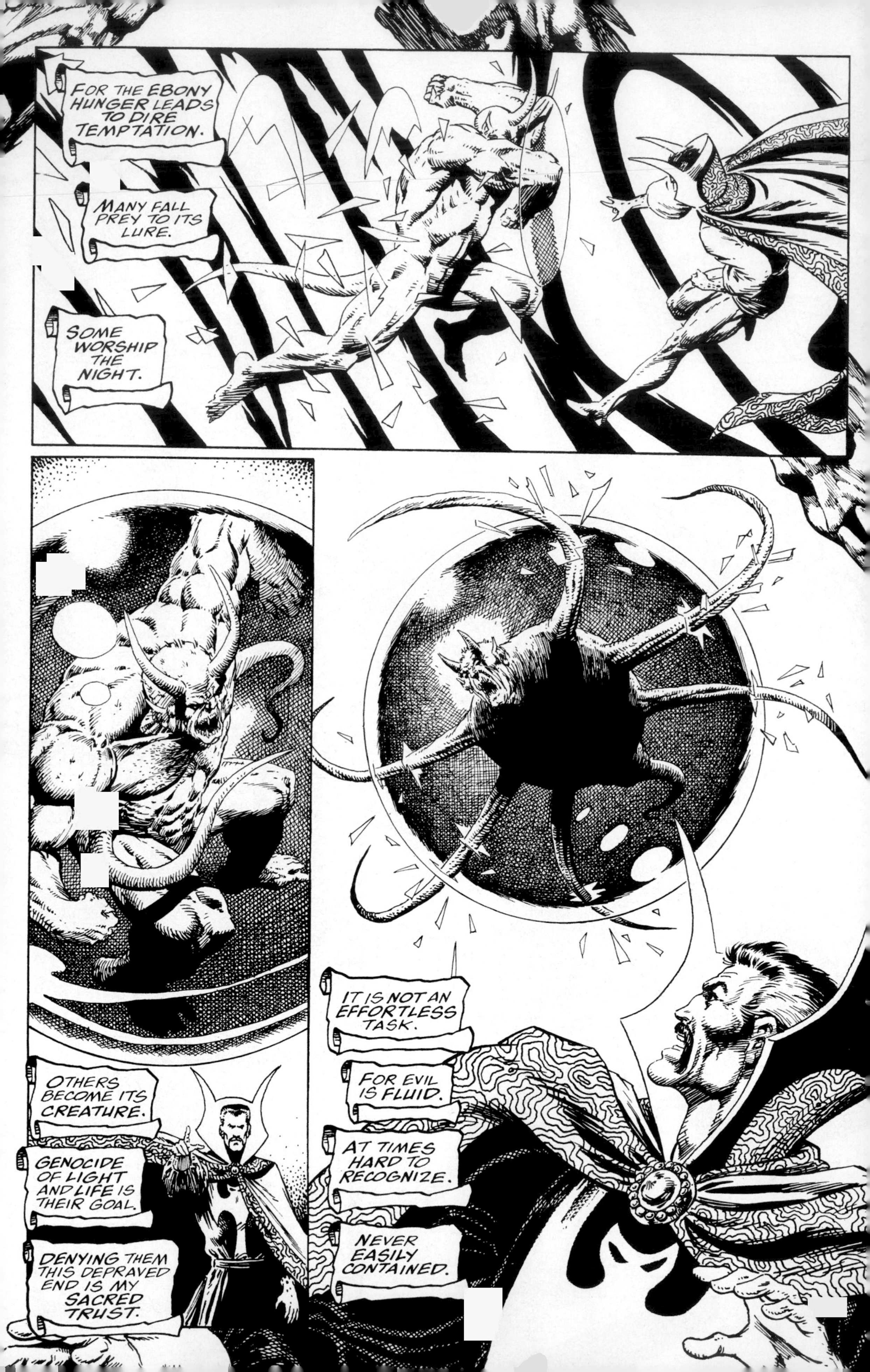

FOR THE EBONY HUNGER LEADS TO DIRE TEMPTATION.
MANY FALL PREY TO ITS LURE.
SOME WORSHIP THE NIGHT.
OTHERS BECOME ITS CREATURE.
GENOCIDE OF LIGHT AND LIFE IS THEIR GOAL.
DENYING THEM THIS DEPRAVED END IS MY SACRED TRUST.
IT IS NOT AN EFFORTLESS TASK.
FOR EVIL IS FLUID.
AT TIMES HARD TO RECOGNIZE.
NEVER EASILY CONTAINED.

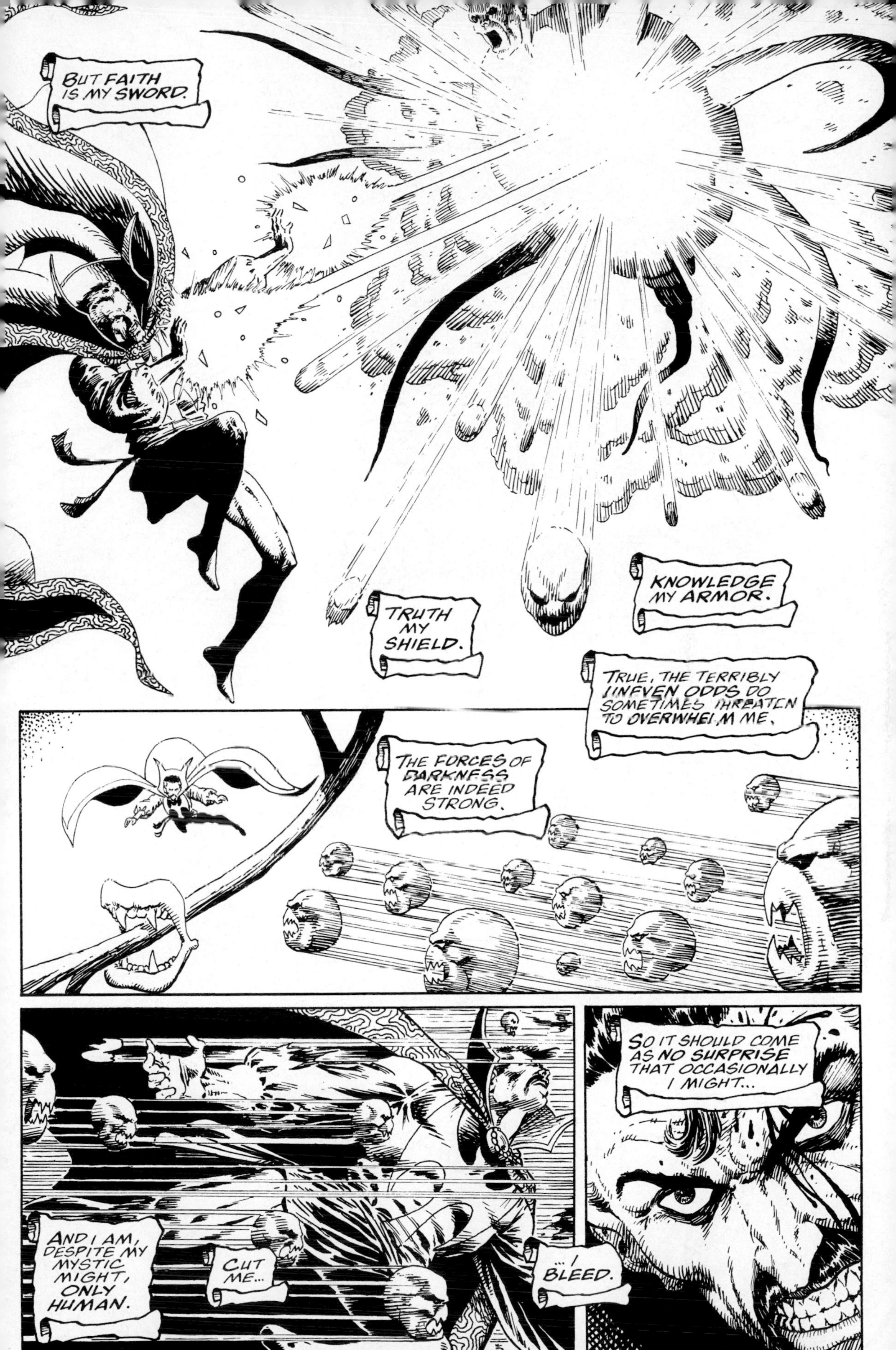
BUT FAITH IS MY SWORD.
TRUTH MY SHIELD.
KNOWLEDGE MY ARMOR.
TRUE, THE TERRIBLY UNEVEN ODDS DO SOMETIMES THREATEN TO OVERWHELM ME.
THE FORCES OF DARKNESS ARE INDEED STRONG.
AND I AM, DESPITE MY MYSTIC MIGHT, ONLY HUMAN.
CUT ME...
...I BLEED.
SO IT SHOULD COME AS NO SURPRISE THAT OCCASIONALLY I MIGHT...

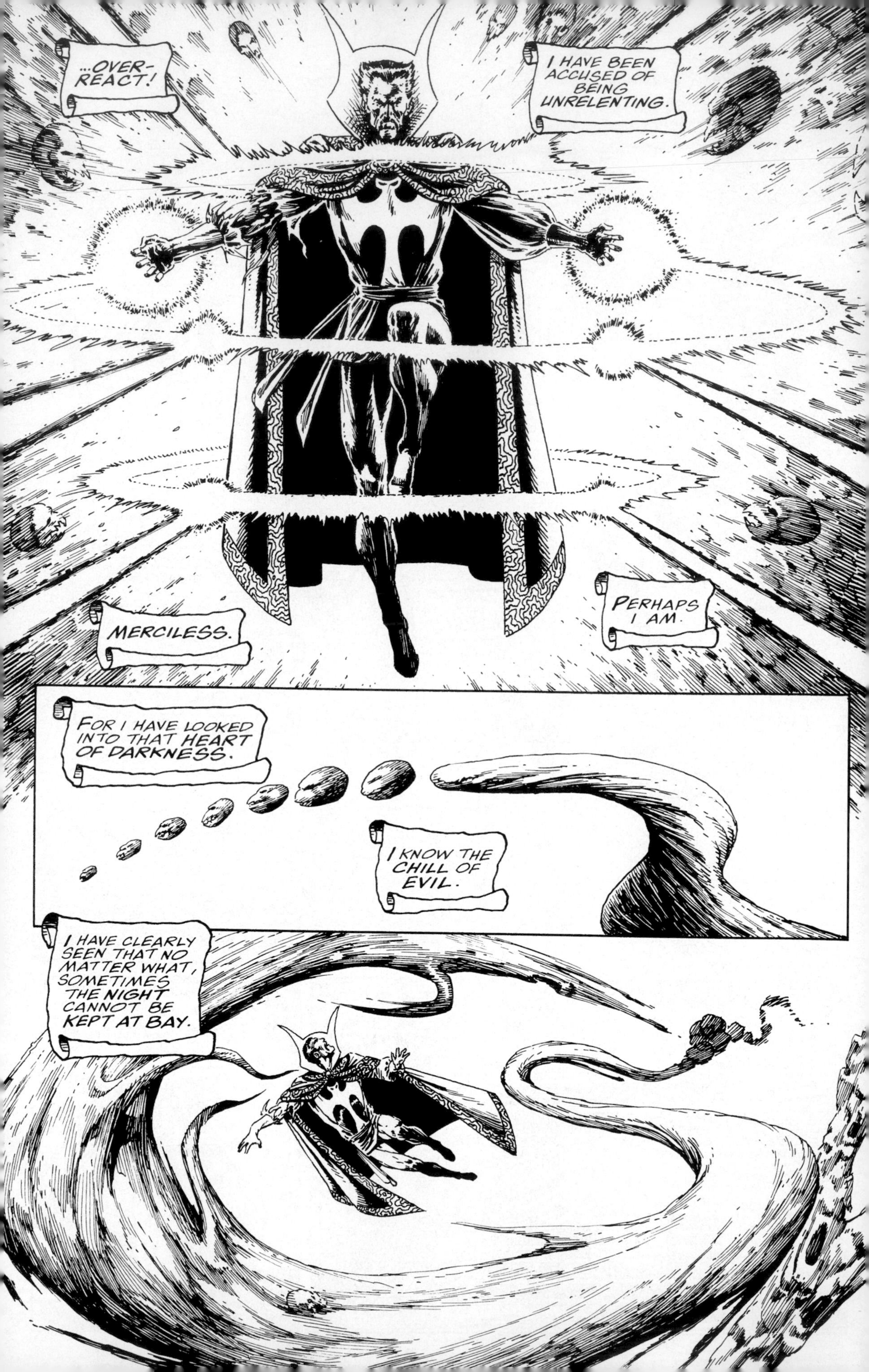

...OVER-REACT!
I HAVE BEEN ACCUSED OF BEING UNRELENTING.
MERCILESS.
PERHAPS I AM.
FOR I HAVE LOOKED INTO THAT HEART OF DARKNESS.
I KNOW THE CHILL OF EVIL.
I HAVE CLEARLY SEEN THAT NO MATTER WHAT, SOMETIMES THE NIGHT CANNOT BE KEPT AT BAY.

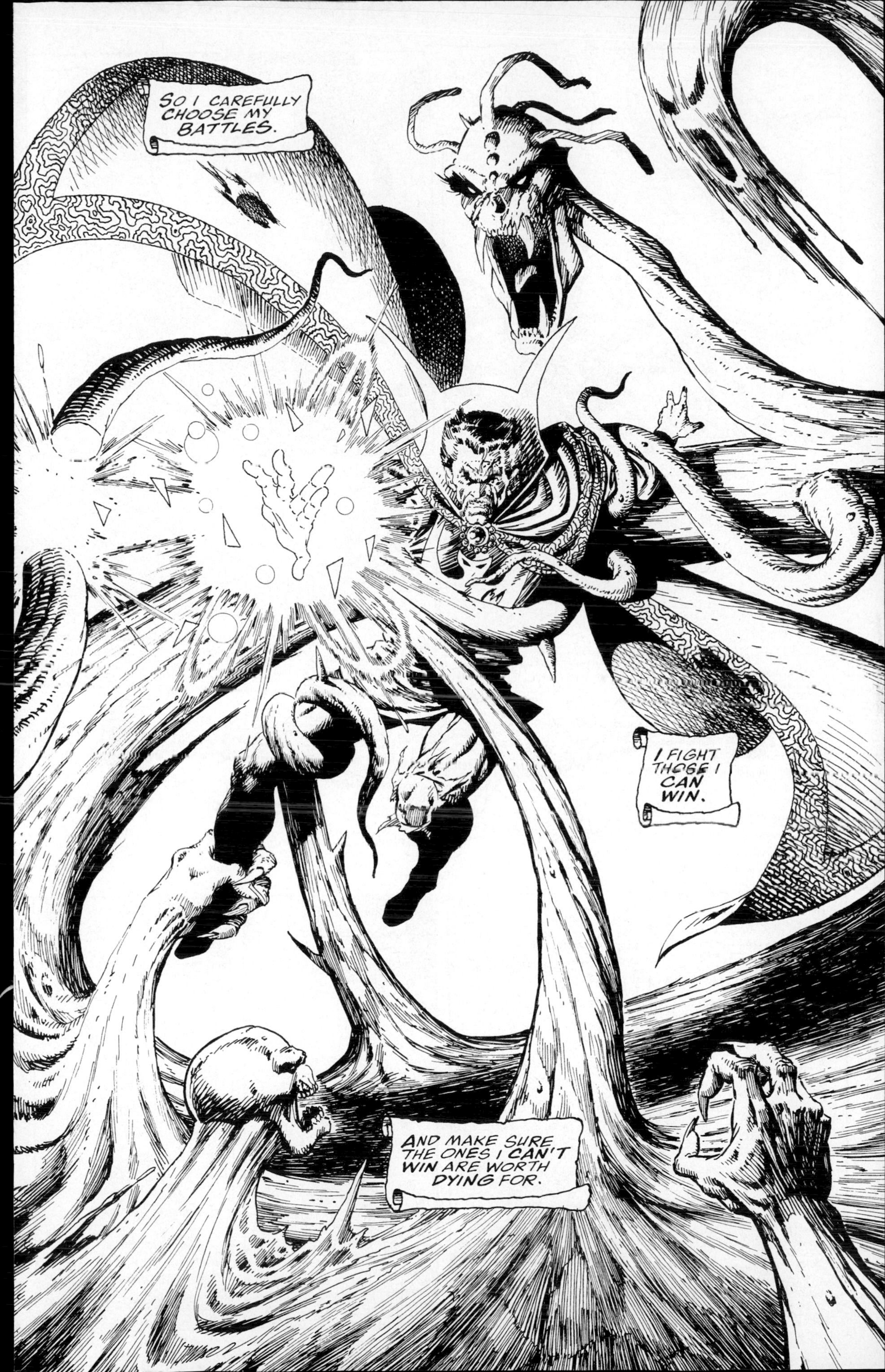
SO I CAREFULLY CHOOSE MY BATTLES.
I FIGHT THOSE I CAN WIN.
AND MAKE SURE THE ONES I CAN'T WIN ARE WORTH DYING FOR.

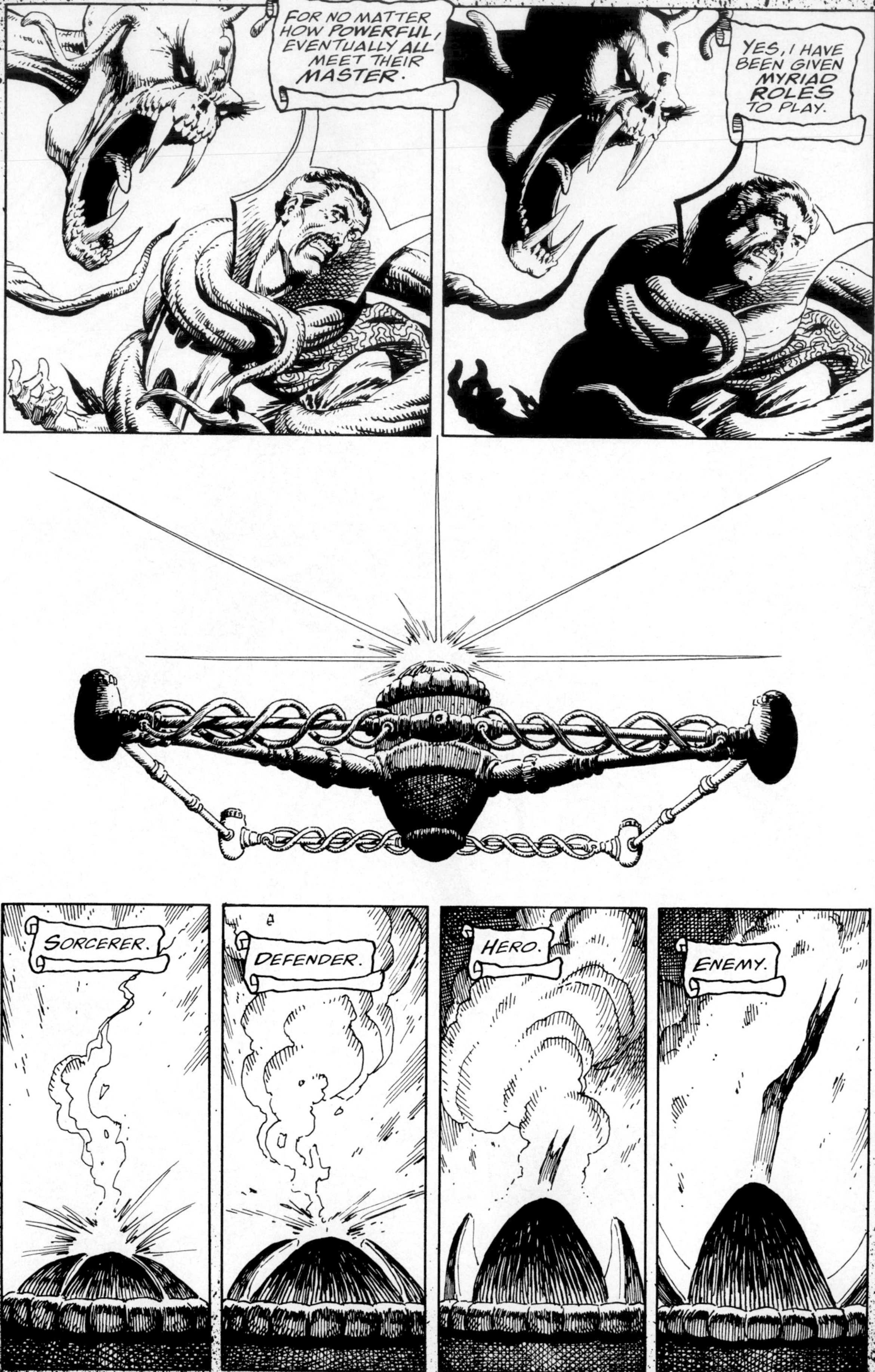

FOR NO MATTER HOW POWERFUL, EVENTUALLY ALL MEET THEIR MASTER.
YES, I HAVE BEEN GIVEN MYRIAD ROLES TO PLAY.
SORCERER.
DEFENDER.
HERO.
ENEMY.

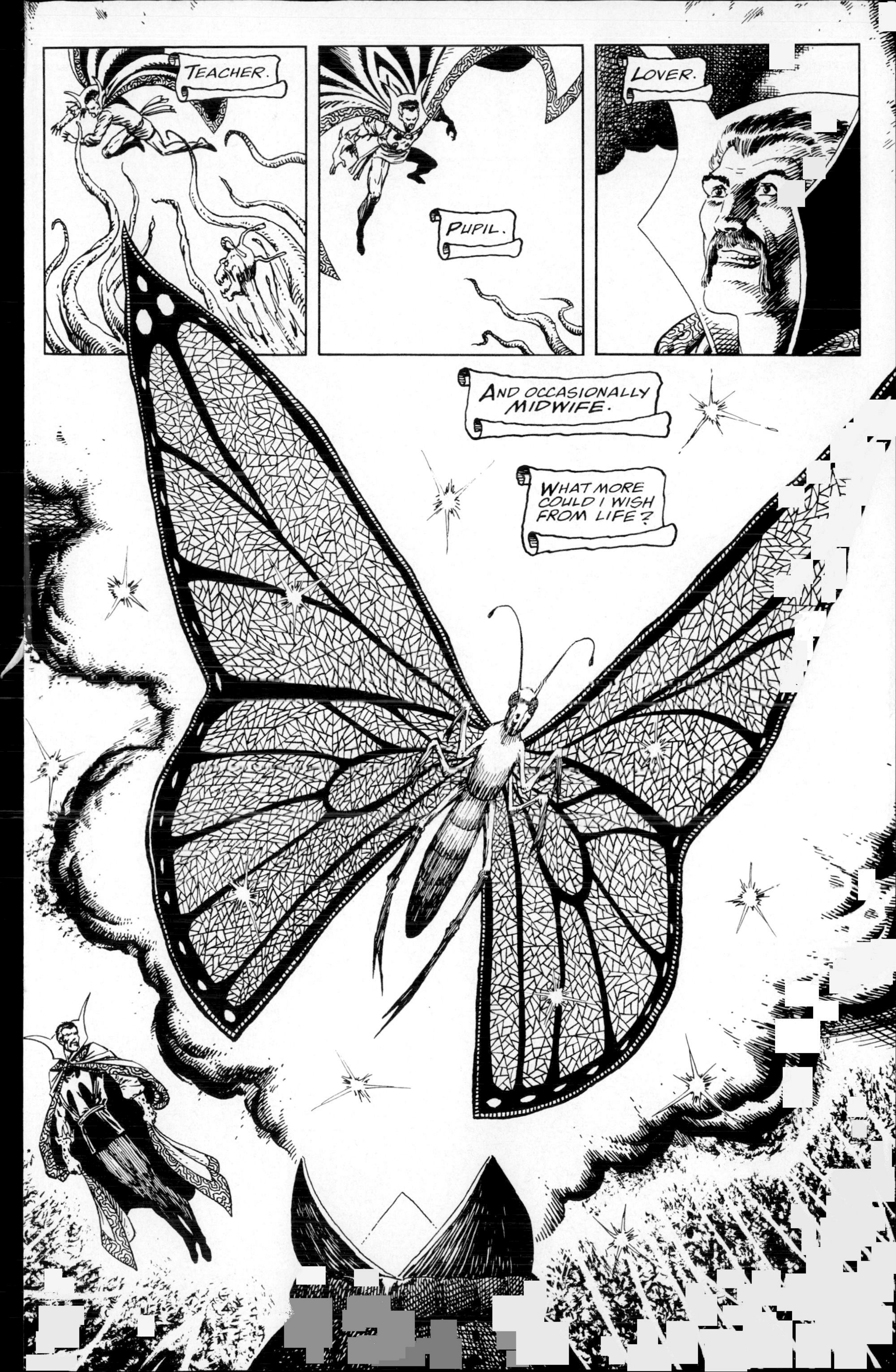
TEACHER.
PUPIL.
LOVER.
AND OCCASIONALLY MIDWIFE.
WHAT MORE COULD I WISH FROM LIFE?

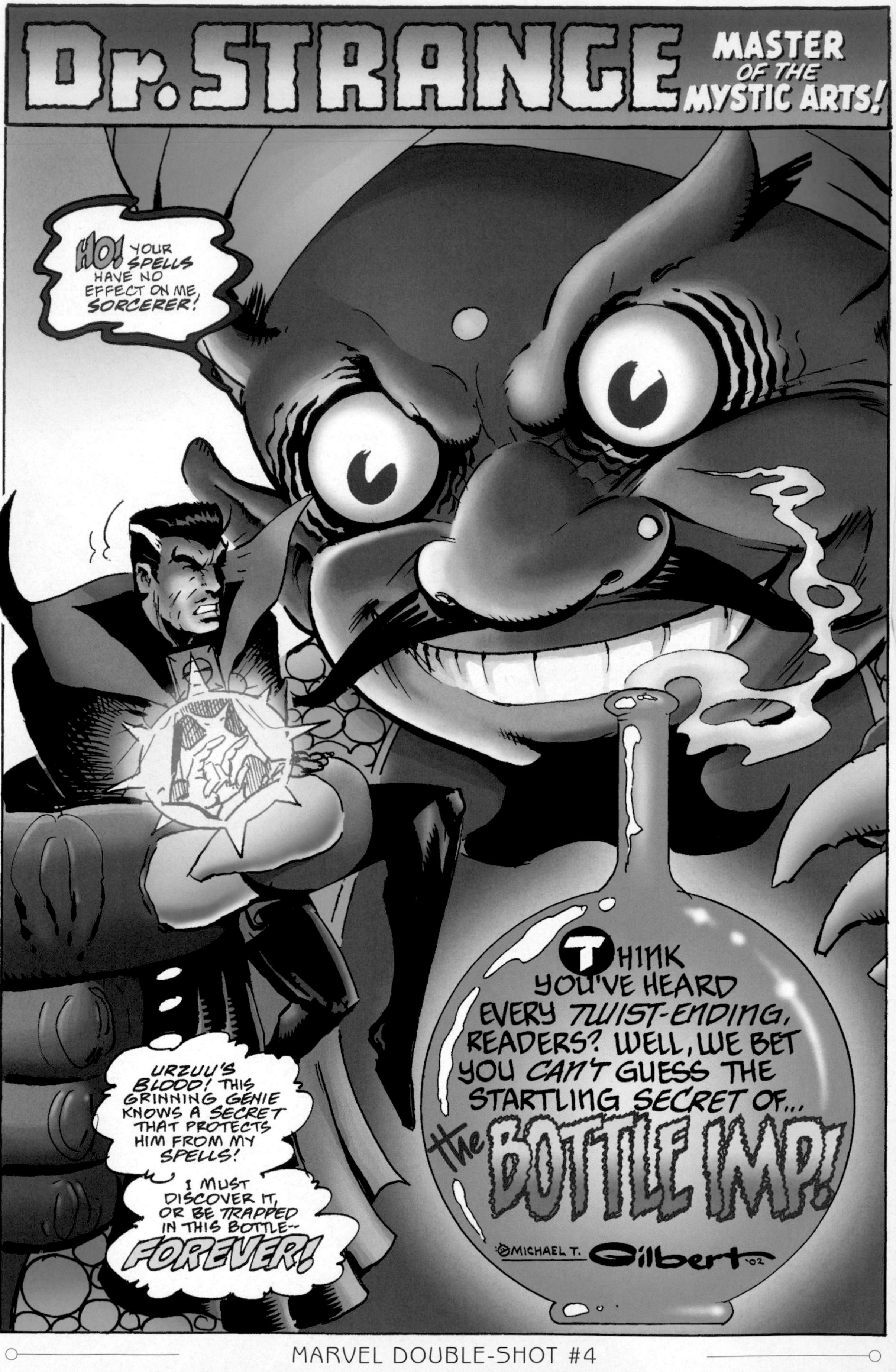

Dr. STRANGE MASTER OF THE MYSTIC ARTS!
HO! YOUR SPELLS HAVE NO EFFECT ON ME, SORCERER!
URZUU'S BLOOD! THIS GRINNING GENIE KNOWS A SECRET THAT PROTECTS HIM FROM MY SPELLS!
I MUST DISCOVER IT, OR BE TRAPPED IN THIS BOTTLE-- FOREVER!
THINK YOU'VE HEARD EVERY TWIST-ENDING, READERS? WELL, WE BET YOU CAN'T GUESS THE STARTLING SECRET OF...
the BOTTLE IMP!
MICHAEL T. Gilbert '02

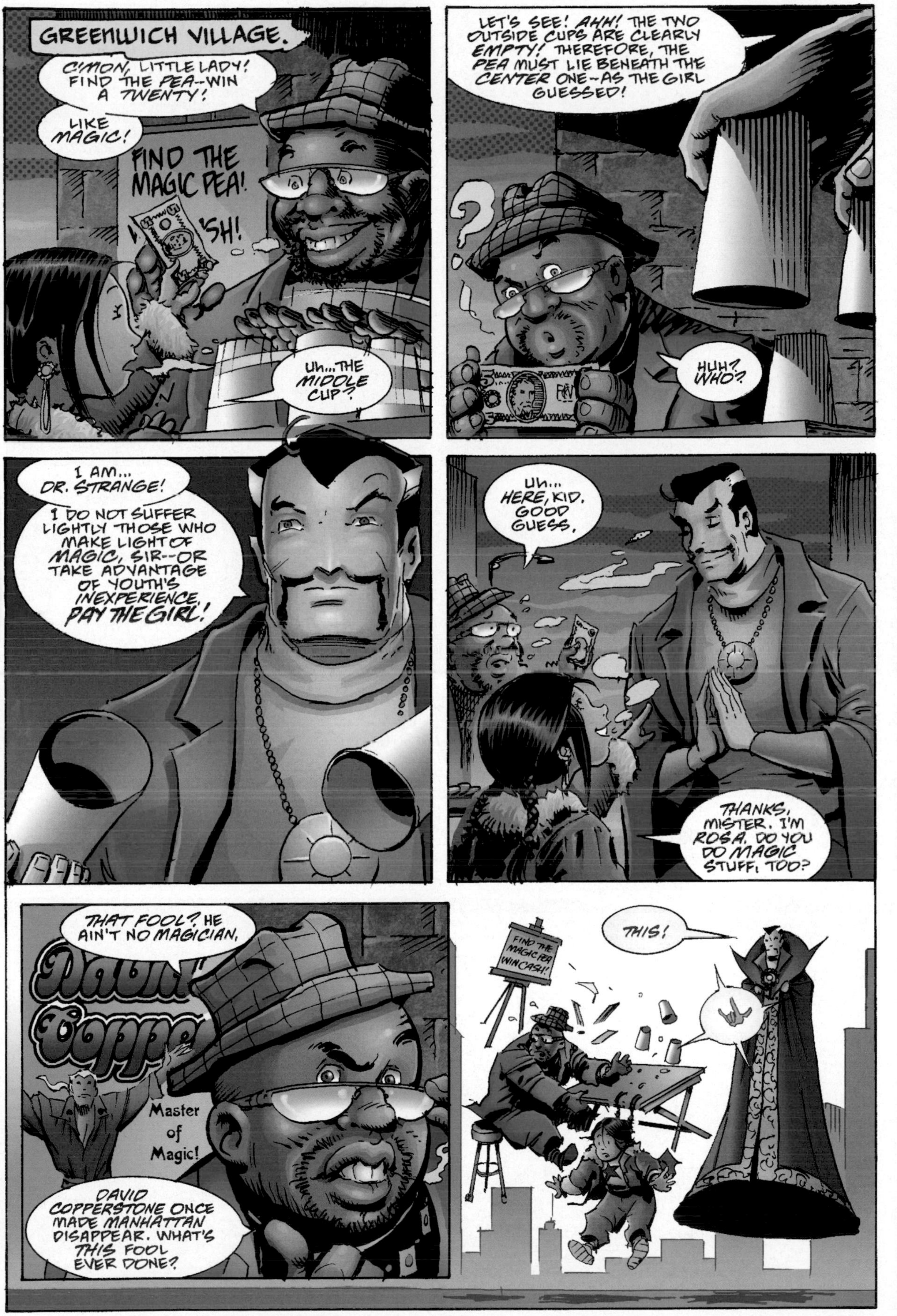
GREENWICH VILLAGE.
C'MON, LITTLE LADY! FIND THE PEA--WIN A TWENTY!
LIKE MAGIC!
FIND THE MAGIC PEA!
SH!
UH...THE MIDDLE CUP?
LET'S SEE! AHH! THE TWO OUTSIDE CUPS ARE CLEARLY EMPTY! THEREFORE, THE PEA MUST LIE BENEATH THE CENTER ONE--AS THE GIRL GUESSED!
?
HUH? WHO?
I AM... DR. STRANGE!
I DO NOT SUFFER LIGHTLY THOSE WHO MAKE LIGHT OF MAGIC, SIR--OR TAKE ADVANTAGE OF YOUTH'S INEXPERIENCE. PAY THE GIRL!
UH... HERE, KID. GOOD GUESS.
THANKS, MISTER. I'M ROSA. DO YOU DO MAGIC STUFF, TOO?
THAT FOOL? HE AIN'T NO MAGICIAN.
Master of Magic!
DAVID COPPERSTONE ONCE MADE MANHATTAN DISAPPEAR. WHAT'S THIS FOOL EVER DONE?
THIS!
FIND THE MAGIC PEA WIN CASH!

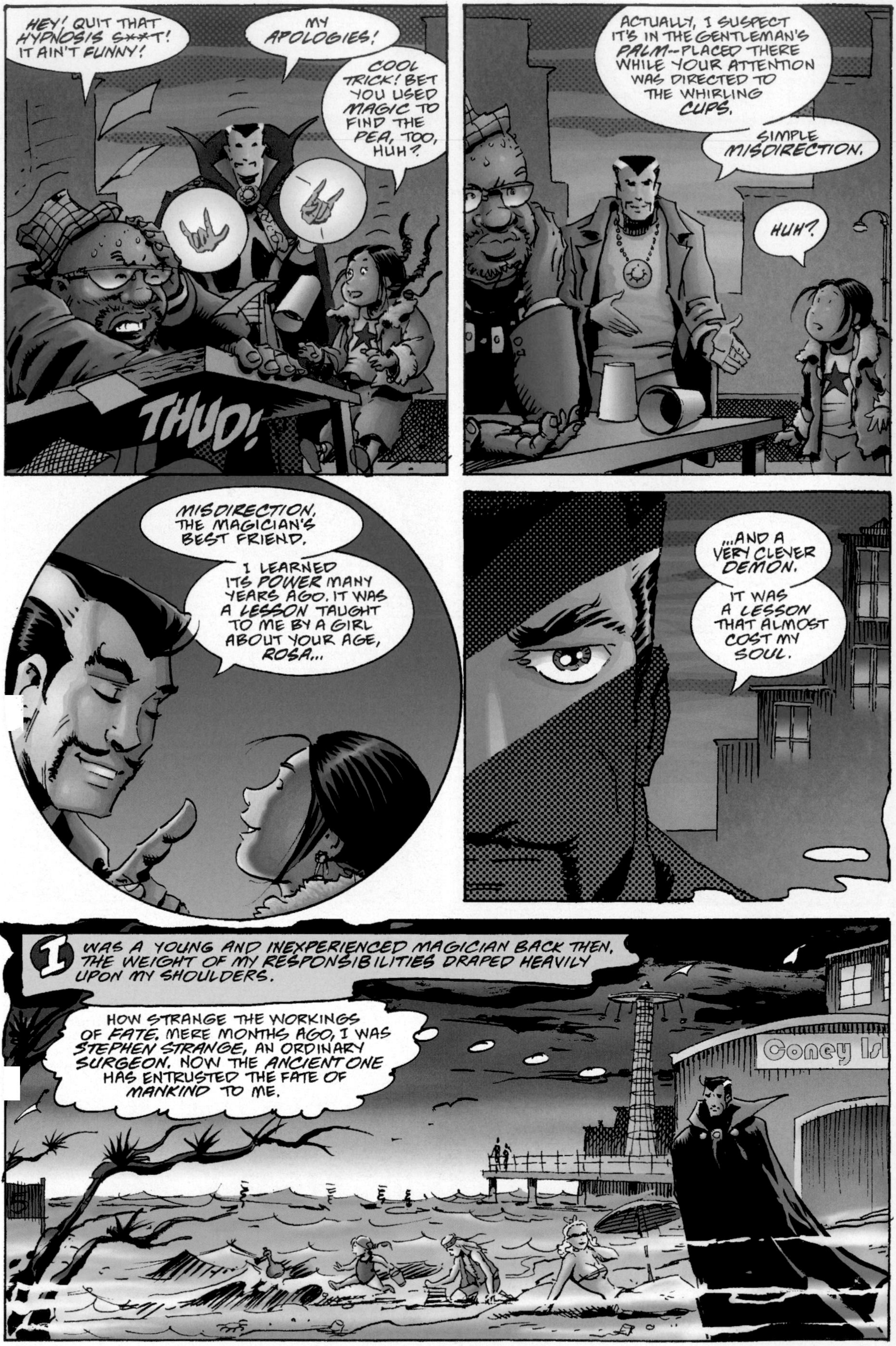
HEY! QUIT THAT HYPNOSIS S**T! IT AIN'T FUNNY!
MY APOLOGIES!
COOL TRICK! BET YOU USED MAGIC TO FIND THE PEA, TOO, HUH?
THUD!
ACTUALLY, I SUSPECT IT'S IN THE GENTLEMAN'S PALM--PLACED THERE WHILE YOUR ATTENTION WAS DIRECTED TO THE WHIRLING CUPS.
SIMPLE MISDIRECTION.
HUH?
MISDIRECTION, THE MAGICIAN'S BEST FRIEND.
I LEARNED ITS POWER MANY YEARS AGO. IT WAS A LESSON TAUGHT TO ME BY A GIRL ABOUT YOUR AGE, ROSA...
...AND A VERY CLEVER DEMON.
IT WAS A LESSON THAT ALMOST COST MY SOUL.
I WAS A YOUNG AND INEXPERIENCED MAGICIAN BACK THEN, THE WEIGHT OF MY RESPONSIBILITIES DRAPED HEAVILY UPON MY SHOULDERS.
HOW STRANGE THE WORKINGS OF FATE. MERE MONTHS AGO, I WAS STEPHEN STRANGE, AN ORDINARY SURGEON. NOW THE ANCIENT ONE HAS ENTRUSTED THE FATE OF MANKIND TO ME.
Coney Isl

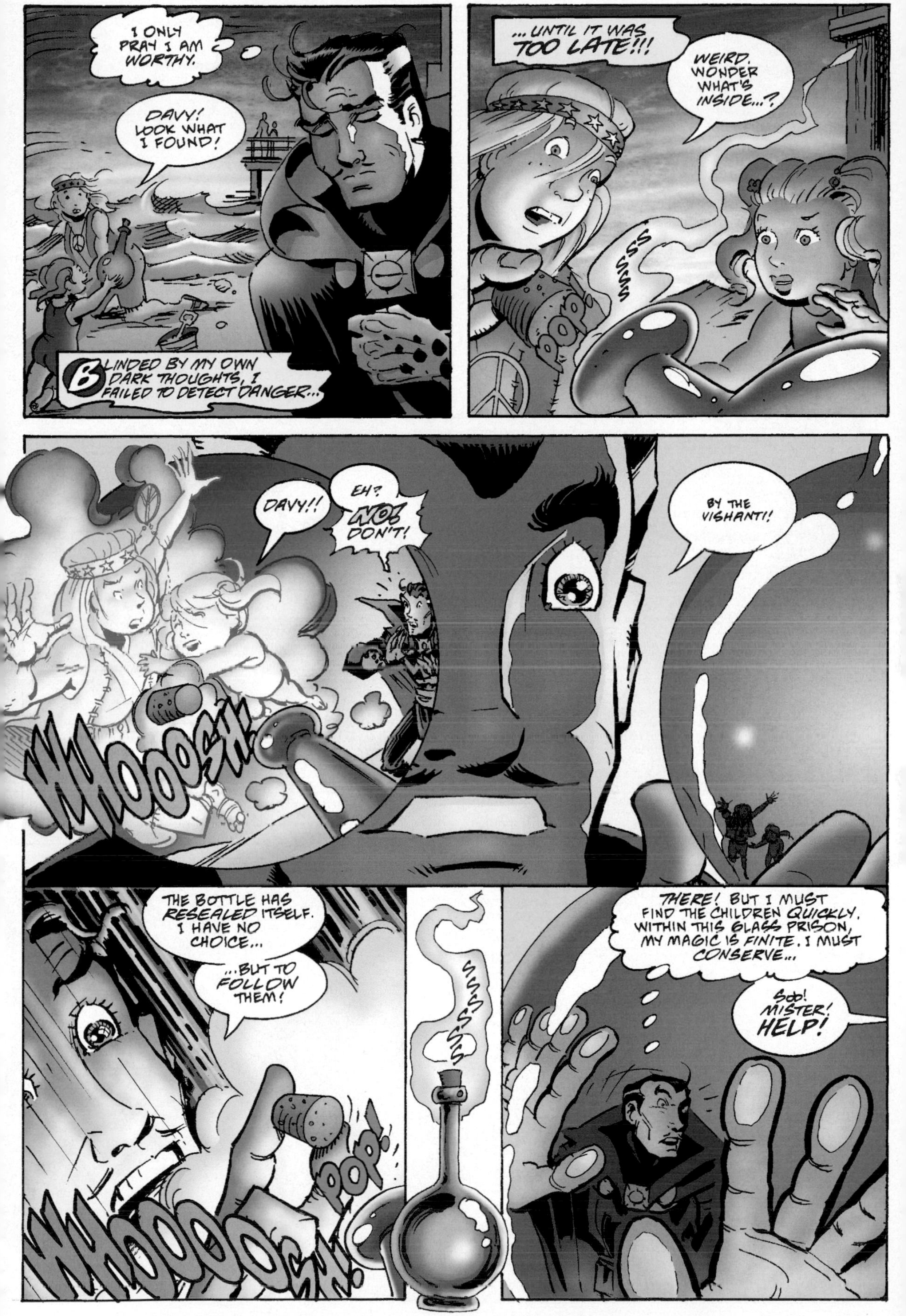
I ONLY PRAY I AM WORTHY.
DAVY! LOOK WHAT I FOUND!
BLINDED BY MY OWN DARK THOUGHTS, I FAILED TO DETECT DANGER...
...UNTIL IT WAS TOO LATE!!!
WEIRD. WONDER WHAT'S INSIDE...?
SSSSSS
POP!
DAVY!!
EH? NO! DON'T!
BY THE VISHANTI!
WHOOOSH!
THE BOTTLE HAS RESEALED ITSELF. I HAVE NO CHOICE...
...BUT TO FOLLOW THEM!
POP!
WHOOOOSH!
SSSSSS
THERE! BUT I MUST FIND THE CHILDREN QUICKLY. WITHIN THIS GLASS PRISON, MY MAGIC IS FINITE. I MUST CONSERVE...
Sob! MISTER! HELP!

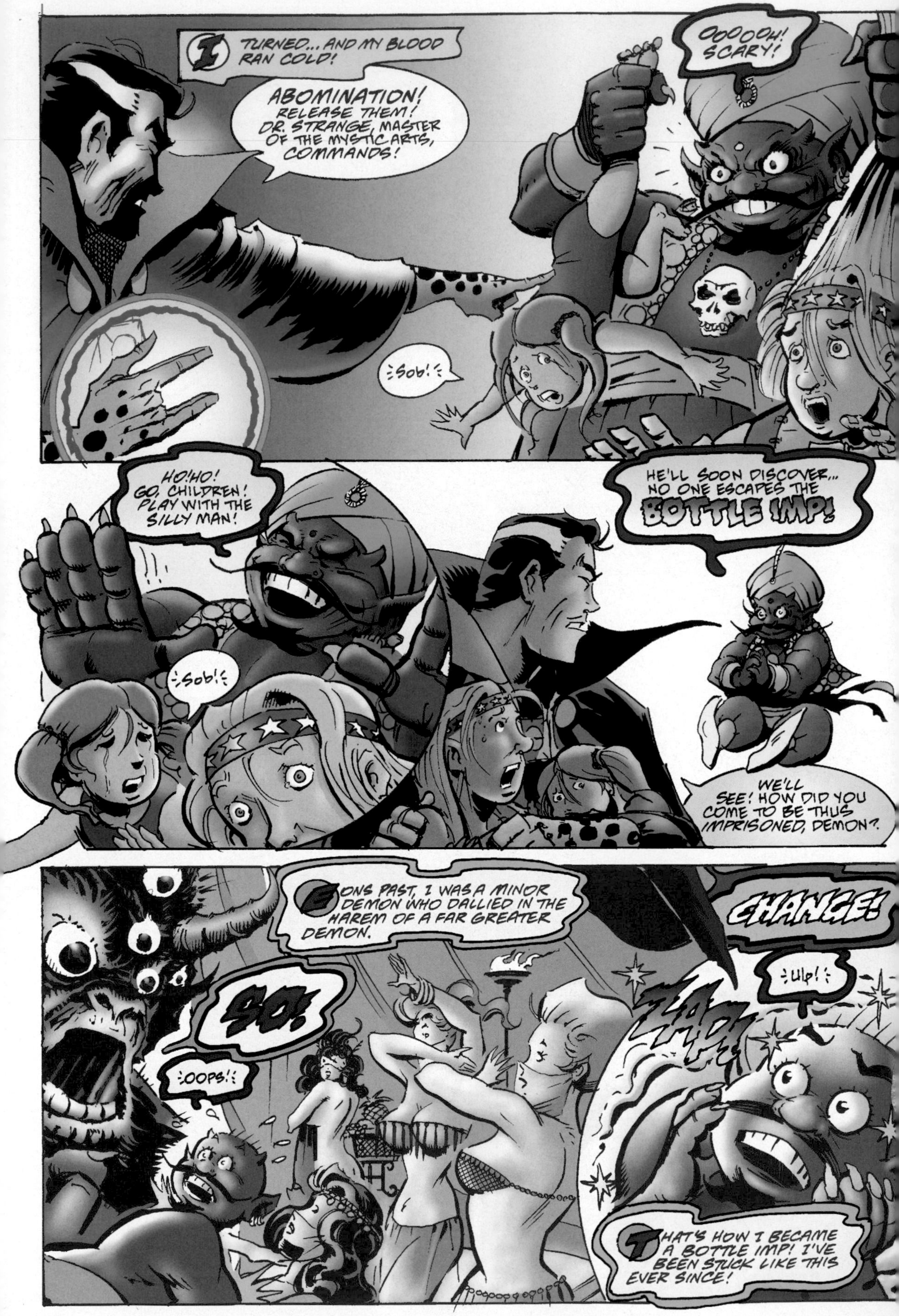
I TURNED... AND MY BLOOD RAN COLD!
ABOMINATION! RELEASE THEM! DR. STRANGE, MASTER OF THE MYSTIC ARTS, COMMANDS!
OOOOOOH! SCARY!
SOB!
HO!HO! GO, CHILDREN! PLAY WITH THE SILLY MAN!
HE'LL SOON DISCOVER... NO ONE ESCAPES THE BOTTLE IMP!
SOB!
WE'LL SEE! HOW DID YOU COME TO BE THUS IMPRISONED, DEMON?
EONS PAST, I WAS A MINOR DEMON WHO DALLIED IN THE HAREM OF A FAR GREATER DEMON.
SO!
OOPS!
CHANGE!
ULP!
ZAP!
THAT'S HOW I BECAME A BOTTLE IMP! I'VE BEEN STUCK LIKE THIS EVER SINCE!

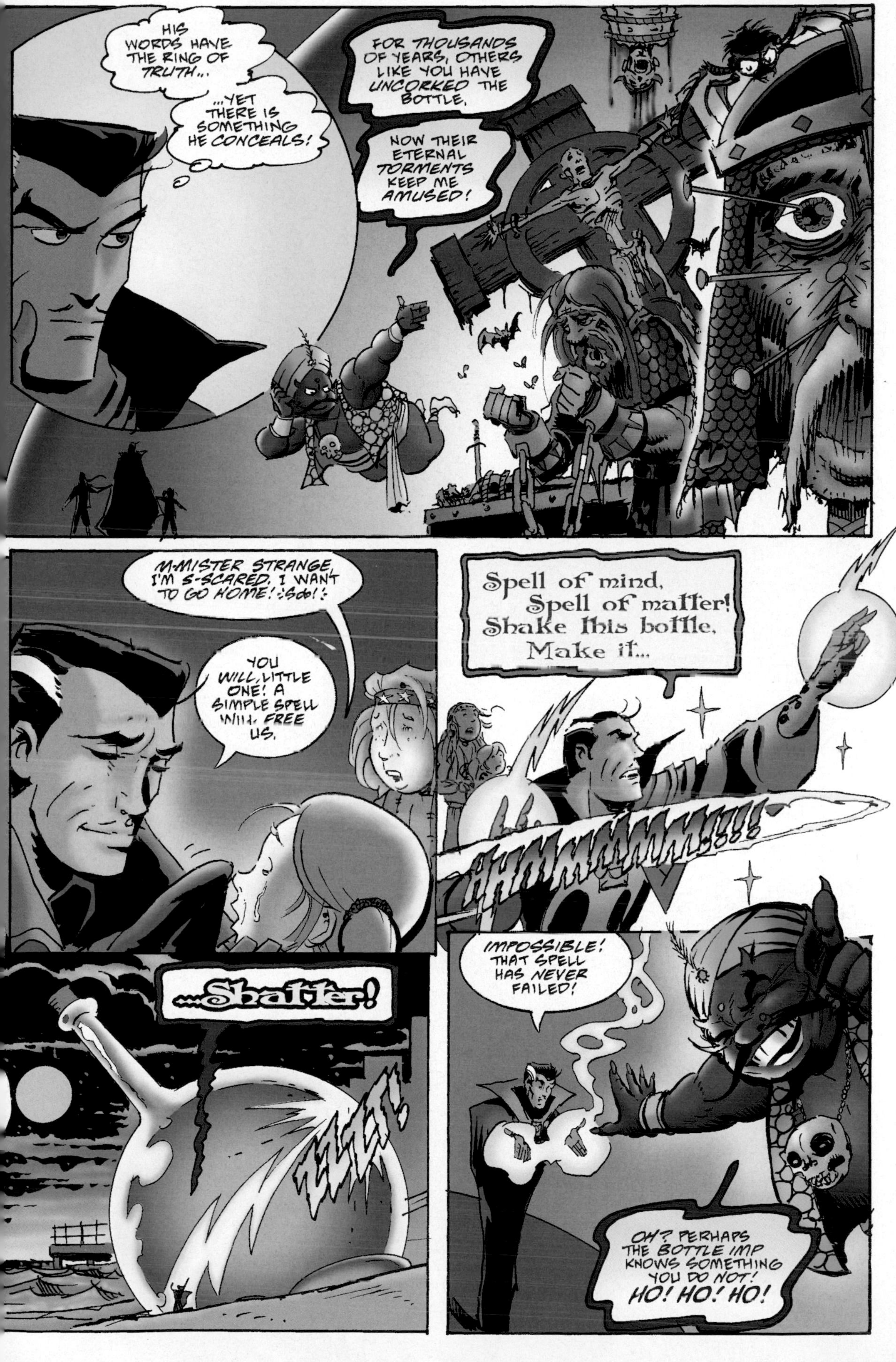
HIS WORDS HAVE THE RING OF TRUTH...
...YET THERE IS SOMETHING HE CONCEALS!
FOR THOUSANDS OF YEARS, OTHERS LIKE YOU HAVE UNCORKED THE BOTTLE.
NOW THEIR ETERNAL TORMENTS KEEP ME AMUSED!
M-MISTER STRANGE, I'M S-SCARED. I WANT TO GO HOME! :Sob!:
YOU WILL, LITTLE ONE! A SIMPLE SPELL WILL FREE US.
Spell of mind, Spell of matter! Shake this bottle, Make it...
...Shatter!
IMPOSSIBLE! THAT SPELL HAS NEVER FAILED!
OH? PERHAPS THE BOTTLE IMP KNOWS SOMETHING YOU DO NOT! HO! HO! HO!

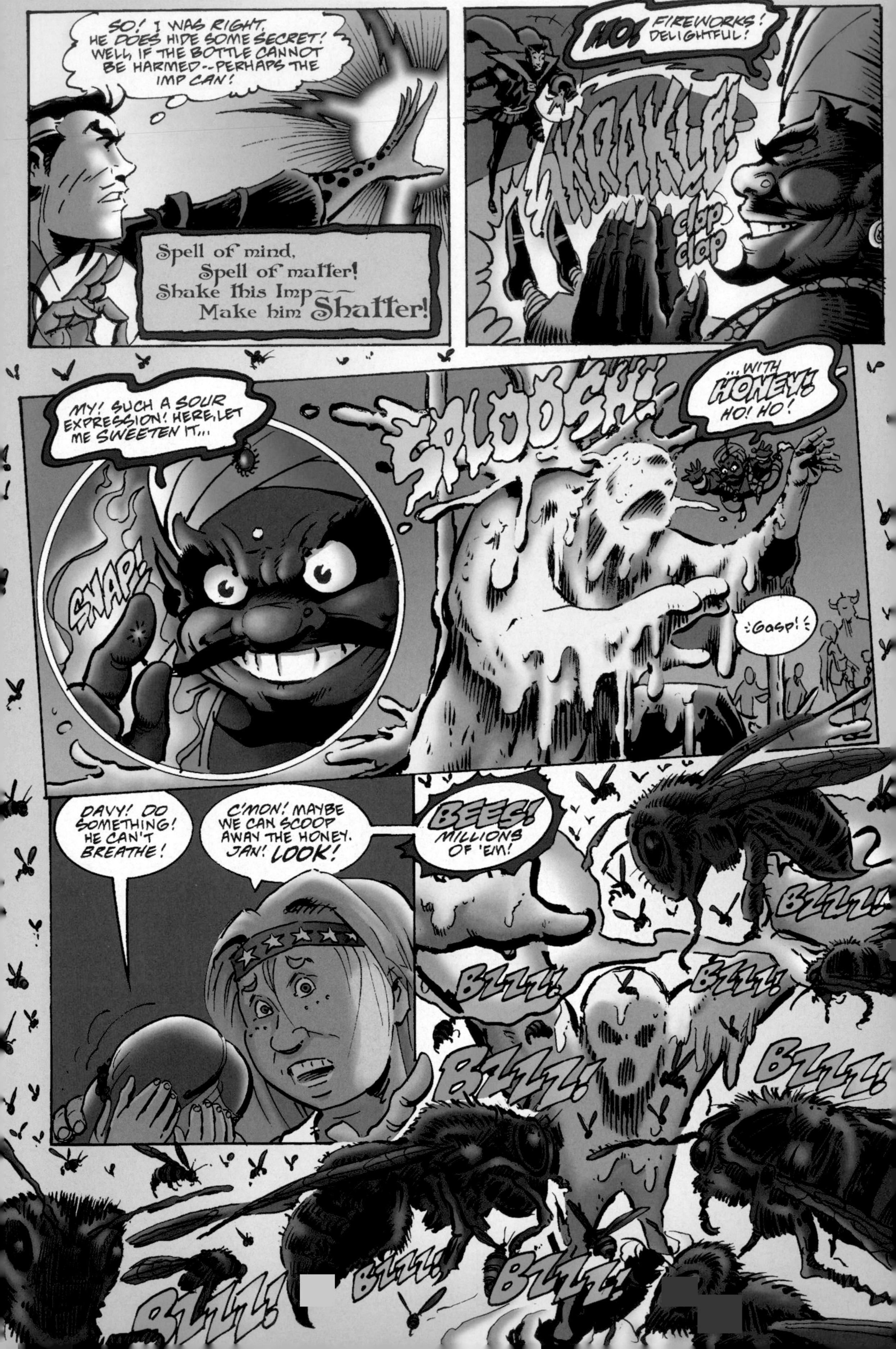
SO! I WAS RIGHT. HE DOES HIDE SOME SECRET! WELL, IF THE BOTTLE CANNOT BE HARMED--PERHAPS THE IMP CAN!
Spell of mind, Spell of matter! Shake this Imp~~ Make him Shatter!
HO! FIREWORKS! DELIGHTFUL!
KRAKLE!
clap clap
MY! SUCH A SOUR EXPRESSION! HERE, LET ME SWEETEN IT...
SNAP!
SPLOOSH!
...WITH HONEY! HO! HO!
Gasp!
DAVY! DO SOMETHING! HE CAN'T BREATHE!
C'MON! MAYBE WE CAN SCOOP AWAY THE HONEY. JAN! LOOK!
BEES! MILLIONS OF 'EM!
BZZZ!
BZZZ!
BZZZ!
BZZZ!
BZZZ!
BZZZ!
BZZZ!
BZZZ!

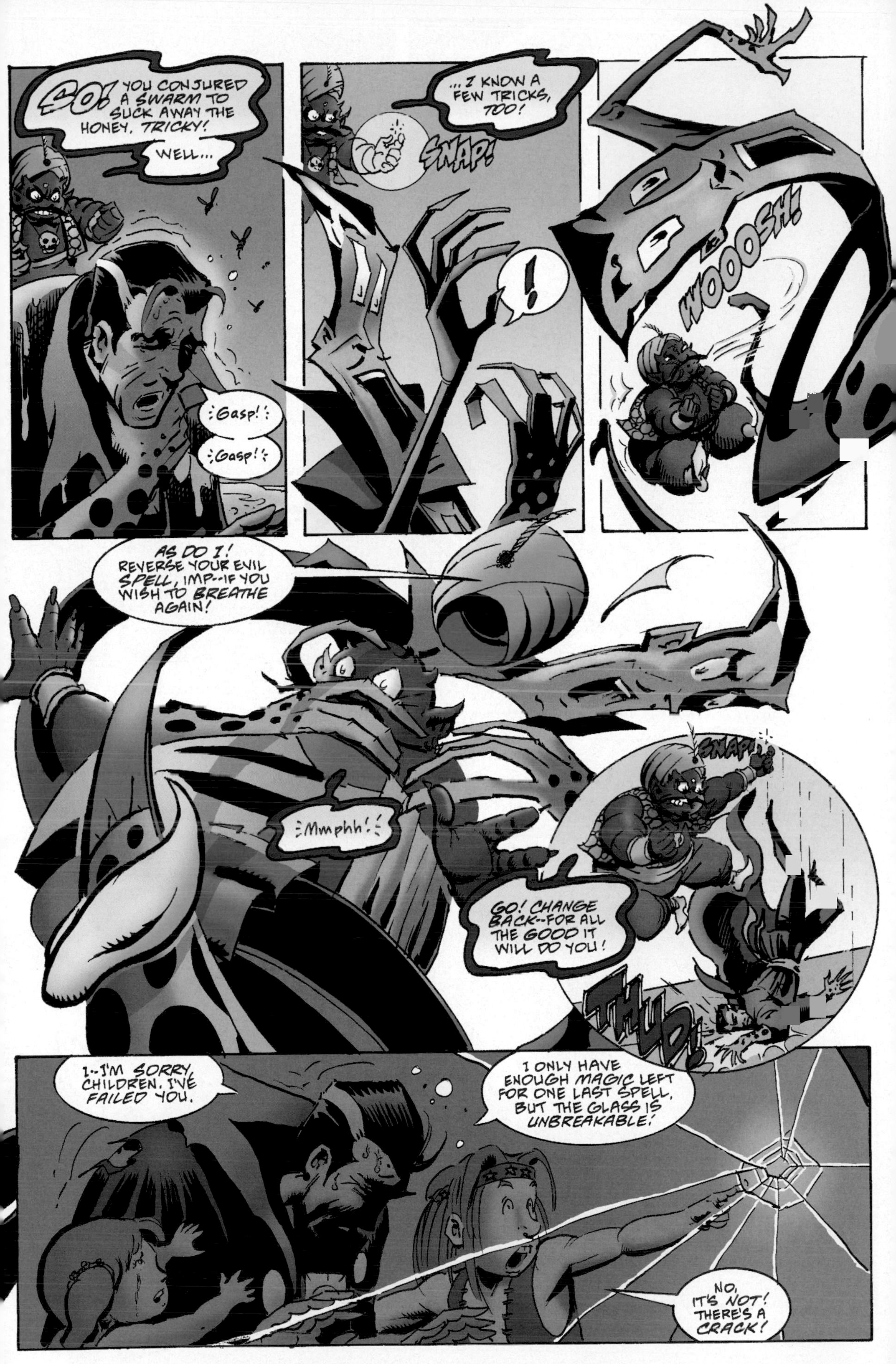
SO! YOU CONJURED A SWARM TO SUCK AWAY THE HONEY, TRICKY!
WELL...
...I KNOW A FEW TRICKS, TOO!
SNAP!
!
WOOOSH!
Gasp!
Gasp!
AS DO I! REVERSE YOUR EVIL SPELL, IMP--IF YOU WISH TO BREATHE AGAIN!
Mmphh!
SNAP!
GO! CHANGE BACK--FOR ALL THE GOOD IT WILL DO YOU!
THUD!
I--I'M SORRY, CHILDREN. I'VE FAILED YOU.
I ONLY HAVE ENOUGH MAGIC LEFT FOR ONE LAST SPELL, BUT THE GLASS IS UNBREAKABLE!
NO, IT'S NOT! THERE'S A CRACK!

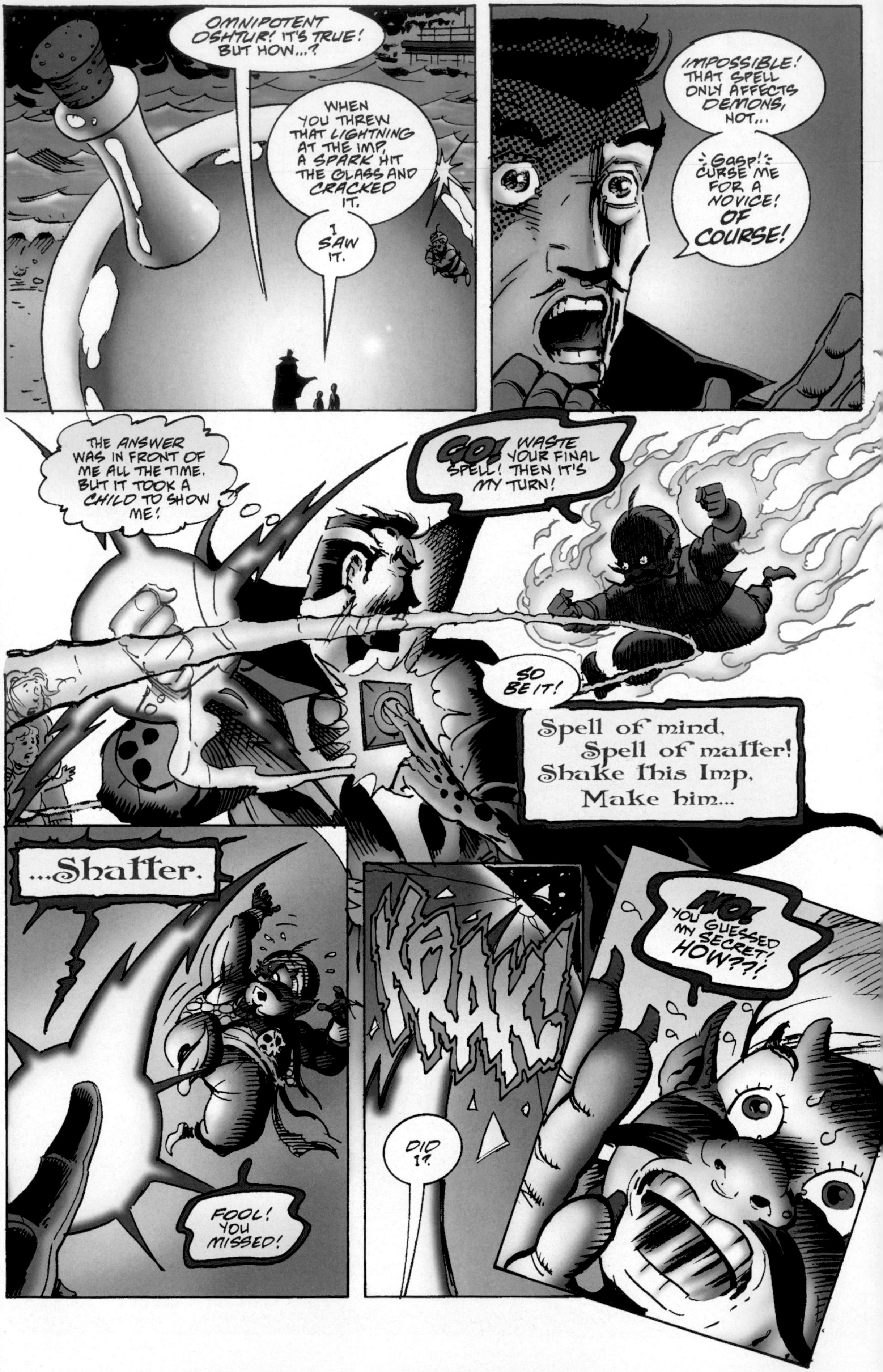
OMNIPOTENT OSHTUR! IT'S TRUE! BUT HOW...?
WHEN YOU THREW THAT LIGHTNING AT THE IMP, A SPARK HIT THE GLASS AND CRACKED IT.
I SAW IT.
IMPOSSIBLE! THAT SPELL ONLY AFFECTS DEMONS, NOT...
Gasp! CURSE ME FOR A NOVICE! OF COURSE!
THE ANSWER WAS IN FRONT OF ME ALL THE TIME. BUT IT TOOK A CHILD TO SHOW ME!
GO! WASTE YOUR FINAL SPELL! THEN IT'S MY TURN!
SO BE IT!
Spell of mind, Spell of matter! Shake this Imp, Make him...
...Shatter.
FOOL! YOU MISSED!
KRAKK
DID I?
NO! YOU GUESSED MY SECRET! HOW??!

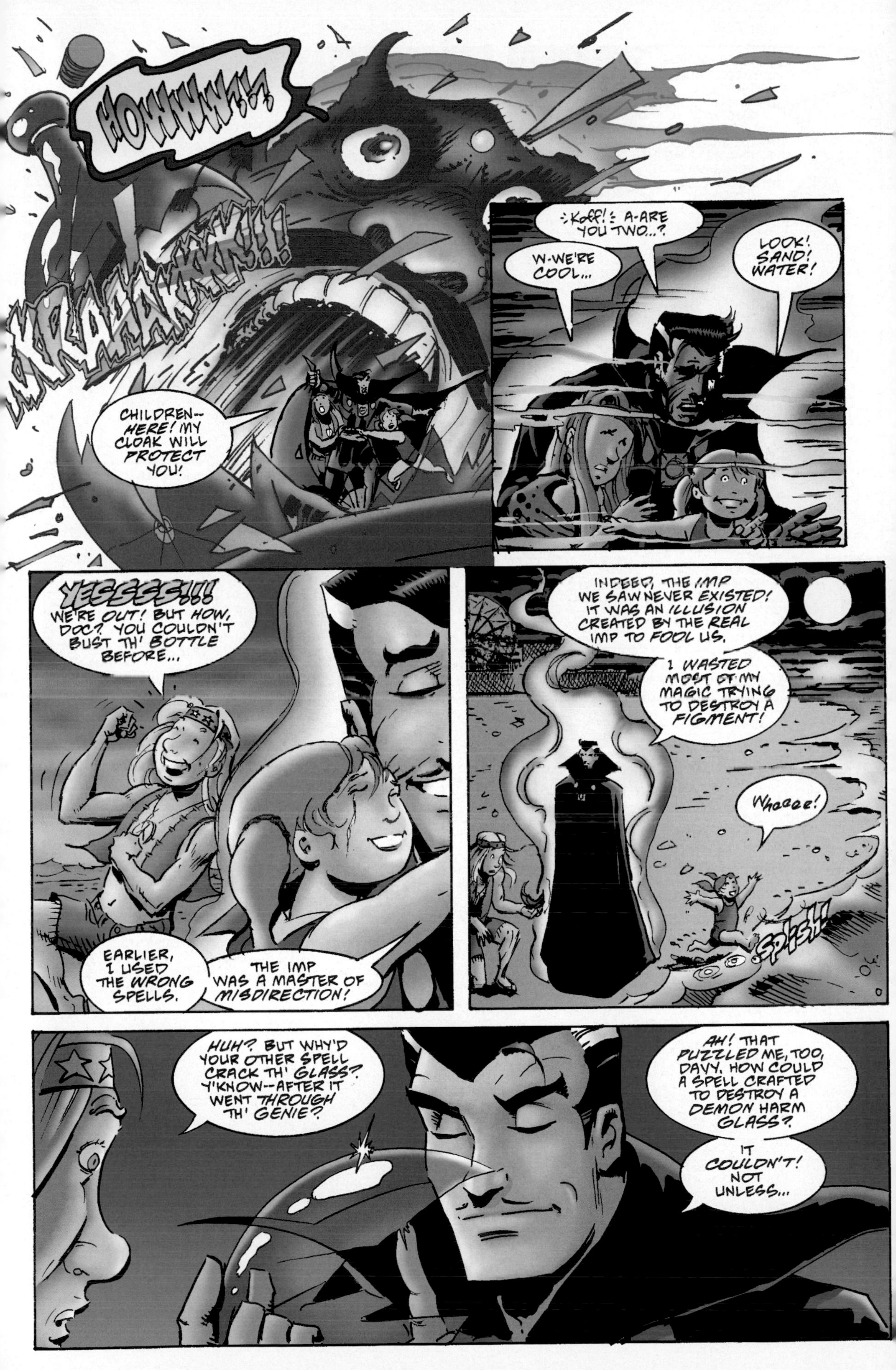
HOWWWW!!
KRAAKKKK!!
CHILDREN-- HERE! MY CLOAK WILL PROTECT YOU!
KOFF! A-ARE YOU TWO...?
W-WE'RE COOL...
LOOK! SAND! WATER!
YESSSSS!!! WE'RE OUT! BUT HOW, DOC? YOU COULDN'T BUST TH' BOTTLE BEFORE...
EARLIER, I USED THE WRONG SPELLS.
THE IMP WAS A MASTER OF MISDIRECTION!
INDEED, THE IMP WE SAW NEVER EXISTED! IT WAS AN ILLUSION CREATED BY THE REAL IMP TO FOOL US.
I WASTED MOST OF MY MAGIC TRYING TO DESTROY A FIGMENT!
Wheeee!
SPLASH!
HUH? BUT WHY'D YOUR OTHER SPELL CRACK TH' GLASS? Y'KNOW--AFTER IT WENT THROUGH TH' GENIE?
AH! THAT PUZZLED ME, TOO, DAVY. HOW COULD A SPELL CRAFTED TO DESTROY A DEMON HARM GLASS?
IT COULDN'T! NOT UNLESS...

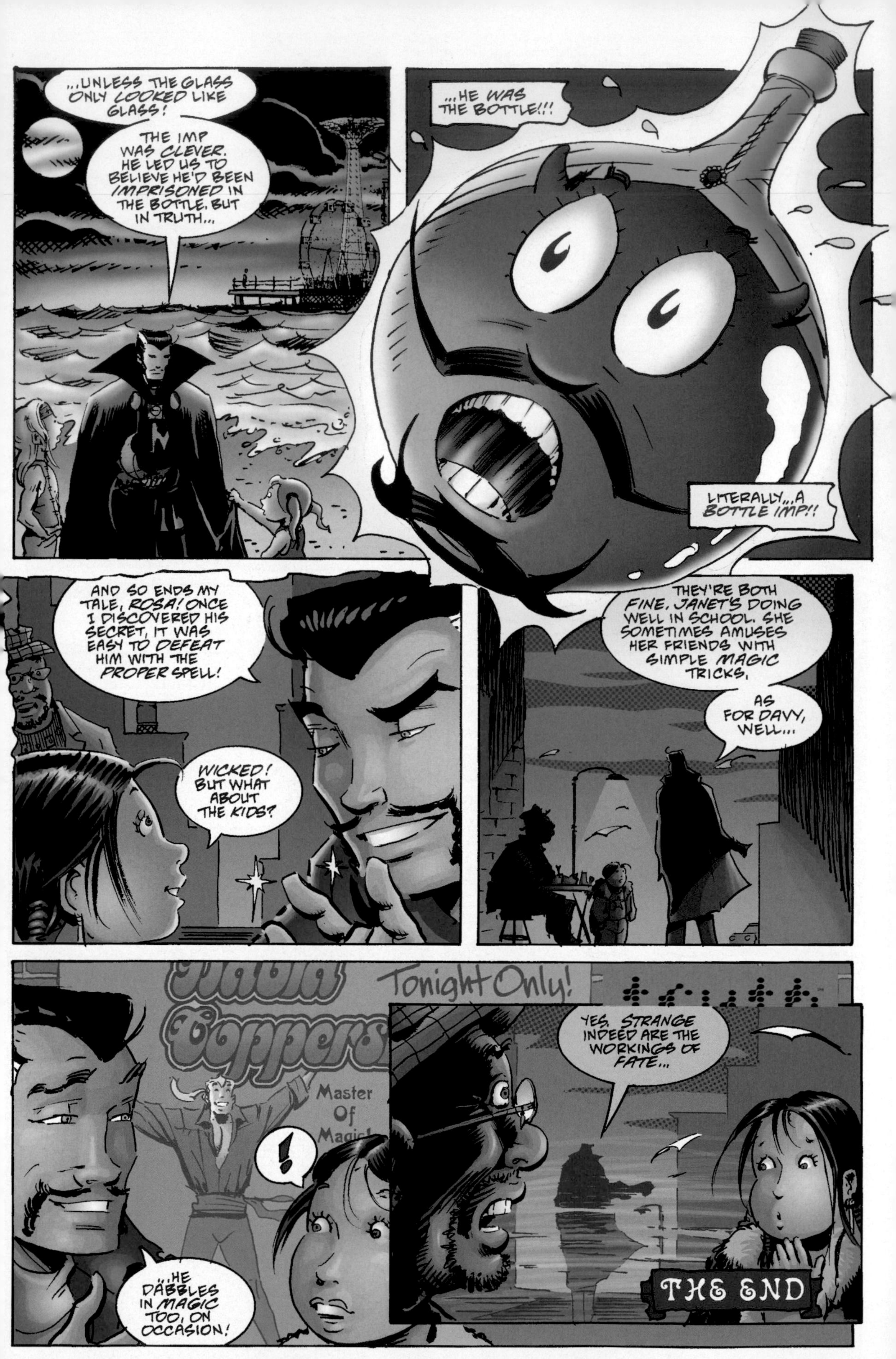
...UNLESS THE GLASS ONLY LOOKED LIKE GLASS!
THE IMP WAS CLEVER. HE LED US TO BELIEVE HE'D BEEN IMPRISONED IN THE BOTTLE. BUT IN TRUTH...
...HE WAS THE BOTTLE!!!
LITERALLY... A BOTTLE IMP!!
AND SO ENDS MY TALE, ROSA! ONCE I DISCOVERED HIS SECRET, IT WAS EASY TO DEFEAT HIM WITH THE PROPER SPELL!
WICKED! BUT WHAT ABOUT THE KIDS?
THEY'RE BOTH FINE. JANET'S DOING WELL IN SCHOOL. SHE SOMETIMES AMUSES HER FRIENDS WITH SIMPLE MAGIC TRICKS.
AS FOR DAVY, WELL...
Tonight Only!
Coppers
Master Of Magic!
!
...HE DABBLES IN MAGIC TOO, ON OCCASION!
YES. STRANGE INDEED ARE THE WORKINGS OF FATE...
THE END

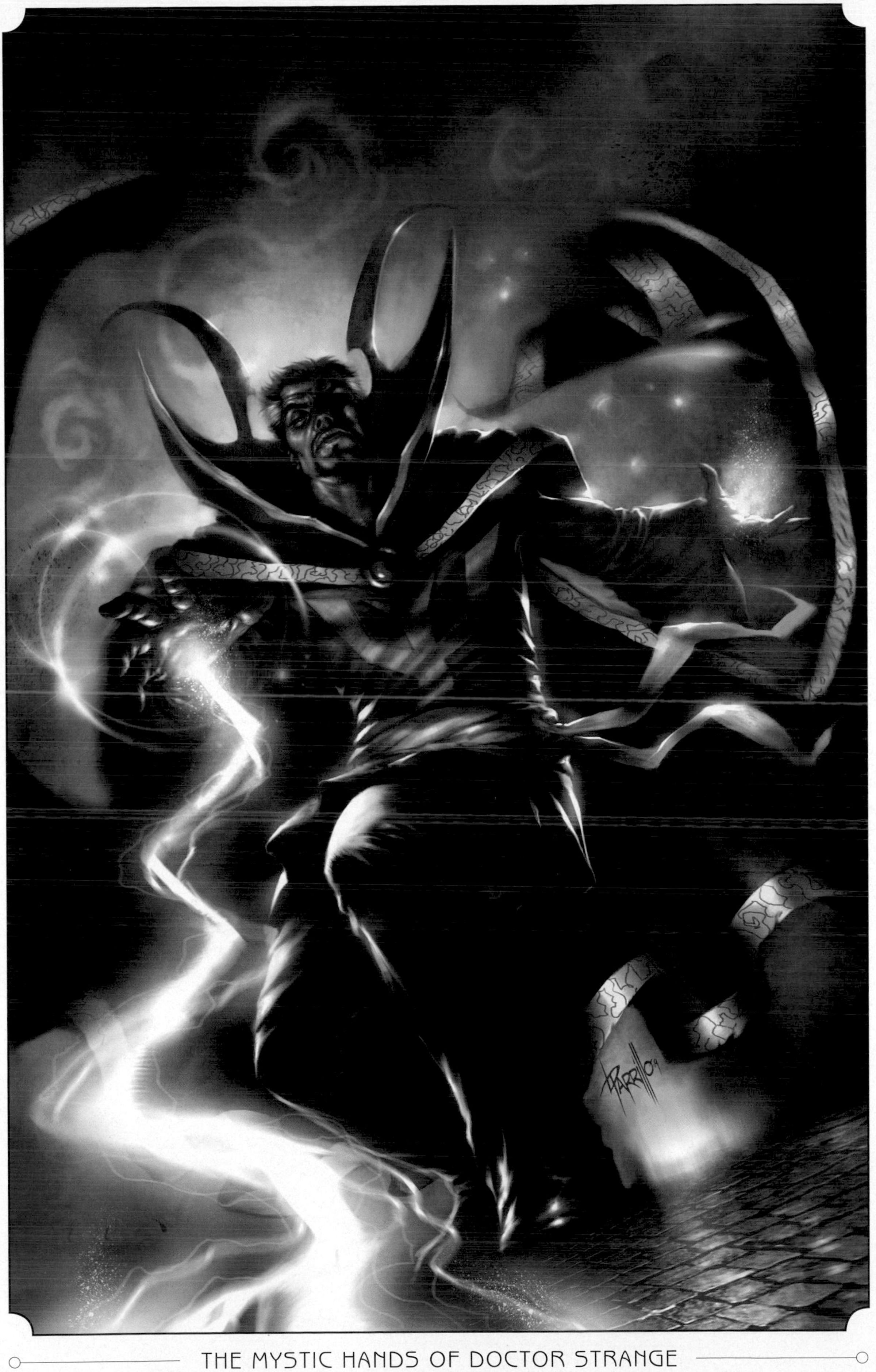

THE MYSTIC HANDS OF DOCTOR STRANGE

Dr. Stephen Strange was the world's finest surgeon, but when a devastating accident caused seemingly irreparable nerve damage to his hands, Strange sought out the healing abilities of the legendary sorcerer known as The Ancient One. The powerful mystic was unable to heal the young and arrogant doctor, but he took Strange on as his student, teaching him humility and the ways of magic. Soon Dr. Strange became Earth's Sorcerer Supreme, Master of the Mystic arts and protector of the world!

THE MYSTIC HANDS OF
DOCTOR STRANGE

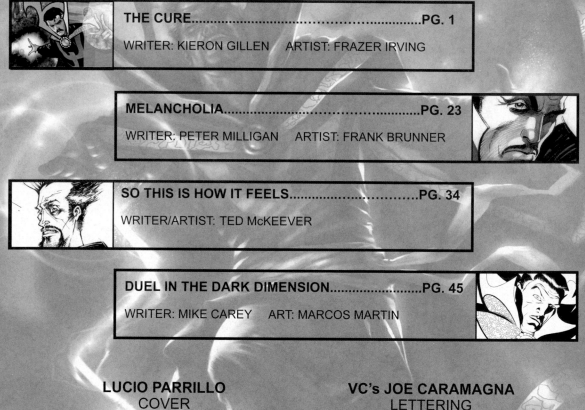

LUCIO PARRILLO
COVER

VC's JOE CARAMAGNA
LETTERING

**JODY LEHEUP &
JOHN BARBER**
EDITORS

JOE QUESADA
EDITOR IN CHIEF

DAN BUCKLEY
PUBLISHER

ALAN FINE
EXEC. PRODUCER

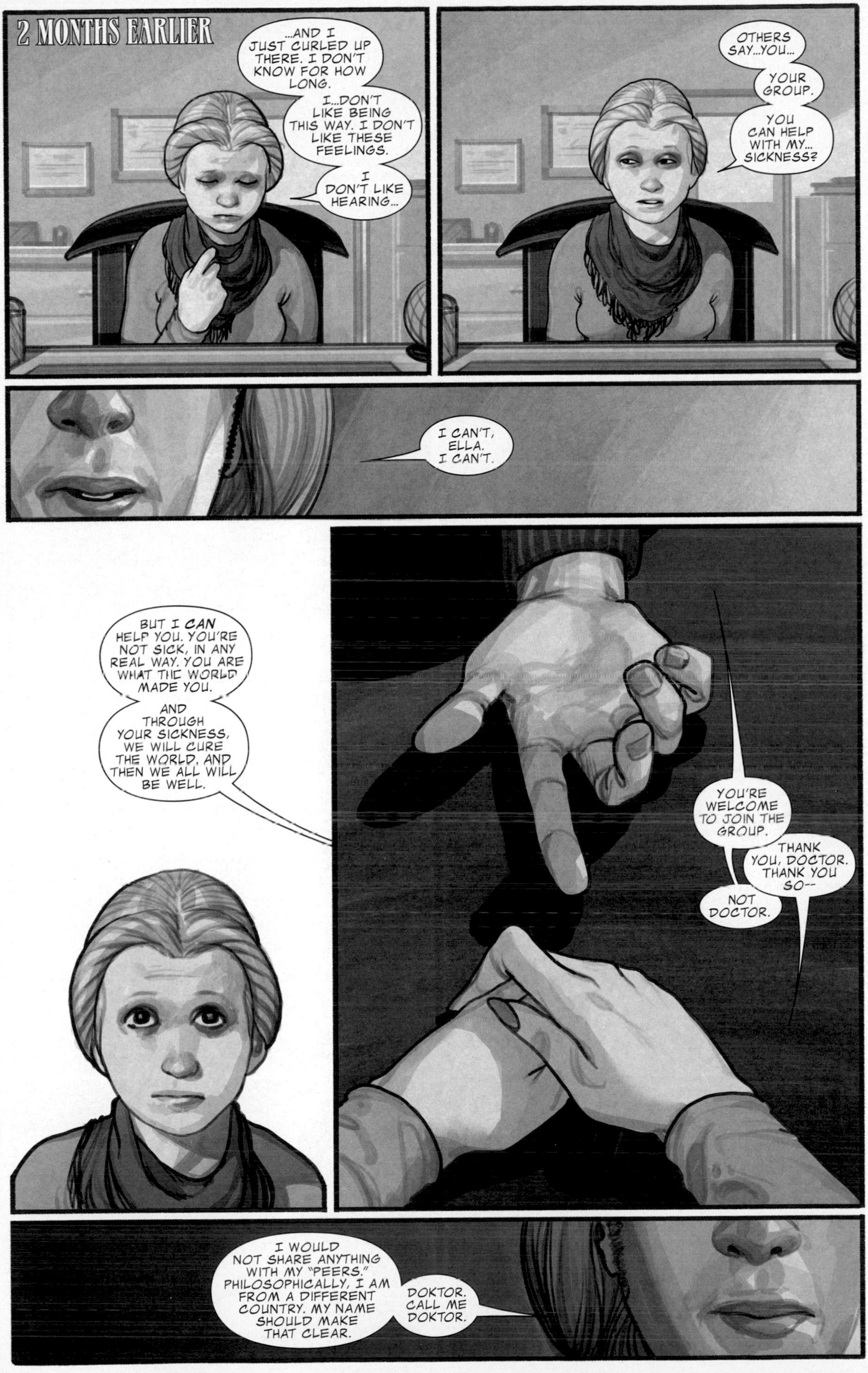
2 MONTHS EARLIER
...AND I JUST CURLED UP THERE. I DON'T KNOW FOR HOW LONG.
I...DON'T LIKE BEING THIS WAY. I DON'T LIKE THESE FEELINGS.
I DON'T LIKE HEARING...
OTHERS SAY...YOU...
YOUR GROUP.
YOU CAN HELP WITH MY... SICKNESS?
I CAN'T, ELLA. I CAN'T.
BUT I CAN HELP YOU. YOU'RE NOT SICK, IN ANY REAL WAY. YOU ARE WHAT THE WORLD MADE YOU.
AND THROUGH YOUR SICKNESS, WE WILL CURE THE WORLD, AND THEN WE ALL WILL BE WELL.
YOU'RE WELCOME TO JOIN THE GROUP.
THANK YOU, DOCTOR. THANK YOU SO--
NOT DOCTOR.
I WOULD NOT SHARE ANYTHING WITH MY "PEERS." PHILOSOPHICALLY, I AM FROM A DIFFERENT COUNTRY. MY NAME SHOULD MAKE THAT CLEAR.
DOKTOR. CALL ME DOKTOR.

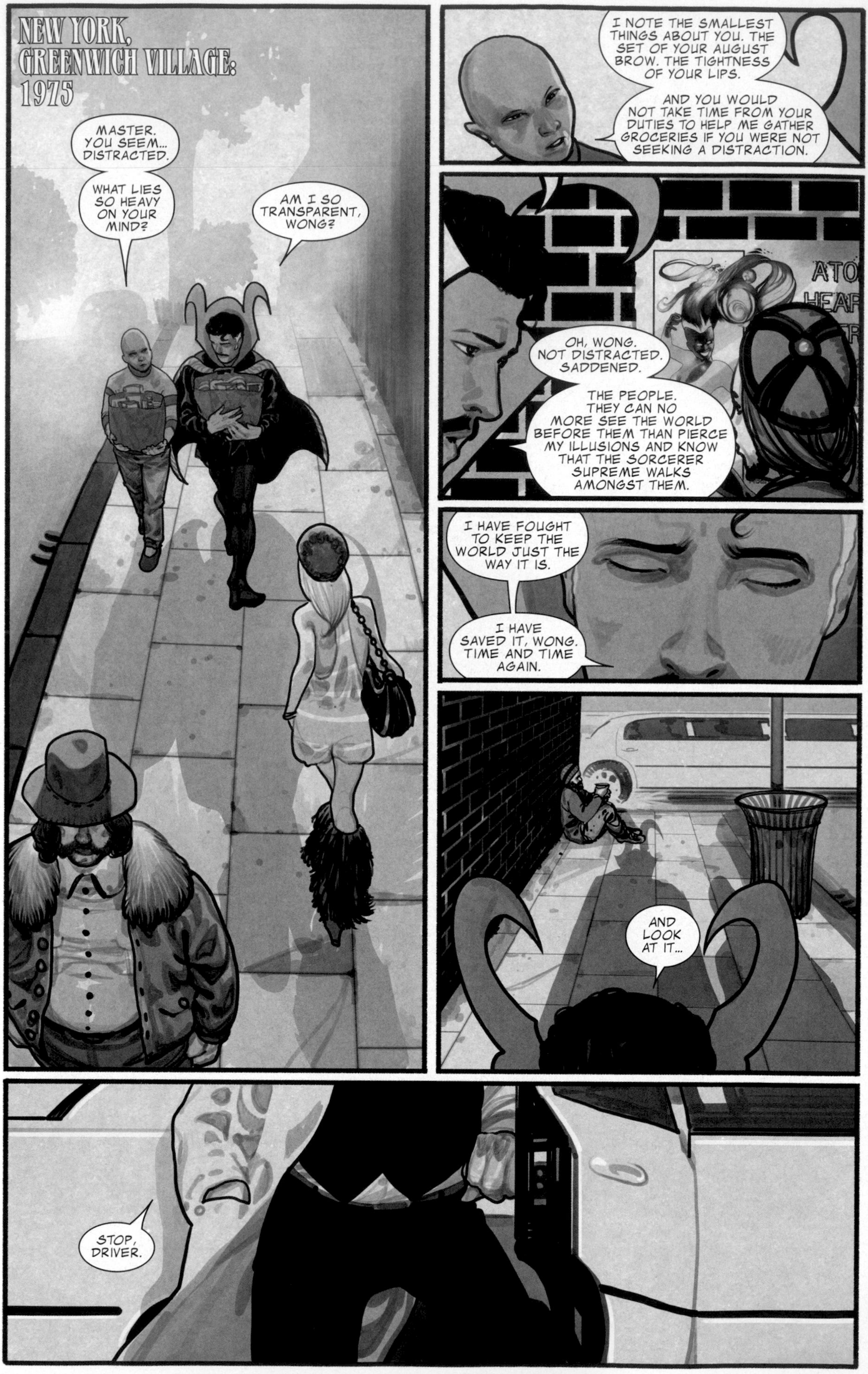
NEW YORK, GREENWICH VILLAGE: 1975
MASTER. YOU SEEM... DISTRACTED.
WHAT LIES SO HEAVY ON YOUR MIND?
AM I SO TRANSPARENT, WONG?
I NOTE THE SMALLEST THINGS ABOUT YOU. THE SET OF YOUR AUGUST BROW. THE TIGHTNESS OF YOUR LIPS.
AND YOU WOULD NOT TAKE TIME FROM YOUR DUTIES TO HELP ME GATHER GROCERIES IF YOU WERE NOT SEEKING A DISTRACTION.
OH, WONG. NOT DISTRACTED. SADDENED.
THE PEOPLE. THEY CAN NO MORE SEE THE WORLD BEFORE THEM THAN PIERCE MY ILLUSIONS AND KNOW THAT THE SORCERER SUPREME WALKS AMONGST THEM.
I HAVE FOUGHT TO KEEP THE WORLD JUST THE WAY IT IS.
I HAVE SAVED IT, WONG. TIME AND TIME AGAIN.
AND LOOK AT IT...
STOP, DRIVER.

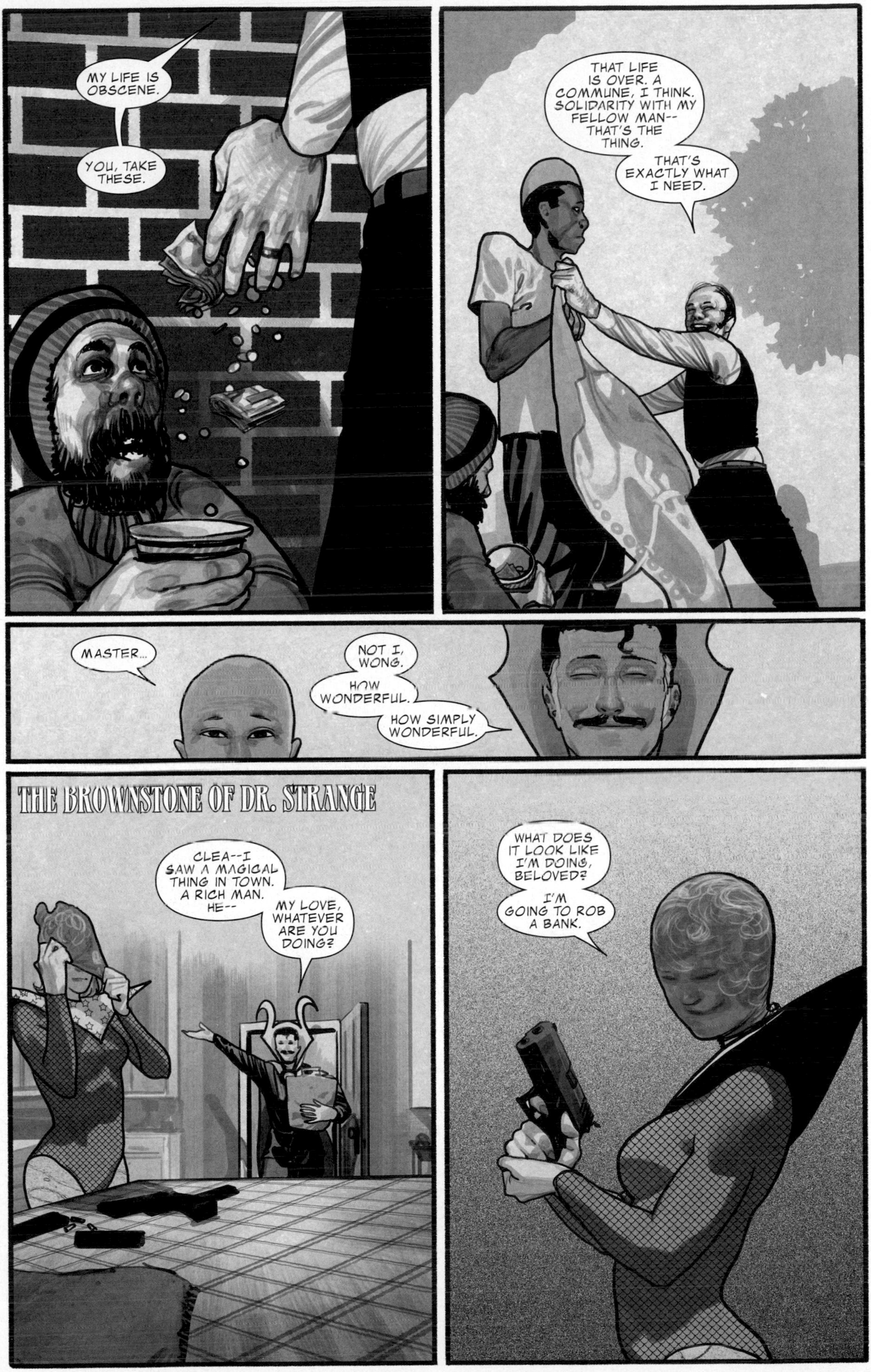
MY LIFE IS OBSCENE.
YOU, TAKE THESE.
THAT LIFE IS OVER. A COMMUNE, I THINK. SOLIDARITY WITH MY FELLOW MAN-- THAT'S THE THING.
THAT'S EXACTLY WHAT I NEED.
MASTER...
NOT I, WONG.
HOW WONDERFUL.
HOW SIMPLY WONDERFUL.
THE BROWNSTONE OF DR. STRANGE
CLEA--I SAW A MAGICAL THING IN TOWN. A RICH MAN. HE--
MY LOVE, WHATEVER ARE YOU DOING?
WHAT DOES IT LOOK LIKE I'M DOING, BELOVED?
I'M GOING TO ROB A BANK.

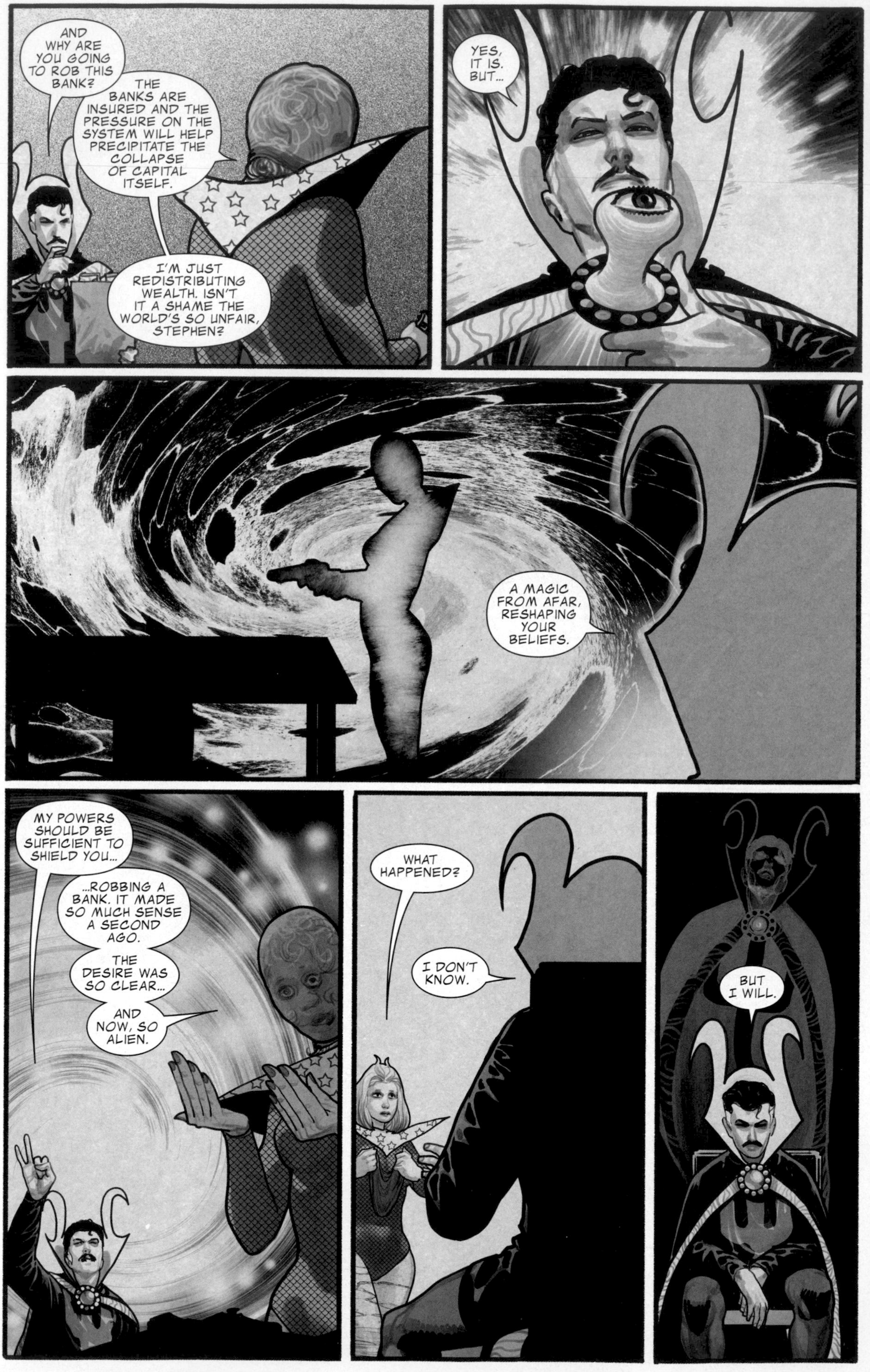
AND WHY ARE YOU GOING TO ROB THIS BANK?
THE BANKS ARE INSURED AND THE PRESSURE ON THE SYSTEM WILL HELP PRECIPITATE THE COLLAPSE OF CAPITAL ITSELF.
I'M JUST REDISTRIBUTING WEALTH. ISN'T IT A SHAME THE WORLD'S SO UNFAIR, STEPHEN?
YES, IT IS. BUT...
A MAGIC FROM AFAR, RESHAPING YOUR BELIEFS.
MY POWERS SHOULD BE SUFFICIENT TO SHIELD YOU...
...ROBBING A BANK. IT MADE SO MUCH SENSE A SECOND AGO.
THE DESIRE WAS SO CLEAR...
AND NOW, SO ALIEN.
WHAT HAPPENED?
I DON'T KNOW.
BUT I WILL.

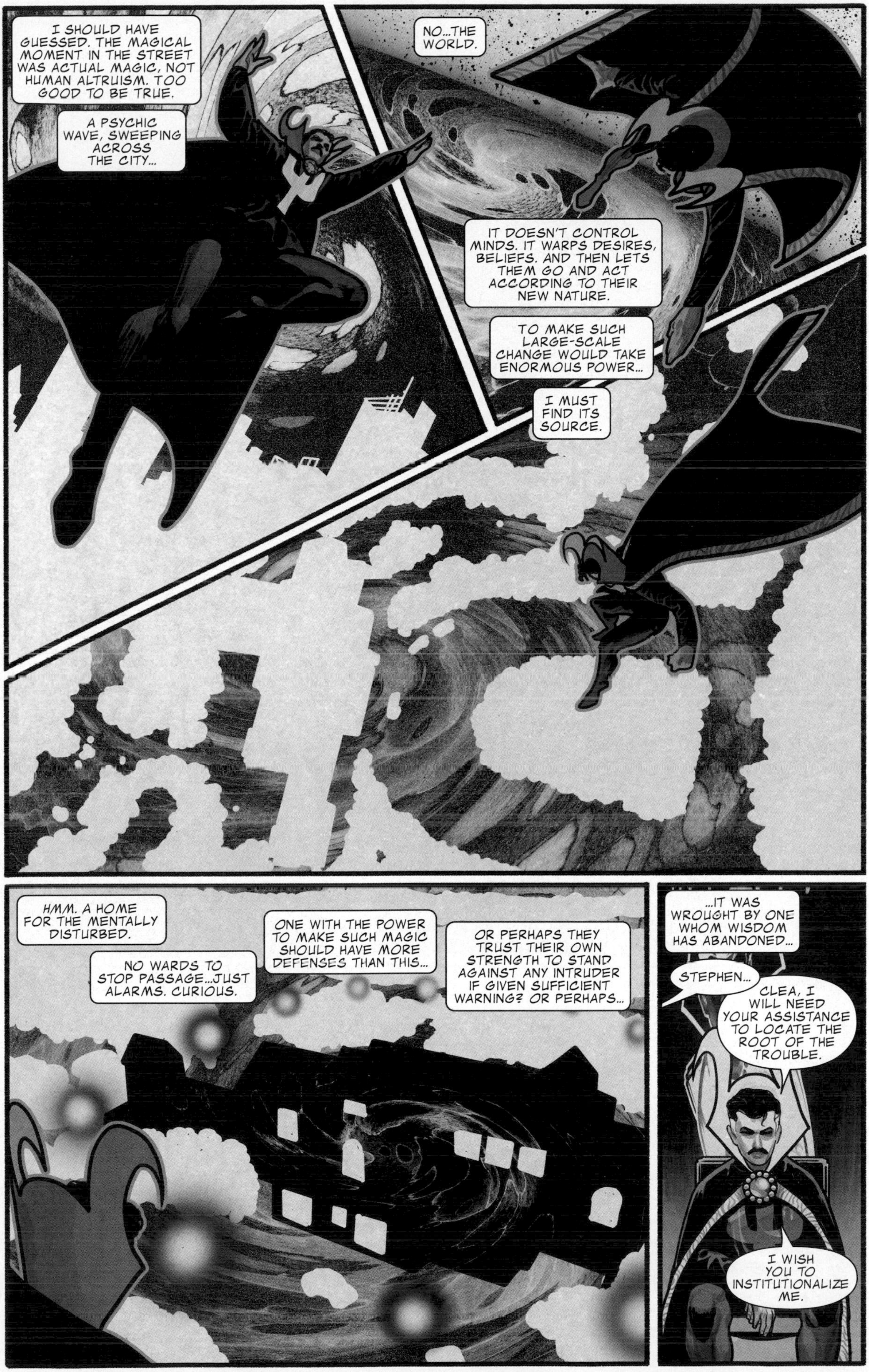
I SHOULD HAVE GUESSED. THE MAGICAL MOMENT IN THE STREET WAS ACTUAL MAGIC, NOT HUMAN ALTRUISM. TOO GOOD TO BE TRUE.
A PSYCHIC WAVE, SWEEPING ACROSS THE CITY...
NO...THE WORLD.
IT DOESN'T CONTROL MINDS. IT WARPS DESIRES, BELIEFS. AND THEN LETS THEM GO AND ACT ACCORDING TO THEIR NEW NATURE.
TO MAKE SUCH LARGE-SCALE CHANGE WOULD TAKE ENORMOUS POWER...
I MUST FIND ITS SOURCE.
HMM. A HOME FOR THE MENTALLY DISTURBED.
NO WARDS TO STOP PASSAGE...JUST ALARMS. CURIOUS.
ONE WITH THE POWER TO MAKE SUCH MAGIC SHOULD HAVE MORE DEFENSES THAN THIS...
OR PERHAPS THEY TRUST THEIR OWN STRENGTH TO STAND AGAINST ANY INTRUDER IF GIVEN SUFFICIENT WARNING? OR PERHAPS...
...IT WAS WROUGHT BY ONE WHOM WISDOM HAS ABANDONED...
STEPHEN...
CLEA, I WILL NEED YOUR ASSISTANCE TO LOCATE THE ROOT OF THE TROUBLE.
I WISH YOU TO INSTITUTIONALIZE ME.

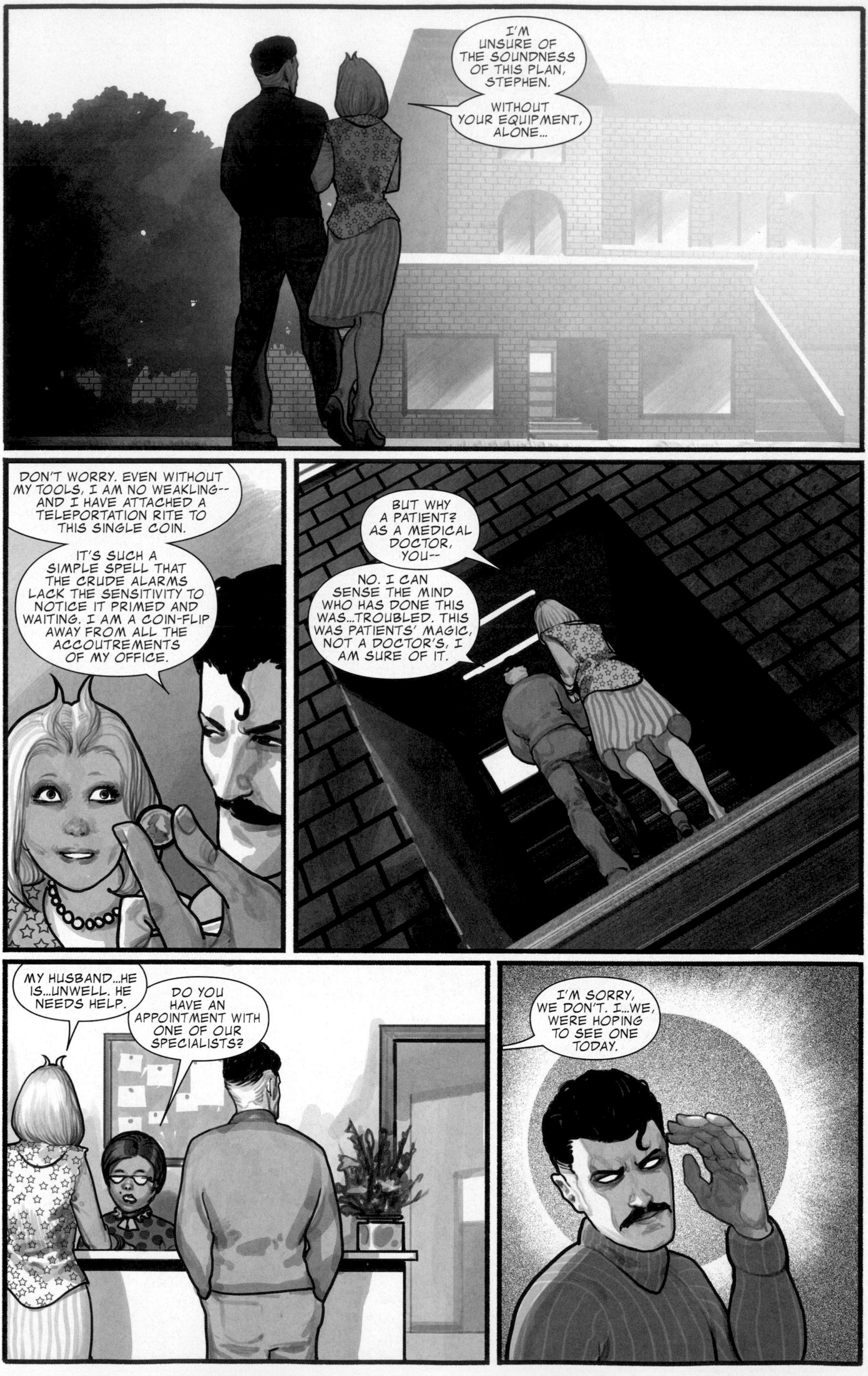
I'M UNSURE OF THE SOUNDNESS OF THIS PLAN, STEPHEN.
WITHOUT YOUR EQUIPMENT, ALONE...
DON'T WORRY. EVEN WITHOUT MY TOOLS, I AM NO WEAKLING-- AND I HAVE ATTACHED A TELEPORTATION RITE TO THIS SINGLE COIN.
IT'S SUCH A SIMPLE SPELL THAT THE CRUDE ALARMS LACK THE SENSITIVITY TO NOTICE IT PRIMED AND WAITING. I AM A COIN-FLIP AWAY FROM ALL THE ACCOUTREMENTS OF MY OFFICE.
BUT WHY A PATIENT? AS A MEDICAL DOCTOR, YOU--
NO. I CAN SENSE THE MIND WHO HAS DONE THIS WAS...TROUBLED. THIS WAS PATIENTS' MAGIC, NOT A DOCTOR'S, I AM SURE OF IT.
MY HUSBAND...HE IS...UNWELL. HE NEEDS HELP.
DO YOU HAVE AN APPOINTMENT WITH ONE OF OUR SPECIALISTS?
I'M SORRY, WE DON'T. I...WE, WERE HOPING TO SEE ONE TODAY.

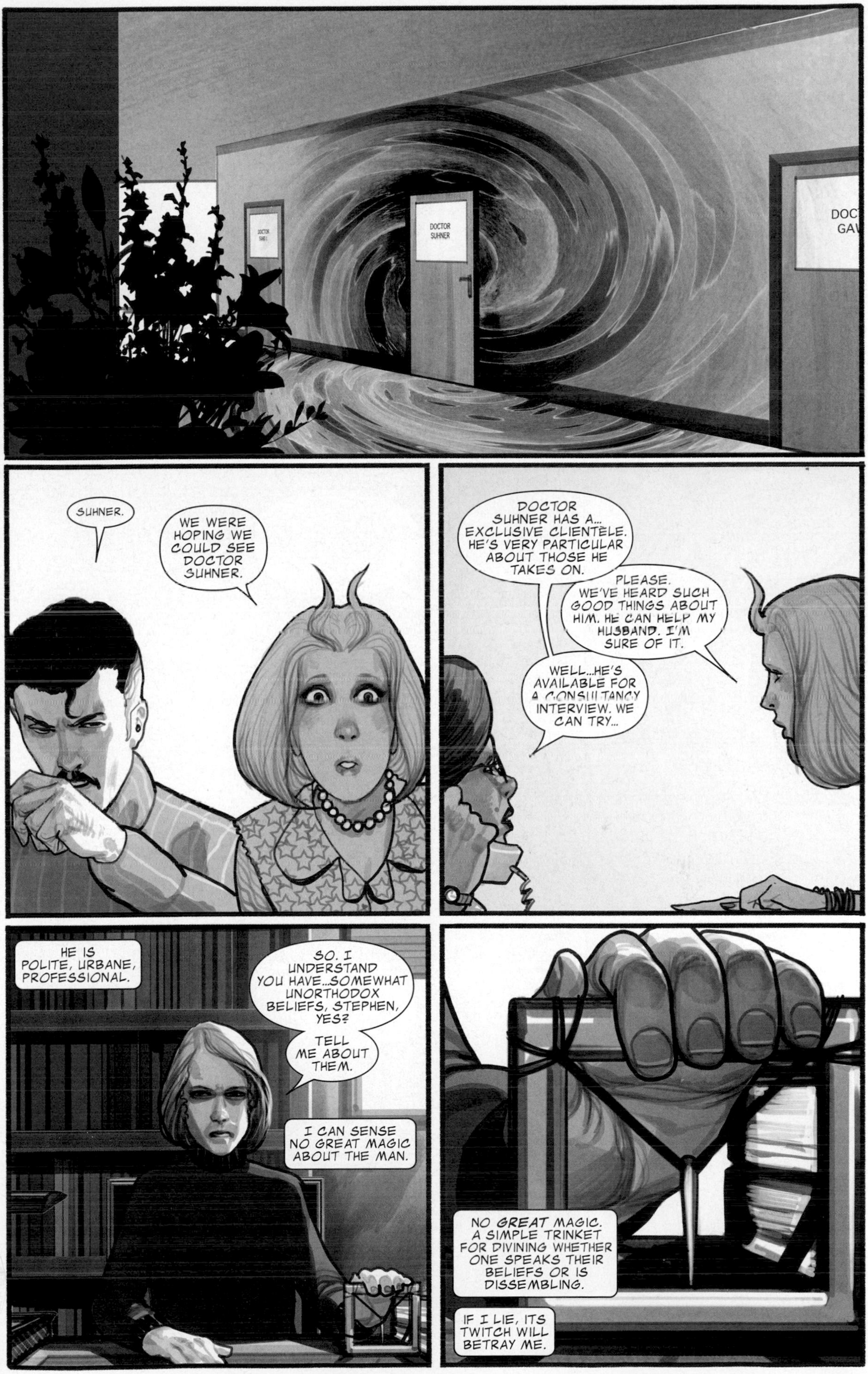
DOCTOR SUHNER
SUHNER.
WE WERE HOPING WE COULD SEE DOCTOR SUHNER.
DOCTOR SUHNER HAS A... EXCLUSIVE CLIENTELE. HE'S VERY PARTICULAR ABOUT THOSE HE TAKES ON.
PLEASE. WE'VE HEARD SUCH GOOD THINGS ABOUT HIM. HE CAN HELP MY HUSBAND. I'M SURE OF IT.
WELL...HE'S AVAILABLE FOR A CONSULTANCY INTERVIEW. WE CAN TRY...
HE IS POLITE, URBANE, PROFESSIONAL.
SO. I UNDERSTAND YOU HAVE...SOMEWHAT UNORTHODOX BELIEFS, STEPHEN, YES?
TELL ME ABOUT THEM.
I CAN SENSE NO GREAT MAGIC ABOUT THE MAN.
NO GREAT MAGIC. A SIMPLE TRINKET FOR DIVINING WHETHER ONE SPEAKS THEIR BELIEFS OR IS DISSEMBLING.
IF I LIE, ITS TWITCH WILL BETRAY ME.

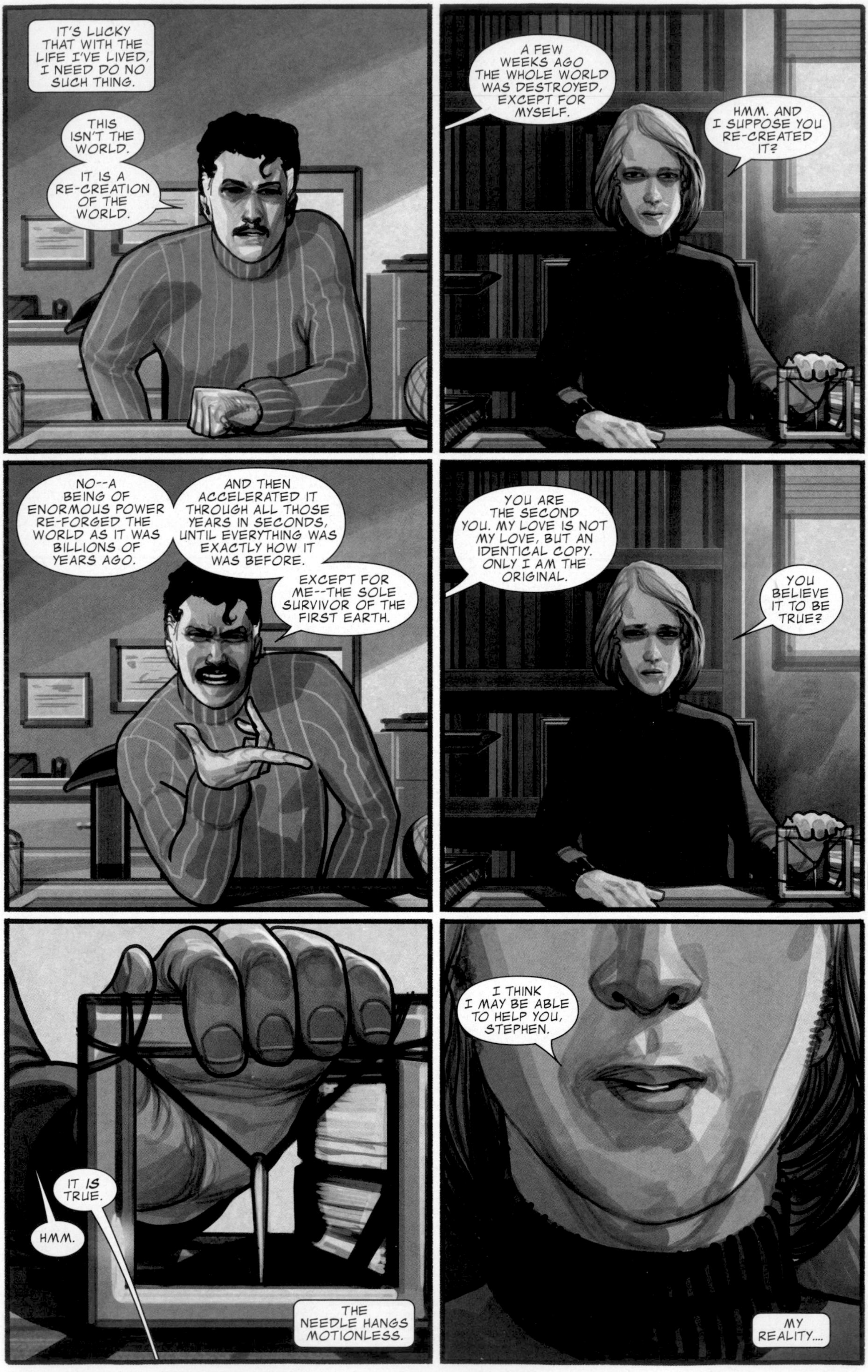

IT'S LUCKY THAT WITH THE LIFE I'VE LIVED, I NEED DO NO SUCH THING.
THIS ISN'T THE WORLD.
IT IS A RE-CREATION OF THE WORLD.
A FEW WEEKS AGO THE WHOLE WORLD WAS DESTROYED, EXCEPT FOR MYSELF.
HMM. AND I SUPPOSE YOU RE-CREATED IT?
NO--A BEING OF ENORMOUS POWER RE-FORGED THE WORLD AS IT WAS BILLIONS OF YEARS AGO.
AND THEN ACCELERATED IT THROUGH ALL THOSE YEARS IN SECONDS, UNTIL EVERYTHING WAS EXACTLY HOW IT WAS BEFORE.
EXCEPT FOR ME--THE SOLE SURVIVOR OF THE FIRST EARTH.
YOU ARE THE SECOND YOU. MY LOVE IS NOT MY LOVE, BUT AN IDENTICAL COPY. ONLY I AM THE ORIGINAL.
YOU BELIEVE IT TO BE TRUE?
IT IS TRUE.
HMM.
THE NEEDLE HANGS MOTIONLESS.
I THINK I MAY BE ABLE TO HELP YOU, STEPHEN.
MY REALITY....

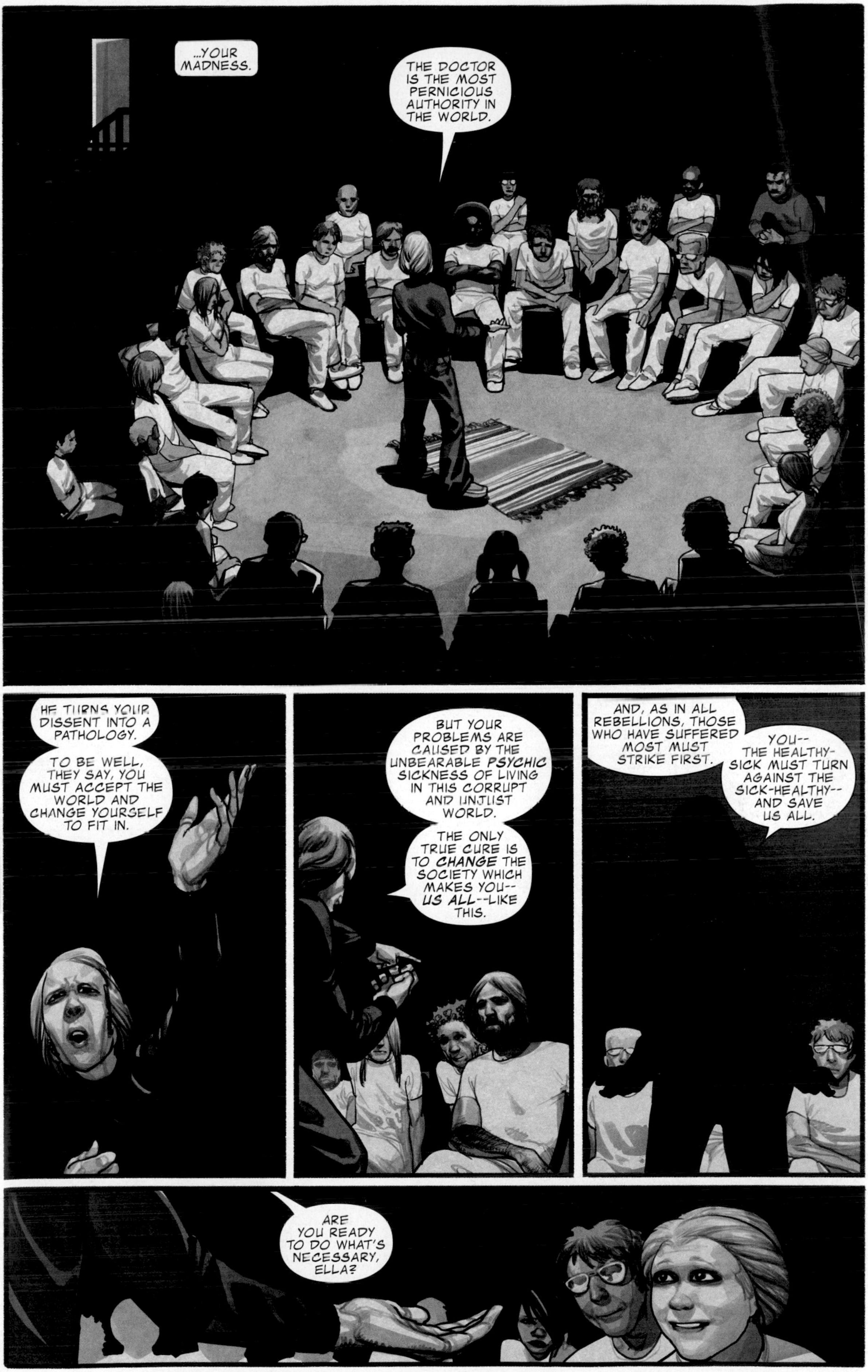

...YOUR MADNESS.
THE DOCTOR IS THE MOST PERNICIOUS AUTHORITY IN THE WORLD.
HE TURNS YOUR DISSENT INTO A PATHOLOGY.
TO BE WELL, THEY SAY, YOU MUST ACCEPT THE WORLD AND CHANGE YOURSELF TO FIT IN.
BUT YOUR PROBLEMS ARE CAUSED BY THE UNBEARABLE PSYCHIC SICKNESS OF LIVING IN THIS CORRUPT AND UNJUST WORLD.
THE ONLY TRUE CURE IS TO CHANGE THE SOCIETY WHICH MAKES YOU-- US ALL--LIKE THIS.
AND, AS IN ALL REBELLIONS, THOSE WHO HAVE SUFFERED MOST MUST STRIKE FIRST.
YOU-- THE HEALTHY-SICK MUST TURN AGAINST THE SICK-HEALTHY-- AND SAVE US ALL.
ARE YOU READY TO DO WHAT'S NECESSARY, ELLA?

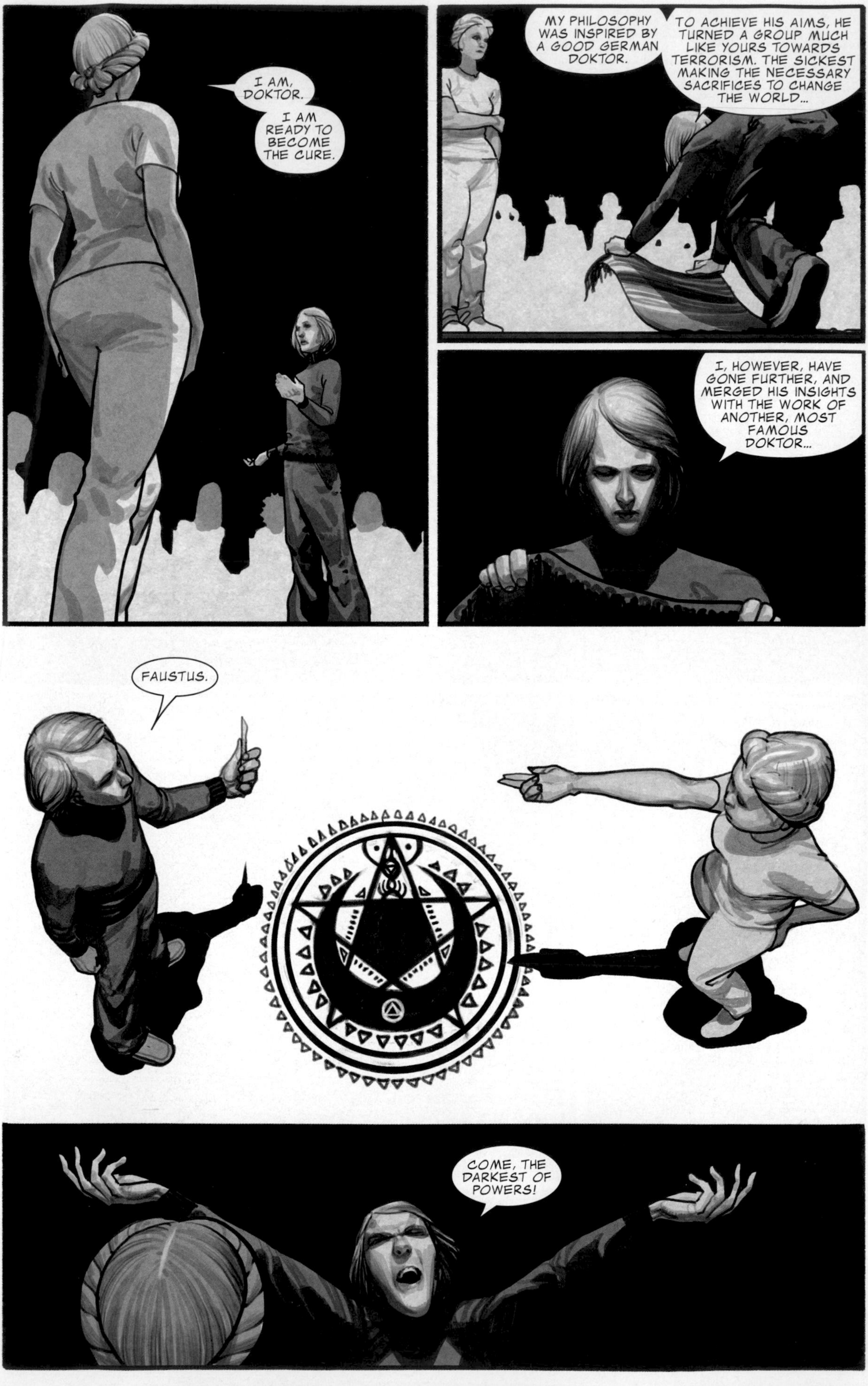
I AM, DOKTOR.
I AM READY TO BECOME THE CURE.
MY PHILOSOPHY WAS INSPIRED BY A GOOD GERMAN DOKTOR.
TO ACHIEVE HIS AIMS, HE TURNED A GROUP MUCH LIKE YOURS TOWARDS TERRORISM. THE SICKEST MAKING THE NECESSARY SACRIFICES TO CHANGE THE WORLD...
I, HOWEVER, HAVE GONE FURTHER, AND MERGED HIS INSIGHTS WITH THE WORK OF ANOTHER, MOST FAMOUS DOKTOR...
FAUSTUS.
COME, THE DARKEST OF POWERS!

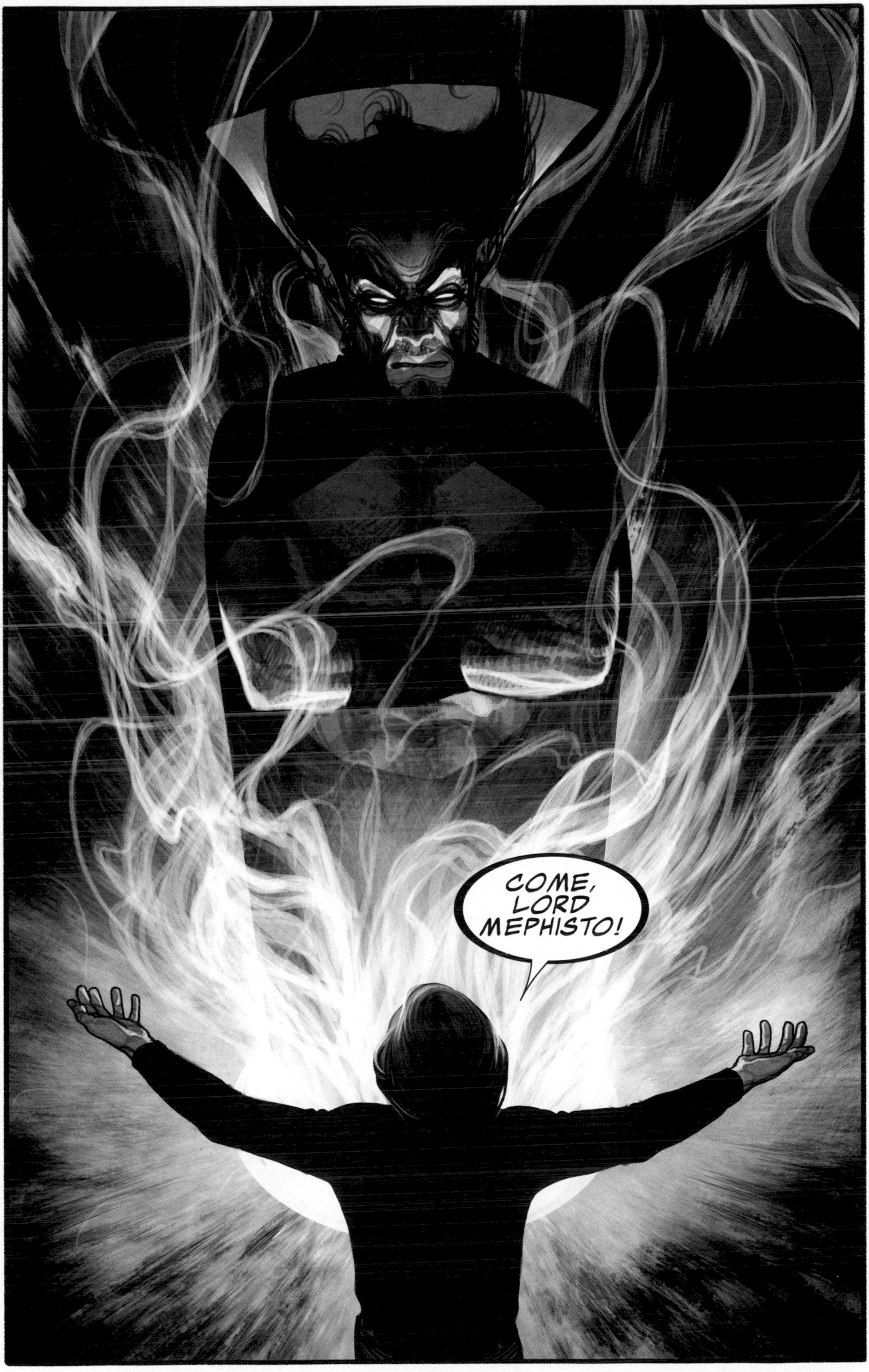
COME, LORD MEPHISTO!

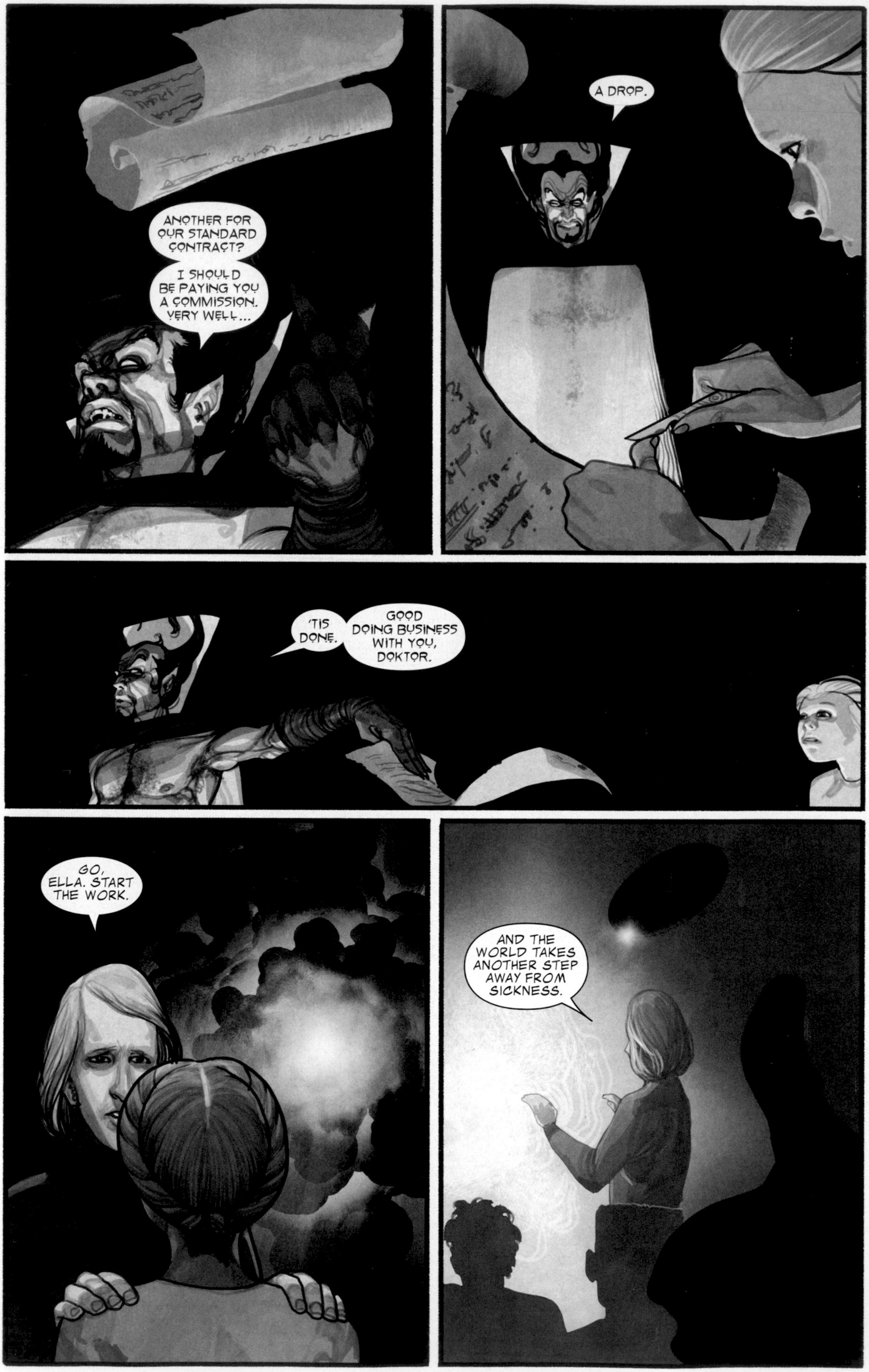
ANOTHER FOR OUR STANDARD CONTRACT?
I SHOULD BE PAYING YOU A COMMISSION. VERY WELL...
A DROP.
'TIS DONE.
GOOD DOING BUSINESS WITH YOU, DOKTOR.
GO, ELLA. START THE WORK.
AND THE WORLD TAKES ANOTHER STEP AWAY FROM SICKNESS.

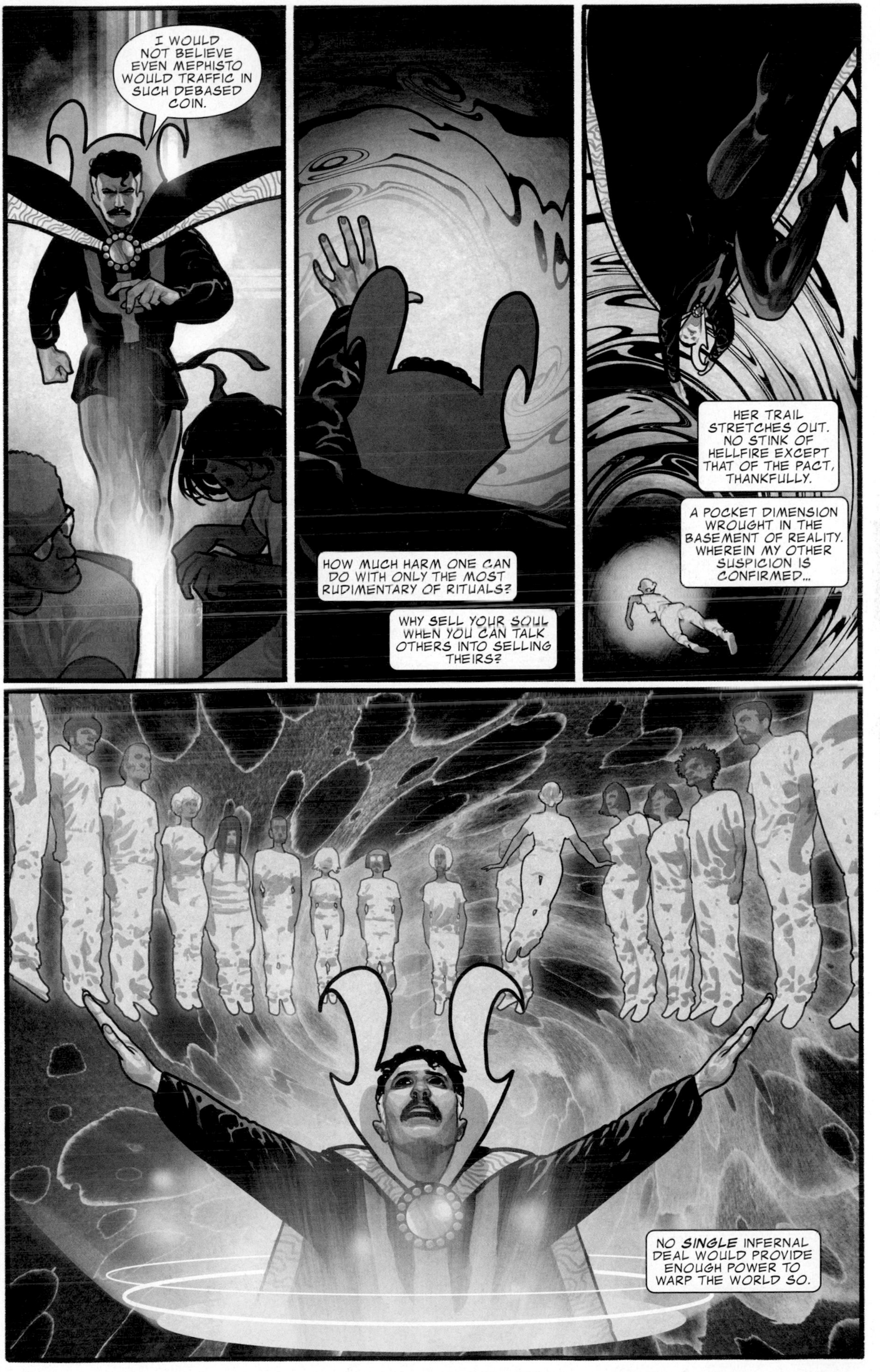
I WOULD NOT BELIEVE EVEN MEPHISTO WOULD TRAFFIC IN SUCH DEBASED COIN.
HOW MUCH HARM ONE CAN DO WITH ONLY THE MOST RUDIMENTARY OF RITUALS?
WHY SELL YOUR SOUL WHEN YOU CAN TALK OTHERS INTO SELLING THEIRS?
HER TRAIL STRETCHES OUT. NO STINK OF HELLFIRE EXCEPT THAT OF THE PACT, THANKFULLY.
A POCKET DIMENSION WROUGHT IN THE BASEMENT OF REALITY. WHEREIN MY OTHER SUSPICION IS CONFIRMED...
NO SINGLE INFERNAL DEAL WOULD PROVIDE ENOUGH POWER TO WARP THE WORLD SO.

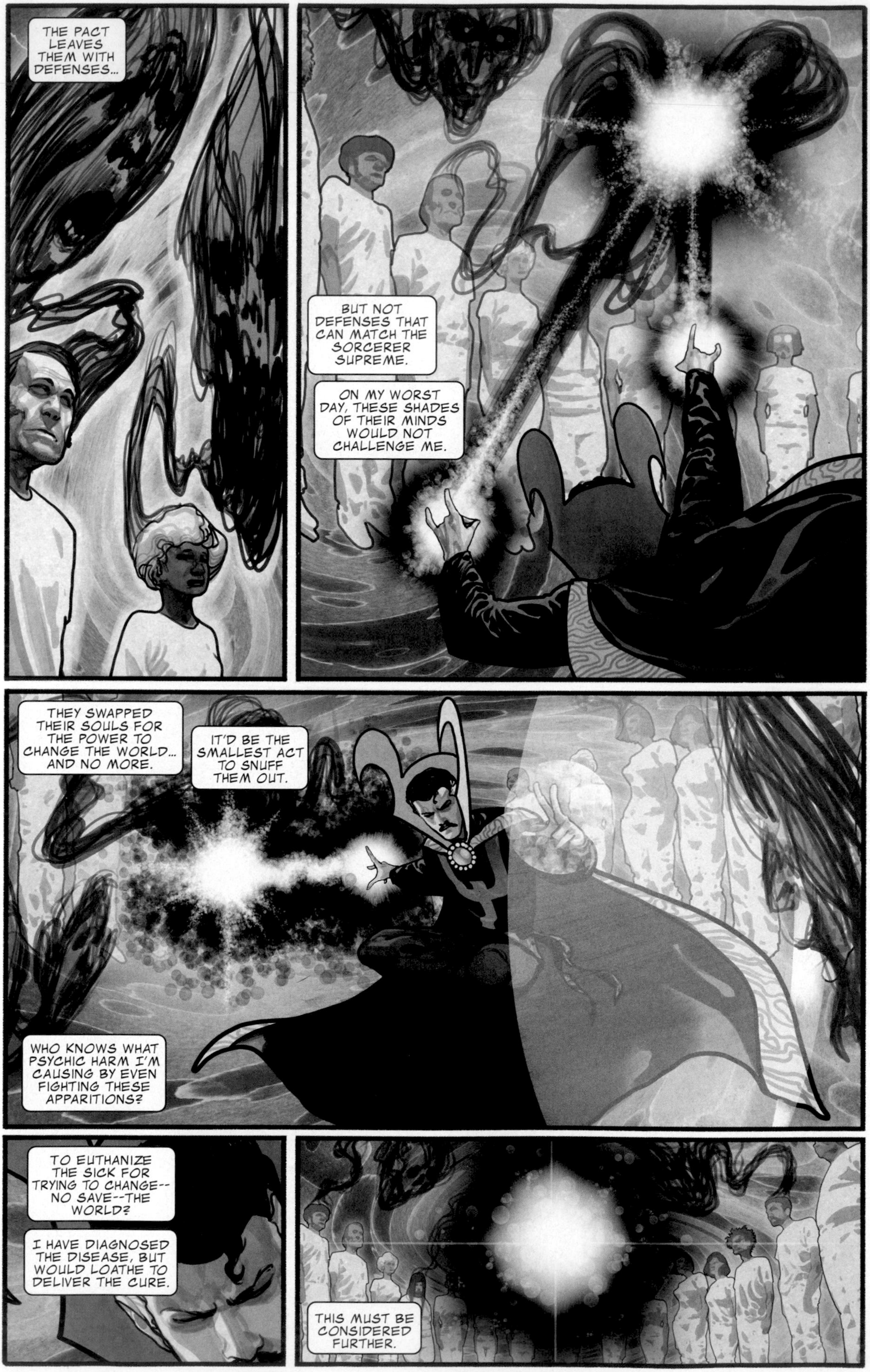
THE PACT LEAVES THEM WITH DEFENSES...
BUT NOT DEFENSES THAT CAN MATCH THE SORCERER SUPREME.
ON MY WORST DAY, THESE SHADES OF THEIR MINDS WOULD NOT CHALLENGE ME.
THEY SWAPPED THEIR SOULS FOR THE POWER TO CHANGE THE WORLD... AND NO MORE.
IT'D BE THE SMALLEST ACT TO SNUFF THEM OUT.
WHO KNOWS WHAT PSYCHIC HARM I'M CAUSING BY EVEN FIGHTING THESE APPARITIONS?
TO EUTHANIZE THE SICK FOR TRYING TO CHANGE-- NO SAVE--THE WORLD?
I HAVE DIAGNOSED THE DISEASE, BUT WOULD LOATHE TO DELIVER THE CURE.
THIS MUST BE CONSIDERED FURTHER.

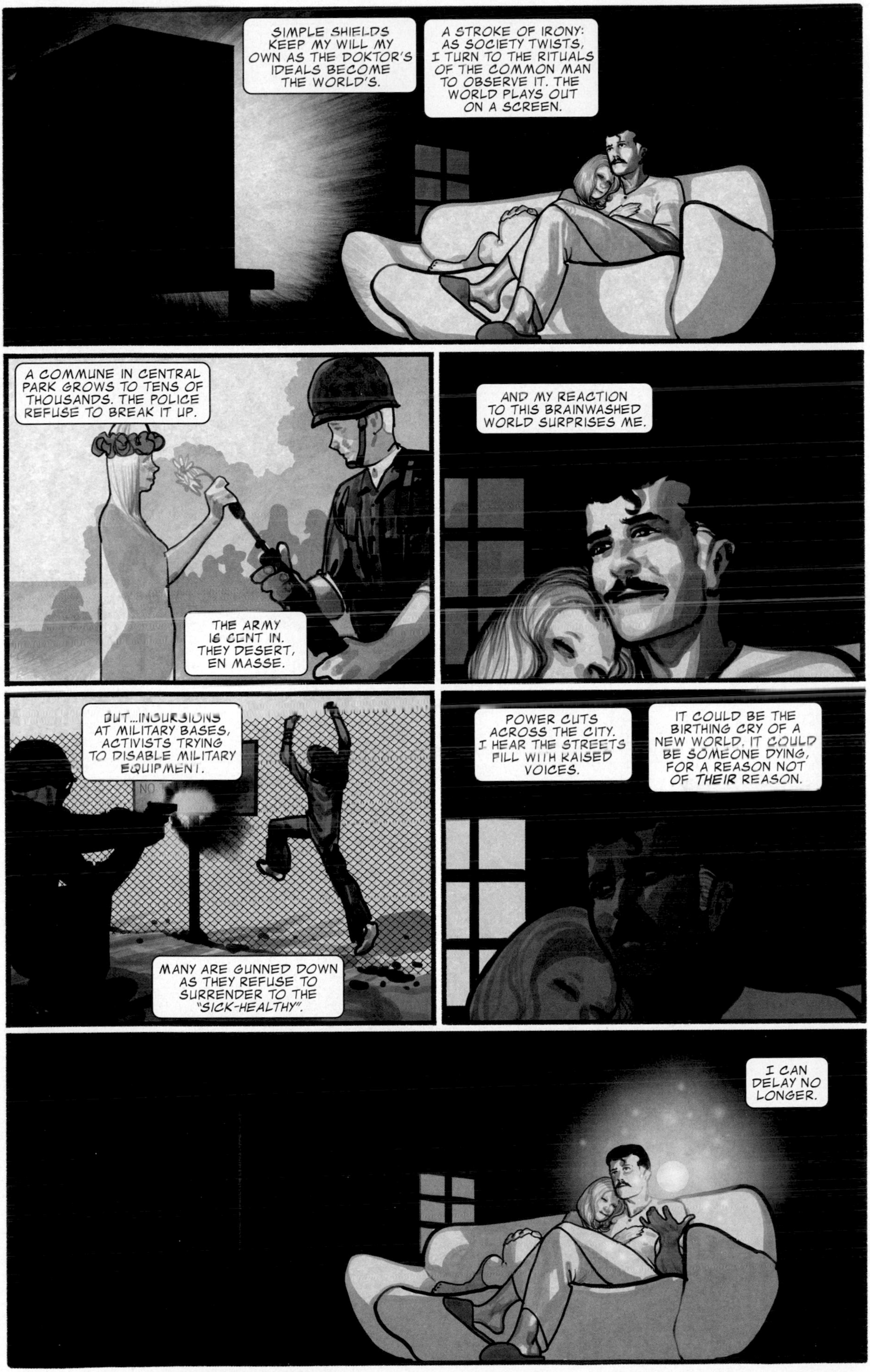
SIMPLE SHIELDS KEEP MY WILL MY OWN AS THE DOKTOR'S IDEALS BECOME THE WORLD'S.
A STROKE OF IRONY: AS SOCIETY TWISTS, I TURN TO THE RITUALS OF THE COMMON MAN TO OBSERVE IT. THE WORLD PLAYS OUT ON A SCREEN.
A COMMUNE IN CENTRAL PARK GROWS TO TENS OF THOUSANDS. THE POLICE REFUSE TO BREAK IT UP.
THE ARMY IS SENT IN. THEY DESERT, EN MASSE.
AND MY REACTION TO THIS BRAINWASHED WORLD SURPRISES ME.
BUT...INCURSIONS AT MILITARY BASES, ACTIVISTS TRYING TO DISABLE MILITARY EQUIPMENT.
MANY ARE GUNNED DOWN AS THEY REFUSE TO SURRENDER TO THE "SICK-HEALTHY".
POWER CUTS ACROSS THE CITY. I HEAR THE STREETS FILL WITH RAISED VOICES.
IT COULD BE THE BIRTHING CRY OF A NEW WORLD. IT COULD BE SOMEONE DYING, FOR A REASON NOT OF *THEIR* REASON.
I CAN DELAY NO LONGER.

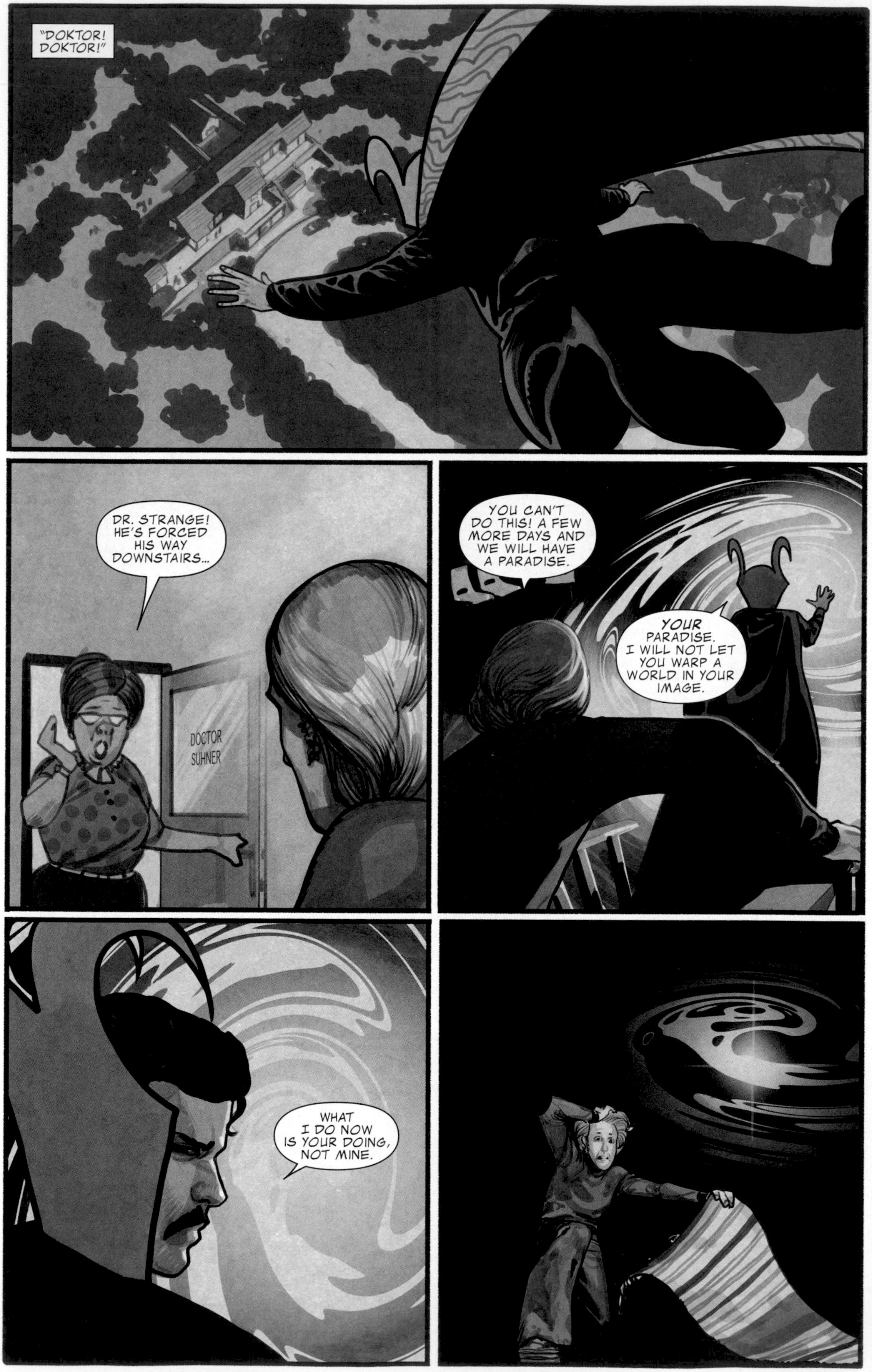
"DOKTOR! DOKTOR!"
DR. STRANGE! HE'S FORCED HIS WAY DOWNSTAIRS...
DOCTOR SUHNER
YOU CAN'T DO THIS! A FEW MORE DAYS AND WE WILL HAVE A PARADISE.
YOUR PARADISE. I WILL NOT LET YOU WARP A WORLD IN YOUR IMAGE.
WHAT I DO NOW IS YOUR DOING, NOT MINE.

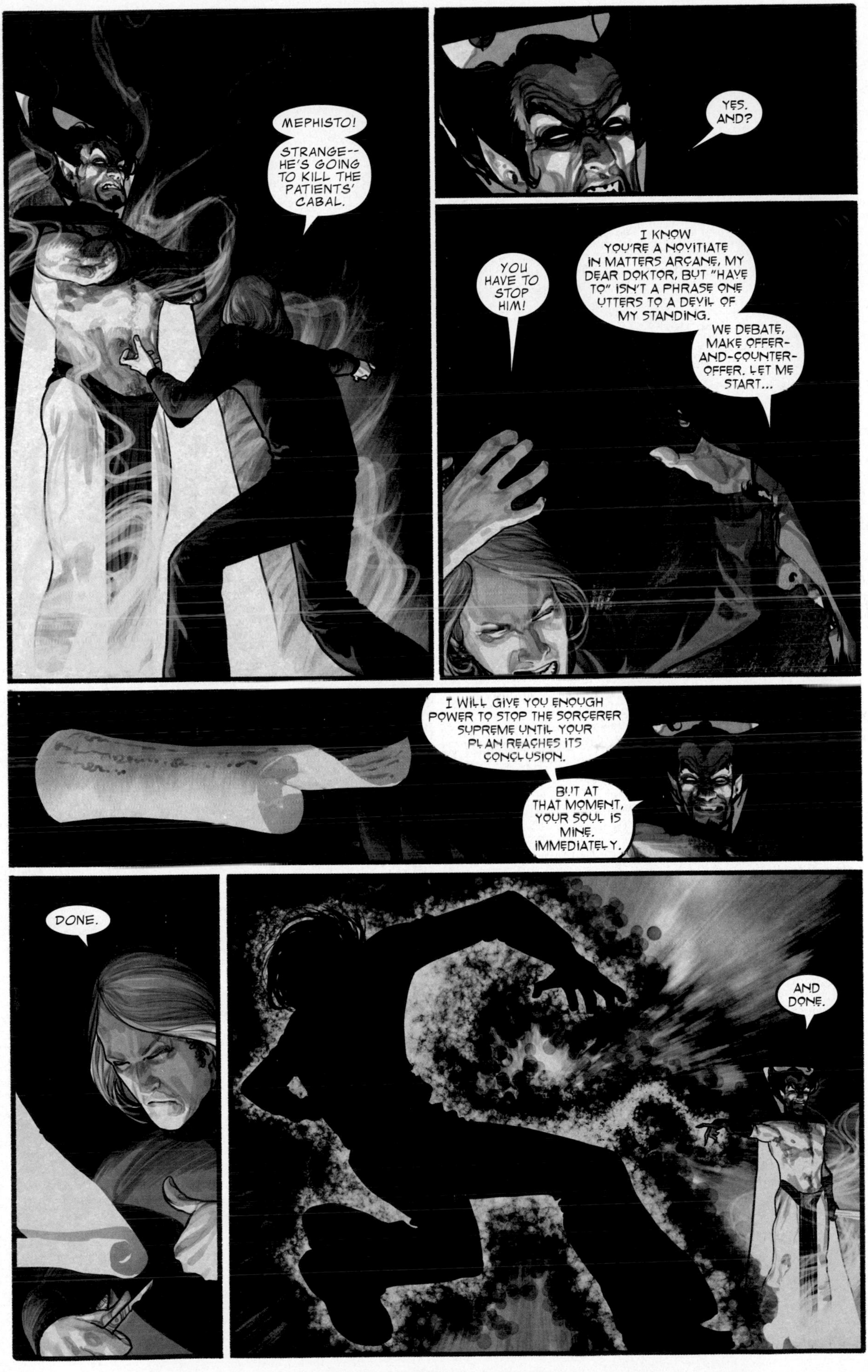
MEPHISTO!
STRANGE--HE'S GOING TO KILL THE PATIENTS' CABAL.
YES. AND?
YOU HAVE TO STOP HIM!
I KNOW YOU'RE A NOVITIATE IN MATTERS ARCANE, MY DEAR DOKTOR, BUT "HAVE TO" ISN'T A PHRASE ONE UTTERS TO A DEVIL OF MY STANDING.
WE DEBATE, MAKE OFFER-AND-COUNTER-OFFER. LET ME START...
I WILL GIVE YOU ENOUGH POWER TO STOP THE SORCERER SUPREME UNTIL YOUR PLAN REACHES ITS CONCLUSION.
BUT AT THAT MOMENT, YOUR SOUL IS MINE. IMMEDIATELY.
DONE.
AND DONE.

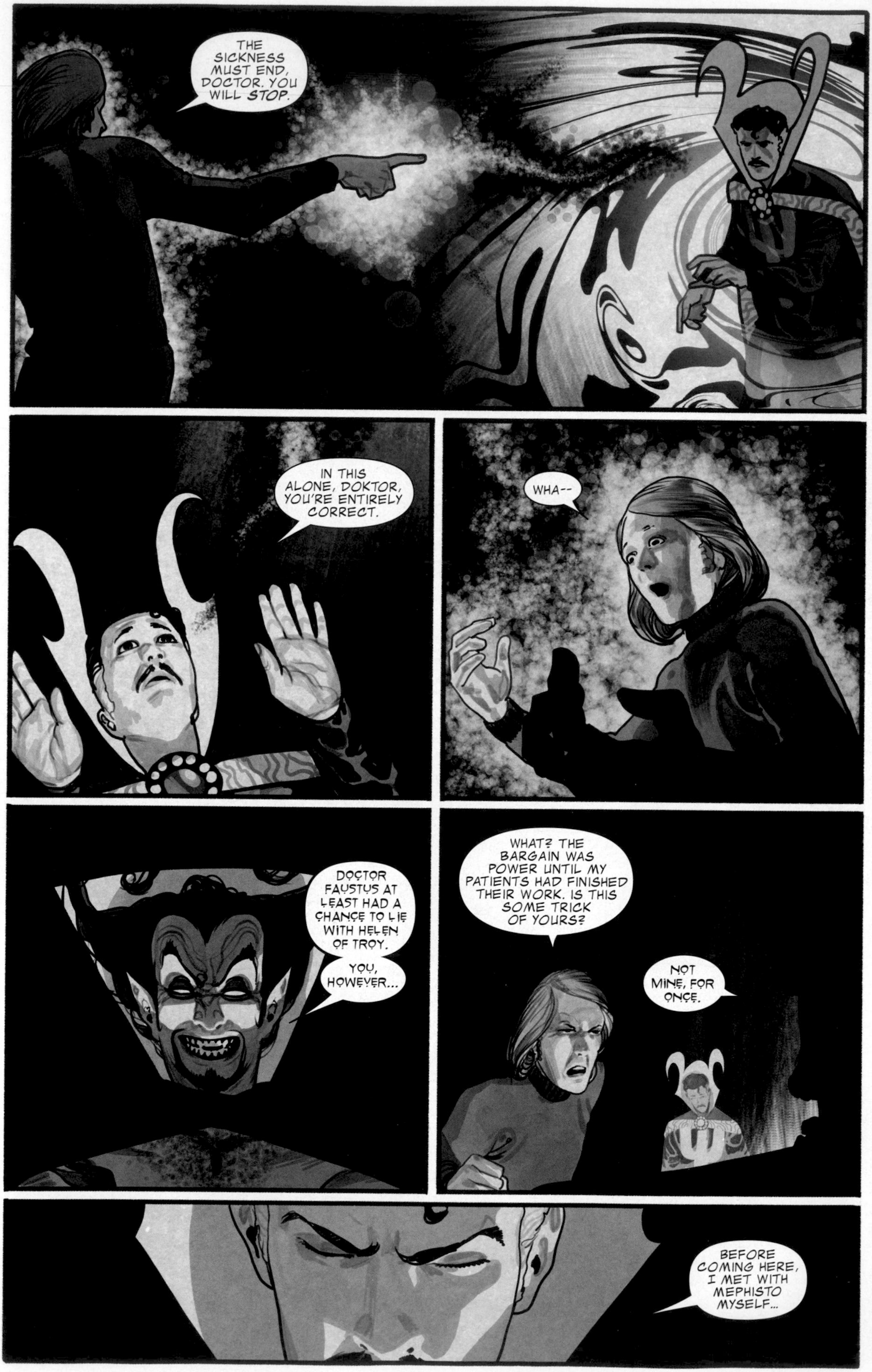
THE SICKNESS MUST END, DOCTOR. YOU WILL STOP.
IN THIS ALONE, DOKTOR, YOU'RE ENTIRELY CORRECT.
WHA--
DOCTOR FAUSTUS AT LEAST HAD A CHANCE TO LIE WITH HELEN OF TROY.
YOU, HOWEVER...
WHAT? THE BARGAIN WAS POWER UNTIL MY PATIENTS HAD FINISHED THEIR WORK. IS THIS SOME TRICK OF YOURS?
NOT MINE, FOR ONCE.
BEFORE COMING HERE, I MET WITH MEPHISTO MYSELF...

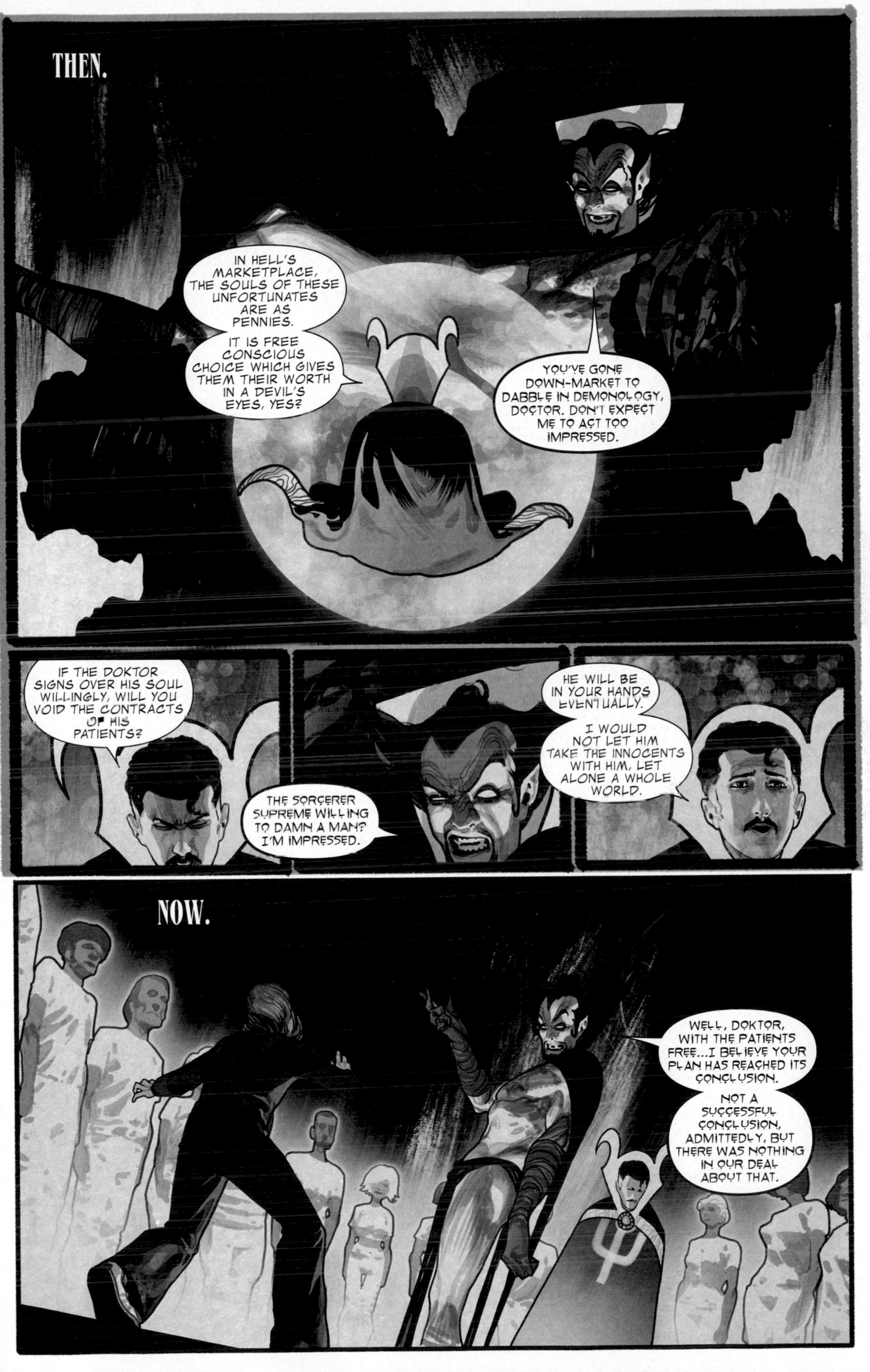
THEN.
IN HELL'S MARKETPLACE, THE SOULS OF THESE UNFORTUNATES ARE AS PENNIES.
IT IS FREE CONSCIOUS CHOICE WHICH GIVES THEM THEIR WORTH IN A DEVIL'S EYES, YES?
YOU'VE GONE DOWN-MARKET TO DABBLE IN DEMONOLOGY, DOCTOR. DON'T EXPECT ME TO ACT TOO IMPRESSED.
IF THE DOKTOR SIGNS OVER HIS SOUL WILLINGLY, WILL YOU VOID THE CONTRACTS OF HIS PATIENTS?
THE SORCERER SUPREME WILLING TO DAMN A MAN? I'M IMPRESSED.
HE WILL BE IN YOUR HANDS EVENTUALLY.
I WOULD NOT LET HIM TAKE THE INNOCENTS WITH HIM, LET ALONE A WHOLE WORLD.
NOW.
WELL, DOKTOR, WITH THE PATIENTS FREE...I BELIEVE YOUR PLAN HAS REACHED ITS CONCLUSION.
NOT A SUCCESSFUL CONCLUSION, ADMITTEDLY, BUT THERE WAS NOTHING IN OUR DEAL ABOUT THAT.

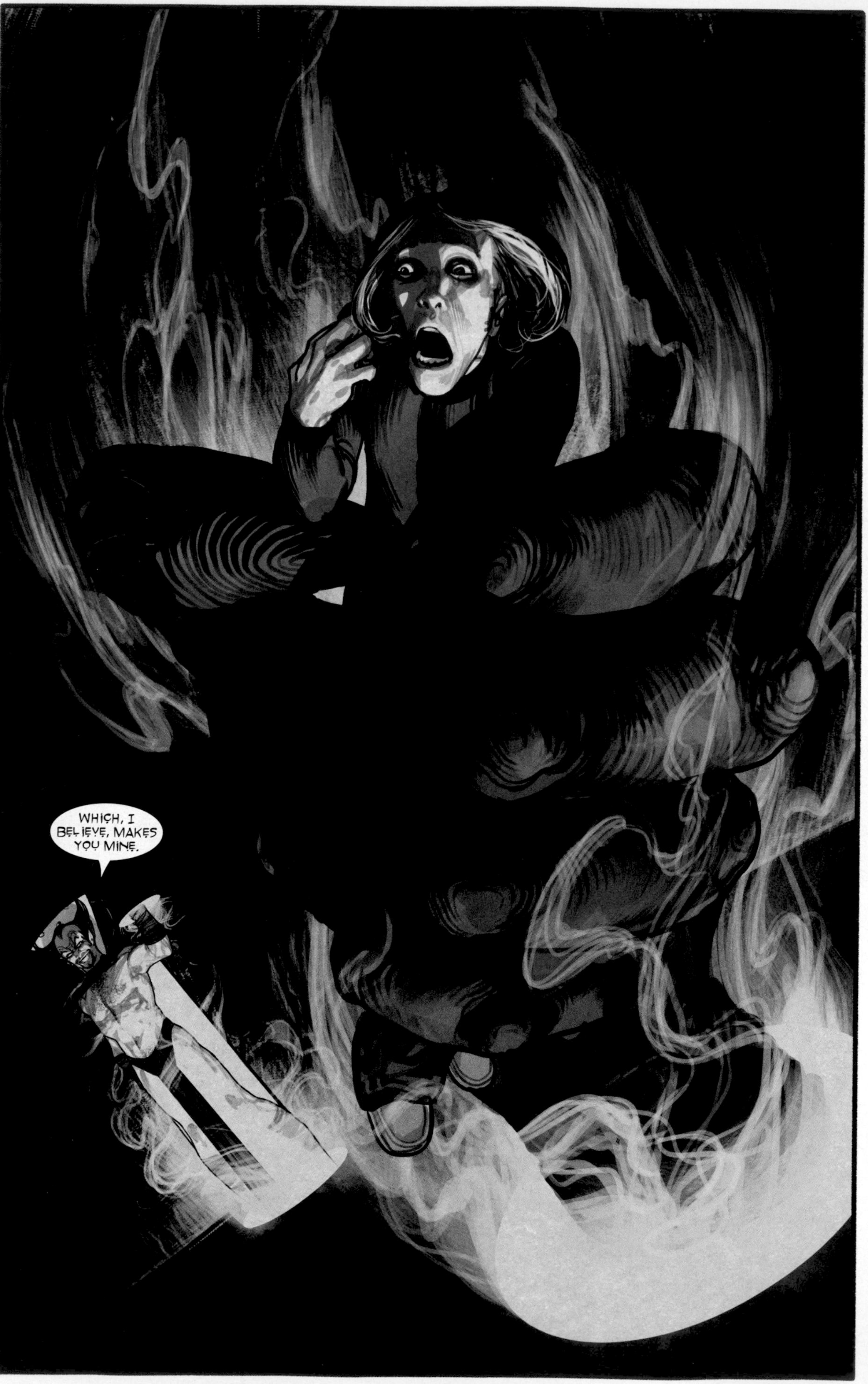
WHICH, I BELIEVE, MAKES YOU MINE.

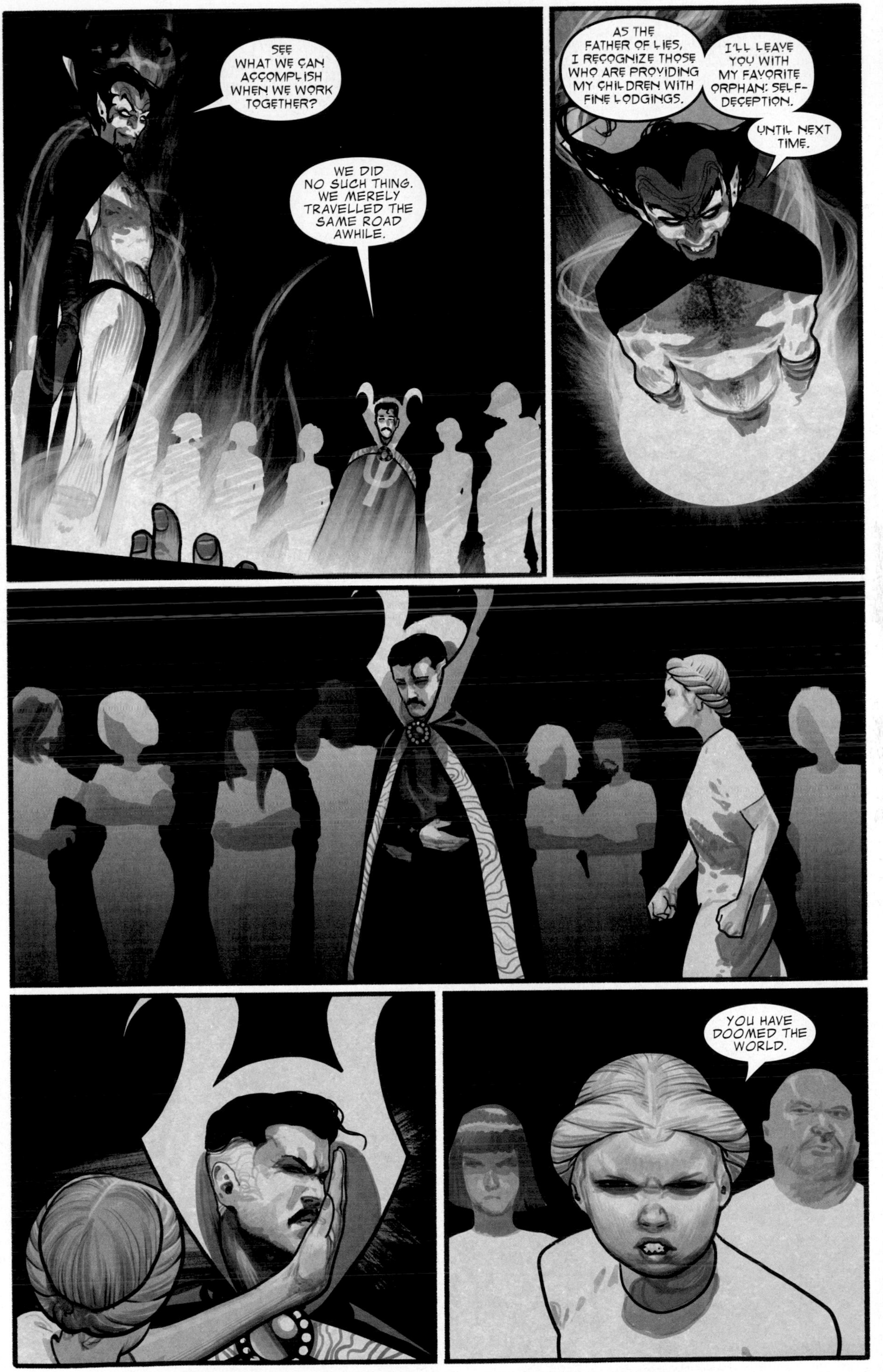
SEE WHAT WE CAN ACCOMPLISH WHEN WE WORK TOGETHER?
WE DID NO SUCH THING. WE MERELY TRAVELLED THE SAME ROAD AWHILE.
AS THE FATHER OF LIES, I RECOGNIZE THOSE WHO ARE PROVIDING MY CHILDREN WITH FINE LODGINGS.
I'LL LEAVE YOU WITH MY FAVORITE ORPHAN: SELF-DECEPTION.
UNTIL NEXT TIME.
YOU HAVE DOOMED THE WORLD.

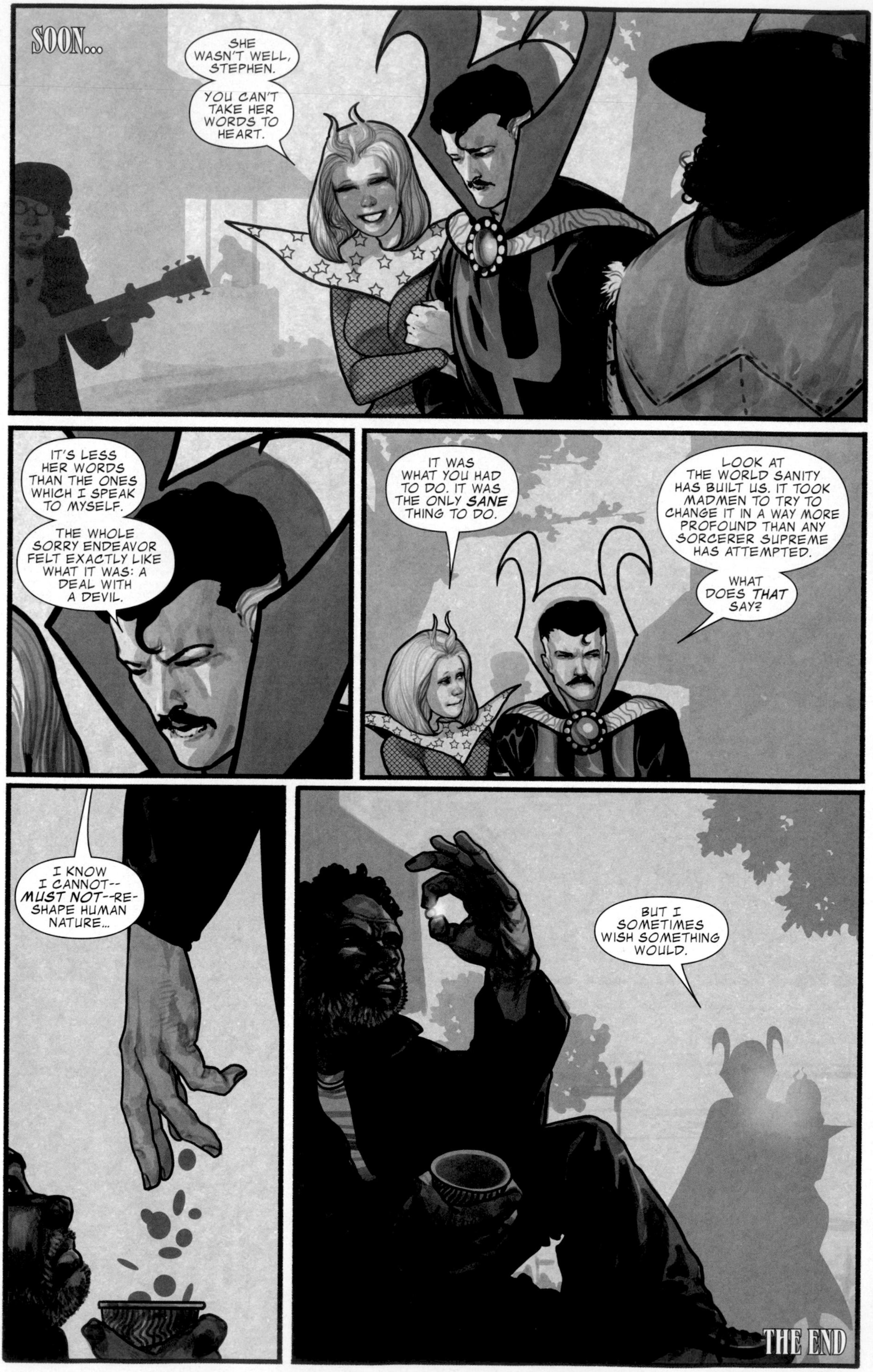
SOON...
SHE WASN'T WELL, STEPHEN.
YOU CAN'T TAKE HER WORDS TO HEART.
IT'S LESS HER WORDS THAN THE ONES WHICH I SPEAK TO MYSELF.
THE WHOLE SORRY ENDEAVOR FELT EXACTLY LIKE WHAT IT WAS: A DEAL WITH A DEVIL.
IT WAS WHAT YOU HAD TO DO. IT WAS THE ONLY SANE THING TO DO.
LOOK AT THE WORLD SANITY HAS BUILT US. IT TOOK MADMEN TO TRY TO CHANGE IT IN A WAY MORE PROFOUND THAN ANY SORCERER SUPREME HAS ATTEMPTED.
WHAT DOES THAT SAY?
I KNOW I CANNOT--MUST NOT--RE-SHAPE HUMAN NATURE...
BUT I SOMETIMES WISH SOMETHING WOULD.
THE END

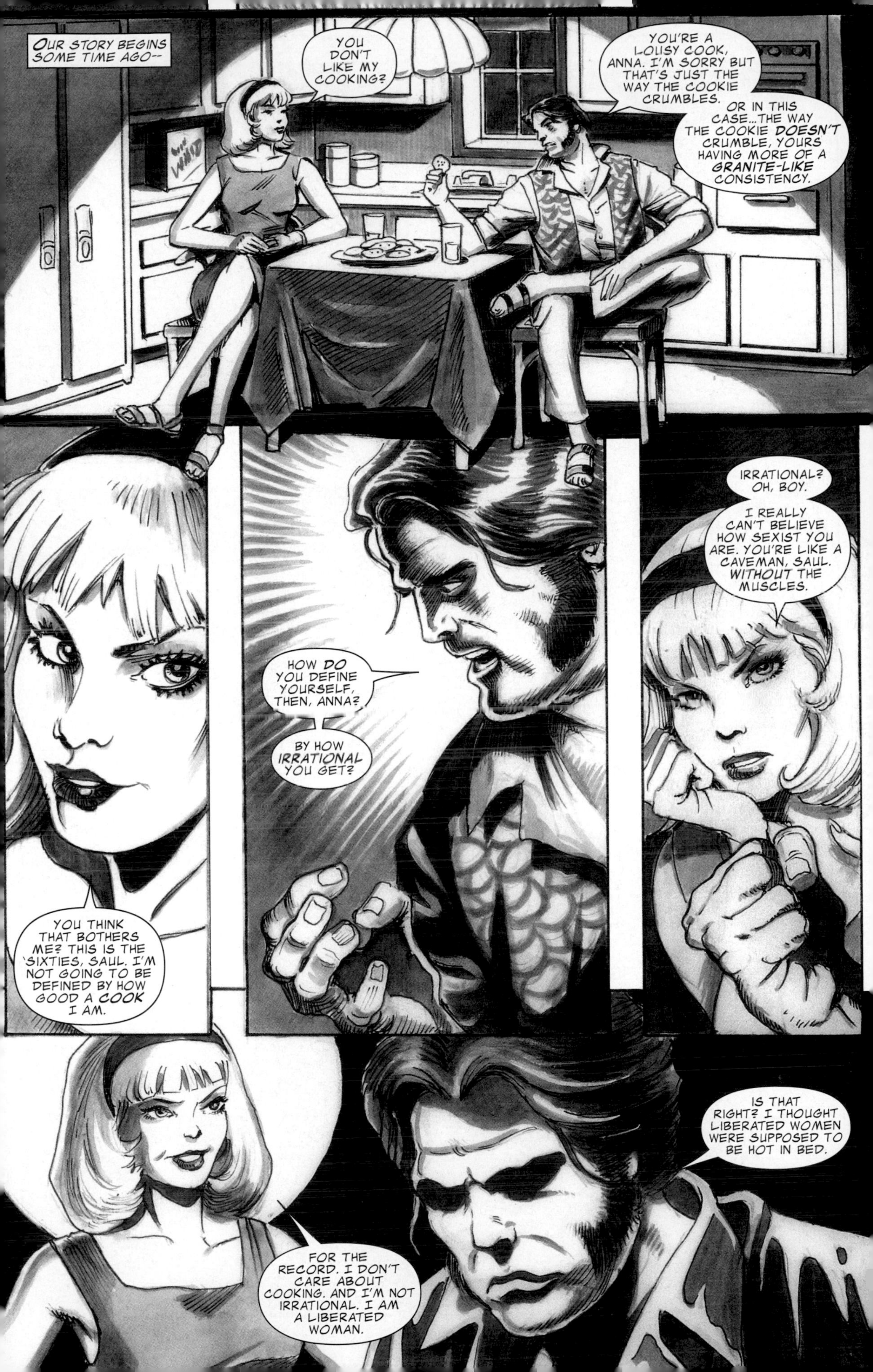
OUR STORY BEGINS SOME TIME AGO--
YOU DON'T LIKE MY COOKING?
YOU'RE A LOUSY COOK, ANNA. I'M SORRY BUT THAT'S JUST THE WAY THE COOKIE CRUMBLES.
OR IN THIS CASE...THE WAY THE COOKIE DOESN'T CRUMBLE, YOURS HAVING MORE OF A GRANITE-LIKE CONSISTENCY.
YOU THINK THAT BOTHERS ME? THIS IS THE 'SIXTIES, SAUL. I'M NOT GOING TO BE DEFINED BY HOW GOOD A COOK I AM.
HOW DO YOU DEFINE YOURSELF, THEN, ANNA?
BY HOW IRRATIONAL YOU GET?
IRRATIONAL? OH, BOY.
I REALLY CAN'T BELIEVE HOW SEXIST YOU ARE. YOU'RE LIKE A CAVEMAN, SAUL. WITHOUT THE MUSCLES.
FOR THE RECORD. I DON'T CARE ABOUT COOKING. AND I'M NOT IRRATIONAL. I AM A LIBERATED WOMAN.
IS THAT RIGHT? I THOUGHT LIBERATED WOMEN WERE SUPPOSED TO BE HOT IN BED.

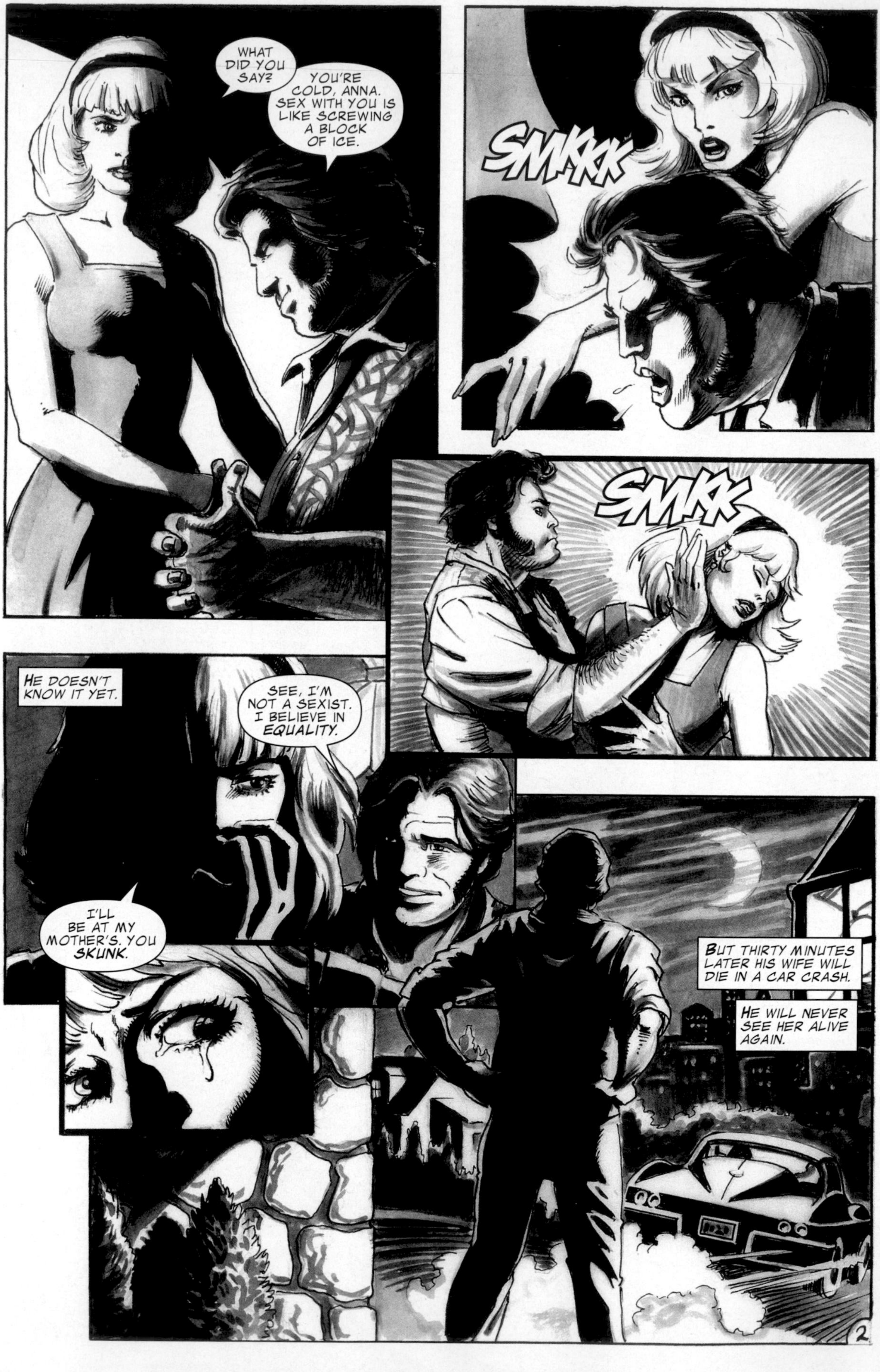
WHAT DID YOU SAY?
YOU'RE COLD, ANNA. SEX WITH YOU IS LIKE SCREWING A BLOCK OF ICE.
SMKKK
SMKK
HE DOESN'T KNOW IT YET.
SEE, I'M NOT A SEXIST. I BELIEVE IN EQUALITY.
I'LL BE AT MY MOTHER'S. YOU SKUNK.
BUT THIRTY MINUTES LATER HIS WIFE WILL DIE IN A CAR CRASH.
HE WILL NEVER SEE HER ALIVE AGAIN.

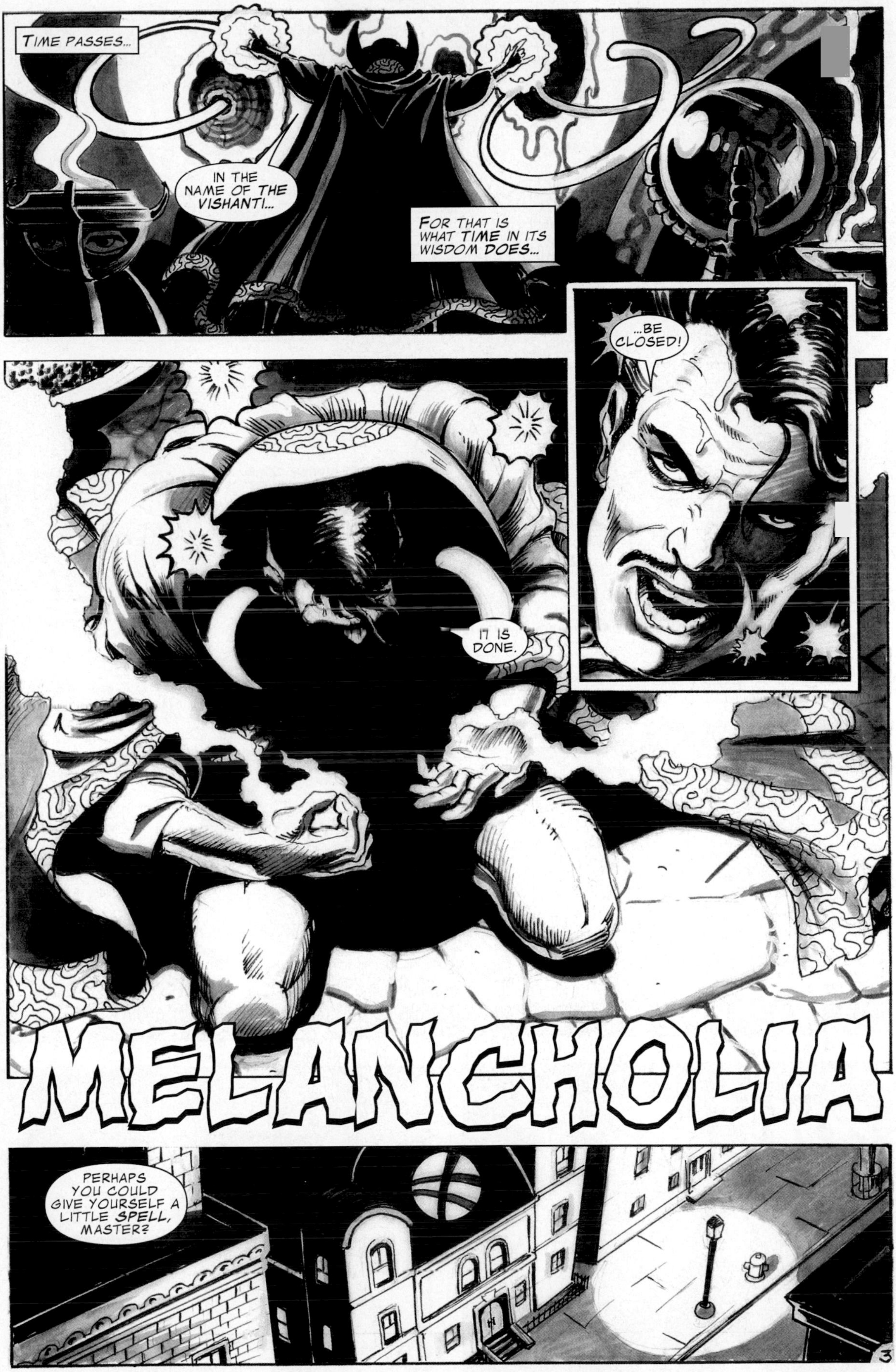

TIME PASSES...
IN THE NAME OF THE VISHANTI...
FOR THAT IS WHAT TIME IN ITS WISDOM DOES...
...BE CLOSED!
IT IS DONE.
MELANCHOLIA
PERHAPS YOU COULD GIVE YOURSELF A LITTLE SPELL, MASTER?

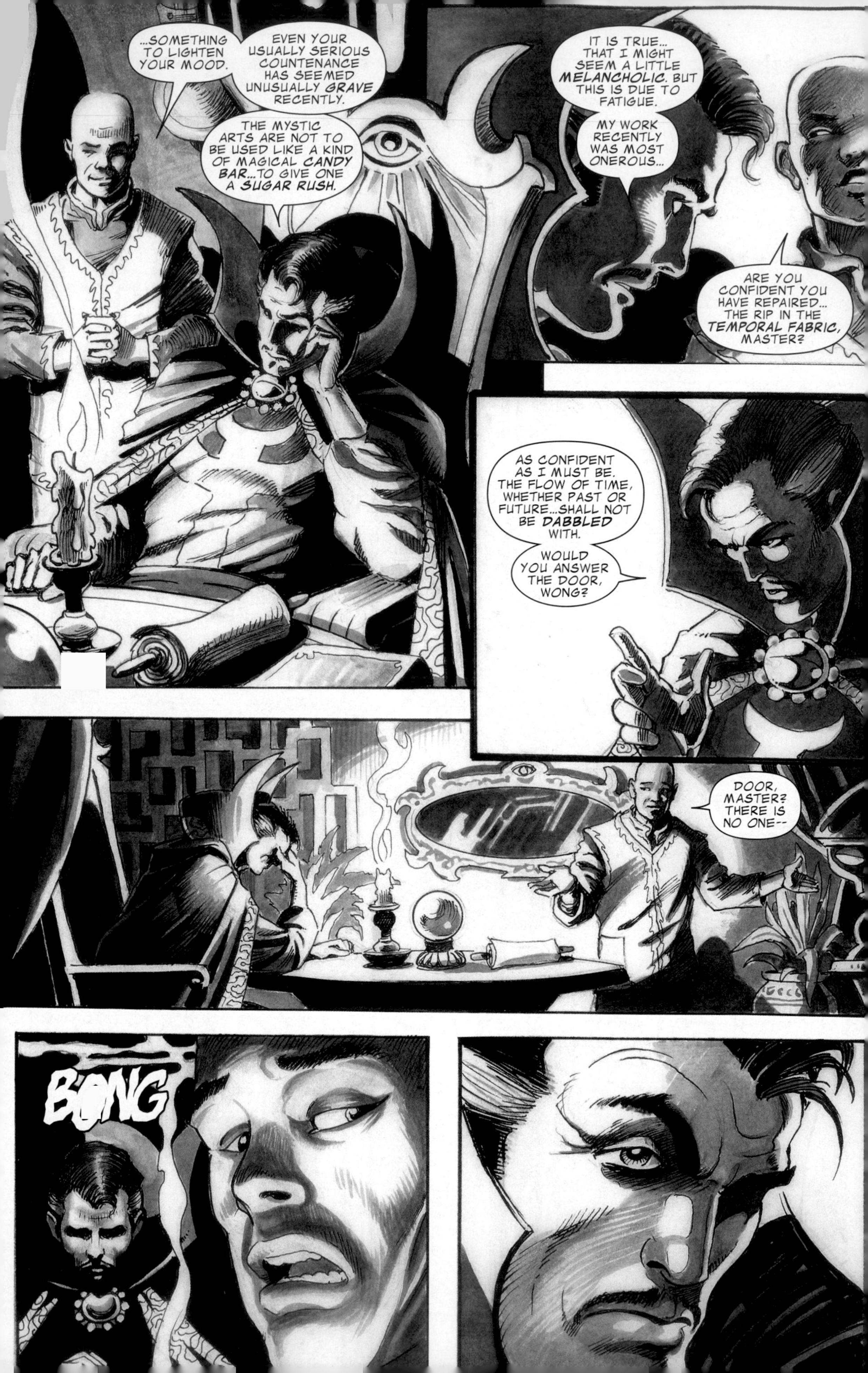
...SOMETHING TO LIGHTEN YOUR MOOD.
EVEN YOUR USUALLY SERIOUS COUNTENANCE HAS SEEMED UNUSUALLY GRAVE RECENTLY.
THE MYSTIC ARTS ARE NOT TO BE USED LIKE A KIND OF MAGICAL CANDY BAR...TO GIVE ONE A SUGAR RUSH.
IT IS TRUE... THAT I MIGHT SEEM A LITTLE MELANCHOLIC. BUT THIS IS DUE TO FATIGUE.
MY WORK RECENTLY WAS MOST ONEROUS...
ARE YOU CONFIDENT YOU HAVE REPAIRED... THE RIP IN THE TEMPORAL FABRIC, MASTER?
AS CONFIDENT AS I MUST BE. THE FLOW OF TIME, WHETHER PAST OR FUTURE...SHALL NOT BE DABBLED WITH.
WOULD YOU ANSWER THE DOOR, WONG?
DOOR, MASTER? THERE IS NO ONE--
BONG

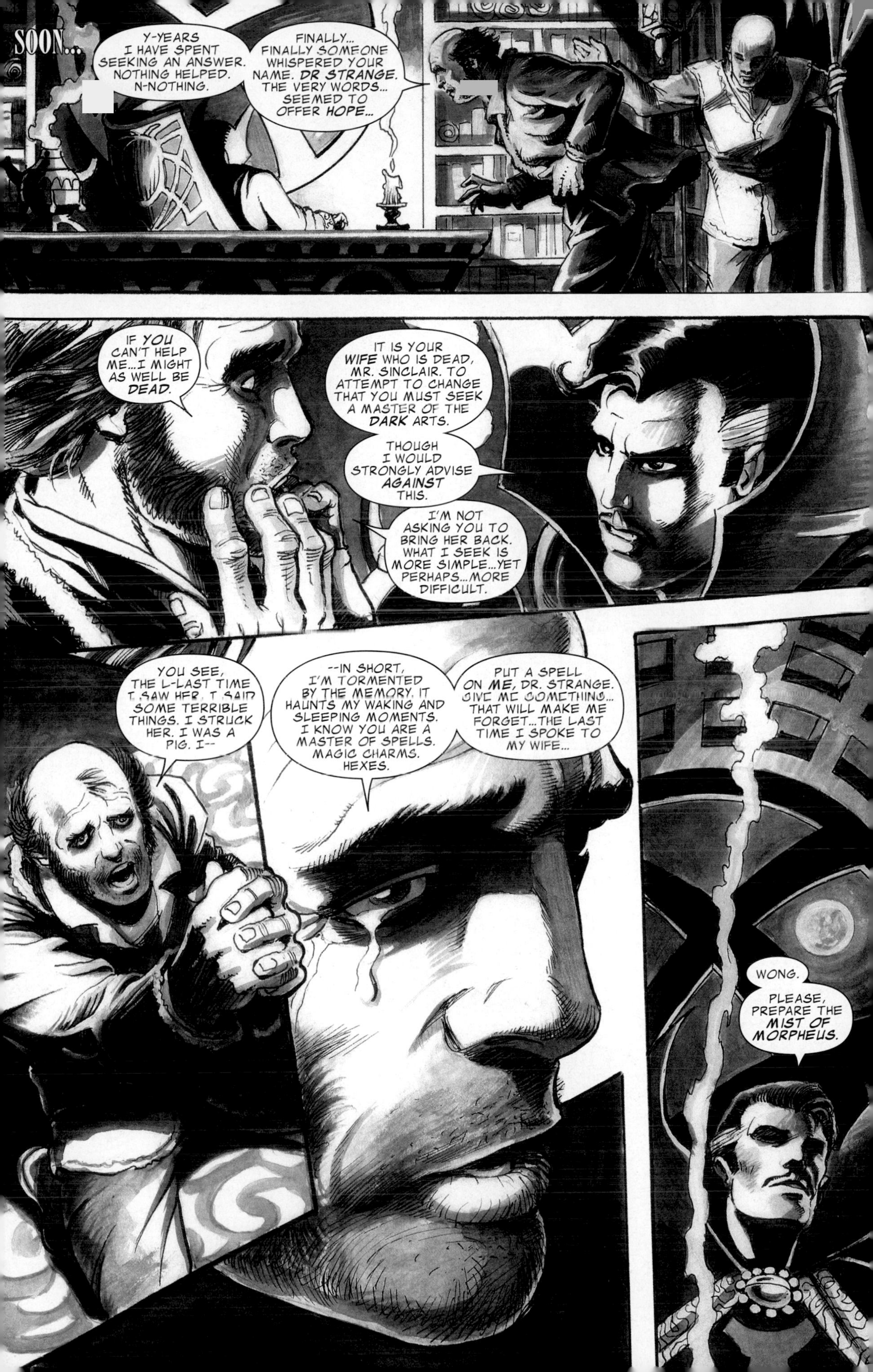
SOON...
Y-YEARS I HAVE SPENT SEEKING AN ANSWER. NOTHING HELPED. N-NOTHING.
FINALLY... FINALLY SOMEONE WHISPERED YOUR NAME. DR STRANGE. THE VERY WORDS... SEEMED TO OFFER HOPE...
IF YOU CAN'T HELP ME...I MIGHT AS WELL BE DEAD.
IT IS YOUR WIFE WHO IS DEAD, MR. SINCLAIR. TO ATTEMPT TO CHANGE THAT YOU MUST SEEK A MASTER OF THE DARK ARTS.
THOUGH I WOULD STRONGLY ADVISE AGAINST THIS.
I'M NOT ASKING YOU TO BRING HER BACK. WHAT I SEEK IS MORE SIMPLE...YET PERHAPS...MORE DIFFICULT.
YOU SEE, THE L-LAST TIME I SAW HER, I SAID SOME TERRIBLE THINGS. I STRUCK HER. I WAS A PIG. I--
--IN SHORT, I'M TORMENTED BY THE MEMORY. IT HAUNTS MY WAKING AND SLEEPING MOMENTS. I KNOW YOU ARE A MASTER OF SPELLS. MAGIC CHARMS. HEXES.
PUT A SPELL ON ME, DR. STRANGE. GIVE ME SOMETHING... THAT WILL MAKE ME FORGET...THE LAST TIME I SPOKE TO MY WIFE...
WONG.
PLEASE, PREPARE THE MIST OF MORPHEUS.

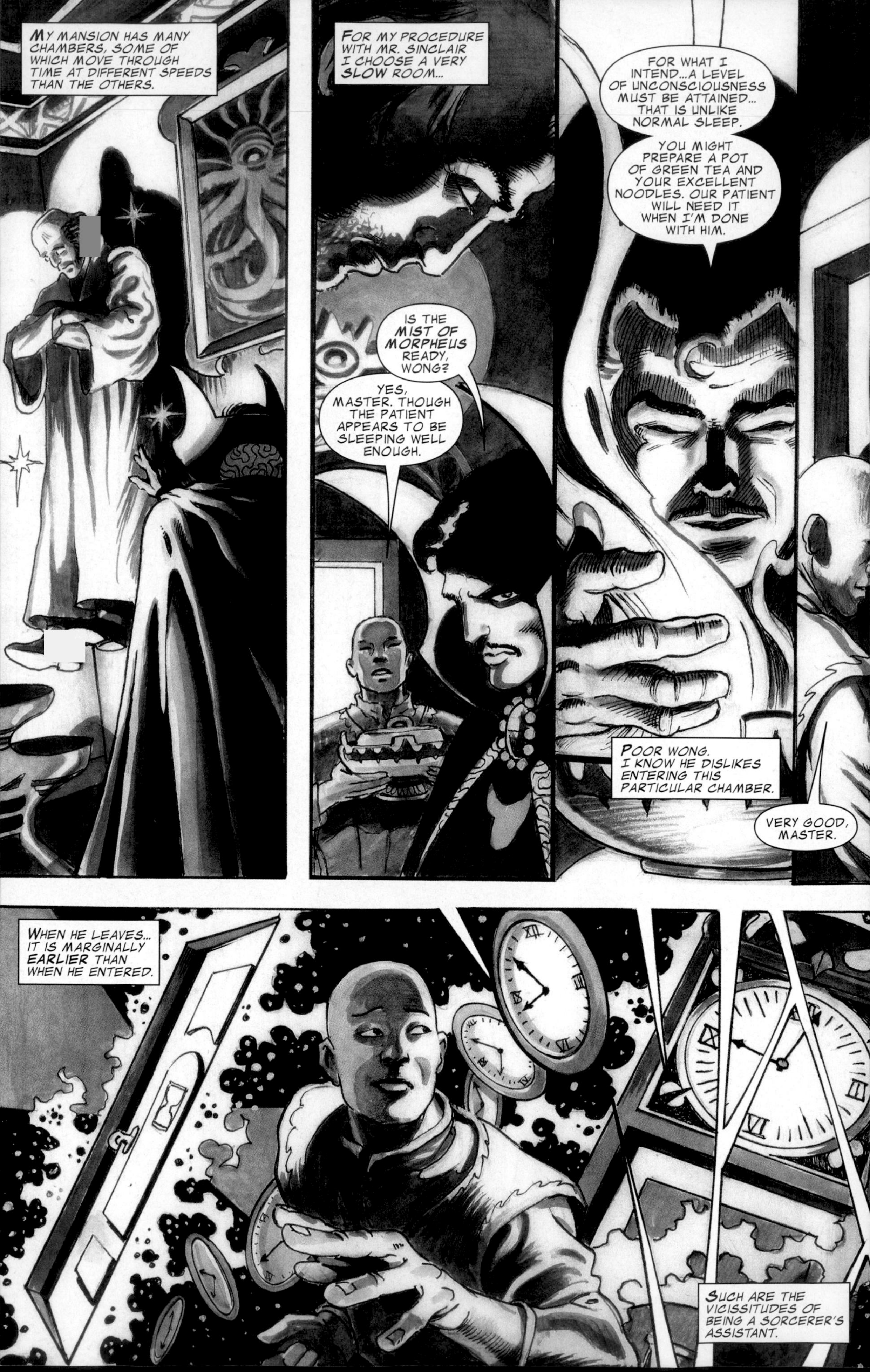
MY MANSION HAS MANY CHAMBERS, SOME OF WHICH MOVE THROUGH TIME AT DIFFERENT SPEEDS THAN THE OTHERS.
FOR MY PROCEDURE WITH MR. SINCLAIR I CHOOSE A VERY SLOW ROOM...
IS THE MIST OF MORPHEUS READY, WONG?
YES, MASTER. THOUGH THE PATIENT APPEARS TO BE SLEEPING WELL ENOUGH.
FOR WHAT I INTEND...A LEVEL OF UNCONSCIOUSNESS MUST BE ATTAINED... THAT IS UNLIKE NORMAL SLEEP.
YOU MIGHT PREPARE A POT OF GREEN TEA AND YOUR EXCELLENT NOODLES. OUR PATIENT WILL NEED IT WHEN I'M DONE WITH HIM.
POOR WONG. I KNOW HE DISLIKES ENTERING THIS PARTICULAR CHAMBER.
VERY GOOD, MASTER.
WHEN HE LEAVES... IT IS MARGINALLY EARLIER THAN WHEN HE ENTERED.
SUCH ARE THE VICISSITUDES OF BEING A SORCERER'S ASSISTANT.

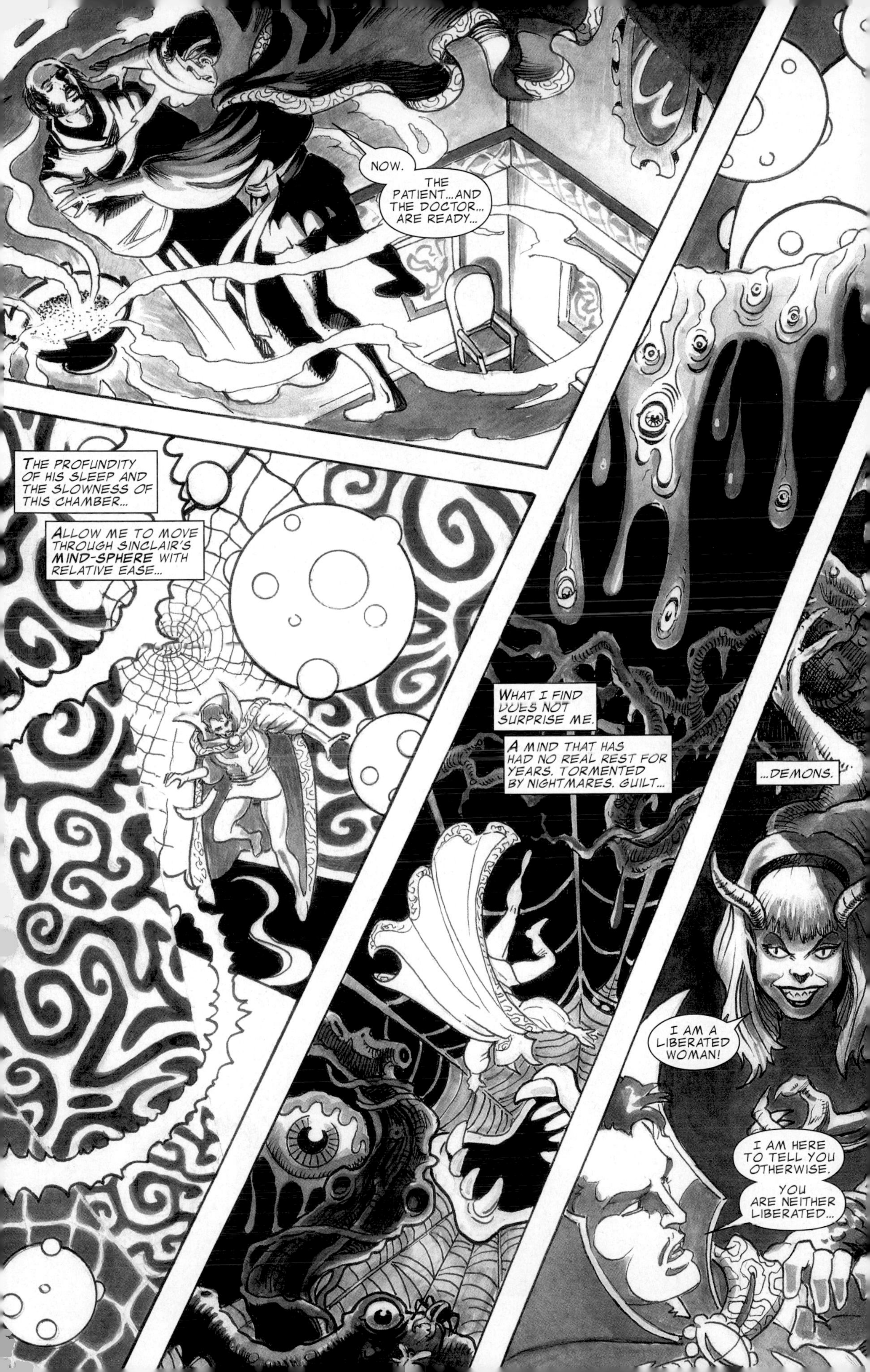
NOW.
THE PATIENT...AND THE DOCTOR... ARE READY...
THE PROFUNDITY OF HIS SLEEP AND THE SLOWNESS OF THIS CHAMBER...
ALLOW ME TO MOVE THROUGH SINCLAIR'S MIND-SPHERE WITH RELATIVE EASE...
WHAT I FIND DOES NOT SURPRISE ME.
A MIND THAT HAS HAD NO REAL REST FOR YEARS. TORMENTED BY NIGHTMARES. GUILT...
...DEMONS.
I AM A LIBERATED WOMAN!
I AM HERE TO TELL YOU OTHERWISE.
YOU ARE NEITHER LIBERATED...

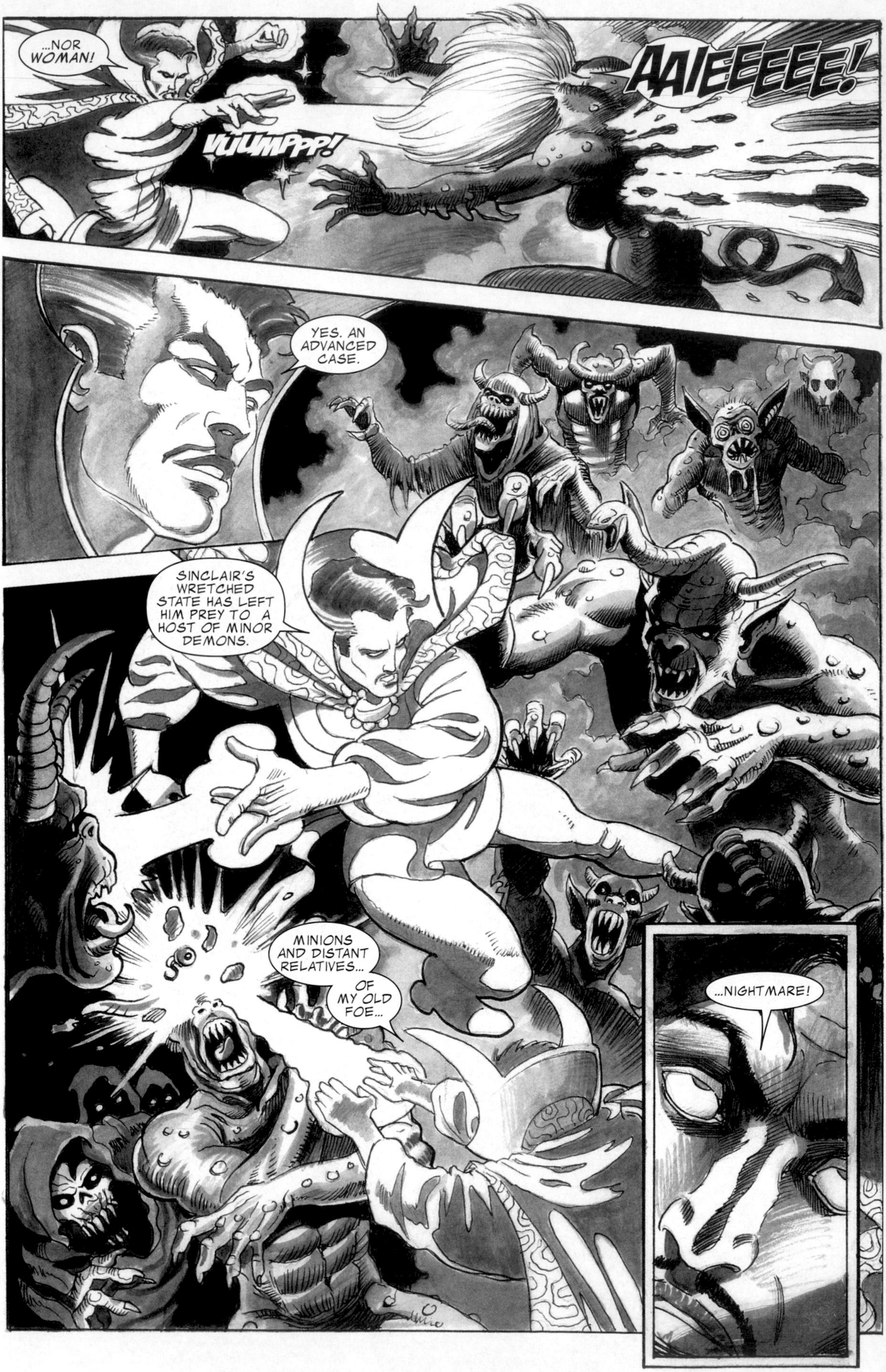
...NOR WOMAN!
AAIEEEEEE!
VUUMPPP!
YES. AN ADVANCED CASE.
SINCLAIR'S WRETCHED STATE HAS LEFT HIM PREY TO A HOST OF MINOR DEMONS.
MINIONS AND DISTANT RELATIVES...
OF MY OLD FOE...
...NIGHTMARE!

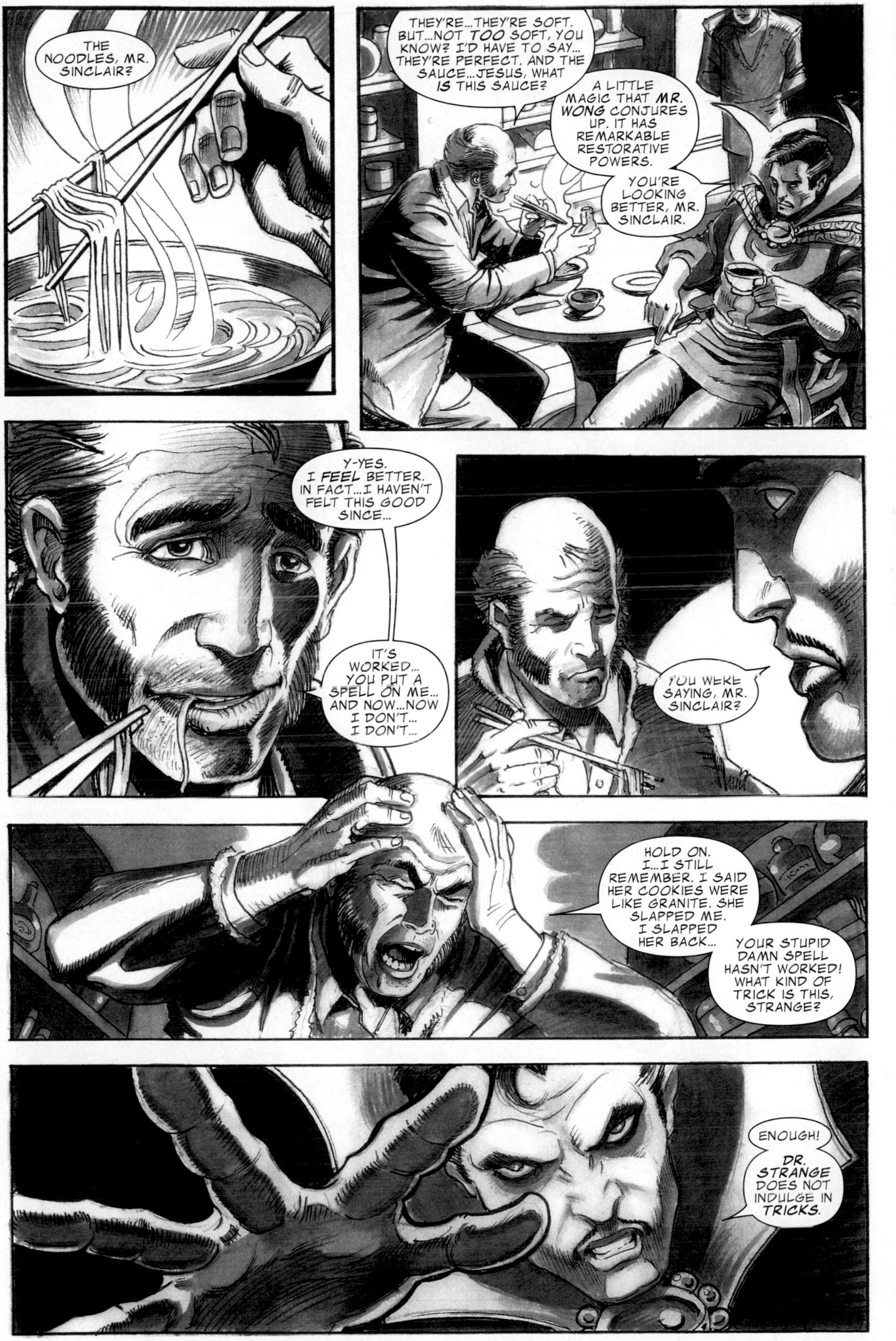
THE NOODLES, MR. SINCLAIR?
THEY'RE...THEY'RE SOFT. BUT...NOT TOO SOFT, YOU KNOW? I'D HAVE TO SAY... THEY'RE PERFECT. AND THE SAUCE...JESUS, WHAT IS THIS SAUCE?
A LITTLE MAGIC THAT MR. WONG CONJURES UP. IT HAS REMARKABLE RESTORATIVE POWERS.
YOU'RE LOOKING BETTER, MR. SINCLAIR.
Y-YES. I FEEL BETTER. IN FACT...I HAVEN'T FELT THIS GOOD SINCE...
IT'S WORKED... YOU PUT A SPELL ON ME... AND NOW...NOW I DON'T... I DON'T...
YOU WERE SAYING, MR. SINCLAIR?
HOLD ON. I...I STILL REMEMBER. I SAID HER COOKIES WERE LIKE GRANITE. SHE SLAPPED ME. I SLAPPED HER BACK...
YOUR STUPID DAMN SPELL HASN'T WORKED! WHAT KIND OF TRICK IS THIS, STRANGE?
ENOUGH!
DR. STRANGE DOES NOT INDULGE IN TRICKS.

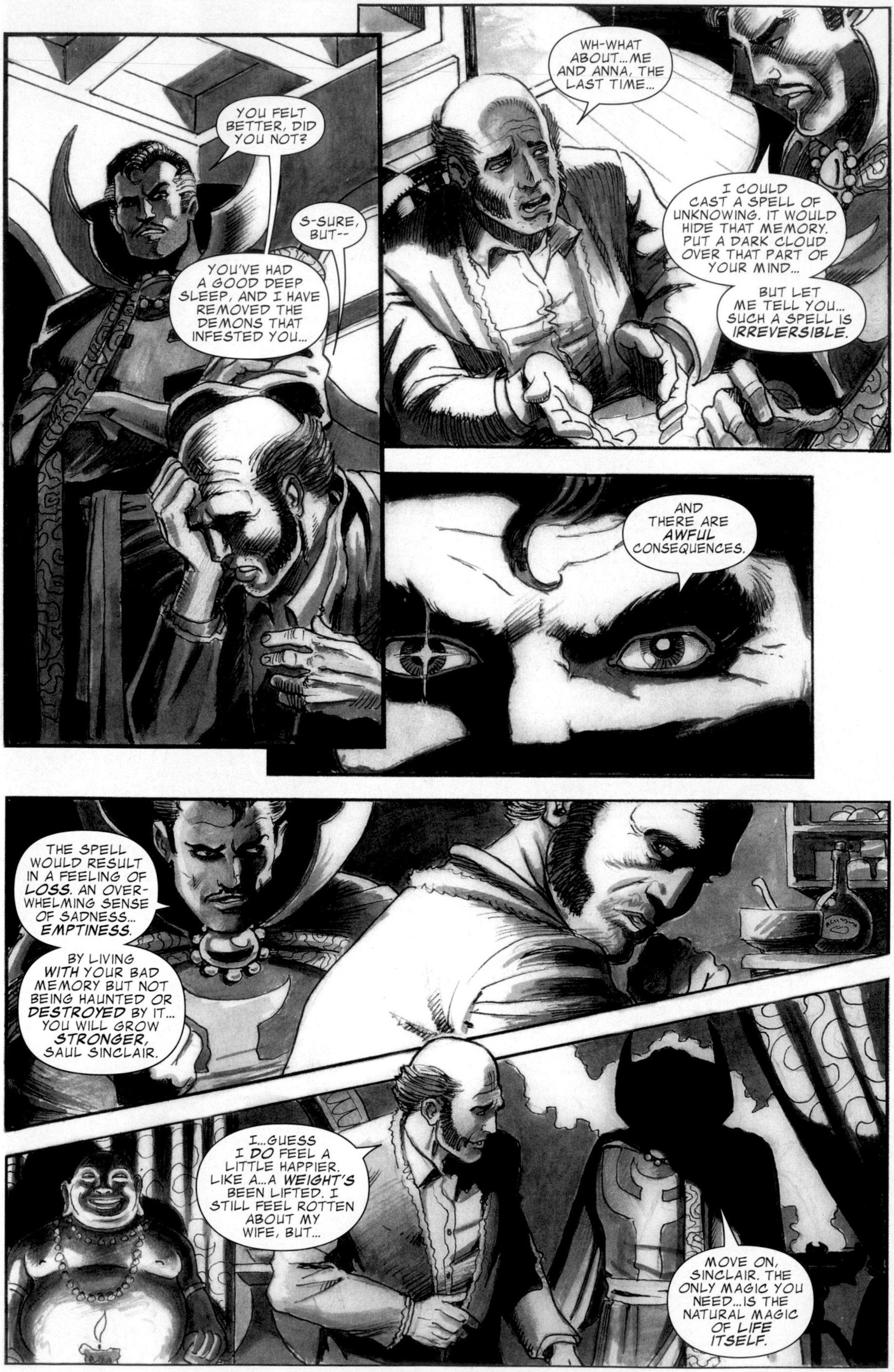
YOU FELT BETTER, DID YOU NOT?
YOU'VE HAD A GOOD DEEP SLEEP, AND I HAVE REMOVED THE DEMONS THAT INFESTED YOU...
S-SURE, BUT--
WH-WHAT ABOUT...ME AND ANNA, THE LAST TIME...
I COULD CAST A SPELL OF UNKNOWING. IT WOULD HIDE THAT MEMORY. PUT A DARK CLOUD OVER THAT PART OF YOUR MIND...
BUT LET ME TELL YOU... SUCH A SPELL IS IRREVERSIBLE.
AND THERE ARE AWFUL CONSEQUENCES.
THE SPELL WOULD RESULT IN A FEELING OF LOSS. AN OVER-WHELMING SENSE OF SADNESS... EMPTINESS.
BY LIVING WITH YOUR BAD MEMORY BUT NOT BEING HAUNTED OR DESTROYED BY IT... YOU WILL GROW STRONGER, SAUL SINCLAIR.
I...GUESS I DO FEEL A LITTLE HAPPIER. LIKE A...A WEIGHT'S BEEN LIFTED. I STILL FEEL ROTTEN ABOUT MY WIFE, BUT...
MOVE ON, SINCLAIR. THE ONLY MAGIC YOU NEED...IS THE NATURAL MAGIC OF LIFE ITSELF.

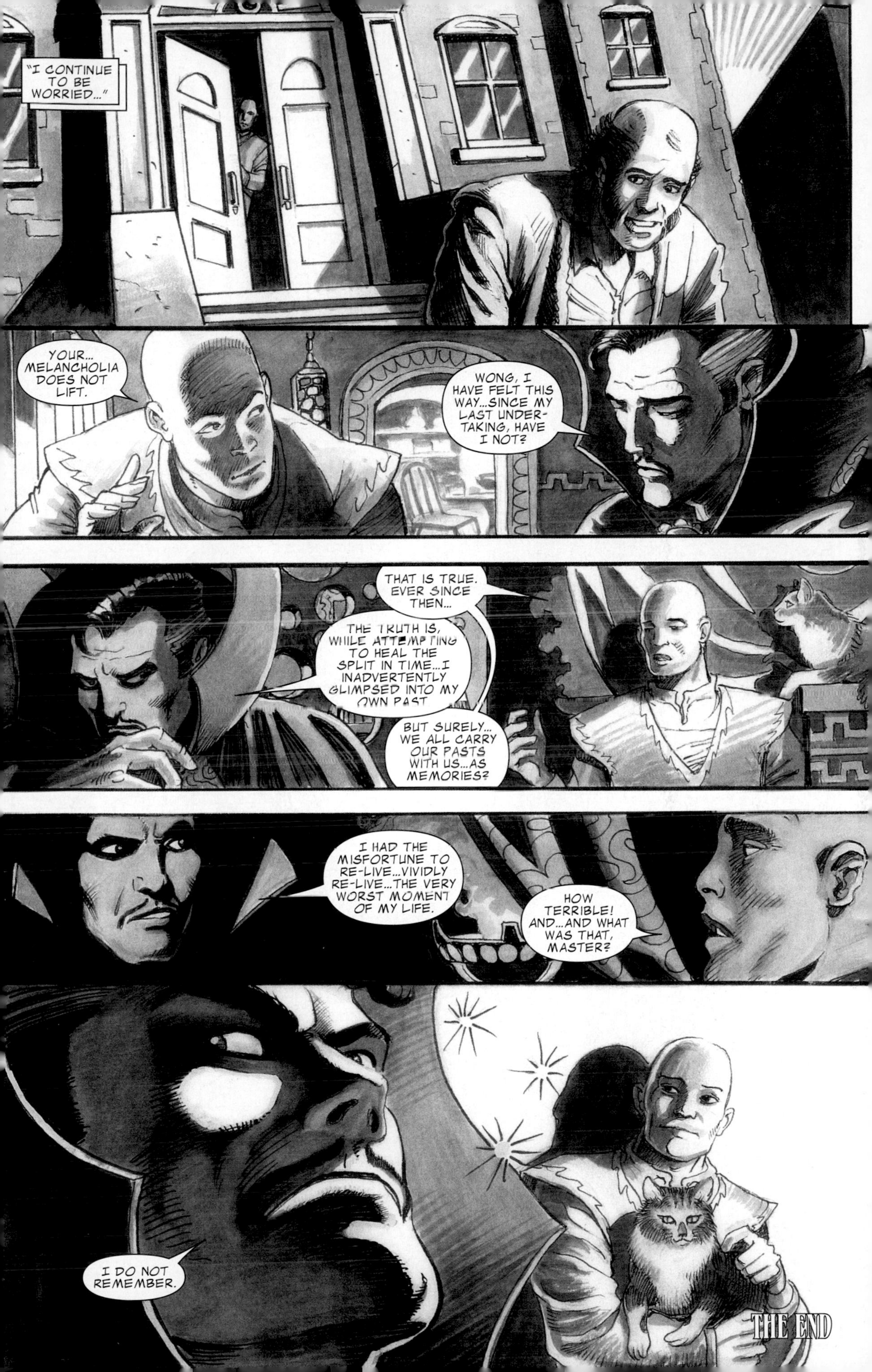
"I CONTINUE TO BE WORRIED..."
YOUR... MELANCHOLIA DOES NOT LIFT.
WONG, I HAVE FELT THIS WAY...SINCE MY LAST UNDER-TAKING, HAVE I NOT?
THAT IS TRUE. EVER SINCE THEN...
THE TRUTH IS, WHILE ATTEMPTING TO HEAL THE SPLIT IN TIME...I INADVERTENTLY GLIMPSED INTO MY OWN PAST
BUT SURELY... WE ALL CARRY OUR PASTS WITH US...AS MEMORIES?
I HAD THE MISFORTUNE TO RE-LIVE...VIVIDLY RE-LIVE...THE VERY WORST MOMENT OF MY LIFE.
HOW TERRIBLE! AND...AND WHAT WAS THAT, MASTER?
I DO NOT REMEMBER.
THE END

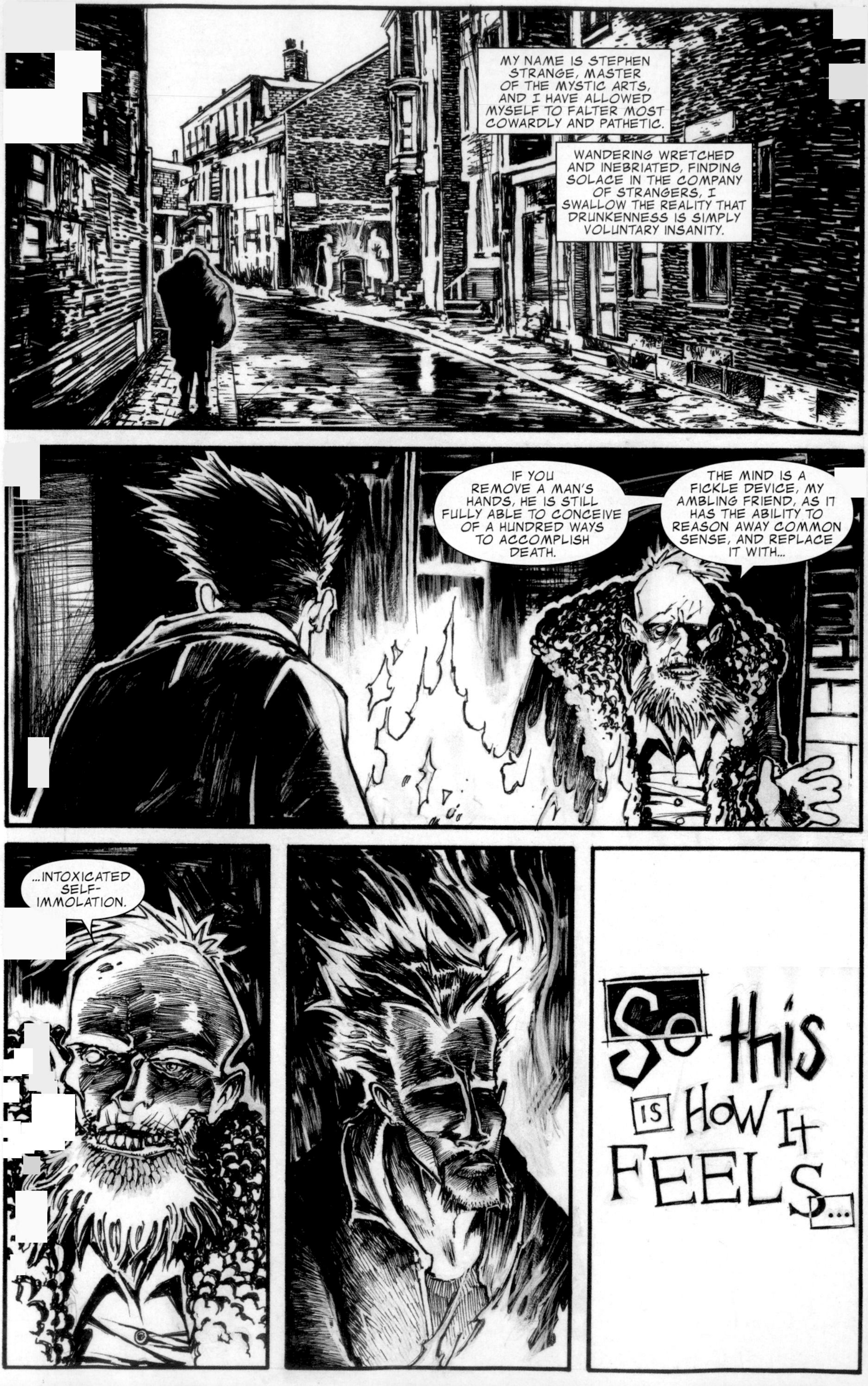
MY NAME IS STEPHEN STRANGE, MASTER OF THE MYSTIC ARTS, AND I HAVE ALLOWED MYSELF TO FALTER MOST COWARDLY AND PATHETIC.
WANDERING WRETCHED AND INEBRIATED, FINDING SOLACE IN THE COMPANY OF STRANGERS, I SWALLOW THE REALITY THAT DRUNKENNESS IS SIMPLY VOLUNTARY INSANITY.
IF YOU REMOVE A MAN'S HANDS, HE IS STILL FULLY ABLE TO CONCEIVE OF A HUNDRED WAYS TO ACCOMPLISH DEATH.
THE MIND IS A FICKLE DEVICE, MY AMBLING FRIEND, AS IT HAS THE ABILITY TO REASON AWAY COMMON SENSE, AND REPLACE IT WITH...
...INTOXICATED SELF-IMMOLATION.
So this is How It FEELS...

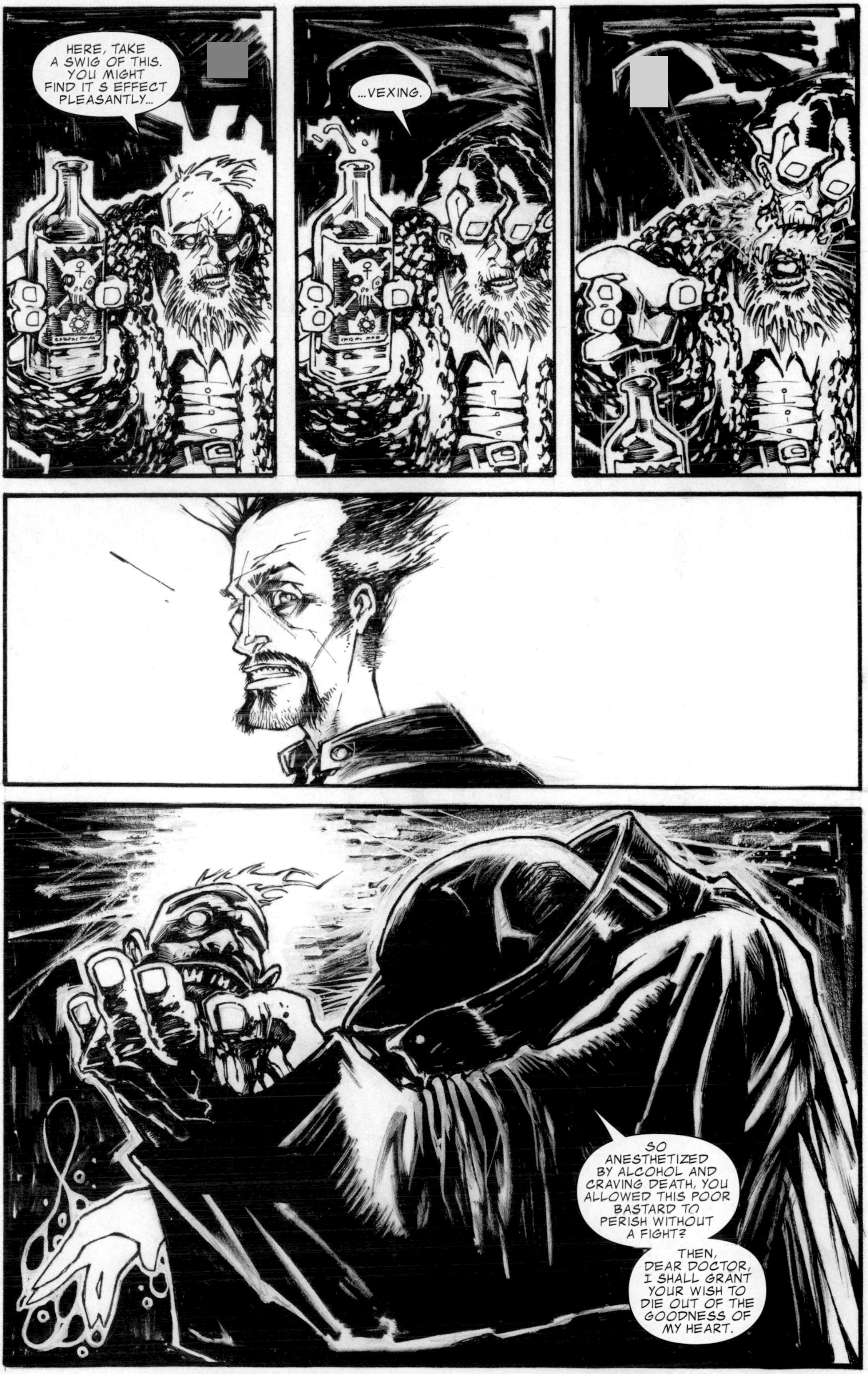
HERE, TAKE A SWIG OF THIS. YOU MIGHT FIND IT S EFFECT PLEASANTLY...
...VEXING.
SO ANESTHETIZED BY ALCOHOL AND CRAVING DEATH, YOU ALLOWED THIS POOR BASTARD TO PERISH WITHOUT A FIGHT?
THEN, DEAR DOCTOR, I SHALL GRANT YOUR WISH TO DIE OUT OF THE GOODNESS OF MY HEART.

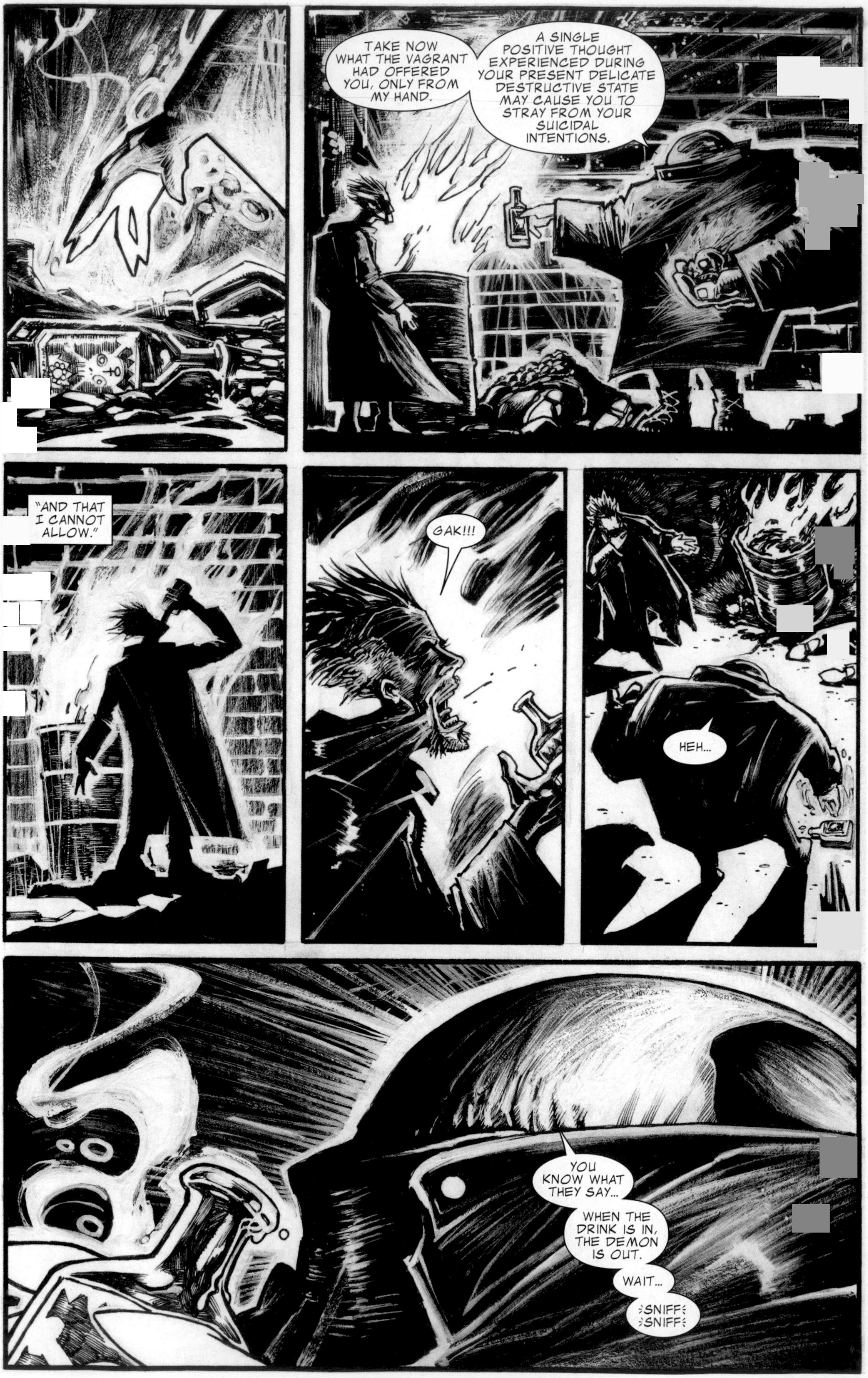
TAKE NOW WHAT THE VAGRANT HAD OFFERED YOU, ONLY FROM MY HAND.
A SINGLE POSITIVE THOUGHT EXPERIENCED DURING YOUR PRESENT DELICATE DESTRUCTIVE STATE MAY CAUSE YOU TO STRAY FROM YOUR SUICIDAL INTENTIONS.
"AND THAT I CANNOT ALLOW."
GAK!!!
HEH...
YOU KNOW WHAT THEY SAY...
WHEN THE DRINK IS IN, THE DEMON IS OUT.
WAIT...
SNIFF SNIFF

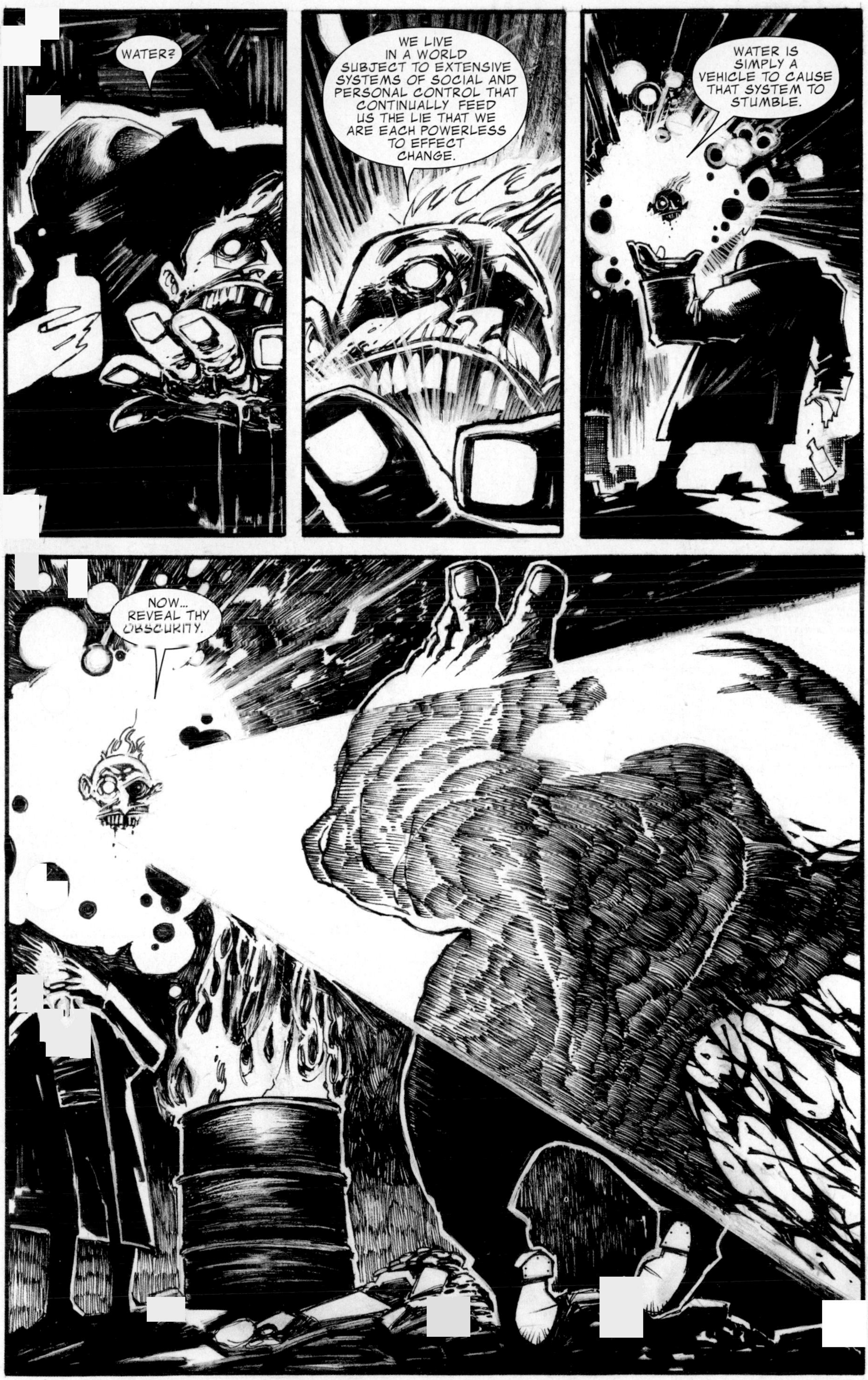
WATER?
WE LIVE IN A WORLD SUBJECT TO EXTENSIVE SYSTEMS OF SOCIAL AND PERSONAL CONTROL THAT CONTINUALLY FEED US THE LIE THAT WE ARE EACH POWERLESS TO EFFECT CHANGE.
WATER IS SIMPLY A VEHICLE TO CAUSE THAT SYSTEM TO STUMBLE.
NOW... REVEAL THY OBSCURITY.

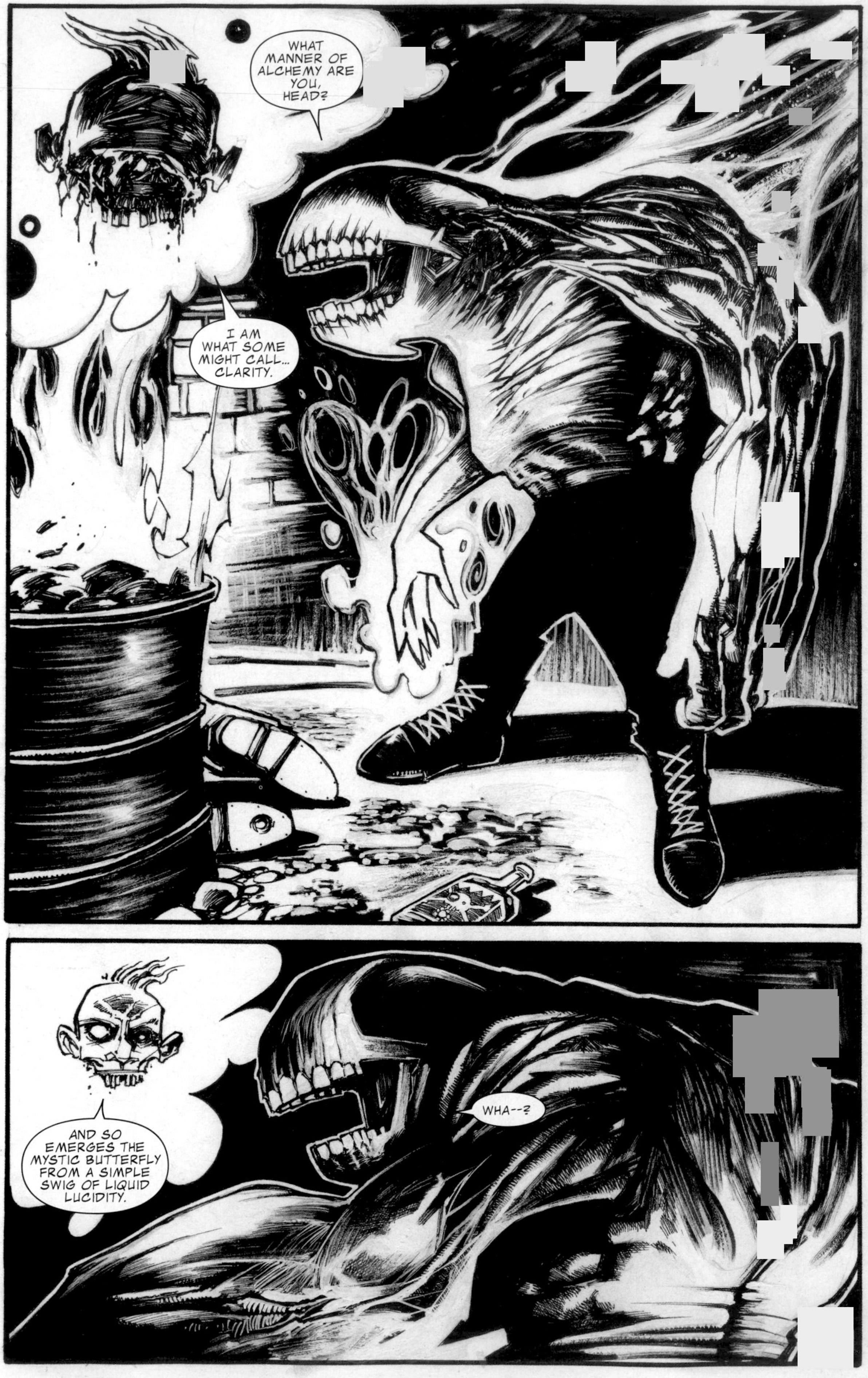
WHAT MANNER OF ALCHEMY ARE YOU, HEAD?
I AM WHAT SOME MIGHT CALL... CLARITY.
AND SO EMERGES THE MYSTIC BUTTERFLY FROM A SIMPLE SWIG OF LIQUID LUCIDITY.
WHA--?

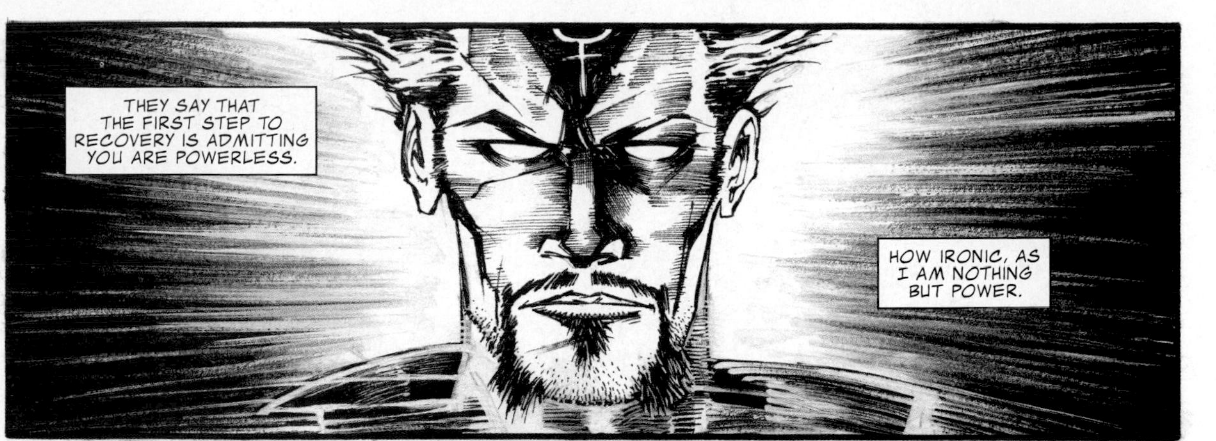
THEY SAY THAT THE FIRST STEP TO RECOVERY IS ADMITTING YOU ARE POWERLESS.
HOW IRONIC, AS I AM NOTHING BUT POWER.
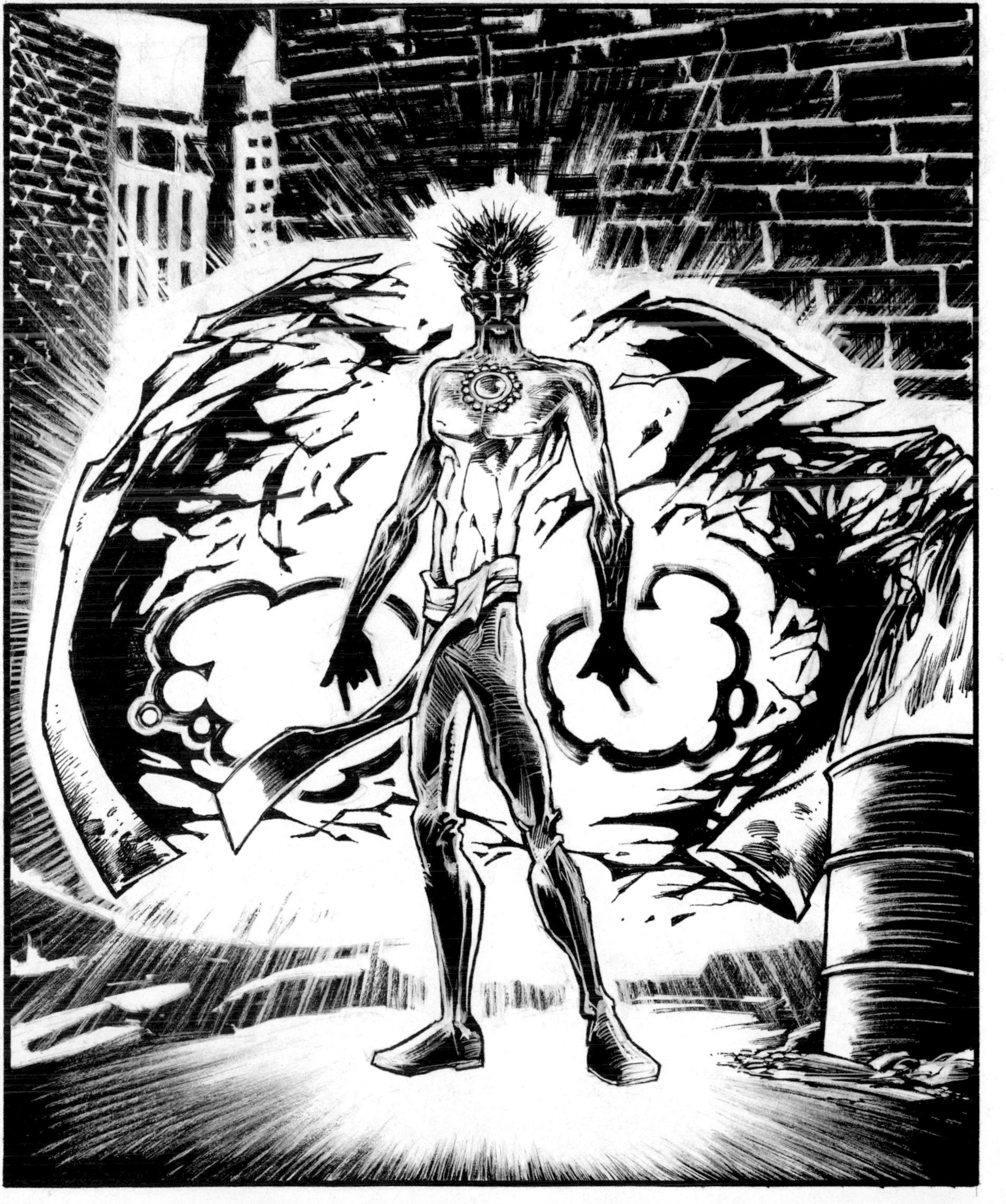

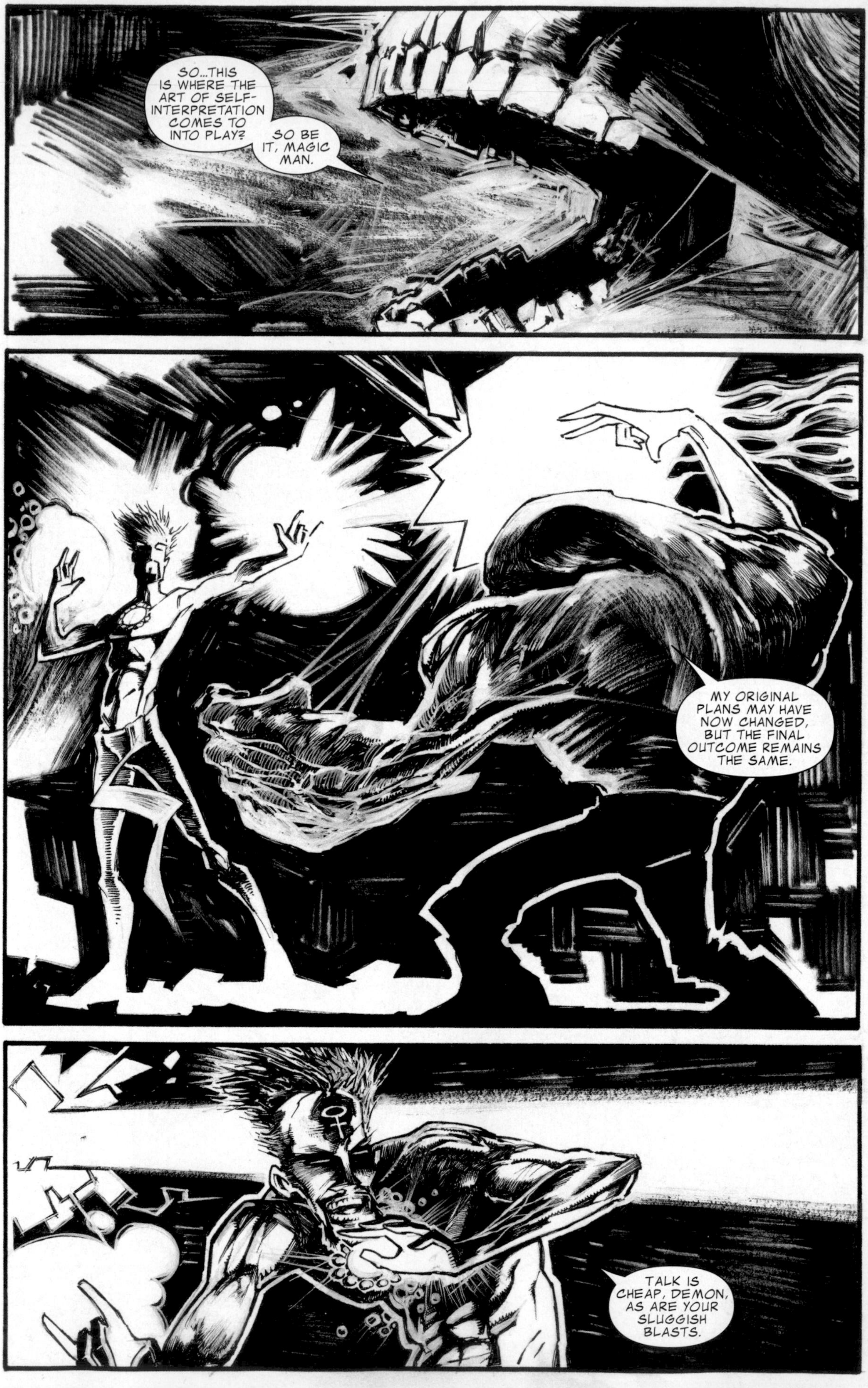
SO...THIS IS WHERE THE ART OF SELF-INTERPRETATION COMES TO INTO PLAY?
SO BE IT, MAGIC MAN.
MY ORIGINAL PLANS MAY HAVE NOW CHANGED, BUT THE FINAL OUTCOME REMAINS THE SAME.
TALK IS CHEAP, DEMON, AS ARE YOUR SLUGGISH BLASTS.

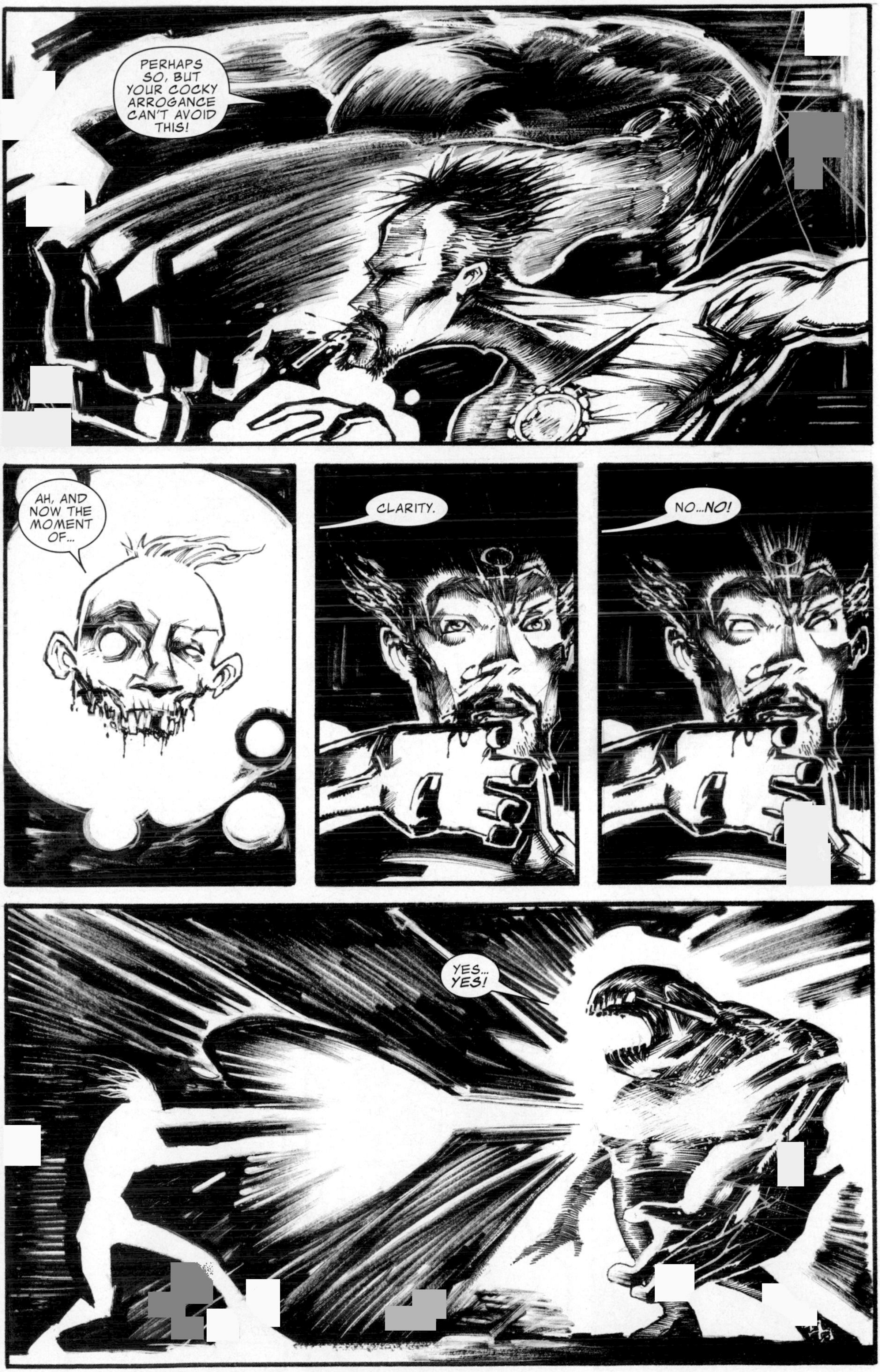
PERHAPS SO, BUT YOUR COCKY ARROGANCE CAN'T AVOID THIS!
AH, AND NOW THE MOMENT OF...
CLARITY.
NO...NO!
YES... YES!

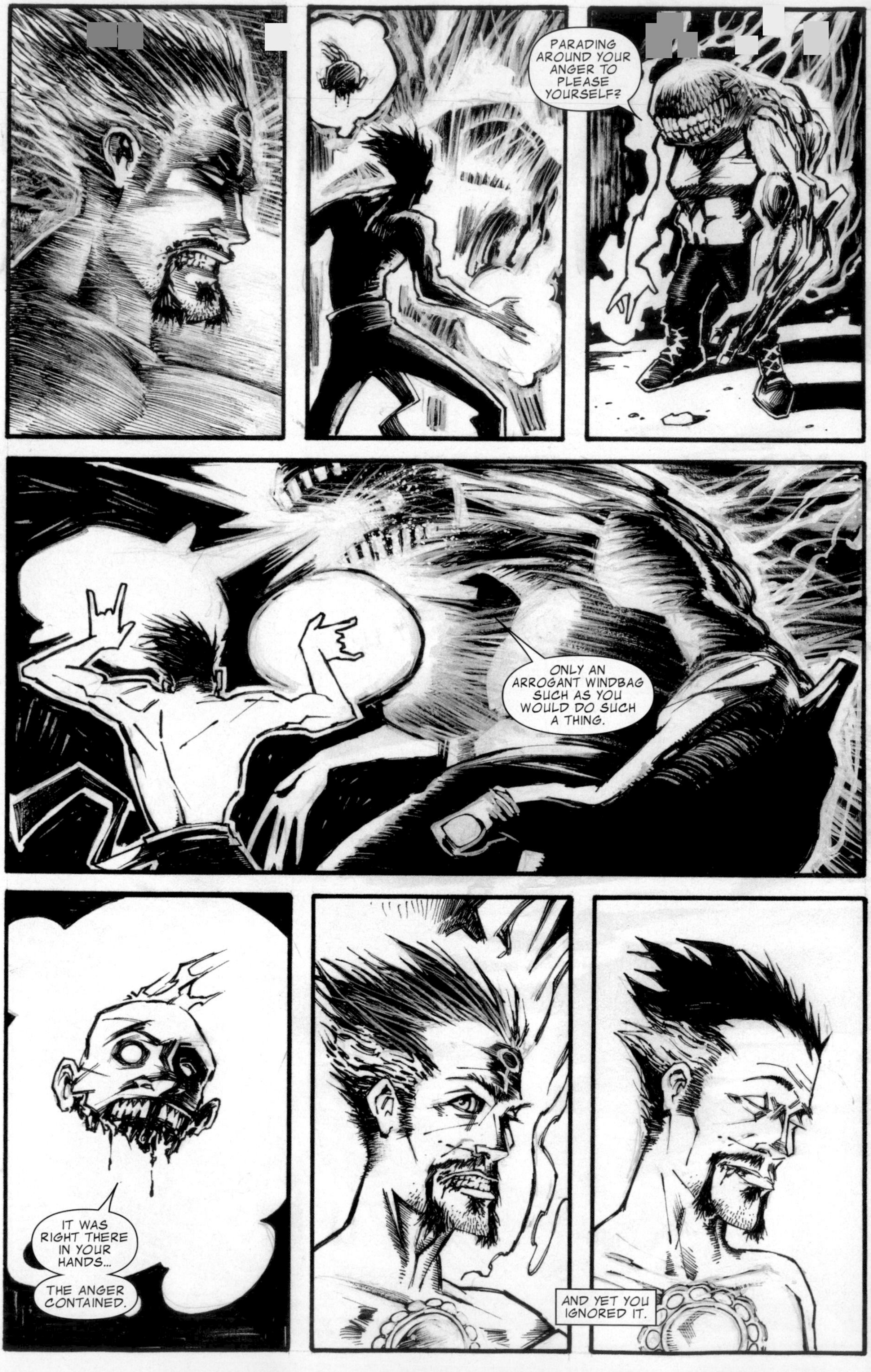
PARADING AROUND YOUR ANGER TO PLEASE YOURSELF?
ONLY AN ARROGANT WINDBAG SUCH AS YOU WOULD DO SUCH A THING.
IT WAS RIGHT THERE IN YOUR HANDS...
THE ANGER CONTAINED.
AND YET YOU IGNORED IT.

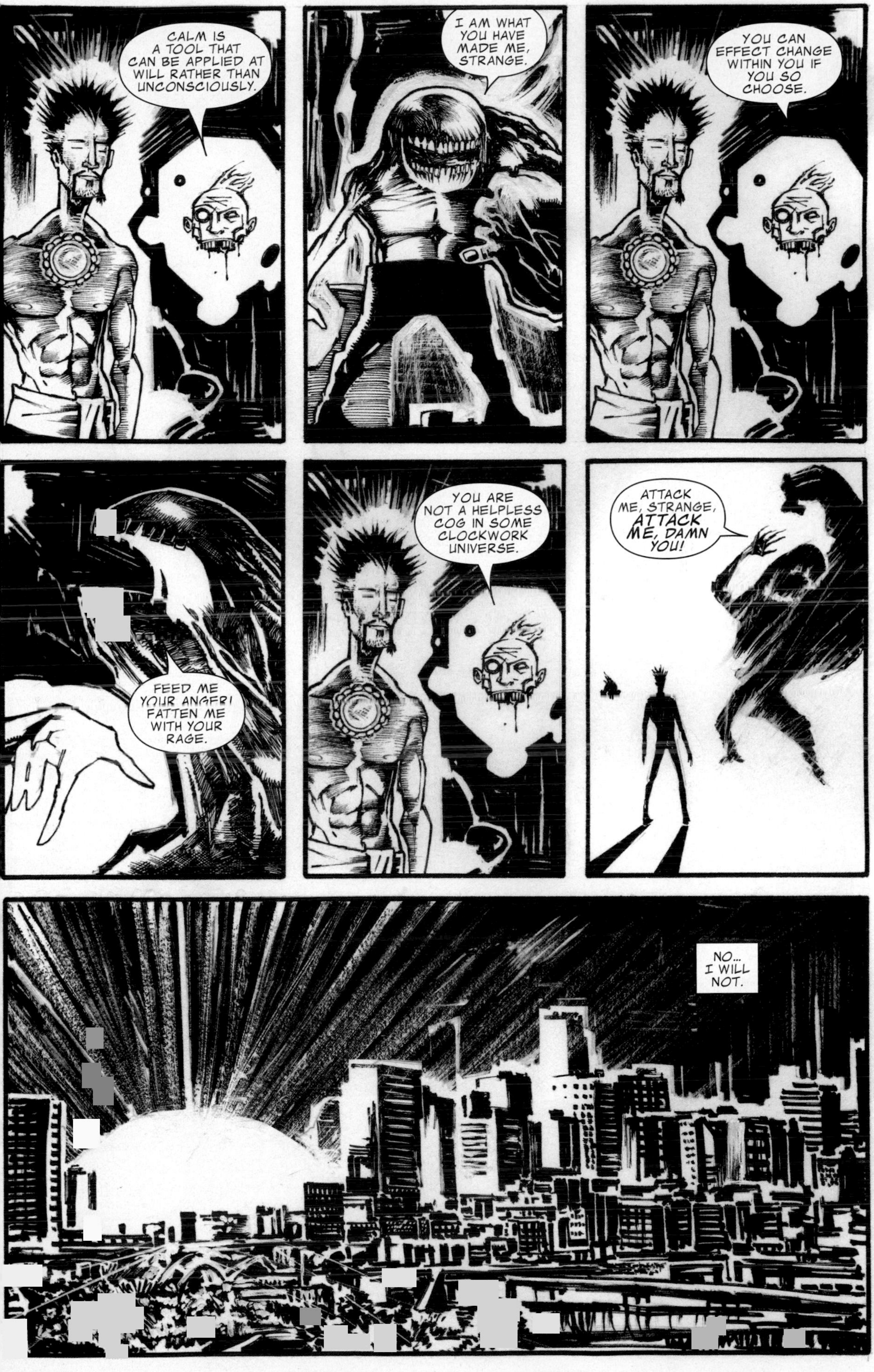
CALM IS A TOOL THAT CAN BE APPLIED AT WILL RATHER THAN UNCONSCIOUSLY.
I AM WHAT YOU HAVE MADE ME, STRANGE.
YOU CAN EFFECT CHANGE WITHIN YOU IF YOU SO CHOOSE.
FEED ME YOUR ANGER! FATTEN ME WITH YOUR RAGE.
YOU ARE NOT A HELPLESS COG IN SOME CLOCKWORK UNIVERSE.
ATTACK ME, STRANGE, ATTACK ME, DAMN YOU!
NO... I WILL NOT.

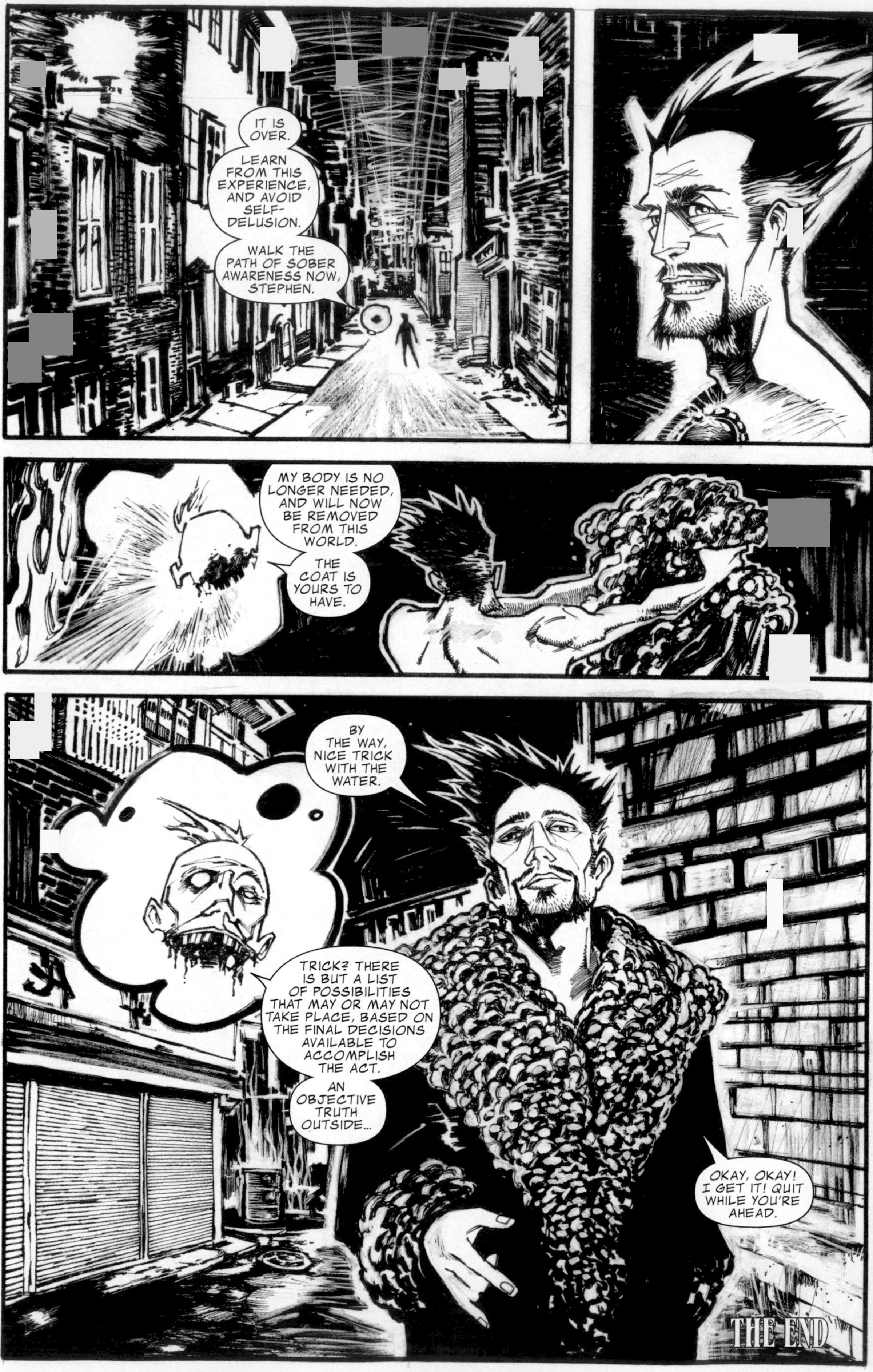
IT IS OVER.
LEARN FROM THIS EXPERIENCE, AND AVOID SELF-DELUSION.
WALK THE PATH OF SOBER AWARENESS NOW, STEPHEN.
MY BODY IS NO LONGER NEEDED, AND WILL NOW BE REMOVED FROM THIS WORLD.
THE COAT IS YOURS TO HAVE.
BY THE WAY, NICE TRICK WITH THE WATER.
TRICK? THERE IS BUT A LIST OF POSSIBILITIES THAT MAY OR MAY NOT TAKE PLACE, BASED ON THE FINAL DECISIONS AVAILABLE TO ACCOMPLISH THE ACT.
AN OBJECTIVE TRUTH OUTSIDE...
OKAY, OKAY! I GET IT! QUIT WHILE YOU'RE AHEAD.
THE END

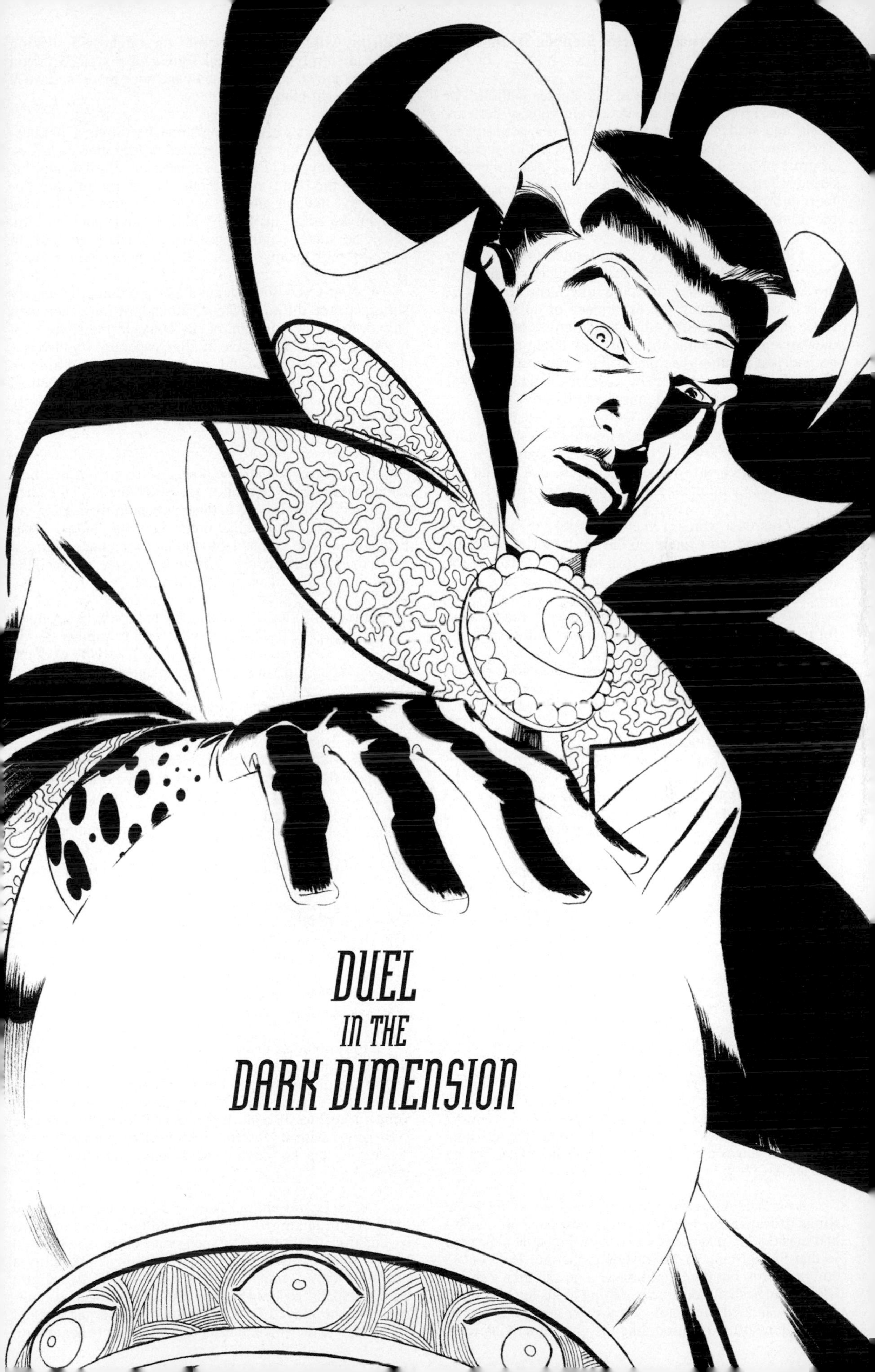
DUEL
IN THE
DARK DIMENSION

From the Journal of Doctor Stephen Strange

In the nineteenth month of my studies with the Ancient One, I tore asunder the deceiving veils of flesh and spirit, and walked for the first time on the astral plane. The sense of freedom that accompanied this shedding of gross physicality was unlike anything else I'd experienced. I felt as though this was a second birth, truer and more profound than the first. Now, I was born again into the subtle realms.

I became a little drunk on this wonderful new power. Every time I crossed over into the baffling topographies of the Astral Dimension, I strayed a little farther and stayed a little longer. I found the experience of unleashing my spirit into those spaces almost addictive. My teacher, the Ancient One, warned me that this might be the case: he had lost another disciple to the rapture of the intra-dimensional depths, and knew their fascination very well, though he himself seemed immune to it.

With a fool's confidence, I assured him that I would take no unnecessary risks; that in every venture I would stay within reach of my physical body, so that I could step back into it at a moment's notice if there was ever a need.

Words. Just words. I knew as I spoke them that they were lies. And most likely, so did he: but he allowed me, as always, to learn from my own mistakes. Quae nocent, docent, as Coleridge said: pain is the great teacher.

A week later, I was exploring once more in spirit form, while my flesh sat empty in my Master's house. I was farther from home than I had ever been, and I had taken a path that I knew was dangerous: the path that leads through the endless realms of the Dark Dimension.

One moment, the path ahead of me was empty. The next, a knight in armor as black as pitch barred my path. He was twice as tall as a man. In place of eye-holes, his helm bore clusters of spikes like the blades of a penknife. The beast he rode on was a red-eyed monstrosity that would have made my stomach lurch with nausea if I had been flesh and blood rather than airy spirit.

He laughed to see me: it was a very unpleasant sound, like the scraping of a surgeon's knife along a knob of bone.

"Well now," he said. "I have roamed far and wide across these borders, and I had all but given up hope of finding a gift to bring home to my master. But the Hosts of Hoggoth provide, do they not? And now I shall not go home empty-handed."

"Who are you?" I demanded, buying a little respite while I readied a spell. "And who is your master?"

"I am Bal Cyphyro," the knight said. He dismounted, his armor shifting in my sight and becoming as red as fire. "Bal Cyphyro, whose sword is a blasphemy, whose lance is despair. My master is the Dread Dormammu, to whom I will give you as a pet, a meal or a sacrifice. The choice I will leave to him."

As he said this, I unleashed my spell: it was the Seven Rings of Raggador, which was the most puissant magic I had mastered to that point. I expected the battle to be over in that first instant, as the ravening energies leapt out to embrace him: but the knight made a gesture like a shrug, and the rings shattered across, falling to his left and to his right in calcined crescents. They even made a sound as they fell: a soft exhalation, like the gasp of a dying man.

"Oh, this will not do, little spirit," the knight said, shaking his head sternly. "How shall I boast of my catch if you make my job so easy? Come by me once more, and we'll see what your mettle is."

His armor shifted a second time, becoming a luminescent green like the rot on the faces of forgotten cadavers. Disgusted beyond measure, I struck out at him again, this time with the Bands of Cyttorak. The knight tutted disapprovingly, making another gesture: the bands expanded like smoke rings, drifting by him without touching him. "No," he said, sounding resigned. "There's no fight in you. But perhaps my master will still find you amusing."

I didn't see his counterattack coming: he barely shrugged, and the air thickened around me into a net, then shrank to fit the contours of my body. In the space of a heartbeat, I couldn't move at all. Desperate, I yelled out the three words that would spit the Fires of Fandral forth from my eyes, but the net in which I was caught seemed designed to negate the power of the spell: it produced only a few pale sparks, and my opponent gave a snort of derision.

He cantered toward me now, towering over me like a father over a wayward child. He hefted me onto the back of his steed, securing me to the pommel of his saddle with a cinch of what looked like braided intestine. Once I was firmly bound, he climbed into the saddle again and turned about the way he'd come. Without a word, he twitched the reins and his foul beast broke into a trot.

I thought furiously. I had no further spells as strong as those I'd already tried. There were smaller cantrips in my repertoire, some of which might conceivably be of some use, but most of them required my hands to be free.

At least, I thought, I had a while in which to plan, because the knight had talked of roaming far from his starting point. But to my dismay, he seemed to have a magic tailor-made for this contingency: he bowed his head every few seconds as he rode, and each time he did so, an immense distance fled past beneath the feet of his mount in a blur, so that its hooves sounded on gravel in one moment, thudded on packed sand in the next, splashed through shallow water in the third. At this rate, it couldn't take us many minutes to reach this Dormammu's domain.

Though my position was desperate, and I ought to have been bending all my thoughts on escape, I was fascinated by this annihilation of distance, and I couldn't resist studying my captor to see how it was done. He seemed to speak no spells, nor to make any gestures of art. There was no clue in his expression or his posture how the miracle was being achieved.

The knight saw me watching him. "You're thinking of escaping me," he said. "But that cannot be. These realms are my hunting grounds, and I know their byways better than anyone. Believe me, little spirit, you chafe yourself needlessly against the inevitable. Better to make your peace with it, and to think of ways to entertain my master, so that he may decide to keep you alive a little longer."

"What is your master like?" I asked—intending only to keep him talking while I observed him. I had realized by this time that it wasn't a spell or a cantrip that allowed him to move so quickly. What was it, then? Possibly a potent artifact, a ring or scarf or the hilt of a sword into which a spell had been woven. But no, he touched nothing when he moved forward in this way: he just ducked his head, and the ethereal distances fell away beneath him.

Gradually, the truth dawned on me. This wasn't magic at all: it was just the exercise of will. The knight had been traveling on the astral planes for far longer than me, and had become far more skilled at negotiating their inexplicable geography. I was like some idiot who has only ever been used to walking, and so when he's offered a donkey as a gift, hoists it on his back and walks on.

"My master is wondrous in every respect," the knight was saying. "To serve him is my glory and my pride. It should be yours, too. If your death affords him some merriment, or your pain some trifling diversion, then your life will have had meaning."

I didn't bother to answer: I was turning over in my mind this matter of will and space, and how the one can mold and shape the other. In the mundane world, obviously, there are other considerations: to move a weight ten miles requires twice as much energy as to move it five, and somehow or other that equation must be balanced. But an astral body has no mass, no weight, and so when it moves there is no relativistic debt to be paid. So in these realms in which I now traveled, space was, if anything, a byproduct of imagination. An adept suitably trained could ignore distance, conquer space with a single thought, and be in an instant wherever he wanted to be.

I turned my attention back to my captor, observing him more closely. The design of his helmet didn't allow me to see whether he closed his eyes, but the frequent bowing of his head suggested a desire to close out external impressions as he focused his mind on what he wished to see. It was as if he was imagining the road in front of us, and bringing it into being by that process.

I began now to harbour some hope of escape, but it was premature. I tried with all the intensity of concentration I could muster to imagine myself elsewhere—in the Ancient One's manse; in the light-gardens of the Cyttorak; even in the very place where I had encountered the knight to begin with. Nothing worked. No amount of thought, of merely willing it, caused me to move as much as an inch.

We had come now to the borders of a realm unlike any we had passed through: a tract of bare and scorched earth, very dark and forbidding, strewn with blasted trees that moved without wind like the clutching hands of drowning men. I sensed that this was Dormammu's domain—and once we passed its border I knew I couldn't expect to return. If I was ever going to escape, I knew it had to be now. But perhaps that very urgency had been working against me. I tried to calm my panic and think the whole thing through calmly, to figure out where I was going wrong.

It was right then that I noticed to the right of the path a sort of pen or corral of huge size, its outer wall a mesh of energy. Behind this mesh, a horde of squat monsters moved. They were shorter in height than a man, but broader in the shoulders, their upper limbs long and muscular. Their skin was the color and texture of sandstone rock. But what was most horrible about them was their faces, or rather the absence of any face at all: instead of features, the front of their head was an open maw from which a stream of vivid energy spewed. These creatures seemed designed only to do harm, and that was what they did: they raged and ravened and attacked anything that moved—which was chiefly each other, but also the very rocks and stones of their pen.

I gasped aloud at the sight: it was all I could do not to cry out.

"The Mindless Ones," the knight said. He made a gesture that might have been a ward against harm, and turned his steed a little way from the border of that terrible place. It was interesting that he was afraid of these creatures: something to bear in mind for the future. But of course, I didn't have much future left now.

I returned to the puzzle, spurred on by desperation. The knight had no trouble in willing himself forward by exercise of will; but try as I might, I couldn't do the same. What was the difference between us? Could it be that I was bound, and he wasn't? Perhaps; although this was only a psychological barrier, it was enough to sabotage my efforts. My mind couldn't think itself free to move when my body was tangled in a net.

So I closed my eyes, and thought again.

At first, nothing.

Again, nothing.

Then the knight gave a terrible oath, and the beast he rode reared up, screaming like a million fingernails dragged down a million blackboards.

I opened my eyes, to see that my stratagem had worked. Unable to move myself, I had moved all three of us—myself, the knight, and the beast on which we rode. I had moved us neither forward nor backward on our route, but sideways; and not a thousand miles, nor a hundred, but a scant few paces. Still, those few paces were enough to take us beyond the barrier to our right.

The Mindless Ones swarmed over us at once in uncountable numbers. Whatever they gazed at with their terrible searchlight faces withered and fell away as though it

had never been. One of them stared through the Knight's right arm, even as he drew his sword. The sword fell to the ground, a mailed hand still gripping it although the arm was now gone. His steed reared high on its hind legs, pawing at the air–but when its hind legs and most of its stomach ceased to be–it tumbled sprawling into the dirt, throwing me headlong.

My hand found the sword, and I turned it on the strands of the net that held me. A few of them gave. Then I was forced to writhe and tumble out of the path of one of the Mindless Ones as its gaze swept across the space where I'd been. Clawing the net away from my legs, I struggled to my feet and was free to run. But the things were converging on me now: to run in any direction was to put myself into the path of those lethal beams.

So I fell straight down, and focused my will at the same time. Translating will into movement means ignoring the primacy of physical law: I fell, and then I was falling sideways, tumbling and rolling along a stone outcrop in a realm of floating monoliths some hundreds of leagues away.

I had made good my escape, although—a thoroughly unintended consequence—I had killed my captor in doing so.

I turned toward home, sore and weary. But my ordeal had taught me a lot about the rules both of travel and of combat in the subtle realms. I would never again make the mistakes I'd made that day.

Nor, I promised myself, would I ever revisit that distant realm where the lord Dormammu dwelled. Having seen how fearsome his servant was, I decided there and then never to make his acquaintance.

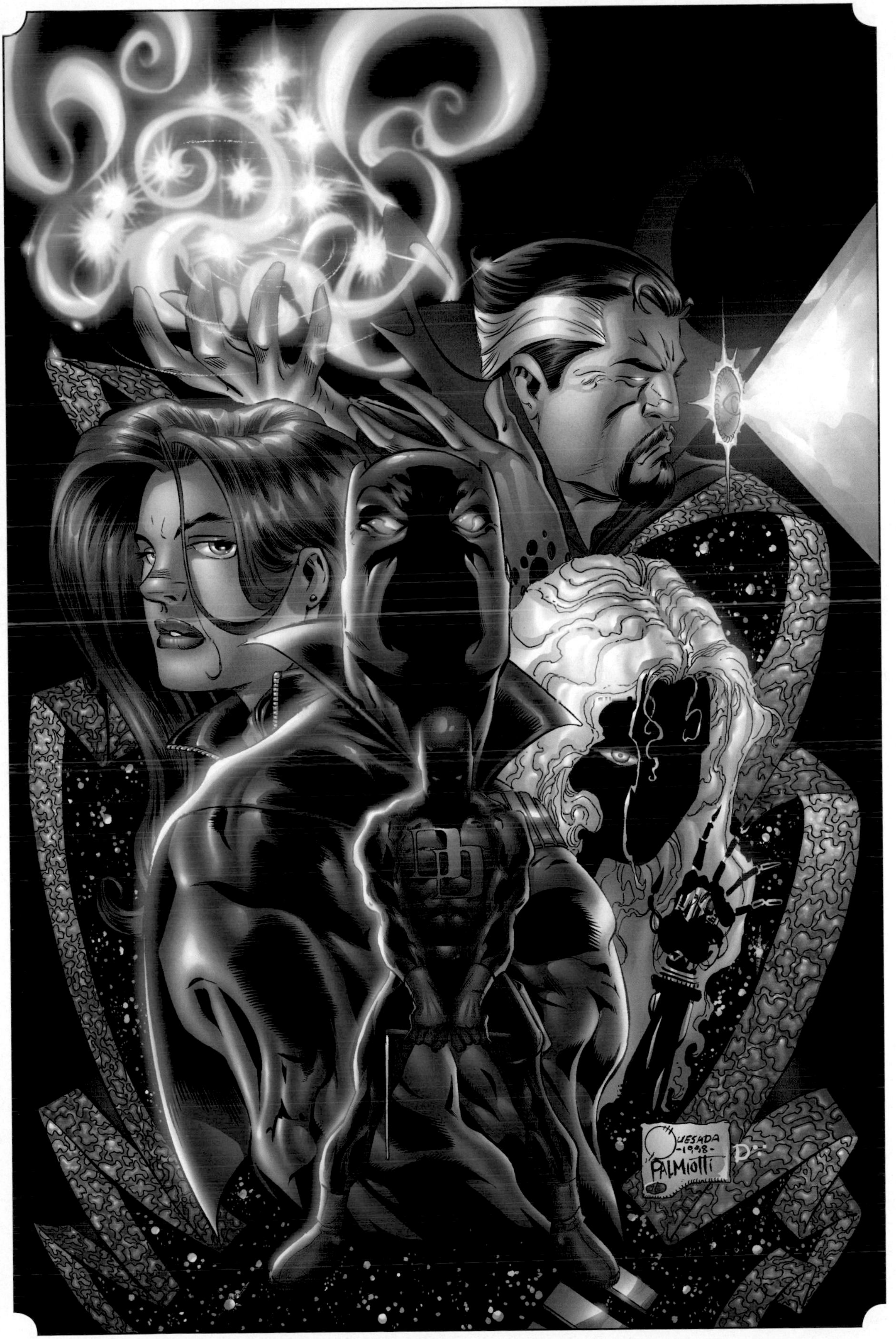
QUESADA
-1998-
PALMIOTTI

MARVEL KNIGHTS WAVE 2 SKETCHBOOK COVER ART BY JOE QUESADA, JIMMY PALMIOTTI & HABERLIN STUDIOS' DAVE KEMP

TONY HARRIS ON:
DOCTOR STRANGE

DOCTOR STRANGE

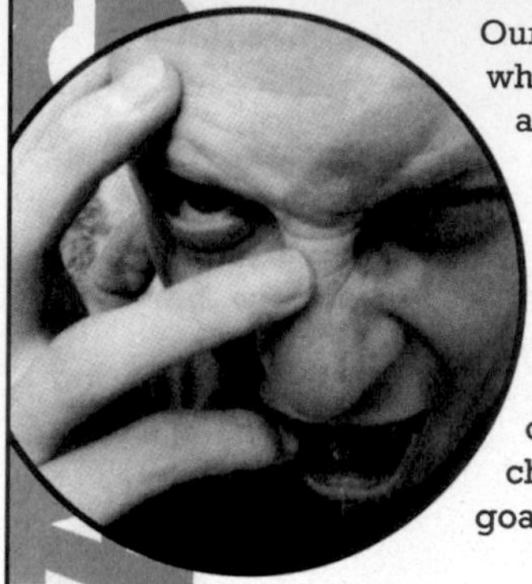

Our villains in the story, The Underchild, are three aspects of the same sub-demon which is, in fact, a physical manifestation of an evil far greater than their own. They are conjured using litergy.

The street clothes Stephen Strange wears in the story reflect the more normal human side of Dr. Strange that we are dealing with. And he is never separated from his talisman. The Eye of Agamotto is worn as a pocket watch. Many times when you see the good doctor in street clothes, it is indeed a cloaking spell to disguise his costume.

Marvel was very gracious in allowing me the freedom to alter the original costume ever so slightly. It's mostly black with a slight change to the icon on his chest, which is now red with a single eye echoing Agamotto. The addition of the goatee is a more distinguished look.

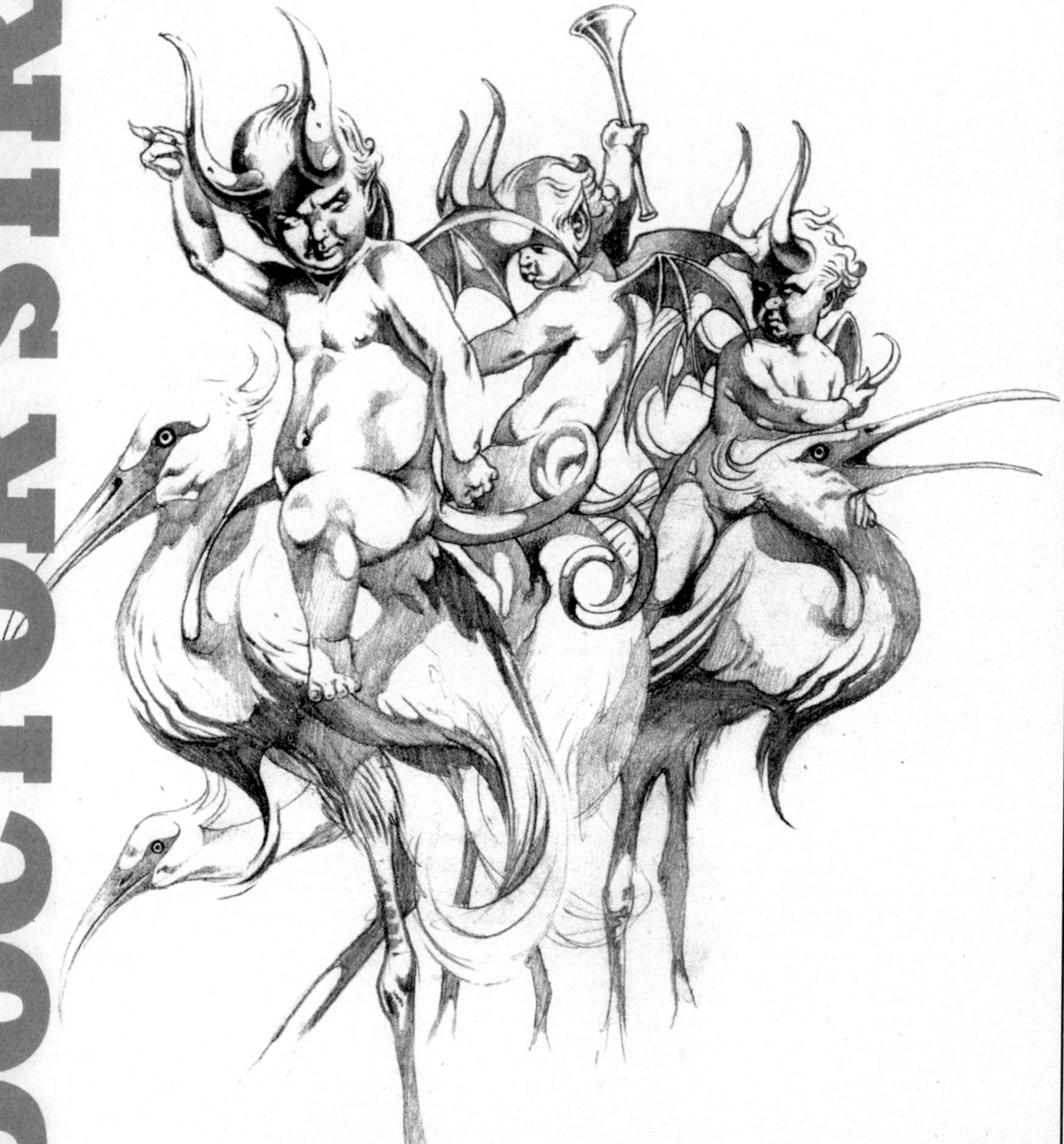

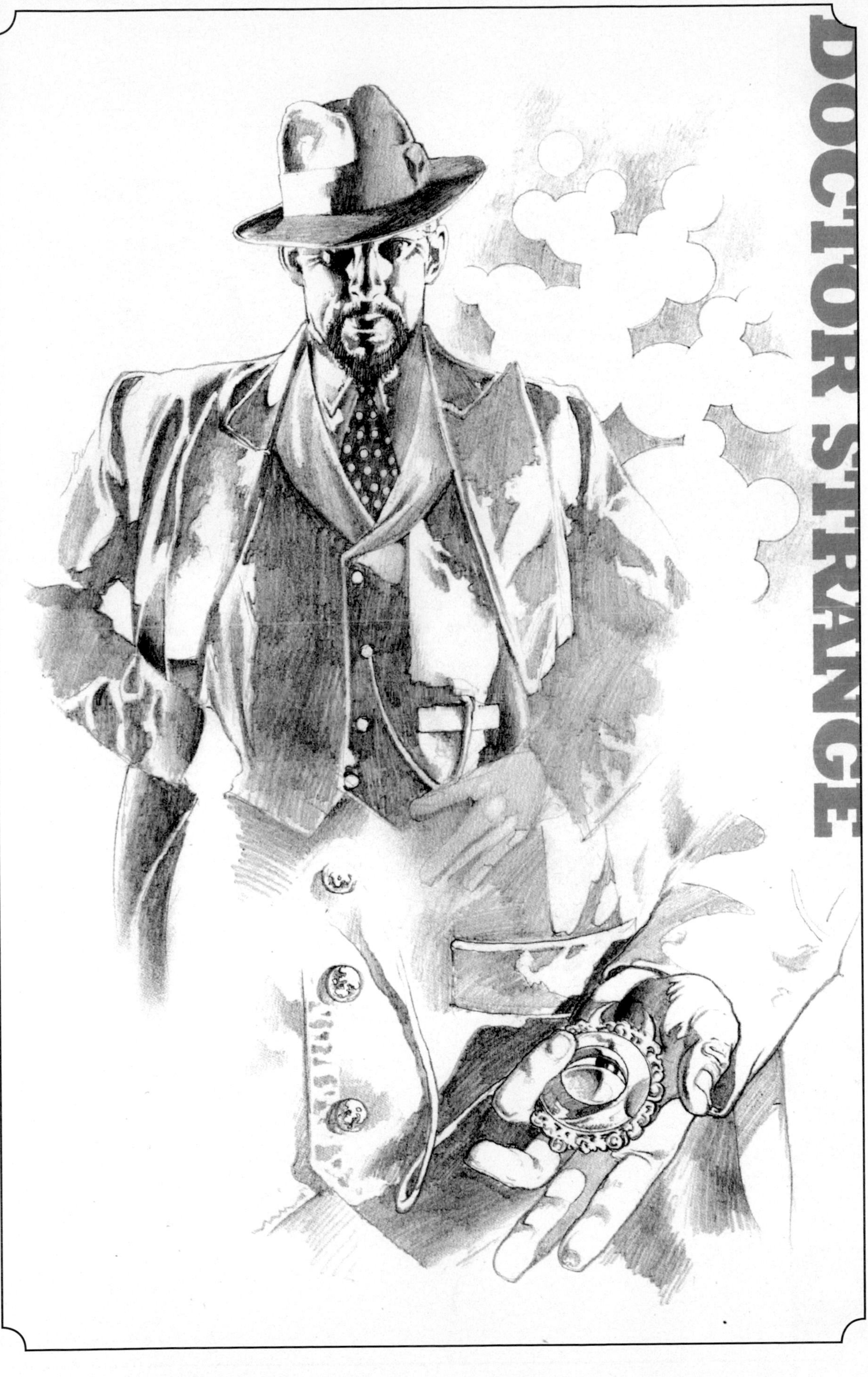
DOCTOR STRANGE

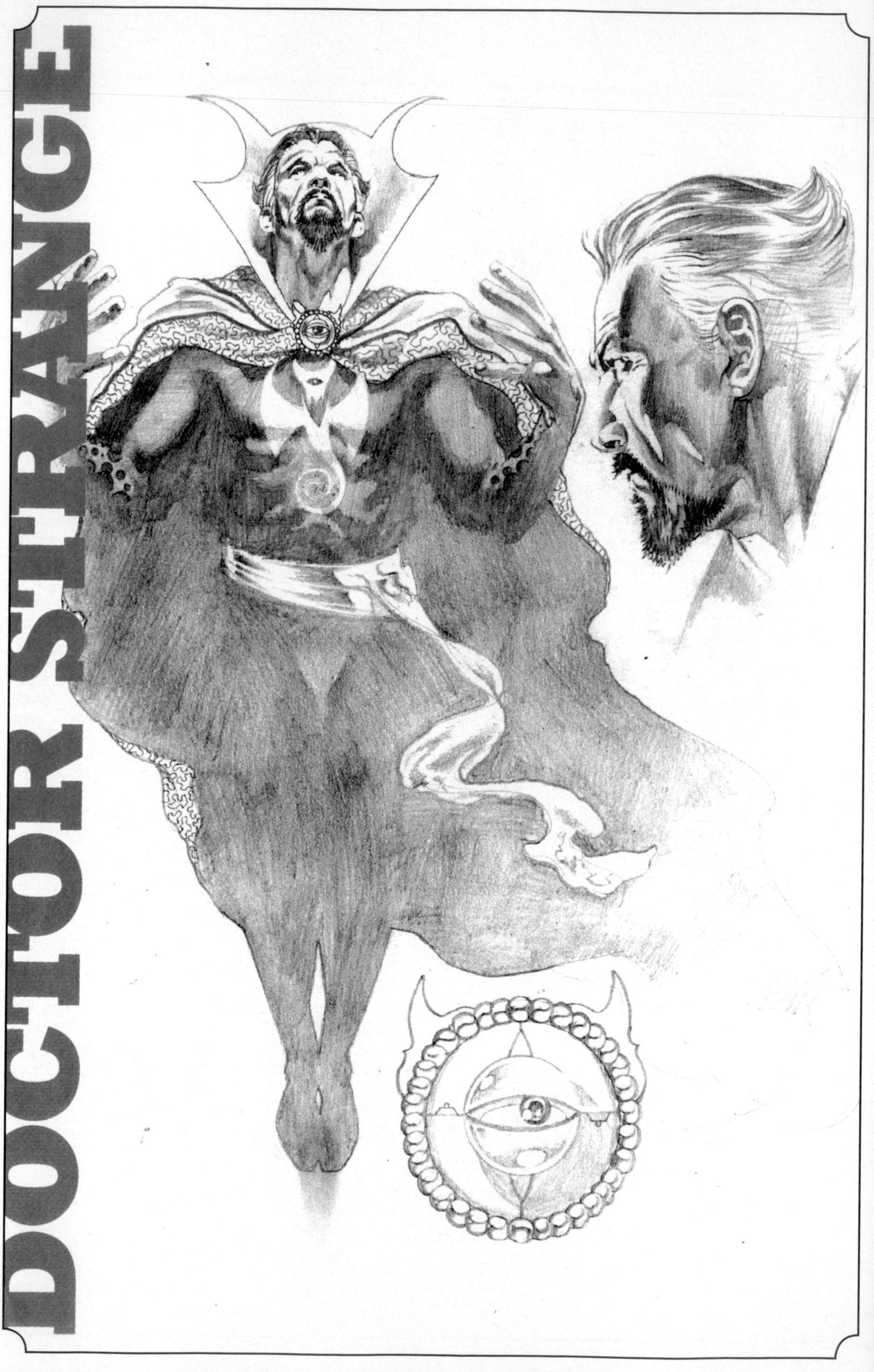
DOCTOR STRANGE

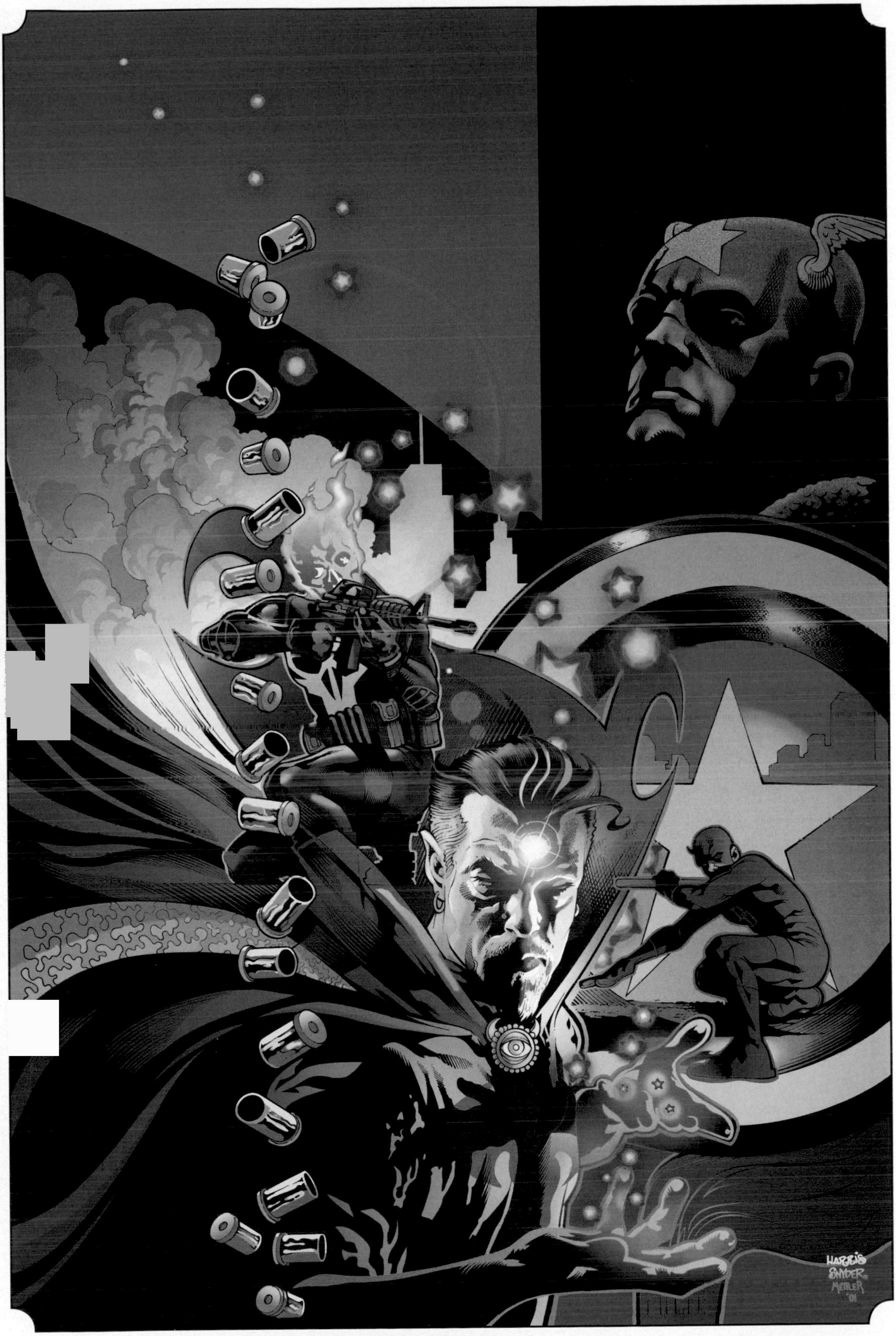
HARRIS
SNYDER
METTLER
'01

MARVEL KNIGHTS: MILLENNIAL VISIONS RE-IMAGINED
THE MARVEL KNIGHTS CHARACTERS IN CREATIVE NEW WAYS.
COVER ART BY TONY HARRIS, RAY SNYDER & J.D. METTLER

S trange!

Who's the Sorcerer Supreme that gets all the chicks?
Strange!

Who's the spell-castin' cat with the phat fro?
Strange!

Who's got a kickin' cloak and the illin' Eye of Agamotto?
Strange!

John McCrea
DR. STRANGE
You Damn Right

Who's got a killer crib in the Village and a kung-fu butler?
Strange!

Who's got a Mindless One on a leash and the world at his feet?
Strange!

Who's got Mistress Clea packin' heat?
Strange!

Who's the Master of the Mystic Arts and the baddest freak there ever was?
Strange!

You damn right.

Colored by Chris Dickey and Text by Bill Rosemann

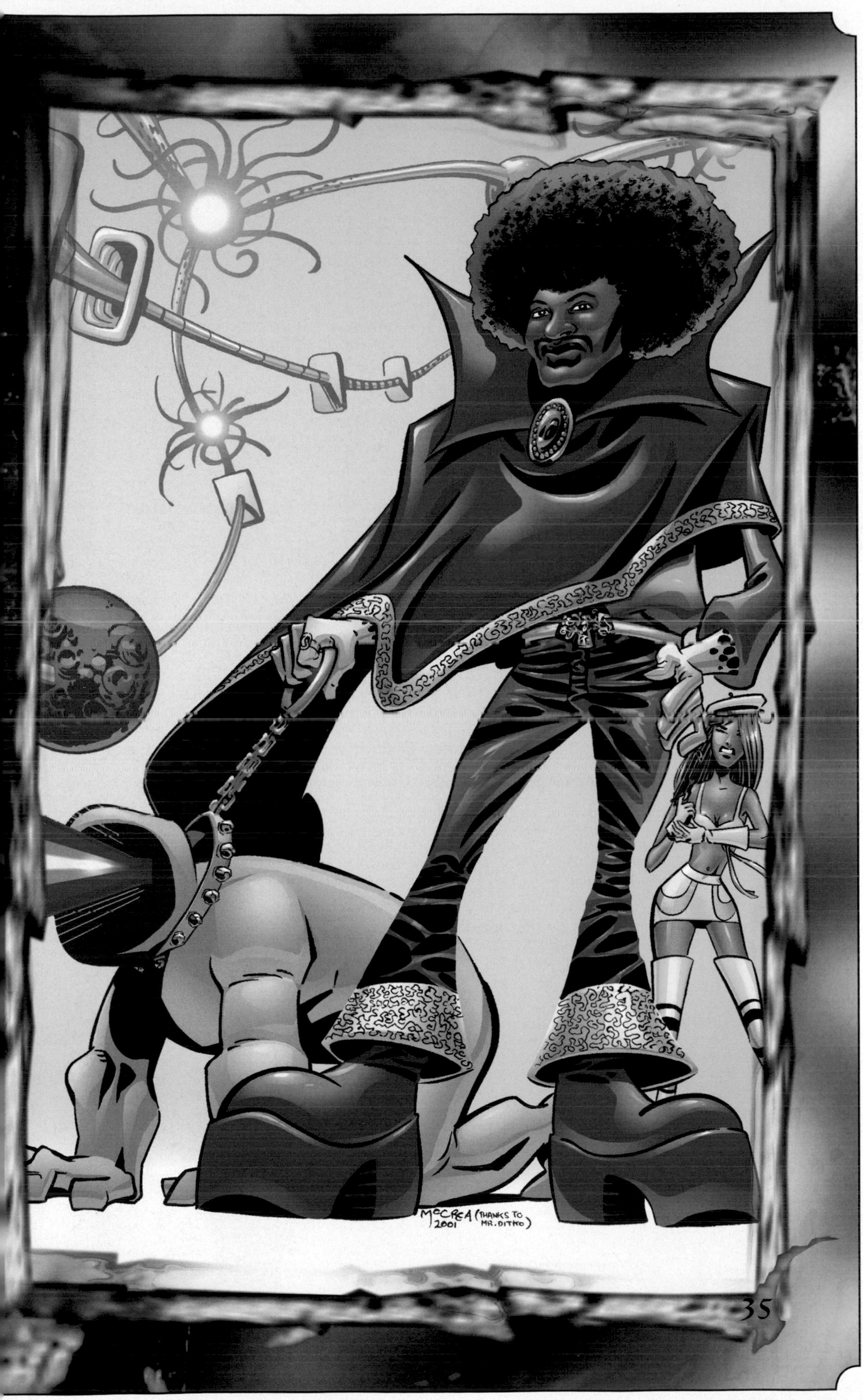
McCREA 2001 (THANKS TO MR. DITKO)

MARVEL KNIGHTS: MILLENNIAL VISIONS FEATURE BY BILL ROSEMANN, JOHN MCCREA & CHRIS DICKEY

TIME SLIP

TIME SLIP offers the chance to see how the original Marvel Universe characters would look if first designed by today's hottest creators.

IT'S 1963 AGAIN... AND STAN LEE HAS JUST HAD A NEW IDEA!

THIS TIME: A COMIC BOOK FEATURING A MAN DRIVEN TO ENTER THE INVISIBLE WORLDS BEYOND OUR REACH. A SORCERER SUPREME. A MASTER OF THE MYSTIC ARTS. THE MAGE CALLED DOCTOR STRANGE.

Your name is Dennis Calero. You've painted MAGIC: THE GATHERING cards and graphic novels, the GAMBIT & ROGUE Marvel press poster, and continue to be one of the foremost comic colorists in the industry with your studio, ATOMIC PAINTBRUSH. But this is different. This is Stan "The Man" who's talking to you. And Marvel Comics is about to be born.

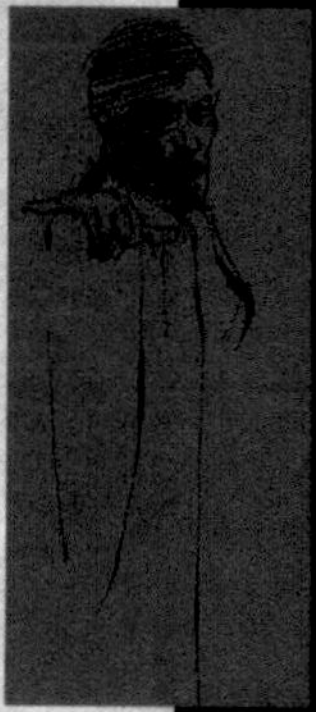

"Now, Dennis. This is how it works. Dr. Stephen Strange is a brilliant surgeon. Far and wide it is thought that his hands themselves can perform modern miracles. But he doesn't have the humility of a healer. He is ruled by his own greed. His pride and lack of compassion will put him on a road that ultimately leads to ruin.

"One night, after having had too much to drink, Strange is in an auto accident. And while he appears unscathed by the process, the truth is, there's a large amount of almost invisible neurological damage, meaning the once-brilliant surgeon will never operate again.

"His world destroyed, Strange finds solace by taking up the life of a vagrant, walking the streets, a derelict. But one day, as fate would have it, Strange hears of an obscure temple in the Tibetan mountains, and of its master, the Ancient One, a wise old monk said to be able to heal any wound.

"Strange, humbled by his time on the streets, yet desiring the life he once had, goes in search of this master only to become the Ancient One's disciple, something greater than he'd ever dreamed.

"He is shown amazing new worlds and becomes the defender of this realm from the dark forces that would invade from the shadows. And where once he saved lives for his own greed, he now, without any thought for himself, performs amazing new miracles of arcane mystery to save the soul of the collective world. He has become the Master Of The Mystic Arts."

Now Dennis, I want to see sketches this afternoon, and a finished Doctor Strange piece tomorrow!"

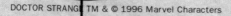

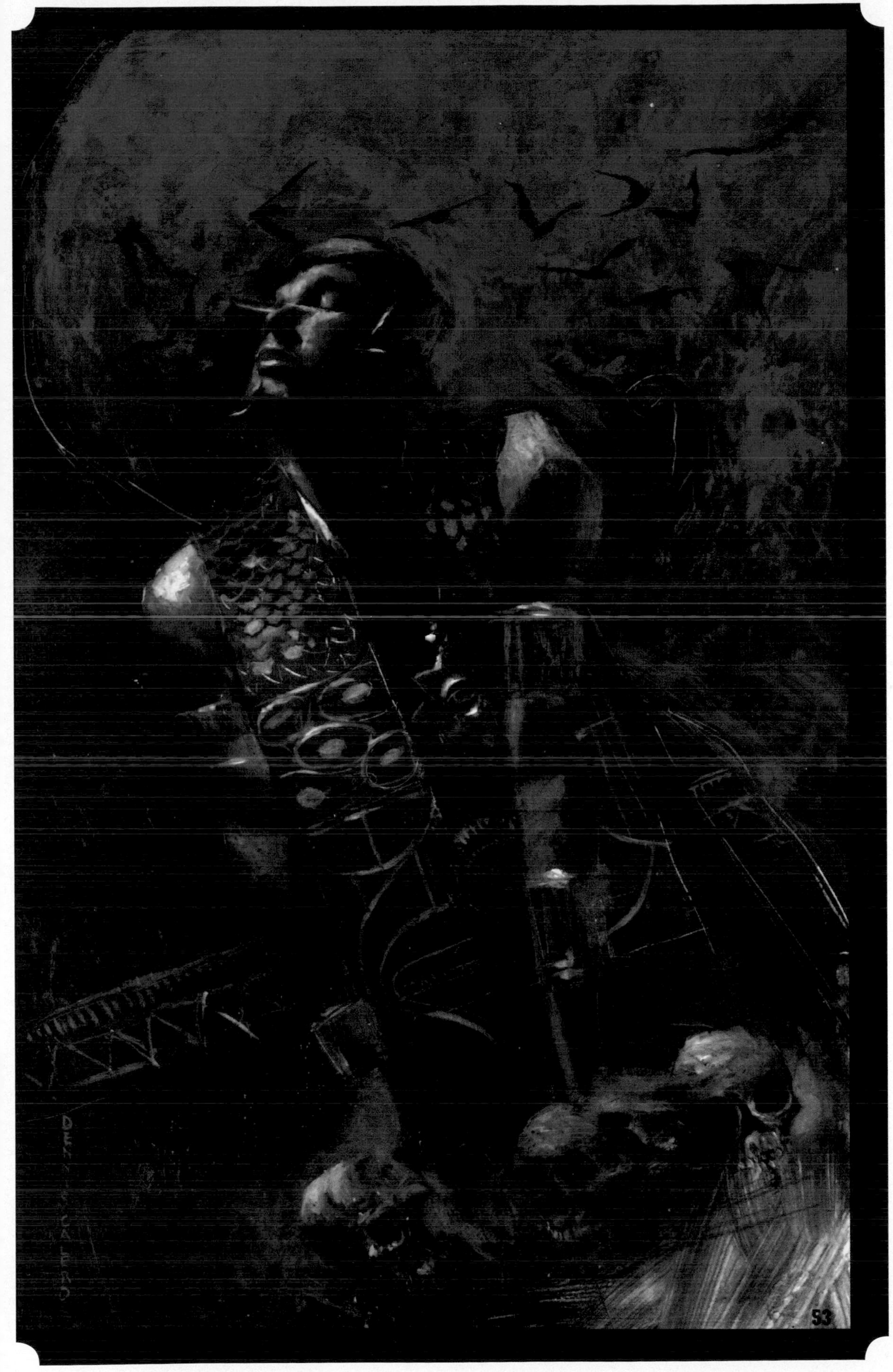

INTERVIEW

with Tony Harris

by Robert Piotrowski

STRANGER IN A STRANGE LAND

Tony Harris doesn't like super heroes very much. Regardless, he's managed to become a well known comic creator through books such as Starman. And he'll prove it in December with the four-issue limited series which he co-wrote, penciled and painted covers for entitled DOCTOR STRANGE. But why does a guy

who isn't crazy about super powers want to co-write and draw a story about another guy who is the Earth's uncontested Sorcerer Supreme? The answer is actually quite simple: because, just like Harris, Stephen Strange has a very humble human side. And if you read on, we'll tell you all about it.

MARVEL MAGAZINE: How did the idea for DOCTOR STRANGE come about?

TONY HARRIS: I'd come up on the end of my run on *Starman* and was talking to (Jimmy) Palmiotti and (Joe) Qeusada about doing something for them on Marvel Knights. When I mentioned to Joe that I didn't have an interior gig at the time, he asked me if there were any main characters at Marvel that I was interested in working on. So I went through the MARVEL UNIVERSE books and kept going back to the same guy, Stephen Strange. So I came up with a story idea with my studio partner Ray Snyder (*Starman, Green Lantern*) and we pitched that to my writing partner, Dan Jolley (*The Mummy, Obergiest*) Dan wrote it up into a great little story and we pitched that idea to Joe, and he got permission from Marvel to use Strange for the second wave in about two days. It was unbelievable.

MM: You're responsible for a lot of the work on this series. Is that 'good' pressure?

TH: Yes, because I'm a control freak (laughs). I didn't really become that way until after I did my run on *Starman*. Working on that was almost like working on a creator-owned property. The late Mr. Archi Goodwin really gave James and me the creative freedom to do what we wanted so I got used to that and loved it. So now the more control I have, the more I like it. That way, if it's wrong I don't have to worry about whose fault it is because it's mine.

MM: Out of all the characters in the Marvel Universe, what drew you to Doctor Strange?

TH: He had the human angle I was looking for and I always try to tap into that. Basically, Stephen Strange was a surgeon who had an accident that caused some neurological damage and he couldn't operate any more because his hands shook. So he started drinking and lost himself. Then he ended up studying magic with The Ancient One and became the Sorcerer Supreme. Since then, I think people have gotten away from that. I mean, he was a brilliant surgeon who had this accident that wrecked his life and then he turned into this magical guy and — Bam! — nobody talked about his hands anymore. There's a great story there!

Also, Strange's got that whole crazy horror, magic, occult, witchcraft element to him and I dig that stuff. To me, Doctor Strange is a wonderfully magical, mystical entity that I think is so underrated and underrealized. There's just immense potential for stories there. If I ever got into it in the right circumstances, I might even be tempted to do a monthly.

MM: What is DOCTOR STRANGE about?

TH: The premise is that there is a freakish cult that's spreading like the plague through New York City and Topaz, an old Doctor Strange character, gets sucked into it. They plan on using her as bait to get to Stephen so that there's nothing standing in the way of their taking over the world. But there's a lot of layered stuff in there too. We're dealing with the friendship Stephen's got with a doctor friend, a young surgeon with personal problems whom he identifies with. Also, he's got this relationship with Topaz. Then we've got this old Marvel villain who's going to show his face eventually, but because of his neurological damage, Stephen's hands will be shaking so badly that he won't even be able to hold a sugar spoon.

The personal story of Stephen Strange is my favorite element of the whole thing. This is really not a story about Doctor Strange, this is a story about Stephen Strange and the stuff that he has to go through on a personal level. The super-hero stuff is all fine and well, but that's not what I'm really interested in. I'm more interested in telling a really human story. Strange actually spends a lot of time in a three piece suit and a fedora with the Eye of Agamotto on a watch chain stuffed in a vest pocket.

MM: It's rather ironic that as a comic book artist, you're more interested in the human side of characters than their super powers.

TH: I think that's what people are crying out for. This medium is saturated with the same old stuff. If you take a long hard look at the new stuff your comic store, you'll find that there isn't much diversity there unless you're looking at the indies. And although I'm working in the mainstream, I think I have an indie mindset.

MM: Tell me about the changes you made to Stephen's costume.

TH: We added a lot more black. His gloves and shirt are black and the symbol on the front looks more like a demon; instead of two eyes it has one which kind of echoes the Eye of Agamotto. His costume kind of alters as his magic intensifies. The cape's the same but we got rid of the moustache and gave him a goatee that comes to a point. I think that's more distinguished and more professor-like. Doctor Strange has that kind of effect on me. And I think these changes fit the story.

MM: What about the horror element you mentioned earlier. Where does that show up?

TH: There's a lot of creepy, creepy stuff in here. I mean, little demon babies with horns three times the size of their heads riding egrets who carry these necklaces that make you theirs if they get one on you. There's lots of crazy stuff like that.

MM: Anything else you want readers to know about DOCTOR STRANGE?

TH: Since it's a limited series, readers are going to see an even higher level of design and detail because I can put twice the amount of time into every page. So readers can look for the ante to be upped a little bit as far as the quality is concerned.

DOCTOR STRANGE #1 is on sale December 16th.

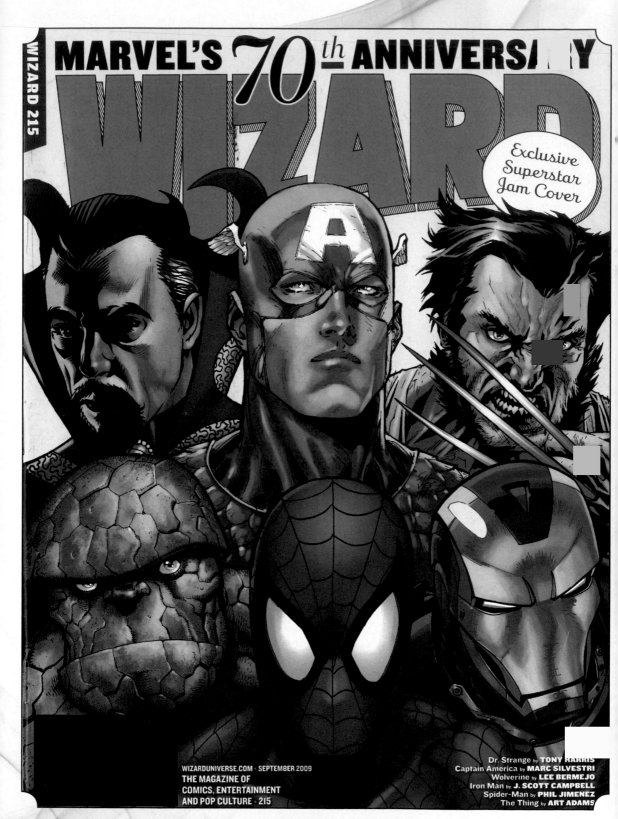

MARVEL'S 70th ANNIVERSARY

WIZARD

Exclusive
Superstar
Jam Cover

WIZARDUNIVERSE.COM · SEPTEMBER 2009
THE MAGAZINE OF
COMICS, ENTERTAINMENT
AND POP CULTURE · 215

Dr. Strange by **TONY HARRIS**
Captain America by **MARC SILVESTRI**
Wolverine by **LEE BERMEJO**
Iron Man by **J. SCOTT CAMPBELL**
Spider-Man by **PHIL JIMENEZ**
The Thing by **ART ADAMS**

WIZARD #215 COVER ART BY TONY HARRIS, MARC SILVESTRI,
LEE BERMEJO, ARTHUR ADAMS, PHIL JIMENEZ & J. SCOTT CAMPBELL